A Magistrate's Court
in

19th Century

Hong Kong

Court in Time

With additional discussion of
"The Opium Ordinance"

The Hon. Frederick Stewart (1836-89), LLD, MA.

*1. Hong Kong Police Magistrate, 26 July 1881 - 29 March 1882.
Educated at Rathen Parish School, Aberdeen Grammar School,
King's College and Divinity Hall, Aberdeen, Scotland.
Stewart rose to head the permanent Hong Kong Civil Service.
He is known as
Founder of Hong Kong Government Education.*

CONTRIBUTORS
21st Century
Gillian Bickley
Verner Bickley
Christopher Coghlan
Timothy Hamlett
Geoffrey Roper
Garry Tallentire

Preface by Sir T. L. Yang

19th Century
Anonymous *China Mail* Reporters

EDITOR
Gillian Bickley

A Magistrate's Court in Nineteenth Century Hong Kong: Court in Time: the Court Cases Reported in *The China Mail* of The Honourable Frederick Stewart, MA, LLD, Founder of Hong Kong Government Education, Head of the Permanent Hong Kong Civil Service & Nineteenth Century Hong Kong Police Magistrate. Modern Commentary & Background Essays with Selected Themed Transcripts.

EDITOR: Gillian Bickley.
CONTRIBUTORS:
21ˢᵗ Century: Gillian Bickley, Verner Bickley, Christopher Coghlan, Timothy Hamlett, Geoffrey Roper, Garry Tallentire.
19ᵗʰ Century: Anonymous *China Mail* Reporter or Reporters.
Preface by Sir T. L. Yang. Index by Verner Bickley.

2nd pbk edition reprint, November 2015, ISBN:978-988-8228-29-4, published by Proverse Hong Kong, P.O. Box 259, Tung Chung Post Office, Lantau Island, NT, Hong Kong SAR, China.
Email: <proverse@netvigator.com>.Website: <www/proversepublishing.com>.
Printed by and available through Create Space.
Copyright © Proverse Hong Kong, 2015.

1st pbk edition, Proverse Hong Kong, 2005. ISBN: 962-85570-4-1.
ISBN-13: 978-962-85570-4-2.
2nd pbk edtion, Proverse Hong Kong, April 2009. (Reformats 1st edition w. slight corrections & additional material.) ISBN-13: 978-988-17724-5-9.

2005 and 2009 pbk editions distributed worldwide by The Chinese University Press, The Chinese University of Hong Kong, Shatin, New Territories, Hong Kong SAR.
E-mail: <cup-bus@cuhk.edu.hk>. Web site: <www.chineseupress.com>.

2005 and 2009 pbk editions also available worldwide through the Aberdeen and North East Scotland Family History Society. Enquiries and orders to The Family History Research Centre, 158-164 King Street, Aberdeen, AB24 5BD, Scotland, United Kingdom. Tel: INT+[0]1224-646323. Fax: INT+[0]1224-639096.
E-mail: publications@anesfhs.org.uk. Website: www.anesfhs.org.uk.

Verner Bickley asserts the moral right to be identified as the author of "Differing Perceptions of Social Reality in Dr Stewart's Court: 'Be Careful: You are in a Court of Justice!'" Christopher Coghlan asserts the moral right to be identified as the author of "Thoughts about the Practice of Law in Hong Kong, arising from the Court Cases of Frederick Stewart, Esq. White Gloves and Patience" Timothy Hamlett asserts the moral right to be identified as the author of "Reporting the Cases of Frederick Stewart: The Public Interest". Geoffrey Roper asserts the moral right to be identified as the author of "The Police Role in Magistrate Frederick Stewart's Court: A Personal Commentary".Garry Tallentire asserts the moral right to be identified as the author of "The Hong Kong (Police) Magistrate in the 1880s and 1990s: A Flavour of the Times".Sir T. L. Yang asserts the moral right to be identified as the author of "Preface".

Original cover design by Mr Charles W. M. Fok. 2009 cover updated by Ms Agnes Po.
Page layout by Proverse Hong Kong.

Proverse Hong Kong
British Library Cataloguing in Publication Data

A magistrate's court in 19th century Hong Kong : court in
time. -- 2nd ed.
1. Stewart, Frederick, 1836-1889. 2. Stewart, Frederick,
1836-1889--Archives. 3. Criminal courts--China--Hong Kong--
History--19th century. 4. Criminal courts--China--Hong Kong-
-History--19th century--Sources. 5. Police magistrates--
China--Hong Kong--History--19th century. 6. Police
magistrates--China--Hong Kong--History--19th century--
Sources. 7. Hong Kong (China)--Social conditions--19th
century. 8. Hong Kong (China)--Social conditions--19th
century--Sources.
I. Bickley, Gillian, 1943-
347.5'125'010264-dc22

ISBN-13: 9789881772459

Also available from CUHK Press and Proverse Hong Kong:
THE COMPLETE COURT CASES OF MAGISTRATE FREDERICK STEWART AS REPORTED IN *THE CHINA MAIL*, JULY 1881 TO MARCH 1882, 2008. *Edited by Gillian Bickley*. CD. Preface by The Hon. Mr Justice Bokhary PJ, Court of Final Appeal. Indexed by Verner Bickley. Supported by the Council of the Lord Wilson Heritage Trust. ISBN-13: 978-988-17724-1-1.

The Court Cases
Reported in *The China Mail*
of The Honourable Frederick Stewart, MA, LLD
Founder of Hong Kong Government Education
Head of the Permanent Hong Kong Civil Service &
Nineteenth Century Hong Kong Police Magistrate

Modern Commentary
Background Essays
Selected Themed Transcripts

Preface to the First Edition by Sir T. L. Yang

In the mid summer of 1842, Chinese and British plenipotentiaries boarded a British warship moored near Nanjing and signed what Chinese even today consider a humiliating treaty, the Treaty of Nanjing, by which the island of Hong Kong was ceded to Great Britain in perpetuity. Under the third clause of the treaty, the island was "given" to Great Britain for "perpetual rule" and laws might be "freely enacted" for the purpose of the island's administration. Little did either party imagine that this "barren rock" called Hong Kong would develop into a gemstone a century or so later.

Some forty years were to pass before we find Dr Frederick Stewart presiding as Police Magistrate in Hong Kong. The colony was by then still a quiet and neglected outpost of the British Empire. The place had not advanced much beyond the ignominious status of a "barren rock". The local population still consisted of farmers and fishermen, with a handful of merchants, craftsmen and others engaged in less respectable activities.

It was an island of two ethnic groups who came from entirely different cultures, customs and religious backgrounds. Whilst the British were blithely – and often conscientiously, it must be admitted – struggling to rule the best they could, adopting as their norms Western codes of morality, governmental practices and traditions and principles of the Common Law, the Chinese on their part, including the thousands who had come to Hong Kong after the establishment of a British administration, carried on with their lives as if nothing important had changed. They tended to ignore their new British masters as they had for centuries ignored their own Chinese masters. If through necessity, the East and the West did meet, it was through trade, domestic requirements, governmental demands – and the brothels. But all these contacts were limited, sporadic, superficial and devoid of any interaction of mind. One learned nothing from the other.

The Magistrate's Court was one of a very few venues, including also the school room and religious meetings, where a handful of expatriates saw the local people as individuals in large numbers and gradually came to gain a little insight into what the Chinese thought and did. This was the place too where the Chinese had a taste of the Westerner's concept of justice. The largely illiterate and tradition-bound Chinese could not understand the ways of the "foreign devils". These pink-skinned and bearded mandarins were fond of flogging, true, but they were so ill-informed as not to comprehend the innovative, diverse and effective means of torture which the apparently much more intelligent Chinese magistrate could devise. Stranger still, they (on the whole) took no bribes and seemed to be content with their meagre pay. When it was time for them to return home, they made no demands on the people for lavish farewell gifts and banquets. And so they came and went, hardly making a ripple on the local scene. Hong Kong thus dragged on, leading an existence that was both uneventful and unexciting. This continued until the 1920s, when western ways slowly and surely gained a foothold, from which we have advanced to become what we are today.

By the mid-1950s, Hong Kong had become an international city. The ethos was a mixture of the East and the West. Moral standards also contained elements of both cultures. International businesses grew, and foreign businessmen came here and did business in much the same way as they did in Europe or North America. Above all, a very comprehensive and fair legal system had firmly established itself, gaining strength and prestige and respect as the city itself was gaining strength, prestige and respect.

It is astonishing that, in his Blue Book Report to London, as Acting Governor, written shortly before his death in 1889, Frederick Stewart anticipated the great changes that, much later, took place in Hong Kong. But Governor Sir William Des Voeux, returning from leave, found the picture Stewart had drawn altogether too fanciful. Des Voeux apparently did not himself foresee the elements that were to make Hong Kong such a story of success, and, unlike Stewart, was unable to dream that Hong Kong would transform itself in such a dramatic way. Perhaps one might put this transformation down firstly to our legal system (by which term I include the judicial system), secondly to our civil service, thirdly to the government's policy of allowing sufficient freedom to the people to trade, fourthly to an environment of security and safety, and fifthly to the determination, persistence and hard work of the people.

Perhaps – just perhaps – too, another reason for our success is the sense of humour of both the British and the Chinese. Also, each group is so convinced of their own superiority over the other that one is able to pooh-pooh the perceived stupidity, backwardness and outlandish ways of the other. Neither side takes the other seriously – at any rate not seriously enough to get really infuriated. So they just shrug and make a rude sign at the other, laugh derisively, call each other names, and forget the other side ever existed. Thus in a hundred and fifty years of colonial rule, except, occasionally, when responding to unrest elsewhere, there have been no racial conflicts, no violence against the government, and no resentment against the British as the colonial government departed.

If Magistrate Stewart were to return to life, he would see a Hong Kong he hardly recognized. Whilst it is difficult to credit him, as a magistrate, with any particular trial or official act, which has made this city great – his work as first Head of the Government Education Department is a different matter – he, and hundreds and thousands like him, has certainly made his mark on this huge golden beach, accumulating grain by grain.

It is therefore with these thoughts in mind that I commend Professor Bickley's book to anyone who is interested in Hong Kong. She has done a great service by introducing us to Dr Stewart as magistrate and allowing us to have a glimpse at different aspects of Hong Kong life at the close of the Nineteenth Century. I congratulate too the contributors, who have written with such insight and understanding, thereby making *A Magistrate's Court in Nineteenth Century Hong Kong: Court in Time* a most readable book. **–2005**

A Magistrate's Court in 19th Century Hong Kong
Court in Time

The Magistrate's Court Cases Reported in *The China Mail*
of The Honourable Frederick Stewart, MA, LLD

Founder of Hong Kong Government Education
Head of the Permanent Hong Kong Civil Service
& Nineteenth Century Hong Kong Police Magistrate

Modern Commentary & Essays
with Selected Themed Transcripts

Table of Contents

SECTION ONE
Modern Commentary

SECTION TWO

Frederick Stewart's Cases as Reported in *The China Mail*: Background Essays with Selected Themed Transcripts

Illustrations, Displayed Text, and Tables
(Pages 2, 142-172, 273, 308, 396, 420-421)

Acknowledgements

The editor is most grateful to the other contributors to *A Magistrate's Court in Nineteenth Century Hong Kong: Court in Time*, Verner Bickley, Christopher Coghlan, Tim Hamlett, Geoffrey Roper and Garry Tallentire, for sharing her interest in the court cases of Frederick Stewart, and – by applying their individuality and specialist knowledge to them – for helping others to understand them, and their significance, more. She is indebted to their friendship, their generosity with their time, their patience in application, and their intuitive sharing of a skill which contemporaries praised in Nineteenth Century Hong Kong Governor, Sir Arthur Kennedy: "He knew when to work, and when to wait". Verner Bickley and Geoffrey Roper are additionally thanked for their help in formulating the model to be followed, Garry Tallentire for hitting on such an apt sub-title for the book. We are all most grateful to Sir T. L. Yang for his Preface and to Chris Hall for his support.

Permission for Garry Tallentire to contribute was kindly received from the Chief Justice of Hong Kong and we acknowledge an element of funding support from the Hong Kong Bar Association.

The Hong Kong Baptist University is acknowledged for a Faculty Research Grant and facilitation by the Department of English Language and Literature. The Information Technology Unit of the Hong Kong Baptist University (Mr Henry So, Mr S. H. Tong, Mr Lawrence Tsang) helped with technical matters. Miss Nicole Ho, Mrs Mildred Marney (England) and Miss Lee Yin Wai, Lilith, helped with the text and tables. Mr Danny K. C. Chow, Mr Charles W. M. Fok and Mr Stephen M. Dingler gave ready advice and assistance. Mr Kelvin Lee and Format Ltd also helped.

The Hong Kong Public Records Office is thanked for their assistance over many years, and similarly, the Inter-library Loan Service of each of the following: the Hong Kong Baptist University, the Chinese University of Hong Kong, the City University of Hong Kong, the Hong Kong Polytechnic University and the University of Hong

Kong. The copying service of the University of Hong Kong has been invaluable.

Helpfully facilitated by Margaret McBryde and Elizabeth Buckley, Dr Ian Grant (National Archives of Scotland) gave early input. Mr N. K. Wong, the Curator of the Hong Kong Police Museum, helped with enquiries. Mr Kwok Hong Lok and Dr Kam Keung Lee assisted with translation and cultural interpretation, while Reverend Carl Smith shared his insights on Nineteenth Century Hong Kong social history. All are warmly acknowledged.

Illustrations are reproduced with kind permission as follows: the Government of the Hong Kong SAR (front cover (inset), Nos 1, 5, 13, 14, 26, 29, 40); the Government of the HKSAR from the collection of the Hong Kong Museum of History (pp. 6 (all), Nos 6, 9, 11, 16, 18, 19, 21, 22, 23, 27, 28, 39, 42); Wellcome Institute Library, London [England] (No. 2); Public Records Office, Government Records Service [Hong Kong] (Nos 12, 14, 55a-d, book-cover background); FormAsia Books (Nos 25, 17, 41, 33); Gillian and Verner Bickley (Nos 31, 32, back cover inset); Hongkong Bank (Nos 3, 4, 7, 8, 43, 44); Bodleian Library, University of Oxford [England] ([RH] MSS.Ind.Ocn.t.10) (Nos 35, 36); Queen's College Hong Kong (No. 34); University of Nottingham Library [England] (Ne C11, 121/18) (No. 10). Other illustrations are from the *Illustrated London News* (No. 24), John Thomson, *Illustrations of China and its People*, 1873-1874 (Nos 37, 38) and William Speer, *The Oldest and the Newest Empire* (No. 30).

Introduction[1]

Unless called for jury service, few Hong Kong residents reading this book are likely to enter the doors of any of Hong Kong's many courts. However, Hong Kong newspapers – like others – carry court reports in the court pages, while everywhere in the world, particularly sensational cases appear in the news pages, as well as on radio and television. Perhaps we should know more than the media tell us about the Hong Kong courts, as about the law under which we live.

A couple of books for the general reader have already offered insider knowledge of this specialised field. In *Myself a Mandarin*, first published in about 1968, and republished in 1987, Austin Coates has written amusingly about his time as a district officer, when one of his duties was magisterial. More recently, in 1998, retired barrister, Patrick Yu Shuk-siu's biography, containing his selected court cases, *A Seventh Child and the Law*, caught the interest of the public, and was followed up, four years later, by his *Tales from No. 9 Ice House Street*. A quite different type of book, published a hundred years earlier, in 1898, Norton-Kyshe's *The History of the Laws and Courts of Hong Kong: from the Earliest Period to 1898*, is only recently being questioned as the last word on the early legal history of Hong Kong.[2]

There are several publications on the policing of Hong Kong. Shortly before the return of Hong Kong to China at midnight, 30 June 1997, two handsome publications appeared, one on the Royal Hong Kong Police Force, and another on the Auxiliary Police. An earlier valuable book on the history of the Hong Kong Marine Police testifies that this is an enduring topic. The Hong Kong Police Museum (at Coombe Road, the Peak) further proves the public interest in these subjects, as does its stream of visitors, a high proportion of whom are Chinese. A collection of informative essays, edited by Harold Traver and Jon Vagg, *Crime and Justice in Hong Kong*, suggests theoretical viewpoints from which to analyse the subject.

The present book, *A Magistrate's Court in*

Nineteenth Century Hong Kong: Court in Time, offers a picture of a Hong Kong magistrate's court and its frequenters in the early 1880s. It also shows, from the personal perspectives of professionals variably involved (a magistrate, a retired senior police officer, a barrister, a journalist, a socio-linguist, a social historian), some aspects of police matters as well as of the Hong Kong magistrate's court in the second half of the *twentieth* century. *Court in Time* draws us into the tense and touching world of the magistrates' courts at two distinct periods of time, and through this, into localities and lives we otherwise might never know and certainly never guess at.

The magistrate whose court is the subject of *Court in Time* is British and Scottish long-term Hong Kong resident, Frederick Stewart, whose significant and admired work in education is the main subject of several scholarly articles and of a biography published in 1997. Stewart's posthumous reputation has received strong support. *The Golden Needle: the Biography of Frederick Stewart (1836-1889)* is introduced by Lord Wilson, penultimate Governor of Hong Kong and contains a Foreword by Lady Saltoun, Chief of Clan Fraser. It was reviewed in *The Scotsman* by Lord Hurd, former British Secretary for Foreign Affairs. In the education field, it was reviewed by Dr Ruth Hayhoe, now Director Emeritus of the Hong Kong Institute of Education, by Mr Colvin Haye, former Hong Kong Director of Education and by Dr Kathleen E. Barker, former Principal of St Stephen's Girls' College and member of the Hong Kong Education Commission. Numerous other reviews and related feature articles have appeared in several languages and several countries. Part of the biography has been translated and serialised in a Hong Kong Chinese daily newspaper. As for Stewart's own writings, the complete series of his official annual reports as Head of the Hong Kong Government Education Department from 1866 to 1879 is available in *The Development of Education in Hong Kong, 1841-1897: as Revealed by the Early Education Reports of the Hong Kong Government, 1848 to 1896*, published in 2002 and sponsored by the Lord Wilson Heritage Trust. The *Oxford Dictionary of National*

Biography, published by Oxford University Press in 2004, includes Frederick Stewart as a new biographical subject. As for the story behind the writing of Stewart's biography, its motivation and research are the main subject of Dr Verner Bickley's book, *Searching for Frederick*, sponsored by the Hong Kong Arts Development Council and published by Asia 2000, in 2001.

In *Court in Time*, that part of Frederick Stewart's work as Police Magistrate, which was reported in *The China Mail*, is brought forward for consideration, supplemented by information from the other daily newspaper of the time, *The Hong Kong Daily Press*. Although this body of material was taken into account in the earlier publications named above to provide an element of completeness and an additional insight into Stewart's life and work, it was directly presented only briefly. Considered now in its own right, it provides a basis for a different focus, on Stewart's work in the Hong Kong courts, while at the same time contributing to our knowledge of Hong Kong society. These two objectives are the reason for the present publication.

Reports of over seven hundred of the cases that Frederick Stewart heard during the period 26 July 1881 to 29 March 1882 have been gathered from surviving archived copies of the contemporary newspaper, *The China Mail*. They were then transcribed, edited, and annotated to form the working document, which was taken as a basis for *Court in Time*. About one hundred and twenty of these reports, relating to about one hundred cases, have been chosen for inclusion here. Further edited, selected and grouped by subject – with introductory essays and explanatory notes – these form the second part of the present book. The variety of people is considerable: sailors, soldiers, police, teachers, men of the cloth, wives, husbands, amahs, cooks, widows, protected women, sons, adopted daughters, burglars, denizens of the domestic scene, prostitutes with their associates and clients, kidnappers and traffickers in human beings, children, students, gamblers, informers and pirates. There is variety of scene also: urban life, country life, and life at sea.

In the first part of *Court in Time*, professionals and academics, distinguished in their own separate fields, with a lively interest in the history of Hong Kong and with well over a century of Hong Kong residence among them, join Stewart's biographer in contributing essays, which explore, from their individual points of view, the full set of court reports, giving a variety of historical perspectives. Some give explicit comparisons with their own, more modern, experience. Taken together, and addressing modern and general readers, their work contributes significantly to an understanding of what these court cases have to tell us. It helps us to understand both the nineteenth and present day Hong Kong social and cultural background, and the happily arcane world (for most of us) of the police and magistrates courts in Hong Kong.

Over twenty magistrates and acting magistrates served in nineteenth century Hong Kong, two of them (Charles May and H. E. Wodehouse) for considerable periods, but most for a handful of years, or even for a few months only. (The only ethnic Chinese magistrate during this period, Ng Choy – a Singapore native, trained for the British bar – is an example of the latter.)[3] Additionally, there were marine magistrates, sitting in separate marine courts.

In *Court in Time* Gillian Bickley considers what sort of magistrate Frederick Stewart was, against the background of what is known of the current practice of the period as well as referring to contemporary opinion. As recorded, Stewart's educational work and the view of his contemporaries convey a picture of a liberal idealist. The evidence of these court case reports, some readers might find inconsistent with this picture. For this shows that Stewart (like the other magistrates of the period) sentenced people to some punishments which today's public opinion generally finds repulsive. As some gesture towards mediating between these two points of view, she uses the evidence of the full set of *China Mail* reports of Frederick Stewart's cases, 26 July 1881 to 29 March 1882, to analyse Stewart's award of the "stocks". (It is not clear whether the cangue – a contraption that fits round the neck, separating it from the rest of the body and making it impossible for the wearer to feed him or herself – was also sometimes meant. – Historical photographs stated to be of Hong Kong show both the cangue and the stocks as methods of punishment.) In another contribution, she offers contemporary perspectives on some nineteenth century Hong Kong legislation, notorious for its discriminatory application – the Light and Pass rules – and considers Stewart's sentencing under these rules.

Verner Bickley takes a cross-cultural perspective, describing the many different types of people who met in magistrate Stewart's court, the widely different views of social reality, which they held, and some of the results of the mixture. Commenting on different ideas about humour, Verner Bickley highlights the contrast between the court reporter's wisecracks and magistrate Stewart's decorum. He confirms part of the rationale for *Court in Time*, when he states, "It is clear that the cultural values of a people may be found in the records of court cases", and he shows how, in the 1880s, the logic of the Hong Kong law sometimes clashed with cultural tradition.

Christopher Coghlan gives a clear overview of Hong Kong courts, law, crimes and sentencing in the early 1880s and the late twentieth century, finding modern-day Hong Kong crime more complex, more sensational and also (comparing like with like) more heavily penalised. He highlights the demands for inexhaustible patience made on a magistrate – both in the nineteenth and twentieth centuries – when dealing with "the ignorant, the mendacious and the unintelligent of all nationalities", descriptions which, he suggests, "would cover probably the majority of witnesses and parties in magistrates' courts". Coghlan suggests that those who comment on the practice of Hong Kong's legal system should imagine themselves in the magistrates' shoes, and should also consider the practical constraints, which, in the past, influenced the choice of official language for the courts. Finally, he looks back with what many laymen will find surprising nostalgia at the image of orderliness he receives from the published records of Frederick Stewart's court.

Geoffrey Roper discusses his analysis of the reports from a police perspective, pointing out that, as late as the 1880s, Hong Kong evidently had many of the policing problems of a frontier seaport. Comparing policing methods in the 1880s and the late 1950s, he draws on his own experience, which in some cases – astonishingly – was almost a replica of what these 1880 court reports describe. For example, Geoffrey Roper took part in an *opium* raid, entering through the roof, in the very same locality in Hong Kong's Central District where members of the police force in 1881 raided for *gambling*,[4] *also* entering through the roof. Roper tells us that he was on duty during the filming of *The World of Susie Wong*, helped line the route during the visit of the Duke of Edinburgh, consort of Queen Elizabeth of Great Britain, struggled with learning Cantonese and – when he retired – took the salute at a Beating of the Retreat at the Central Police Station compound, very near the site of Stewart's magistrate's court. This is the same compound whose fate – demolition for a shopping mall or preservation as a heritage site – was at issue at the end of 2004. Finally, he comments approvingly on the changed roles of Chinese and non-Chinese members within the present-day Hong Kong Police Force.

Tim Hamlett comments on the conditions under which a court reporter works and on the striking similarity between work in the 1880s in Hong Kong and his own early days as a reporter in the 1970s in England. Showing how circumstances affected what appeared in the paper, that, "lengthy contemplation of news values or composition was not wanted, and would be wasted if supplied", he asserts that the primary need was for speed. Hamlett describes the formula to which *The China Mail* reporter or reporters worked. He comments that many of the short stories produced would still be perfectly at home in a modern newspaper, and points out the testimony this gives to the durability of plain English prose. Hamlett also comments on the restrictive impact of the Law of Libel Amendment Act, passed in the United Kingdom, in 1888, telling us by implication, that these reports of the cases Frederick Stewart heard, a handful of years before the passing of this Act, are very much more colourful and racy than most were after this date. Hamlett considers the evidence given by these reports for signs of racism and heavy-handed colonialism, but – somewhat reluctantly, this writer thinks – comes to the conclusion that, "the proceedings do not look grossly unfair considering the circumstances". He also comments on the interesting challenge to journalism theory, which the full group of reports poses.

Garry Tallentire uses his first-hand experience as a Hong Kong magistrate, to comment on differences in the magistrates and their work, as between 1880 and 1990. As Christopher Coghlan also does, Tallentire comments on the relative simplicity of offences in the 1880s and the fact that sentencing today is seen from a rehabilitation, rather than a punitive point of view. The catchment area for Tallentire's court at the time of writing includes the famous vice area of Wanchai, and Tallentire comments on the comparative absence of vice and vice-related crimes in the 1880s (when brothels were licensed, as they are not, now). He also remarks on the relative absence in the early 1880s of corporal punishment. Tallentire concludes with some stories from among the cases he himself has heard in Hong Kong, and wonders whether, in a further one hundred years time, another magistrate will scour the newspaper reports of today, to try to get a flavour of *our* times.

Court in Time, then, gives insights into the law, the practice of law, and the newspaper reporting of the law, into the personalities of the magistrates' courts (and the character of magistrate Frederick Stewart, in particular), into police personnel and policing. It does this in relation to a particular period of Nineteenth Century Hong Kong; as well as bringing into light late twentieth century Hong Kong and British practice and practitioners. Furthermore, it introduces us to some late twentieth century Hong Kong personalities and scenes. Above all, it creates a vivid picture of Hong Kong people and Hong Kong life *beyond* the courts in the 1880s and – occasionally – in the late twentieth century; giving a clear sense of a developing community where all sorts are thrown into contact: people of many nationalities, religions, and ways of life – the grist for the mill that produced and produces the modern, international city of Hong Kong, still constantly evolving.

The cases, which give the main basis to these discussions, were heard during the period July 1881 to March 1882. This was within the period when John Pope Hennessy was Governor of Hong Kong, and this adds further interest. As is well known, Hennessy instigated much talk of changes and some actual changes in both the practice and rules of Hong Kong's legal system. He was concerned about discriminatory legislation, and about the Contagious (Venereal) Diseases Ordinance, and he set up a Commission to enquire into the latter. He was an advocate for "the separate system" for prisons. He expressed concern about aspects of prison discipline, including the flogging of prisoners. On questions of law and order, Hennessy so alarmed and angered sections of the Hong Kong public – who believed that his harmful leniency was causing an increase in crime – that a public meeting was called, and high emotion displayed. A contemporary account of Pope Hennessy's intervention in Hong Kong's legal, police and prison systems is given in *Europe in China*, the early history of Hong Kong, written by E. J. Eitel, whose own residence in Hong Kong was contemporary with some of the period he discusses.[5] Eitel also describes the public reaction to these and the contemporary view that the likely consequences of these changes would be a very marked increase in crime. Unfortunately for those interested in Frederick Stewart, he was absent on his only home leave at the time.

Immediately before, as well as during the period when Frederick Stewart heard the court cases presented in *Court in Time*, some of the legislation prompted by Hennessy's interests was actively being considered. *The Hong Kong Government Gazette*, published on 19 November 1881, contains the text of a new "Ordinance . . . to amend and repeal certain ordinances relating to branding and to the punishment of flogging", as well as the text of correspondence, following an initial recommendation, made by Hennessy in a despatch to the Colonial Office, dated 17 October 1879.[6] By this Ordinance (Number 3 of 1881), the following Ordinances were repealed: Ordinance Number 12 of 1845 "for the suppression of the Triad Society"; Number 4 of 1872 "to make provision for the branding and punishment of criminals in certain cases"; and Number 8 of 1876, "The deportation and conditional pardons consolidation ordinance."

Also repealed under the new Ordinance was Section 7 of Ordinance Number 12 of 1856 "to regulate the Chinese burials, and to prevent certain nuisances within the colony of Hong Kong"; part of Number 8 of 1858 "for regulation of the Chinese people, and for the population census, and for other purposes of police" ("To regulate Chinese people"); part of Number 1 of 1868 "to make provision for the more effectual suppression of piracy"; Section 1 of Number 3 of 1868 "to empower the Supreme Court to direct offenders to be whipped and to be kept in solitary confinement in certain specified cases"; and Section 7 of Number 16 of 1875 ("The Magistrates Ordinance, 1875"). Read for the first time on 3 June, the new Ordinance (Number 3 of 1881), "The Penal Ordinance Amendment Ordinance, 1881", was passed on 24 June 1881. Soon after, Ordinance Number 12 of 1881, the "Banishment and Conditional Pardons Ordinance, 1881", was passed on 23 August 1881.

The present book gives an opportunity to see how one part of the system operated during Hennessy's time. It throws everyday light on part of a subject where a vocal part of the Hong Kong public came to express deep dissatisfaction about a controversial Governor. This study is relevant to any who seek to evaluate in depth the reality of Hennessy's contribution, based on a detailed understanding of his times in Hong Kong.

Little use has been made as yet of Nineteenth Century Hong Kong Police Court Reports; yet they are a rich resource, illuminating Hong Kong life and society and giving glimpses of past lives, some famous, most unknown. Written at a time when the English-language press carried detailed reports of Police Court cases, they provide a substantial opportunity to view and feel active compassion for several aspects of Hong Kong lives, long gone. They have a vividness and intimacy, which (for various reasons) is less frequently offered on such topics today in Hong Kong's English language press. Additionally, the reports give examples by which to test the general ideas about Hong Kong law and its practice, expressed in some well-known writings about Hong Kong.

There are already a number of scholarly books in English on aspects of the Nineteenth Century social history of urban Hong Kong before 1898, when the New Territories were acquired. There are also some interesting articles, for example, in the *Journal of the Royal Asiatic Society (Hong Kong Branch)*. Introducing his own article in this Journal, "Condition of the European Working Class in Nineteenth Century Hong Kong", H. J. Lethbridge (former Reader in Sociology at the University of Hong Kong), justifies his topic by the comment that, "questions raised by . . . [the] existence [of the European working class in Hong Kong] are important sociologically and some attempt must be made to answer them".[7] In his interesting essay, however, although he admits that court cases such as those in this present book are the major available source of information, Lethbridge makes little use of them, and in fact quotes only one.

In a more recent work, Tsai Jung-fang comments that, "Scholarly publications on the working people in Hong Kong during the period from 1842 to 1913 have been extremely rare,"[8] and suggests that, "Perhaps this is partly because of the scarcity of materials about them." [9] Jung-Fang Tsai himself is one of the few commentators, previous to the present publication, to have drawn on reports from the Hong Kong Police Magistrates' courts. Like Lethbridge, Tsai clearly shows his understanding of the importance of magistrates' court cases, but, again, the number he actually discusses is rather small.[10]

The present book, *Court in Time*, thus supplies a clear need. Those newspaper reports of cases before the Hong Kong Police Magistrates' courts, which *Court in Time* reproduces, provide abundant materials about individuals within both the European and Chinese working classes (as well as from other ranks of society) in Hong Kong. They describe incidents from their lives, and occasionally give translations or transcriptions of what defendants, complainants, witnesses – as well as prosecutors and magistrate – actually said.

To the present writer's knowledge, the only other published work, which makes use of a large number of newspaper reports of Hong Kong court cases (but deriving from the *Supreme* Court, not a *magistrate's* court, as in the present book), is Christopher Munn's "The Criminal Trial under Early Colonial Rule". In his interesting and determinedly revisionist essay, Munn bases his discussion mainly on what he describes as "an exhaustive survey of 566 reported criminal cases involving 1,132 defendants tried by the Supreme Court in the ten years between 1848 and 1857."[11] The period Munn *considers* is longer, 1841 to 1866; and he chooses 1866 as the terminal point because, he says, "it marks the culminating point at which . . . reforms were consolidated into a system that was to serve the colony for the rest of the century and beyond".[12] It is a pity that evident constraints of length have permitted Munn to quote fewer than ten extracts from the newspaper reports of these cases, although he does seem to give references to several more.

In his interesting and well-written book, *Hong Kong in Chinese History: Community and Social Unrest in the British Colony, 1842-1913*, published in 1993, Tsai Jung-Fang considers Hong Kong history from a modern historical perspective which very cleverly balances different (post-colonial) points of view. In relation to the courts, however, he starts from the implicit premise that Chinese persons would not have received "justice" in Hong Kong courts, as indicated by his grudging statement, "In some ways British justice did protect coolies".[13] The premise may or may not be one that he personally accepts. Tsai also writes, "There were, of course, important judicial cases in the history of Hong Kong that served to illustrate the capability of the British judges to administer impartial justice on some occasions."[14] The final phrase, "on some occasions", carries the resonance that the number of these was few. This resonance is obviously what Tsai intends; the sentence does not otherwise need this phrase at all. Tsai quotes cases approvingly – as demonstrating that justice was done – when Europeans were punished for crimes and offences against Chinese persons. I do not believe he cites a case when a Chinese person was punished, approving the justice of any such finding of guilt.

This is obviously an emotive topic. As quoted by Tsai, in 1908, Lai Wing Sheng, shroff at the Hong Kong police magistracy for more than twelve years (1895 to 1908) requested a transfer to another position. In explanation, he wrote that he did not like seeing defendants cry and weep who did not have sufficient money to pay their fines, and he also did not like the treatment he himself sometimes received from the Police.[15] Nineteen years later, in 1927, Eric Blair (best known as the writer, George Orwell) resigned from the Burma Police, later using these experiences in the short stories, "A Hanging" and "Shooting an Elephant", and in his novel, *Burmese Days*. The world-view presented in his final novel, *Nineteen-Eighty-Four*, also owes much, it has been suggested, to Orwell's experience of law-enforcement in an eastern British colony. Orwell himself indicates rather, that he was concerned at totalitarian tendencies wherever they were evident in the world.

Published in 1924, E. M. Forster's *A Passage to India* posits the view that the colonial situation in itself distorts all human relationships; that, while a colonial situation remains, even the best of personal relationships disintegrate through accumulative misunderstandings. It would be a pity if – in a *post*-colonial situation – we continue the discussion in these terms, thereby reinforcing attitudes that we apparently (as we should) condemn. Avid watchers of police dramas are familiar with the similar polarity of some television series, where the old politics of class and the newer politics of gender give the additional tension and conflict that the genre requires.

As a first step towards the cross-cultural position discussed in Verner Bickley's essay, "Be Careful! You are in a Court of Justice", it is valuable to seek to view circumstances and events from the perspective of other people, and therefore Tsai's presentation of the attitudes he imagines as those of the labouring Chinese in Hong Kong is valuable: – "To the masses of coolies, the 'foreign devil's' rule in Hong Kong often seemed arbitrary and unjust."[16] It is of the nature of the case, however, that little – if any – record, by such a Chinese working-man or woman, of what his or her feelings and attitudes really were, as recorded by him or herself, can exist.

Stewart's biographer succeeded in finding only two relatively personal letters, written by Frederick Stewart himself, and even these are written to a senior official, addressed as a friend.[17] The message firmly brought home is that the erosions brought by time, natural disaster and human interference give little respect to the writings and opinions of those formerly respected and held in warm affection. They give little more respect to the writings and opinions of the rich and powerful. How much less likely is it that the views of the poor and illiterate will be preserved! With no counterbalancing information, those who put words in their mouths may – from what may be the best of motives – set up an unreal and false picture.

Of course, *Court in Time* also offers its own commentary on the large body of court cases, which it includes from among a carefully edited[18] typescript corpus of more than seven hundred reports. Even so, the people appear and speak as themselves, obscured only slightly by the verbal gauze constructed by that original *China Mail* reporter or reporters in Frederick Stewart's court. It may be only here that an authentic picture can be derived. Given existing interest in such material, *Court in Time* is likely to give several scholars the green light, while providing the general reader with much that is fresh and new.

This book is offered to a varied readership. To the *general* reader, interested in Hong Kong, present and past, particularly in its social history. To those professionally or personally involved, in or with the legal profession, in any capacity, whether in Hong Kong or elsewhere. To those involved in or studying the newspaper reporting of the law. Those interested in the history of law; those interested in comparisons and contrasts between and among *various* legal systems; and in comparisons over time within the *same* legal system. To those professionally or personally involved in police-work in Hong Kong and elsewhere, or interested in police history. Those interested in the historical persons (high and low), mentioned in the text, or in the professional experience of the contributors themselves. Those interested in the development of newspapers and in journalistic styles. Colonial historians. China historians. There is much to interest all.

The present book, deriving from reports of Magistrate Frederick Stewart's court cases in 1881 and 1882, provides an additional dimension from which to consider the Honourable Dr Frederick Stewart's work in education, and this is particularly true when we reflect on the close link between a government education system on the one hand and the legal system and policing on the other, particularly in a colonial or developing society. Furthermore, all the evidence seen suggests that Stewart's court work – like his work in education – was widely approved in the community, as well as by Colonial Office officials in London. Knowledge of his work provides considerable insight into Hong Kong society and some insight into the Colonial Office ethos at his time.

The editor and other contributors believe that this book will be both interesting and useful to different people in varying ways, and that it will continue to be used and referred to, as well as enjoyed.

Magistrate Frederick Stewart[19]

"Dr Stewart would do well for the magistrateship"[20]

Gillian Bickley

After twenty-five years in the Hong Kong Government, Frederick Stewart became Colonial Secretary, head of the permanent Hong Kong Civil Service (the position now named "Chief Secretary"). Immediately previously, he occupied the very important substantive posts of Registrar General and Protector of Chinese. Yet contemporaries named him "Founder of Hong Kong Education", and – until now – he is mainly remembered for his important work, from 1862 onwards, in Hong Kong education.

Although Frederick Stewart held the substantive post of Police Magistrate for approximately three years, from 19 May 1881 until April or May 1883,[21] resigning from the Headship of the Hong Kong Government Central School (which he had established) to take up this new position, his actual work as Police Magistrate was limited to the period, 26 July 1881 to 29 March 1882. The reason for this is both complex and straightforward. For twelve months or so before his appointment, since May 1880, Stewart had been Acting Colonial Secretary and Auditor General.[22] Following a disagreement with Governor Pope Hennessy (who had criticised Stewart's support for Jardine's leader, William Keswick, with whom Hennessy had personal and political differences), and being – as a newspaper supposed – too independent-minded to please the flattery-loving and obedience-seeking Governor, Stewart resigned from these acting positions, on 26 July 1881, taking up his substantive position as Police Magistrate. However, as soon as Sir John Pope Hennessy had left Hong Kong, at the end of his term as Governor, Stewart – well liked by his former colleagues, and respected by the community – was reappointed Acting Colonial Secretary and Auditor General, on 28 March 1882. On that day, besides reporting the swearing in as Administrator of W. H.

Marsh,[23] *The China Mail* highlighted Stewart's appointment. "After the oath had been administered to the Hon. W. H. Marsh, he at once rose and announced that Dr Stewart would take up the duties of Acting Colonial Secretary."[24] In another column, *The China Mail* welcomed Stewart's appointment in place of M. S. Tonnochy (previously Stewart's successor in the same post after Stewart's earlier resignation from it). "Now that Dr Stewart resumes his position, the wheels of Government may be expected to revolve with a smoothness to which the Service and the community have been comparative strangers for the last five years."[25] The last cases reported in *The China Mail* as "Before Frederick Stewart, Esq." appeared the following day, 29 March 1882.

Stewart continued in these positions until the arrival of a new Governor, Sir George Bowen, on 30 March 1883,[26] when Stewart took up another acting position as Registrar General. In time, Stewart was confirmed as Registrar General, a post which the Colonial Office had previously recommended him for, and he thus never resumed his work as Police Magistrate.

Contrary to what this history might suggest, the position of Police Magistrate was one which Stewart had actively sought and one for which he had considerable relevant experience, having served as Acting Coroner and Coroner for well over four years (1867 to 1871, 1876 to 1877), at the same time as he held his main positions as Headmaster of the Hong Kong Government Central School and Inspector of Schools. Not surprisingly, his resignation from the position of Coroner was because the work load finally became far too great, particularly as a result of the increasing success and expansion of the Hong Kong Government education system, for which Stewart was responsible. However, as a result of a need in the service, Stewart did later accept for a while the temporary positions of Acting Police Magistrate and Acting Coroner, which he held for some months from late 1876 to early 1877.

Not long after the British administration of Hong Kong began (in 1841), the position of Police Magistrate was created in 1844, first occupied by William Caine. Shortly after this, Caine was joined by an Assistant Magistrate, and he himself was given the new title of Chief Magistrate. This pattern of Chief and Assistant Magistrates continued until 23 July 1862, when a new pattern was established of two Police Magistrates of equal status.[27]

In November 1875, Ordinance Number 16 of 1875, "The Magistrates Ordinance, 1875" was passed,[28] "to amend and consolidate the laws concerning the jurisdiction of Magistrates over indictable offences and for other purposes". It lists clearly those offences for which a Magistrate was obliged to commit the alleged offender for trial in the Supreme Court, which included offences punishable with death; any offences (except burglary) punishable with penal servitude for life; offences committed within the jurisdiction of the Admiralty; blaphemy and offences against religion; perjury and subornation of perjury; composing, printing, or publishing blaphemous, seditious, or defamatory libels; defamation; bigamy; bribery; arson; forgery, etc. The Magistrate had the power to convict and sentence other offenders to a maximum of six months imprisonment with or without hard labour, to a fine not exceeding fifty dollars, or to be imprisoned with or without hard labour and to pay a fine, for any term and amount not exceeding six months and fifty dollars respectively. He could direct that the offender be kept in solitary confinement for any portion of his term of imprisonment, not exceeding fourteen days at any one time and not exceeding one month altogether. In cases of common assault, the Magistrate could, however, sentence an offender for up to a year. For certain other offences, he could sentence a male offender to a public or private whipping. In no case, could the number of strokes exceed thirty-six, and they were to be inflicted with a rattan. Males under sixteen, convicted of larceny, could be sentenced to up to twenty strokes only. Offenders could be sentenced to be publicly exposed in the stocks for up to six hours, in lieu of the whole or any part of any punishment to which the offender would otherwise be liable. If anyone was convicted of any offence by which injury or loss to person or property had accrued, the Magistrate could order the offender to pay to the aggrieved person reasonable compensation not exceeding fifty dollars, in addition to any penalty of punishment to which he was sentenced. In some cases, the two Magistrates, sitting together, could impose a prison term of up to two years with or without hard labour.

Some months later, Ordinance Number 8 of 1876, "The deportation and conditional pardons consolidation ordinance, 1876", was passed on 11 December 1876. It consolidated and amended the ordinances relating to deportation, conditional pardons, the branding and punishment of certain criminals, and the Ordinance Number 9 of 1857, entitled "An amended ordinance for better securing the peace of the colony". Under this Ordinance, Magistrates could still sentence certain offenders to be "once or twice publicly or privately flogged with the regulation instrument: Provided that not more than thirty-six lashes be inflicted on any one occasion." Others could be sentenced to be "whipped thirty-six strokes with a rattan, and [to] be sent to his native place".

The whole of Ordinance Number 8 of 1876 and Section 7 of the Magistrates Ordinance, 1875 (which provides that magistrates might sentence male offenders to whipping in certain cases), were scheduled for repeal under the draft ordinance "to amend and repeal certain ordinances relating to branding and to the punishment of flogging", as published in *The Hong Kong Government Gazette* on 19 November 1881. The repeal was first raised by Hennessy to London in a Despatch dated 17 October 1879,[29] and it quite likely had an impact on sentencing in the meantime.

One of the two equal Police Magistrates appointed on 23 July 1862 was Charles May, who – having arrived in Hong Kong in 1845 as Captain Superintendent of Police – had previously been acting assistant Magistrate from March 1853, and acting Chief Magistrate from October 1861. When he died on 25 April 1879,[30] he was the British resident who had lived the longest in Hong Kong. After a career in Hong Kong police work, which had lasted thirty-four years, including his magistrate's career of twenty-six years, the place he left empty was considerable.

No substantive Police Magistrate had been

appointed since 1870, when a former Cadet, James Russell (who became Chief Justice in 1888), was appointed. It is not surprising then, that, when May's post was being filled, in 1879, Colonial Office officials reminded each other of the nature of the posts and the qualifications of previous occupants of the posts. One minuted that, "The two Magistracies at Hong Kong are of equal value ($3,840), and have not of recent years been filled by English barristers, but by trained Hong Kong Civil Servants."[31]

In about February 1879, Stewart, who had respected Charles May, his opinions, and knowledge of Hong Kong, applied for his post,[32] but – at least partly due to the opposition of Governor Sir John Pope Hennessy, which the Colonial Office could not ignore – Stewart was not successful. Stewart's letter of application [33] had been forwarded to London by Governor Hennessy on 2 May 1879.[34] (Governors had the obligation to forward all such correspondence, but they also had the privilege of attaching to it their own point of view.) Hennessy wrote: "By this mail, I am transmitting to you, at Mr F. Stewart's request, an application he has made for the post of Police Magistrate in Hong Kong. I cannot, however, recommend Mr Stewart for this Office. The records of Mr Stewart's actions as Acting Police Magistrate[35] convince me that he is not fitted to deal with the Chinese as a Magistrate. Mr Stewart is an able man. I think, however, it would, at any time, be a mistake to transfer him from the Office of Head Master of the Central School to the Magistracy. At the present moment, it would be especially unfortunate to do so."[36]

This Despatch arrived at the Colonial Office on 17 June 1879. After passing through the hands of C. P. Lucas, it reached Mr Meade, who minuted John Bramston as follows: "I should like something more definite than the bare statement here made before deciding against the claim of an officer of Mr Stewart's standing for an office not requiring special qualifications and of whose character we have hitherto had the highest opinion. But all Mr Hennessy's statements in regard to his officials are to be taken with a very large grain of salt."[37] The only further mention of Stewart's application was made by Sir Michael

Hicks Beach, who seems simply to have rubber-stamped Governor Hennessy's decision: "I don't think Mr Stewart would do for this post".[38]

There was in fact considerable uncertainty at the Colonial Office as to whom to appoint. H. E. Wodehouse was mentioned: but, again, there was a barrier to any promotion for him, in the face of a previous despatch that Hennessy had written.[39] There was talk of offering May's post to an officer in Trinidad; of making a transfer from the Straits Settlements. In the end, Mr Plunkett, the Registrar of the Supreme Court at Hong Kong, a trained lawyer, was offered the post. His name was put forward to Sir Michael Hicks Beach by Mr Herbert, who stated that Plunkett had, "proved himself an excellent magistrate in the Straits." Mr Herbert also felt that, "He would also be a good man for the Legislative Council".[40] Plunkett was appointed. However, the Hon. C. B. Plunkett died on 21 December 1880, after less than two years in the post. He is now remembered by the name of a road in the Hong Kong residential area, known as The Peak.

On 2 February 1881, following Plunkett's death, Frederick Stewart applied again for a post as Magistrate,[41] and Pope Hennessy forwarded the application three days later. This time, he gave qualified support, doing so in terms which suggest that either his memory of his previous objection was faulty, or that he now accepted that his written reason for his objection at that time had been based on a mistake, or otherwise in error: "Whilst adhering to the opinion that the post of Stipendiary Magistrate in this Colony should be held by a Barrister, I have much pleasure in again drawing attention to Dr Stewart's long and valuable services as Headmaster of the Central School, and, in the event of Your Lordship not selecting a Member of the Bar for the post, I venture to recommend Dr Stewart's application to Your Lordship's most favourable consideration."[42]

Initially, however, this request could not be granted, since, as C. P. Lucas of the Colonial Office minuted, "The post has been already filled up".[43] (It had been given to Wodehouse.) Lucas was a supporter of Stewart, and in response to this application, put forward the suggestion that Stewart should be appointed Registrar General, instead. However, although Lucas's colleagues at the Colonial Office endorsed his suggestion, and an instruction was issued to Governor Pope Hennessy to put this into effect, Stewart was not appointed Registrar General at this time. The appointment was aborted through the manipulations and deviousness of Governor Pope Hennessy,[44] who was still working to create within the Hong Kong Government a system more dedicated to his own will, and who had ideas (never in fact carried out) about permanently transferring the work of the Registrar General's Office to a new Interpretation Department.[45]

Some months after Stewart's second application for the post of Police Magistrate was received, James Russell (who had been one of the two Police Magistrates since 1870) was appointed Registrar General and Colonial Treasurer, and a new vacancy therefore occurred. With no further objections from Governor John Pope Hennessy and with effect from 19 May 1881, Stewart was appointed (possibly retroactively) to the substantive post of Police Magistrate. Two months later, on 26 July 1881, following his resignation from the post of Acting Colonial Secretary, Stewart took up the duties of this post.[46]

Police Work and Education

At least during the early period of British administration in Hong Kong, and in the minds of some administrators, the connection between education and policing (perhaps between educated and law-abiding citizens) was close. Both were areas where contact was made with the mass of the population. Hong Kong's second Police Magistrate (at the time when there was one magistrate only), C. B. Hillier, was appointed one of the Committee who reported on the proposal that the Hong Kong Government should provide a subsidy to a small number of Chinese schools in Hong Kong. Following the decision to award the subsidy, Hillier was appointed as one of the small number of members of the Hong Kong Government's first Education Committee, and he served from 1848 until 1855.

A few years after Frederick Stewart arrived in Hong Kong as Headmaster of the Government Central School and Inspector of Schools, the Board of Education (which had succeeded the Education Committee) was disbanded and Stewart became head of the Government's Education Department. Later, he combined this work with additional work as Coroner (1867-1871) and, for a few months, that of Acting Coroner and Acting Police Magistrate (late 1876 to early 1877). Subsequently – by now the *previous* Head of the Education Department – Stewart became *substantive* Police Magistrate. It could be suggested that these periods in Stewart's career represent the apogee of the link in Hong Kong between police work and education.

The function of the Magistrate has common ground with that of the schoolmaster. His role is to teach as well – or as much – as to punish. Although true in any court, this seems particularly apparent in a colonial court, where (as Verner Bickley comments) many of the people in the courts are even further separated from the rules and logic of the society where they live[47] than are the "clients" of the courts in today's urban societies.

Stewart is certainly at pains to explain matters to defendants. For example, in Court Case Number 563,[48] where Yau Chung Ping was charged with neglecting to give correct information to the Postmaster General – and admitted his error – Stewart explains why this was such a serious offence.

In "The Embezzlement Case,"[49] Stewart's words to the defendant, Conner, who had spent ten years in the Artillery and four in the Naval Yard police, show that his advice was offered to Chinese and non-Chinese alike. The report of this case additionally shows that Stewart was careful to explain legal matters in court that needed explaining, and also his alertness to matters of legal practice that needed amendment.

On at least one occasion, Stewart's sentencing was taken up by *The China Mail* as a means of educating a whole group in society. On Tuesday, 15 November 1881,[50] when a jinricksha coolie appeared on a summons, "at the instance of Mr. Franco", charged with creating a disturbance at his house a few days earlier, Stewart fined him fifty cents or two days' imprisonment. In a separate column, "Local and General", published the same day, *The China Mail* elaborated the story further and used it as a means of suggesting several changes in the regulation of rickshaws,[51] which had been introduced into Hong Kong only in 1880.[52]

On other occasions, Stewart's judgements or comments about a case suggested administrative and legal amendments and did in fact lead to changes in how things were done. When a large number of defendants appeared (27 September 1881),[53] charged with using the wrong weighing or measuring instruments, Stewart fined them all the small sum of fifty cents, and expressed a hope that the law they had transgressed would be translated into Chinese. As reported in *The China Mail*, "His Worship said he inflicted this nominal penalty, as the trade had been representing to the Government a 'custom' not recognised by Ordinance. He did not know that the 'custom' would ever be recognised by the Legislature, but he hoped the Ordinance would be translated and circulated so as to remove all doubt as to what the Law on the subject really was."[54]

Although I have said elsewhere that personal sentiment seems not to have influenced Frederick Stewart in court, nevertheless the fact that his own father, in Scotland, was a tradesman (a tailor) must have helped him to understand these tradesmen's difficulties.

Stewart's remark had an impact. Soon after this, the Law was translated, as he had urged.[55] *The China Mail* of 3 October 1881 reports that, "Ordinance Number 22 of 1844, entitled, 'An Ordinance for establishing standard weights and measures and for preventing the use of such as are false and dishonest', with a translation of the same into Chinese, is published in the 'Gazette' by command of H. E. the Administrator. We noted the other day, in our Police Intelligence columns, in reporting eighteen cases in which Chinese shopkeepers were fined fifty cents for each false measure in their shops, a remark made by the presiding Magistrate, Dr Frederick Stewart, to the effect that he 'inflicted this nominal penalty, as the Trade had been representing to the Government a "custom" not recognised by Ordinance adding that he did not know that the "custom" would ever be recognised by the Legislature, but he hoped the Ordinance would be translated and circulated so as to remove all doubt as to what the Law on the subject really was.' It is satisfactory to see the ordinance in [question?] was promptly published in the form [required?]."[56]

Some days after this, a Chinese translation of the "Ordinance for Establishing Standard Weights and Measures, and for preventing the Use of such as are false and deficient", dated 30 December 1844, appeared under Government Notification Number 349 in *The Hong Kong Government Gazette*, 8 October 1881.[57] Stewart's Court Case Number 285, "False Measure", heard on October 1881, refers to the fact that the translation had appeared. The Defendant admitted having heard of the translation, but had been absent from Hong Kong. He was fined double the amount that was awarded prior to the translation of the Ordinance, one dollar or two days in prison.

On another occasion, a number of "chair coolies" appeared in court (1 February 1882) for standing at hire at an unauthorised place and Stewart cautioned and discharged them since the evidence included comments that there were not enough stands to accommodate all the chairs in Hong Kong. A later comment in the newspaper shows that this problem also was being addressed.[58]

Paradoxically, some were concerned lest exposure to western education itself was a cause of crime,[59] although Stewart himself – quoting a biblical example – took the more informed view that it was exposure to a whole new culture that might have this effect.

Frederick Stewart's conduct as Police Magistrate
The *China Mail* reports are generally spare and give little direct impression of Frederick Stewart's authority as presiding magistrate. Yet there is *one*, which shows that he was quite capable of taking prompt and decisive measures to keep order in his court. On this occasion, he silenced an unruly defendant – one of a group charged with repeated

piracy – by threatening, if he persisted in calling out, to have him removed outside and placed in the stocks.[60]

It is clear also, that Frederick Stewart was careful in handling his cases, could stand up to suggestion and pressure from counsel and outside authorities, and that he knew his own mind. Two cases, where Stewart mentions a jury, give examples of this.

References to a Jury[61]

On occasion, Stewart is reported as saying from the bench that he had to see a case as a jury would see it. Magistrate Garry Tallentire has explained that Stewart, when sitting alone, deciding a trial where the defendant has pleaded "Not guilty", had to decide law and fact, as Hong Kong Magistrates and District Court Judges today also do.[62] However, in England and Wales, fact was – and is – decided by the jury. Stewart's comments served to alert or remind those in court to this difference.

In "Alleged Attempted Shooting", when John Bryant, boatswain, was charged with firing a revolver at Samuel Bryant,[63] fireman, on board their ship, the "S.S. Ashington", the barrister acting for John Bryant said that he did not think that there was any necessity for sending the case to the Supreme Court.[64] Stewart however said, that "he thought the question of the defendant's intention was one which he would like to be left to a jury, and he would endeavour to have the case brought up before a special sessions". The Special Sessions was arranged. John Bryant was unanimously found not guilty of shooting with intent to murder and not guilty of shooting with intent to do some grievous bodily harm but he was found guilty of common assault. The sentence, also given on 10 March 1882, was three months' imprisonment with hard labour.[65]

In "Assault with Intent",[66] Francis Wyley and Robert Whitley, Privates in Her Majesty's Royal Inniskilling Fusiliers, were arrested on a warrant and charged with unlawfully assaulting three Parsee gentlemen with intent to commit a felony. The men appeared in Stewart's court on 10 and 12 December 1881. It was an important case. British soldiers were involved. Leading

Hong Kong residents had been assaulted taking a popular walk. The Acting Deputy Superintendent of Police was a witness. The lengthy newspaper report and Stewart's concluding words reflect the considerable interest of the community: "He had gone into the case most fully both for the sake of the prisoners and of the public". But the evidence was not sufficient to convict these particular men. "He must look at the case as a jury would look at it, and there certainly was not enough evidence for him to convict them." "Looking at it in every aspect as a jury would do, he saw nothing for it, but to dismiss the case."[67]

This case also illustrates a different point. It seems clear that the jurisdiction of the Magistrate in this case was not clear-cut and that there was considerable pressure on Stewart behind the scenes. Although the men were brought before him on 10 December and formally charged, the investigation was remanded at the request of the Military authorities, and the prisoners were not at this stage handed over to the Civil Authority. As the *Mail* explained, "Colonel Geddes [Lieutenant Colonel Andrew David Geddes commanded the Royal Inniskillings][68] is instituting enquiries of the most stringent and searching nature into the whole of the circumstances of the case . . . and to enable him to do so with more facility the prisoners are permitted to be retained for the present in the Regimental Guard Room."[69] Continuing a careful balancing act, the *Mail* wrote soothingly: "while every effort is being made to bring the guilt home to the guilty parties, no one would wish that others should be unduly brought to punishment by injudicious hurry."[70] It further states, that "The Magistrate's investigation will . . . not be resumed until the Military authorities are thoroughly satisfied that they have the right men."[71]

The *Mail* may have somewhat misrepresented the situation. Two days after this was written, Stewart did hear the case. He himself pronounced the evidence insufficient to find any of the accused men guilty, although, he said, "There was no doubt soldiers had been there". Stewart did however state, in concluding, that he "would refrain from making any remarks on the case". It seems clear that there were several remarks that he would have liked to make.

Stewart's demeanour from the bench

Stewart's demeanour from the bench seems to have been unexceptionable. During the James and Jane M'Breen hearings, where much domestic unhappiness is revealed, when tempers were lost and witnesses upset, Stewart did his best to smooth the waters, and was himself polite and conciliatory. For example, when Inspector Adams and the barrister representing Mrs M'Breen bandied words, and Adams refused to answer a question, Stewart pointed out that the barrister, Mr Mossop, had "a very delicate duty to perform, and Mr Adams should answer the question properly", which Adams then did. When the second dependent was upset by what the barrister had said, Stewart soothed both men: "Of course Mr Mossop was acting under instructions, which was quite a different thing from what Mr Mossop might do individually. It was a delicate matter, and he was bound to say that Mr Mossop had conducted the case very properly." The second defendant was upset by a statement which he felt suggested that he had done something improper. Stewart reassured him. He "was sure that Mr Blake would do nothing which was not proper". Nevertheless, Stewart was clearly in charge of the court. And when, on one occasion, Mr Mossop objected to some evidence, Stewart admitted it nevertheless.

There is evidence that Stewart was anxious for people to settle their differences out of court, rather than go to the extreme of a police court sentence. In the same case, arising from the M'Breen marriage, we read, "Remanded until tomorrow..., to see if the parties could come to some arrangement."

In the case of the quarrel between Mrs Driscoll and her amah, where there seems to have been fault on both sides, Stewart opened the door for the Driscolls to drop the case, although in vain. There was a better outcome in the "Penitent Servants" Case.[72] The case of Fong Akum and two other chair coolies, employed by the merchant, Mr J. D. Hutchison (one of Stewart's friends), was remanded on 9 August 1881, to see if they would obey the orders of their employer. When it was called again a week later, on 16 August, Mr Hutchison stated that the culprits had since obeyed orders, and the case was dismissed.

Extra-court relationships

As might be expected in the small place that Hong Kong was, at this time, some of those who appeared as defendants, complainants and witnesses in his court were people whom Stewart already knew. There is nothing to suppose that he treated them differently from others, whether with greater or less severity. For example, although Frederick Stewart had more than once praised highly the educational work of the Basel Mission school for Chinese girls, in his Annual Reports when Inspector of Schools, he does not seem to have allowed this to affect his judgement of the "Straying Cattle" case[73] in which the Basel Missionary, Revd Lechler, appeared and was sentenced to pay a two dollars fine, in default one day's imprisonment. Lechler had been summoned by Mr Ford, Superintendent of the Botanical Gardens, charged with unlawfully permitting three cows to stray on Crown lands and destroy young trees planted there. Mr Lechler said that he had told his cowboy[74] to be careful not to allow the cows to touch the young trees, but he had allowed the cows to stray while he was taking his breakfast.

Similarly, the sentence in the "Chair Coolie in Liquor" case,[75] where another teacher, Mr George Piercy, once a teacher at Stewart's Government Central School for Boys and now head schoolmaster of the Diocesan Home and Orphanage, is the same as that in the similar "Disobedient Servant" case,[76] where Mr J. H. Dos Remedios was the employer.

On the other hand, Mr John Joseph Francis, the Roman Catholic barrister, was considered by some as an opponent of Stewart's educational policies, when he served in the Education Department. (Historian E. J. Eitel asserts that J. J. Francis was the author of the Pamphlet, *The Central School: Does it justify its Raison d'être?*, published in 1877, which had attacked Stewart's Central School. Yet, in the reporting of the case, "Public Obstruction", heard on 16 November 1881, when Mr Francis acted for the defendant and Stewart supported the Police, there is no evidence that any personal feeling was involved.)[77]

Similarly, there is no evidence that Stewart expressed the undoubted disappointment he felt, when he committed for trial at the next Criminal Sessions Anthony Santos Spencer, former Central School pupil,[78] on one charge of stealing a clock from a house and another of obtaining goods by fraudulent means from Messrs McEwen Frickel & Co., Queen's Road, on various dates.[79]

Police Magistrate's work:
26 July 1881 - 29 March 1882

During the period, 26 July 1881 to 29 March 1882, Stewart's fellow police magistrate was H. E. Wodehouse, whose appointment also had been rejected earlier by Governor John Pope Hennessy, and whose distinguished service on the bench was to extend from 15 January 1881 to 1898, when he retired on pension. Frederick Stewart and H. E. Wodehouse each had separate courts; and cases were reported in the newspapers as, "Before Frederick Stewart, Esq.",[80] or "Before H. E. Wodehouse, Esq., Police Magistrate". On one or two occasions, however, the reports state "both magistrates sitting". Magistrate Garry Tallentire states that there is no provision in Hong Kong now for more than *one* magistrate to sit. He finds an analogy for the Hong Kong practice in the 1880s with the magistrates' courts in the United Kingdom today. As was the case with Stewart, these magistrates have no formal legal qualifications. They sit as benches of two to seven, with three regarded as the ideal number. He suggests that on the occasions when Stewart and his colleague heard cases together, this was because of the complexity or interest of the case. And, in fact, both Ordinance Number 2 of 1869 and Ordinance Number 16 of 1875[81] refer to jurisdiction vested in two magistrates sitting together.[82]

What sort of magistrate was Frederick Stewart?

Many factors need to be taken into consideration in deciding what sort of magistrate Frederick Stewart was. And, in their essays, Verner Bickley, Christopher Coghlan, Tim Hamlett, Geoffrey Roper and Garry Tallentire all contribute information and insights, which help – both directly and indirectly – in forming a picture of the man in this work, against the particular background of his time. The selected cases, given in Section Two, together with the various introductory essays and notes by the present writer, also supply considerable material for you, the reader, to form your own impressions. One caveat is needed, however. The cases as presented here are mediated by the voice of the *China Mail* reporter (or reporters), who occasionally adopts a facetious tone. Very occasionally, we appear to hear Stewart's own voice, but we need to be careful to distinguish between the two.

Public Opinion of Stewart a Magistrate

Long before Stewart was appointed substantive Police Magistrate and some months before he was appointed Acting Police Magistrate, the view was expressed that he would do well on the bench. On 25 February 1876, speaking about the replacement for Mr Alexander, Registrar, Supreme Court, *The China Mail* writes: "Current report mentions three gentlemen as . . . eligible for the post – Messrs Huffam, Russell, and Stewart." It comments: "That Mr Stewart should by many be deemed an admirable candidate is, after the thorough success he has achieved in his own department, but natural. We should much prefer, however, to see Mr Stewart on the bench, for which his knowledge of Chinese, his promptitude and decision, and his wide range of general knowledge preeminently qualify him. In truth, it would be a pity were the Government in selecting an officer to perform the duties of Registrar to depart from the original intention of the cadet system,[83] and wastefully throw away the Chinese scholarship of either Mr Russell or Mr Stewart on an office which may adequately be filled as efficiently by one possessing no such acquirements."[84]

On 28 February 1876, *The China Mail* mentioned

the support given by the *Daily Press* for the appointment of Huffam as Registrar, Supreme Court. "With regard to the two other valuable and highly-esteemed gentlemen whose names have been mentioned in connection with the vacancy, there can be but one opinion. They are capable of adorning almost any post under Government, but they have no special claim upon this . . .."[85]

When finally able to announce Stewart's appointment as Police Magistrate, on 16 May 1881, *The China Mail* was glad that he had been given the post, but expressed concern for education now he was leaving that department: "The general anxiety for the welfare of Education and the prosperity of the Central School may thereby be increased".[86] The writer hoped that a special appointment would be made so that Stewart could remain on the Legislative Council, where he had in recent years held a position, by virtue of being Acting Colonial Secretary. "His experience, clear-headedness, and high character peculiarly qualify him for a place in that body."[87] The appointment, *The China Mail* reported, "will be hailed as thoroughly satisfactory in every way".[88]

Still looking out for Stewart's interest, a week later, 23 May, *The China Mail* responded to the wording of the announcement in the *Hong Kong Government Gazette* of Stewart's appointment, with surprise that he was not named as "Chief Magistrate".[89] "The *Gazette* records the late appointment of . . . the Hon. Frederick Stewart as follows: – the Governor has been pleased to appoint . . . the Honourable Frederick Stewart to be a Police Magistrate. We should have thought that Dr. Stewart would have been Chief Magistrate." And in fact, in its announcement of the appointment, *The China Mail* had earlier stated that Stewart had been appointed, "First Police Magistrate".[90]

By 2 June 1881, however, *The China Mail* had clarified the situation. There was now no such thing as "Chief Police Magistrate". Mr May had continued to be referred to in this way even when the post was abolished (presumably because of his far greater seniority as a magistrate). Both Police Magistrates were now on the same footing.[91]

There is evidence that, when Stewart was finally active as magistrate, public opinion endorsed his conduct in the post. For example, on 15 November 1881, the "Local and General" column of *The China Mail* [92] supported Stewart's decision in relation to a rickshaw case. In the case, "Public Obstruction", reported on 16 November 1881, [93] in which Stewart supported the Police, his handling of the case was praised by *The China Mail*. We have already seen that some of his comments from the bench were acted on to effect improvements in the way Hong Kong did things then. Attention was also paid, on Thursday 9 March 1882, when Stewart highlighted an alarming aspect of a case, when a rumour was repeated about, "a gang numbering about one hundred men, organised for the purpose of fighting". [94] *The China Mail* sided with Stewart against Inspector Fleming – in charge of the case – who said that the statement was merely founded on rumour. "This may be so", *The China Mail* commented, "but as Dr. Stewart remarked, it is a rumour which should be most carefully inquired into, as the existence of gangs such as this is a danger to the peace of the Colony." [95]

<u>Familiarity with Chinese people, customs and language</u>
There is no doubt that, over the years, Stewart's work in education and the courts gave him considerable experience of Chinese people and knowledge of their ways of life and thought, and a corresponding reputation. Even so, there are no signs that Stewart was reluctant, when necessary, to refer in court to his interpreter (probably Bedell Lee Yun, who had been First Chinese Interpreter since March 1876), as cultural expert, just as Garry Tallentire states that he uses his court interpreter today. [96] For example, in the counterfeit coin case, which Stewart heard on 6 January 1882, the interpreter – a gentleman who had worked for the Hong Kong Government since 1861 and at the Magistrates' Courts since at least 1862 [97] – is reported as explaining that the wooden label in Court, with the words, "I collect silver taels" on it, was used by those who collected old silver ornaments and bad dollars. [98]

Although not all previous holders of the position

had had a knowledge of the Chinese Language (Charles May is a notable example),[99] knowledge of Chinese was nevertheless regarded as important for Hong Kong Magistrates at this time.[100] And know it Frederick Stewart certainly did. It had been one of the requirements of the concurrent positions of Headmaster of the Central School and Inspector of Schools, that the appointee should learn Chinese. Stewart had a private teacher of the language (paid for by the Hong Kong Government, as in the case of other Government officers) from the time of his arrival in Hong Kong in 1862. And there is clear evidence that Stewart was diligent and successful in this study, using Cantonese as a medium of instruction in the Central School and examining Village School students in the recitation of the Chinese Classics. Combined with this experience, his time on the magistrate's and coroner's benches would itself also have led to continuous improvements in these skills.[101]

It is because of the good opinion in which the public held him, together with the view that he was close to the Chinese population, combined with his knowledge of the Chinese language and the good opinion of the Colonial Office in London, that Stewart was later appointed Registrar General, a position that also required knowledge of the Chinese language and a good relationship with the Chinese inhabitants.

The Cases

On his first day in court as substantive Police Magistrate, 26 July 1881, several of Stewart's cases are reported. The captions indicate the content well: "Without a [Hawker's] Licence", "Assault", "Cruelty to a Dog", "Theft of an Umbrella", "A Medicine Man" (the defendant had damaged some trees), "Earring Snatching", "Buying a Soldier's Greatcoat", "Furious Driving [of a jinricksha]".

Stewart dealt with these as follows. One case ("Furious Driving") was dismissed for insufficient or unclear evidence. And for the others, the sentences ranged from the fine of one dollar or four days in prison ("Cruelty to a Dog") to three months imprisonment with hard labour ("Earring Snatching"). On 27 March 1882, at the end of his service as Police Magistrate, a similar variety of cases is reported: "Leaving Service without Notice", "A Disorderly Amah", "Drunk", "Larceny", "Disturbers of the Peace", and "Attempted Robberies on Board the 'Mary Tatham'". The range of sentences – from a fine of 25 cents or one day in prison to four months imprisonment – is very similar to that on Stewart's first day. In between the first day (26 July 1881) to the last day but two (27 March 1882), there was a scattering of serious cases, which Stewart committed for trial at the Supreme Court: kidnapping, piracy, murder.

The Sentences

In his essay here, Garry Tallentire comments that there seemed to be few sentencing options at Stewart's disposal.[102] The description given above of the sentences available to Magistrates under Ordinance Number 16 of 1875 confirms that the range was indeed narrow, compared to today. In their essays, both Tim Hamlett and Christopher Coghlan comment on the mildness of the sentences passed. And Hamlett seeks to explain this by commenting that Stewart's service as Police Magistrate in the early 1880s, "coincided with the period of controversial gentleness", imposed by Governor John Pope Hennessy.[103] However, as shown above, magistrates still had the power to sentence some offenders to whipping or a number of strokes with the rattan.

Historical Context

To give a historical context for Stewart's work and the court reports reproduced in Section Two, a short overview of earlier Hong Kong practices in relation to corporal and some other punishments, awarded by magistrates at that time but unfamiliar today, is useful.

The first number of *The Hong Kong Government Gazette* was published on 1 May 1841, only three months after Commodore Bremer of HMS *Sulphur* hoisted the Union Flag at Possession Mound (on 26 January 1841). It announced the appointment, as Chief Magistrate of Hong Kong, of Captain William Caine of the 26th Cameronion Regiment. [104] He was to exercise authority over all non-Chinese inhabitants (those of the Army and Navy excepted) according to the customs and usages of British police law, and over all Chinese inhabitants – as far and as closely as possible – according to the laws, customs and usages of China, "every description of torture excepted". [105]

However, Caine's jurisdiction was not unlimited. When cases required punishments exceeding a fine of four hundred dollars, imprisonment over three months, flogging of more than one hundred lashes, [106] or capital punishment, he had to remit them to the judgement of the Head of the Government. [107] Evidently, then, at this time, the Chief Magistrate had the power to award flogging of up to one hundred lashes. Also, as Eitel states, Caine awarded the bamboo for minor offences committed by Chinese. [108]

In its early years, Hong Kong was a rough and violent place. Bad elements poured into Hong Kong, particularly from Canton, attracted by what Hong Kong residents correctly [109] saw as their much softer penal system than that of Imperial China. – As late as 1897, *The Daily Press* reported speculation that an eleven year old child, who had accidentally caused the death of his mother, would either be beheaded or, after detention to the age of sixteen, would be put to death by the "lingchi or slicing process". [110] The continuing discrepancy between the punishments imposed in Hong Kong and Imperial China led to a state of mind, to be found among some of the non-Chinese population in Hong Kong, favourable to the adoption of

Chinese methods in Hong Kong: a view which the missionary, Revd James Legge, speaking publicly in 1872, found "outrageous".[111]

Writing from a modern, sociological, perspective, H. J. Lethbridge gives a balanced view of this early Hong Kong society. He suggests that the original Chinese inhabitants of Hong Kong in 1841 were *incorrectly* perceived by some Englishmen of the time as "a chance collection of poor peasants, piratical fishermen and unkempt quarrymen – a lawless and potentially dangerous class of people".

Lethbridge presents a different picture. "Like their fellow countrymen in *Hsin-an hsien* (a county which then comprised the future British Kowloon Peninsula and New Territories)", he suggests, they "formed a socially well-organised community, knit together by ties of family and kinship and involved, apart from the boat people, in wider forms of social organisation such as the clan and the lineage. They were constrained by the type of in-built social controls found typically in any rural Chinese community."[112]

On the other hand, the picture Lethbridge draws of the society that rapidly formed after the establishment of the British administration is consistent with contemporary opinion, although differently expressed: "Immigrant Chinese arriving after 1842, who came mostly from Canton and the delta counties, formed a purely urban population, lacking roots and sentiments of belonging: they had necessarily few attachments at first to their new area of residence. Congregated in the mushrooming city of Victoria and soon outnumbering the old, established Chinese population of the island, they were not subject to any in-built system of social control."[113]

Lethbridge presents better-off and wealthy Chinese and European new residents – the two main urban groups – as each faced with the problems of maintaining public order and protecting their families and properties.[114] (Governor Pope Hennessy publicly regretted that so few "respectable" Chinese brought their families to live in Hong Kong; and he adopted measures to change this situation.[115] Indeed, for decades, the population of Hong Kong as a whole was heavily skewed to males. Christopher Munn, for example, describes it as, "a port city populated largely by sojourners with a heavy preponderance of men".)[116]

The better-off Chinese merchants and traders, Lethbridge comments, were – soon after the formation of the British colony – compelled to employ their own guards; while some householders and shopkeepers engaged their own street watchmen, and these were paid for either by the individual householder or collectively by subscription.[117] In time, the District Watch Committee evolved, managed by the Chinese residents themselves.[118]

In the early years, piracy – often heavily organised in pirate fleets – was rife.[119] That the activities of pirates threatened not only those at sea is indicated by the name, "Taipingshan" (quiet mountain), given to their area in the Central district by Chinese residents, as an expression of relief after the removal of a pirate gang.[120] As a further example, two of the five cases of murder, reported for 1877, arose from piratical attacks on villages.[121]

Violence was quite common and personal, and – directed against non-Chinese – included the withholding of the means of life – food – and the conveniences and activities of life represented by the Chinese labour supply. During the 1850s, there were calls from Canton to boycott the food supply to Hong Kong, for shops in Hong Kong to close down and for the Chinese to return to China. The violence was also directly physical. A large group of two thousand Chinese was formed in Kowloon to harass the British stationed in Hong Kong.[122] On 15 January 1857, an attempt was made to poison all the foreigners in Hong Kong by lacing the daily bread supply with arsenic,[123] and the plan to do this was certainly known in advance by at least some among the general Chinese population. On an early tour of inspection of village schools (in 1862), Frederick Stewart himself was set upon by a group of men, one with a personal grudge against him.[124] However, the Chinese population itself – the vast majority – was at least equally at risk, and most of the reports of the cases involving violence, which Frederick Stewart heard in his court, involve acts of violence by Chinese against Chinese. In 1889, fourteen persons were banished as, "dangerous to the peace and good order of the Colony, in that being without other visible means of subsistence, they practice organised extortion by threats upon the villagers of Hunghom".[125]

In response to this situation, quite ordinary individuals armed themselves, ready for self-defence. Respectable English ladies carried pistols when out and about. Householders kept firearms in the house. People took swords and other deadly weapons with them when there was a fire in the street and this caused so much disorder that, in September 1882, Frederick Stewart (as Acting Colonial Secretary) issued a notification that the Police would disarm all such persons and charge them with a breach of the law.[126]

In the face of this initial, and continuing, situation, the heavier sentences, beyond a magistrate's jurisdiction, were certainly not spared. In the 1850s, for example, an eyewitness records how he, "'saw the pirates brought in, tied together with their queues, and later executed hanged in three rows of three'."[127]

The nature of punishments in Hong Kong was a subject of discussion – whether in Hong Kong itself or in Great Britain – from the early days. Following a motion introduced into the British Parliament by Dr Bowring, then Member of Parliament for Bolton and later (April 1854 to May 1859) Governor of Hong Kong – public flogging was suspended from 23 January to 8 May 1847.[128] During the governorship of Sir George Bonham (March 1848 to April 1854) a Draft Ordinance on flogging was published in January 1849, to test public opinion for change, but the response was such that the question was shelved.[129] In 1865 and 1868, Governor Sir Richard MacDonnell (March 1866 to April 1872) applied whipping and solitary confinement to cases of armed or violent assault, kidnapping and child-stealing, [130] and to criminals returning from deportation.[131]

The public nature of the punishments shows that they were intended to have a deterrent as well as a punitive effect. For example, previous to a public flogging that had taken place on 6 September 1870, the Chinese had been notified by placard of the names, offences, and other particulars of the prisoners.[132] Although there had been a mistake in the announcement of the time, so that, "a large number of foreigners arrived too late for the spectacle", *The Daily Press*, the following day, explained clearly what the offences had been, and what had happened. Nine prisoners had been flogged, for sentences ranging from one year's hard labour and thirty lashes for kidnapping, to three years' penal servitude and seventy-five lashes, for robbing with violence. The strokes administered on this occasion (by turnkeys of West Indian origin and under the supervision of Dr Murray, Colonial Surgeon and Mr Douglas, Warden of the Gaol)[133] ranged from fifteen to twenty-five. Each prisoner screamed under the lash. Except for two, the prisoners were all young men and two were "mere boys". Doubtless, the "immense" crowd of Chinese present drew some conclusions from what they saw, just as they did from the public executions and public torture inflicted on the Chinese Mainland.

According to Eitel, the branding (tattooing) of convicts was originally introduced into the Hong Kong legal system at the request of the Chinese authorities. Eitel records that, from before the beginning of British administration in Hong Kong, secret political societies, the most important of which was called the Triad Society (now familiar to us in a more unambiguously criminal context), were aiming to overthrow the Manchu Empire. Apparently, the Mandarins persuaded Governor Sir John Davis into passing an Ordinance (Number 1 of 1845), the effect of which was that the Hong Kong Police should search out and arrest political refugees as being members of the Triad and other secret societies. After a term of imprisonment, they should be branded on the cheek and deported to Chinese territory. (Their fate on their return was predictable. The Mandarins would arrest, torture and execute them. And this sequence of events was a weighty factor in the minds of the Hong Kong administrators of justice.) Branding on the cheek was modified nine months later (20 October 1845) by substituting, in an amendment (Number 12 of 1845), branding under the arm.[134]

In autumn 1866, to control the prison population, MacDonnell introduced a system under which prisoners were induced to petition, that they might be liberated on condition of their voluntarily submitting to be branded (in effect, tattooed)[135] and also to be deported, with the understanding that, if they were thereafter again found in the Colony, they would be liable to be flogged by order of a Magistrate and remitted to their original sentence. This Ordinance, in its original form, was disapproved by London. Sir Richard then abandoned the system of bringing branded and deported criminals, who returned to the colony, before a Magistrate, but continued the original system of branding and deporting prisoners, before the expiration of their sentences, in accordance with the engagements voluntarily entered into by prisoners, and ratified in each case by the Executive Council. Criminals thus liberated and deported were, on being found again in Hong Kong, remitted to their original sentences and then flogged in gaol as a matter of gaol discipline. This system continued until 25 May 1870,[136] when it was stopped on the recommendation of the Chief Justice Sir John Smale and the Attorney General, during MacDonnell's period of leave, out of Hong Kong.[137]

The branding, deporting and flogging system was reintroduced in 1872,[138] at the beginning of the administration of Sir Arthur Kennedy,[139] and made law by Ordinance Number 4 of 1872. At the same time, prison discipline became more severe.[140]

Shortly after John Pope Hennessy arrived, to become Governor of Hong Kong (23 April 1877), two men were flogged at the public whipping post near the Harbour Master's Office, the event having previously been announced by paragraphs in the local newspapers.[141] Possibly as a result, Hennessy directed his attention to the topic of flogging early in his term, and the following of his views are among those recorded: "the use of the lash [. . . seems to be excessive in this Colony];[142] and (as he wrote in a despatch to the Earl of Carnarvon, dated 6 July 1877), "As far as I am aware there is no code of laws in any part of her Majesty's Empire in which the power of flogging is so extensively given to Magistrates and Judges as in Hong Kong."[143] Under Hennessy's administration, flogging was practically abolished and only a few whippings, privately administered within the walls of the Gaol, took place.[144] Papers relevant to the "Penal Laws Amendment, Abolition of Branding and Public Flogging, Etc." were laid before the Legislative Council on 3 June and 19 November 1881.[145] On 3 March 1882, *The China Mail* relates that, "The much-abused and lately neglected whipping post near the Harbour Master's Office is now in course of removal."[146]

However, Hennessy's actions were not all in the direction of more humanity, although his habit of "always thinking how he can put his best foot forward in the House of Commons",[147] and the impact this has had on some commentators, has led to a substantial body of opinion in this direction. He introduced a new rule in 1879. "All old offenders should be tried in Supreme Court, where they might receive sentences commensurate with habitual indulgence in crime, instead of the frequent short sentences inflicted by the Police Magistrates."[148] In the interests of better prison discipline, he also reduced the Gaol diet for Chinese prisoners (it had previously been too generous, he believed) and reintroduced the treadmill.[149]

Public Opinion and Opinions of the Public

According to Eitel, Sir Richard MacDonnell's severely deterrent treatment of Chinese criminals was unambiguously approved, by Chinese and European residents alike, including the unofficial Members of Council.[150] Similar approval was given to Sir Arthur Kennedy's measures. As one might expect, however, the community violently disagreed with Hennessy's change in policy – an unprecedented public meeting was called to protest – and the evidence suggests that an *increase* in crime was the result. Eitel claims that there is evidence that Pope Hennessy manipulated the statistics to suggest that his own package of measures (which included increased discipline for prisoners in gaol) had *reduced* crime, but – as stated by Eitel – the true facts were that crime significantly *increased.* [151] This is confirmed by a reading of the contemporary statistics, published in *The Hong Kong Government Gazette*. A specific instance, as perceived by Hong Kong opinion, related to the snatching of earrings from Chinese females. [152] *The China Mail*'s comment, published on 20 September 1881, gives a fair sample of the contemporary tone.

"From our Supreme Court report it will be seen that the far too common crime of ear-snatching [*sic*] is beginning to attract the attention of the Judges. Mr Justice Russell, from his experience of the Police Bench, speaks with considerable authority when he says that the offence of ear-snatching was at one time rampant, and that the number of such offences was then reduced by the application of the "cat". If the ears of the woman from whom the articles were wrenched or snatched were at all injured, the Court was wont in those days to construe that fact to mean that a robbery with personal violence had been committed; and the ear-snatcher, having thus been brought within the provisions of a certain local ordinance, he was flogged in accordance with that decision, at the discretion of the Judge. The application of this wholesome rule Mr Russell does not hesitate to say had the direct effect of deterring Chinese from committing such offences; and, as the learned Puisne Judge goes on to remark that he will not be slow to apply the same rule when he can possibly do so, we can only say that the public will doubtless recognise the fact that common sense and legal knowledge need not necessarily be divorced from each other, but may live and reign together. It is well known that different impressions have been conveyed from certain quarters as to the increase of late in this offence of ear-snatching; but we fully believe that since flogging has been but sparingly dealt in, this crime has become again a confirmed nuisance and a constant source of anxiety to Chinese females in the streets. If a clear case of ear-snatching with violence were but detected – for a large number of these cases are never even reported to the Police – and a sound dose of corporal punishment were administered to the thief, the effect would no doubt be as wholesome as at a former period it was shown to be."[153]

Not surprisingly, the flogging controversy made waves in the United Kingdom. In view of the tone of discussion there, Sir Edmund Hornby, formerly Her Majesty's Chief Judge for China and Japan, felt impelled to write a letter to the Editor of the *Spectator*. In this, Hornby defends Hong Kong residents against the impression currently being given (as a result of Pope Hennessy's interventions) that they were brutal towards Chinese criminals and prisoners. "The lower class of Chinese who inhabit the colony, and who flee to it from the mainland, are amongst the most dangerous, persistent, and insubordinate of any criminals I know of, and the amount of crime committed by them in Hong Kong is astounding, bearing no comparison with that committed in any other part of the world; while the difficulty of detection and bringing offenders to justice is almost beyond belief, as the more respectable Chinese dare not give evidence, in consequence of the terror exercised over them by the gangs of ruffians living in their midst."[154]

Within the constraints of the system, there is evidence of compassion, both in the treatment of defendants and prisoners and in the newspaper response to this treatment. One example is the case of Wong Alo, a carpenter, who appeared before Frederick Stewart on Tuesday, 13 December 1881, charged with unlawful possession on the previous day.

As the report of the case states, "He was seen in Hollywood Road carrying a spar of timber, but when he observed the constable he threw it down and ran into Square Street, where he was pursued and arrested. He said he had been engaged by another man to carry the timber. He also admitted two previous convictions for larceny in 1879. Fined five pounds [*sic* for "five dollars"], in default six weeks' imprisonment with hard labour."[155] Wong Alo opted for imprisonment.

Sadly, on 24 January 1882, Wong Alo died in prison, ironically, on the last day of his sentence. *The China Mail* report of the inquest that was held, reads: "An Inquest was held this afternoon in Victoria Gaol before the Coroner, H. E. Wodehouse, Esq., and the following gentlemen as a jury: – Messrs G. D. Böning, J. F. Mardtfieldt and J. R. White, on the body of Wong A-lo, aged twenty-eight, a prisoner, who died in the Hospital Ward this morning.

"The prisoner was admitted to the gaol on the 13th December on a six weeks' sentence for stealing wood. Dr Ayres examined the deceased then and found him in a very emaciated condition, as he had found him twice previously within the last year. Instead of being placed on penal diet and condemned to hard labour, he was, on account of his debilitated condition, given an extra diet and only required to execute as much work as he was able to accomplish. He was removed to the Hospital Ward on the 10th of this month, suffering from bronchitis. He had recovered from that and had asked for some additional food, which was granted, and seemed to be improved yesterday, but this morning at half-past five, when the Hospital Warder visited him, he exhibited signs of extreme exhaustion. The Doctor was sent for, but before he arrived, at a quarter past six, the prisoner had died. During the whole confinement he had made no complaints, and yesterday was walking about along with some other patients. The Jury returned a verdict of death from natural causes. The prisoner's sentence expired today."[156]

In November 1880, Lord Kimberley sanctioned the final abolition of all branding of criminals, permanent discontinuance of *public* flogging, repeal of all Ordinances providing for the flogging of Chinese, prohibition of all flogging except in cases where it would be inflicted in the United Kingdom, and an order that flogging of Asiatics should in all cases be on the breach and not on the back.[157]

In 1884, however, the Minutes of an Executive Council Meeting show that both flogging and the prevalence of earring snatching were still hot topics. For both a report from the Colonial Secretary on the topic and "a return by the Registrar General showing the feeling of some of the leading Chinese inhabitants as to the reintroduction of flogging for offences of this nature" were read.[158]

In 1886, a Hong Kong Government Commission considered introducing the measure of cutting off the queue – a punishment practiced in Imperial China – in the case of all those admitted into prison, no matter how short the sentence.[159] In 1887, a Bill entitled, an *Ordinance Empowering the Courts to Award Whipping as a Further Punishment for Certain Crimes* was passed on 18 March. The prison diets were reduced further in both 1886 and 1887. Prisoners sentenced to one year or more in prison were now to be "secured by fetters of a pattern to be approved by the Governor".[160]

Considering all the evidence, Samson Chan concludes that the measures taken by the Hong Kong Government in the Nineteenth Century are not surprising. Citing Spierenburg's view,[161] that the early modern state had to resort to violent and exemplary punishment to frighten potential criminals and to demonstrate the state's monopoly of authority, Chan concludes: "Hong Kong during the formative years . . . [had] major public order difficulties and it is therefore not surprising that deterrent and public punishments were needed in enforcing the authority of this newly ceded Colony."[162]

This outline of early nineteenth century Hong Kong practices in relation to capital and corporal punishment in particular, suggests that magistrates never had the power to sentence convicts to hanging. But, in addition to fines and sentences of imprisonment (with or without hard labour and periods of solitary confinement), at various times, magistrates did have the power to give sentences of deportation, branding (tattooing), flogging and strokes of the bamboo. Frederick Stewart himself gave a few sentences of flogging during his few months as Acting Police Magistrate in 1876 and 1877. For example, he awarded Ho Alo, "two months' hard labour and to be flogged ten strokes" for robbing a Malay seaman of five rupees tied up in a handkerchief which he had in his trousers pocket,[163] and he awarded Thomas Louis ten strokes for Larceny on 31 October 1876 and again on 28 December 1876.[164] In 1885, the rattan replaced the cat for Chinese offenders.[165] It seems to have been ordered by the Governor of the Gaol to enforce prison discipline, and not as ordered by the Magistrates. Although not commenting on whether or not it has consistently remained on the Statute Books as a sentencing option from early days, Garry Tallentire reports that, only recently has *caning* been removed as a sentencing option in Hong Kong."[166]

Other evidence suggests that, during some periods, magistrates had powers to sentence to the rod,[167] the cangue (a wooden board somewhat like a film clapper board, worn round the neck) or the stocks.

Magistrates also took evidence in cases, which they later remitted to the Supreme Court, where the sentences could – at various times – include not only flogging and deportation, but hanging. Capital punishment remained on the Hong Kong Statute Books until the Crime Amendment Ordinance came into force in April 1993: Section V abolished the death penalty and substituted life imprisonment. However, for a considerable period before that, the death sentence was usually commuted to a prison term.

The China Mail reports no sentences of flogging, rod, branding or deportation, given by Magistrate Stewart during the period 1881-1882. But it does report eleven cases (with an overall total of fourteen defendants), where the sentences include some hours in "the stocks". Since, as reported, seven of these sentences specified the place where the sentence was to be served (which, reflecting the different places where the offences were committed, were various), these seven at least may have referred to the cangue, a much more mobile instrument of punishment than the much heavier stocks. Each of the other sentences, also, could appropriately have been served at the place where the offence was committed. Possibly they were served there; and if so, it is likely that they also may have referred to the cangue.[168]

The Stocks and the Cangue

Those of us who have had a long-term interest in Hong Kong history will be very familiar with photographs of men in the stocks or wearing a cangue in Nineteenth Century Hong Kong. Some of these photographs suggest that the crime committed was written down and displayed about the prisoner's person.[169] We may not be equally familiar with images of the stocks in Europe or elsewhere, where their use may have ceased prior to the advent of photography. After all, as Frederick Stewart wrote, "The Nineteenth Century in England is not the Nineteenth Century in Hong Kong".[170] We tend therefore to regard these forms of punishment as another peculiarity of the system of law and punishments in early Hong Kong, and some of us at least may find it embarrassingly distasteful, because the conjunction of time, place and régime makes it appear a colonial rather than a universal punishment.

However, we may also remember the disguised Earl of Kent in the stocks in Shakespeare's play *King Lear*. An exhibition of documents from the national archives of Scotland, held at General Register House, Edinburgh, in 1998, also gave exposure to now obsolete forms of punishment. *Crime and Punishment*, the text of the exhibition, published as a booklet, includes an image of a man, in what might be sixteenth or seventeenth century dress, standing in the pillory, his head and hands fixed into a perpendicular board of wood, attached to a wooden pole.[171] A similar image (but the period of dress is not equally clear) appears on the front cover of the booklet. A paragraph in the text, referring to an incident which occurred in 1674, refers to the jougs (iron collars) and stocks, "where minor felons were chained up and put on public display" at the tolbooth or mercat [market] cross, both public places where public humiliation was part of the punishment. Apparently, "Petty theft, drunkenness, brawling, 'flyting' or gossip-mongering were dealt with in this way."[172] It was common for people so punished to have "a paper" pinned to their chest describing the offence for which they had been convicted.[173]

In fact, the stocks and pillory were common in early modern times in England and in colonial America, and continued to be used as late as the mid-nineteenth century. In Puritan England and New England the stocks were a favoured punishment for frivolous behaviour in violation of the Sabbath. Women scolds also were frequent victims. In the southern states of America, disobedient slaves were sent to the stocks. Confinement sometimes lasted several days.

Some take the view that the effect on the prisoner was more psychological than physical, for he or she was exposed to public ridicule. Frequently, however, prisoners confined in stocks or pillories were also flogged or branded and additionally stoned by passers-by.[174]

The China Mail quotes Lemprière in the *China Review*, as stating that the cangue, "so well known in China was also an instrument of punishment at Rome."[175] The quotation continues: "It was in the form of a fork, hence its name arose. It also bore the shapes of H or V and was placed on the culprit's neck, while his hands were fastened to the two ends. It is at least curious that Rome and China should have hit upon the same punishment." The piece ends with a question, "What is the earliest date of the introduction of the cangue into China, or is it a punishment purely native in its origin?" The *Nouveau Petit Larousse Illustré* (1924) gives two illustrations of cangues in use and explains: "En Chine, table percée de trous dans lesquels on introduit la tête et les bras d'un condamné: le poids de la cangue varie avec la gravité de la faute commise." ["In China, a board pierced with holes into which are introduced the head and arms of a condemned person: the weight of the cangue varies according to the gravity of the fault committed."] A folk museum some hours' journey out from Seoul, Republic of Korea, shows examples of the cangue.

Among the seven hundred or so reports of Magistrate Stewart's cases in the period 1881-1882, eleven cases, with a total of fourteen defendants, resulted in a sentence, which included a minimum of two hours and a maximum of six hours "in the stocks" (or the cangue).[176] In five of the sentences, nothing is reported about the position of the stocks; but in nine sentences, the time in the stocks (or cangue) was to be served at the place where the offence occurred.

In none of these cases was the stocks (or the cangue) the only sentence given. Associated sentences ranged from a fine of one dollar to six months imprisonment with hard labour, the first and second fortnights of the imprisonment to be in solitary confinement.

From the nature of the cases, it seems clear that this punishment was used to teach not only those convicted of the offences, but those who saw the offenders punished, about what they should not do. They should not commit larceny from the person, or theft, or attempt to pick pockets. They should not cut earth and undermine walls, behave in a disorderly manner at a public hydrant, steal a chopper and two brass ladles, fight and create a disturbance, be armed with a deadly weapon, steal an umbrella, or snatch a pair of trousers and two silver dollars.

All defendants were Chinese. Their occupations are not stated in all cases, but the defendants included an earthcutter, two coolies, a fisherman and a seaman. As for the complainants, although some of them were not Chinese – Mr Watts of the Survey Department and H. Gustave (a scholar at St Joseph's College), for example – they were mainly Chinese, and they included people referred to or indicated to be a Chinese girl, a Chinese man, a Chinese ship's cook, a Police Constable, a street coolie, a lukong (a Chinese policeman), another Chinese man, and a Chinese hawker.

Branding and deportation

In none of those cases, for which we have a report, did Stewart sentence a guilty party to branding or deportation. (We have no adequate record of his cases during his few months as acting magistrate, in 1876 to 1877.) The absence of branding is consistent with the passing, on 24 June 1881, of the "Penal Ordinances Amendment Ordinance, 1881" which incuded the abolition of branding (as provided for in Ordinance Number 4 of 1872 and Ordinance Number 8 of 1876). Similarly, the absence of deportation is consistent with the passing of Ordinance Number 12 of 1881, the

"Banishment and Conditional Pardons Ordinance, 1881", on 23 August 1881.

Remitted to the Criminal Sessions

Among the seven hundred or so reports of Stewart's court cases in 1882 and 1883, we find that Stewart remitted several of the defendants to the Criminal Sessions.[177] The charges in these cases were very varied. They included obtaining money under false pretences,[178] stealing a clock,[179] highway robbery,[180] theft of a twenty-five dollar note,[181] stealing a piece of brass from auction rooms,[182] stealing an umbrella, [183] stealing a bundle of clothing, [184] embezzlement,[185] being in a dwelling house for a supposed unlawful purpose,[186] trafficking in human beings[187] willful damage to a garden, [188] murder, [189] passing counterfeit coin, [190] robbery (of thirty dollars) from the person, [191] armed burglary,[192] piracy,[193] snatching from the person,[194] dealing in counterfeit coin, [195] stealing a coverlet, [196] robbery of one hundred dollars,[197] alleged kidnapping,[198] being in possession of burglarious instruments and deadly weapons, [199] larceny of two brass smoking pipes, [200] receiving stolen property knowing it was stolen,[201] and stealing a clock. [202] Some were remitted because the defendant chose to be tried by a jury.[203] Others were remitted because the offence was beyond a magistrate's jurisdiction at this time.

As Headmaster of the Hong Kong Government Central School, Stewart had been known and admired as a strict disciplinarian. This was achieved, however, by moral example and moral suasion, and the cane – at a time when its use was common in Great Britain – Stewart hardly ever used in the School. What view should we reach, now, about the severity or otherwise of the sentences he gave when Police Magistrate? The court case reports given in Section Two provide a considerable body of information to assist each reader to form an opinion.

Differing Perceptions of Social Reality in Dr Stewart's Court

"Be Careful: You are in a Court of Justice!"
– Mr Mossop, Hong Kong Barrister, representing the Chinese wife of an Irish husband

Verner Bickley

There are many different definitions of "culture". For our present purpose, we shall assume it to be the fabric of meaning in terms of which human beings interpret their different experiences and by which their actions are guided. Some anthropologists have claimed that the institutions and values of particular cultures can only be self-validating[204] and therefore it is difficult to interpret and evaluate the beliefs and practices of societies and cultures other than one's own. We are, however, often obliged to judge the actions of members of other cultures by standards which are not theirs. This is often the case in both adversarial and inquisitorial applications of the law which may be exposed to the particularities of another culture, or cultures.

There is a substantial literature relating to "culture learning" and cross-cultural contact, including many studies of negative and positive interactions between members of different national, social and ethnic groups.

Such interactions among persons in Dr Frederick Stewart's courtroom took various forms, involving persons of the same racial and ethnic group (for example, persons from among the Hakka Chinese community), persons of the same race but of different ethnicity (for example, Chinese of Hokkien and Tanka origins), and persons of markedly different races and cultures (for example, Europeans from various countries and Indians from different communities).

In a majority of cases the complainants, defendants and witnesses were of Chinese origin, although they did not necessarily come from the same language group.

Cross-cultural transactions in the court often took place among individuals from quite different cultures, as in the case, "Theft of a Watch, etc.", heard on 2 September

1881,[205] in which the magistrate, a Scot, with the help of a Chinese interpreter, presided over the trial of a man of the Islamic faith, accused of theft by a former policeman of Indian origin.

Persons engaging in inter-cultural interactions in different settings sometimes occupy positions of unequal power. Such was the case in Stewart's court in which the magistrate was duty bound to uphold English legal practices, albeit tempered and modified to some extent, to suit local conditions. There is, however, no indication in the printed reports that Stewart's decisions were affected by the differences between the "in-group" (of which he was a representative) and the members of the different "out-groups" who appeared before him – persons of different social class, race, religion and skin colour.

Our definition of culture is all-embracing in that the "fabric of meaning" reflects all of a country's habits and values, including its laws. Countries, societies and cultures are not necessarily the same thing but, generally, a national legal system applies across cultural and social boundaries within the same country. In nineteenth century Imperial China, a set of precepts derived from Confucian thought was applied universally, despite the social and linguistic differences that existed between ethnic groups. "The ruler was expected to sway the people by virtuous conduct and moral example, not by legal regulation."[206]

Conformity with the ideas known as *Li* (customs, rituals, etiquette, virtue and propriety) "induced by education and example", was, "of greater importance than compliance with *fa*, or positive law in the Western sense . . .".[207] *Li* did not include the capacity for recognising and reacting to situations that might be regarded as amusing in another culture. Therefore, *humour* was regarded, at least in literature, as an inappropriate form of expression, fit only for the "common people".

Although, no doubt, capable of appreciating an earthy parable or an appropriate aphorism in their own language, many, if not most, of the persons who appeared before Magistrate Dr Frederick Stewart were illiterate in Chinese and ignorant of English. They were, therefore, spared the ironic and sometimes flippant manner in which their peccadilloes were often reported in *The China Mail*, of which the case, "Theft of an Umbrella" is an example:[208]

> ### THEFT OF AN UMBRELLA
> Wong Ahong, who (as he alleged) only went into the house of the complainant to enquire for a friend who was at the U. S. Consulate, and departed in company with an umbrella belonging to the occupant, was relieved of the necessity of having an umbrella by getting six weeks' imprisonment with hard labour.

Reporting of this nature would rarely be possible in today's sanitised newspapers – ruled out largely by the perceived need to observe "political correctness" and perhaps by the belief that humour, especially that involving sarcasm, exaggeration and satire, transfers uneasily across cultural boundaries.

Proceedings in Frederick Stewart's court were conducted with decorum, but sensitivity to the feelings and "rights" of persons from other cultures and nationalities was not paramount in the *reporting* of those proceedings. Words were used and descriptions were given which would be unacceptable today. There is the headline, "A Drunk and Violent Darkie",[209] in the case of an African seaman accused of soliciting alms. "Darkie" was used in Hong Kong, until recently, as the name of a popular toothpaste, but it has now been re-named "Darlie". In "A Goose Plucked",[210] the (Chinese) complainant is described in further unflattering terms as a "gullible young man", "the poor simpleton" and "the farmer fool". Worse, the same report makes a slighting reference to Sikh policemen, somewhat grudgingly described as, "not *always* awanting when their good offices are serviceable." [211]

Cases were sometimes heard in which the observance of ritualistic practices resulted in offences being committed because the logic of the law clashed with cultural tradition. Qing Ming (All Souls' Day) falls at the beginning of the third moon of the Chinese calendar,[212] coinciding roughly with the Christian festival of Easter. During the Chinese festival, it is imperative for families to deposit "money" in the Bank of Hell by burning joss paper for the benefit of their ancestors. Sometimes this was (and is) done in the streets, rather than in the cemeteries. It was, however, a breach of the law (and a danger to the public) to start fires in the streets. For this reason, in the case, captioned "Joss Pidgin" (heard in August 1881),[213] three Chinese were charged with unlawfully making a bonfire in the public street. In a similar case, captioned "More Bonfires" (heard the following day),[214] twenty Chinese admitted having made bonfires in the public streets.

Later in the year (October 1881), one Pong Atin found to his cost that firing crackers in the street was illegal,[215] despite the cultural demands of the Autumn (Mooncake) Festival − the "Moon pidgin" − held on the fifteenth night of the eighth moon.[216] And a clash of cultures occurred in February 1882 when Ng Asum was fined one dollar, with the option of four days' imprisonment, for firing crackers on a Sunday,[217] a day particularly respected by Christians.

A relaxation of similar rules relating to noise-making celebrations was however authorised at Chinese New Year in 1882, when permission was given for crackers to be fired within a clearly stated period of time.[218]

It is clear then that the cultural values of a people may be found in the records of court cases. David Bayley has illustrated this in an article on the modes and mores of policing in Japan, in which he describes some of the social values of the Japanese.[219] Similarly, in his analysis of certain capital cases in India, A. R. Blackshield provides a graphic account of Indian life. − "Beyond the bloody stories of violence and tragedy in these cases, there are constant glimpses of ordinary, undistorted life in the day to day village milieu; and even in the actual murders, there is much to learn".[220]

From among the cases heard by Frederick Stewart in Hong Kong, I have already given, above, examples of breaches of the law brought about by the performance of certain rituals, long practised by the Chinese community. Other cases touch on the spiritual beliefs of both complainants and defendants. So, in the case, "Theft of a Watch, etc.",[221] referred to above, the defendant is Ahmed, from Malacca. He is deposed by an Indian, Ameer Khan, who saw "the defendant for the first time in the Mahomedan Cemetery". He (the complainant) went "to a well to wash his hands and feet before saying his prayers. Left his coat and belt on the table in the Mosque".[222]

On 8 November 1881, an unmarried Chinese woman attempted to commit suicide. Found "dripping wet" at the Harbour Master's Office, she pleaded in court on 9 November that a devil had told her to jump into the harbour. The magistrate remanded her for a report by the Colonial Surgeon.[223]

The defendant in another case[224] had committed sacrilege. Consequently, today, he would doubtless have become the victim of a *fatwa* at least as serious as that which affected the author, Salmon Rushdie. Charged with being a lunatic and dangerous, Syed Ahmed allegedly kicked his wife and threatened to kill her. "He went into the kitchen for a knife, and as he could not get one he threw the Koran at her".

At least one case reflects the attitude of a member of one Chinese community towards a member of another Chinese community; a conflict across cultures within the same society. In "Wilful Damage to a Garden", the accused in the case was charged with destroying his late employer's garden. He is reported as having told a witness that "a punti man" had taken his situation, indicating that he was resentful of a person who came from a Chinese community other than his own.

Contradicting the view that each culture has its own – different – standards, there were certain types of offence which were quite unacceptable in *both* China and Hong Kong. In China, the sale of women for prostitution and kidnapping was subject to the legal sanctions of *fa*. However, these would not necessarily have applied in China, or in Hong Kong, to the selling either of boys for adoption, or of girls as *muitsai* (bonded maid servants). In her comprehensive history of the Tung Wah Hospital in Hong Kong, Elizabeth Sinn notes that, "There were various kinds and degrees of bondage operating in Chinese society over wives, concubines, apprentices, *muitsai*, sons, brothers, nephews, and so forth which were incomprehensible and repugnant to English law. But these social principles had to be upheld, even in Hong Kong and the Tung Wah Hospital Committee . . . was guardian to them. In other words, the Committee enabled Chinese in Hong Kong to have justice dispensed according to accepted Chinese principles wherever the legal machinery of the British could be bypassed".[225] And, we might add, if they *wished* to bypass it. (This corpus of court cases shows that in many cases Chinese people actively *sought* a decision by means of the British legal system in Hong Kong.)

This "legal machinery" made trafficking in human beings a criminal act in Hong Kong when The Protection of Chinese Women and Female children Ordinance (Number 2 of 1875) was introduced.[226] It was this Ordinance, which governed the conduct of cases in the magistrates' and higher courts.

In one such case – "Alleged Trafficking in Human Beings" – two women and three men were charged with detaining a Chinese woman for the purpose of selling her. After a preliminary hearing, Frederick Stewart sent the case to the next Criminal Sessions of the Supreme Court.[227]

Another, more complicated, case of kidnapping was brought to the magistrate's court four times, between 27 January and 11 February 1882.[228] Two women, one Pang Asun and one Chan Acheung, were charged with bringing Chan Nui, the wife of a coolie, into Hong Kong for the purposes[229] of prostitution. The account of the first hearing in court reads like a perverted "fairy story".

> On the 23rd September an old woman, who lived in
> the same village but whose name she did not know,
> came to her [the complainant, Chan Nui's][230]
> father-in-law's house and asked her to accompany
> her to Canton, which she did in the expectation of
> meeting her husband. . . . When they arrived in
> Canton the old woman placed her on board a small
> boat . . . occupied by two women, and she remained
> there until the 28th September . . .. On that date, the
> first defendant came on board the boat and asked
> the boatwomen if they had a woman for sale, to
> which they replied in the affirmative and pointed to
> the complainant. After some disputing the bargain
> money was settled at $245, and this woman left in
> the boatwomen's hands three gold rings, and the
> gold earring as earnest money.

Stewart committed these defendants also for trial in the
Supreme Court. Their lawyer (Mr Holmes of Messrs
Stephen and Holmes) reserved their defence.

The case against Pang Asun and Chan Acheung
was conducted by Frederick Stewart and Mr Holmes in the
English language. Pang Asun and Chan Acheung, when
asked to speak, would have replied in Chinese.

It seems certain that Frederick Stewart possessed a
good command of Cantonese.[231] Despite this, the case was
probably mediated by an interpreter, whose role was crucial,
as it still is today. The interpreter's duties were taxing, since
a typical day's work could involve translating (and
sometimes glossing) statements from different witnesses,
complainants and defendants. All of these statements were
taken down in longhand by the magistrate himself.

In 1989, in an article, which focussed on the ways
in which languages can be used by individuals for
mediating purposes across cultures, the present writer
described the proceedings of Court Number Six in the South
Kowloon Magistracy, one day that year. "The first case (of
the morning) had to do with the possession of dangerous

drugs for the purpose of trafficking. The interpreter begins the proceedings by making a statement in Cantonese. The magistrate, using a variety of Australian English, then points out to the defendant that there is a significant difference between the date of the alleged offence and the date he first received a prescription for the drug, the date of the alleged offence coming *before* the issue of the prescription. An explanation is given in Cantonese by the interpreter and then the magistrate announces in English that he will take a plea. The interpreter confirms (in English) 'record admitted' and the magistrate asks the defendant (in English) if he has anything to say. The defendant (in Cantonese) replies 'I was drunk but I admit the offence. I really did obtain the prescription'. The interpreter repeats this in English. The defendant then pleads (in Cantonese) 'I hope that your Worship will give me a chance'. This is repeated in English by the interpreter. The magistrate (in English) concludes the proceedings by instructing the defendant to appear for sentencing in three weeks' time".[232]

It is reasonable to suppose that a similar set of circumstances prevailed in the 1880s, in Frederick Stewart's court. In some cases, the defendants – and less frequently – the complainants, spoke different varieties of English, but the majority of complainants, defendants and witnesses did not have English as a first language and, in the case of the Chinese persons who appeared in court, they could, in most cases, probably communicate only in a Chinese language, or in "pidgin".

In his ground-breaking book on pidgins and creoles, the linguist, Peter Mühlhäusler, accepts that several different meanings have been ascribed to the term "pidgin" which, he believes, are not in conflict with his definition of pidgins as "partially targeted or non targeted second language learning, developing from simpler to more complex systems as communicative requirements become more demanding". Pidgin languages (he suggests) have no native speakers. "They are *social* rather than individual solutions, and hence are characterised by norms of acceptability."[233]

Many of the linguistic exchanges that took place in

Stewart's court were between Chinese persons and/or persons of other nationalities who could speak Chinese. In *The China Mail*, these exchanges were usually rendered in English for the readers' benefit. Even the cross-cultural exchanges between Chinese speakers and non-Chinese speakers were, for the most part, reported in English, although the word *Pidgin* appeared in the caption, "Joss Pidgin", meaning business or activities related to the illegal burning of joss sticks.[234]

Although rare, there are however at least two examples of verbatim reporting when pidgin was used. In one case, a German woman was charged with assaulting a tailor who forcefully demanded payment of $100 owed to him. "The complainant . . . persisted on having immediate payment . . . 'You must pay me money just now, what for you keep me? You wantee things, you must pay money!'"[235] The second case, involving the use of pidgin, illustrates some of the difficulties that can occur in a cross-cultural marriage. In August 1881, an Irishman named James Joseph M'Breen was charged, together with George Blake, a staff sergeant, with assaulting M'Breen's wife, a Chinese lady. An unhappy marriage of nine months' duration had culminated in charges and counter-charges and some lively exchanges between a witness and prosecuting council, unlikely to be heard in today's courts:

> *Mr Mossop:* I think you said something about them walking away.
> *Witness:* I think you have made a mistake.
> *Mr Mossop:* Perhaps I have; you may correct it.
> *Witness:* No, I won't.
> *Mr Mossop:* Be careful; you are in a Court of Justice.
> *Witness:* I think you had better be careful.

O'Breen, the first defendant in the case, referred to an incident which revealed a cultural difference between his wife and himself. On "the afternoon of the day in question", Mrs O'Breen persuaded her husband to accompany her to a cemetery in Happy Valley. There, after considerable bickering between the two – and, presumably, to make a point – she threw herself down upon her late husband's grave, and remained on it for two hours. A further example of cultural incompatibility between the two was reported by another witness, at odds once again with Mr Mossop:

> *Witness:* The noise was most disgraceful . . .. She tried to incite him to strike her.
> *Mr Mossop:* Be careful.
> *Witness:* There is no careful about it. She said "You likee flog me".
>
> . . .
>
> *By Mr Mossop:* — Complainant did try to incite
>
> defendant to flog her. The words were "You wancheee flog my; You likee flog my".[236]

The case of Irishman James Joseph M'Breen and his Chinese wife, Jane, illustrates the misunderstandings that can occur and the problems that can arise when the values of cultures and societies differ. These values often influence the way people behave. Types of behaviour, which are acceptable in one culture, may offend in another culture. This is revealed very clearly in the records of Dr Frederick Stewart's magistrate's court. By the standards of nineteenth century Hong Kong, the verdicts of the court were necessary, fair, right and just, yet it is certainly possible that some of the defendants failed to perceive these rulings as consonant with their own perceptions of social reality.

Thoughts about the Practice of Law in Hong Kong arising from the Court Cases of Frederick Stewart, Esq.

White Gloves and Patience

Christopher Coghlan

The first point that struck this writer on reading the *China Mail* reports of the Court cases of Frederick Stewart, as gathered together and edited by Gillian Bickley, was the style of the reporting – clear, limpid, factual (but with the occasional hint of irony[237] or humour).[238] What a contrast to the present style of our English-language press, full of strangulated Americanese – "beat up on him" instead of "beat him" – and euphemisms – "helper" for "servant", "boss" for "master". All reporters of course will at some stage fall victim to the temptation to make a story out of an incident where the facts barely support their interest, but nowadays the interest is likely to be pruriently salacious so as to make the story more sensational. However it may be said that today – life being more complicated and sophisticated than it was in the 1880s – our crimes themselves have perforce become more sensational. In these reports there are constant tales of theft of clothing – usually single items or small bundles of workmen's apparel – with the motive no doubt of using them for their proper purpose or selling them as second-hand.[239] Nowadays the clothing is likely to be womens' underwear – occasionally a uniform – stolen for rather more nefarious purposes.

Another fact that strikes the knowledgeable reader forcibly is the comparative leniency of some of the sentences passed by Stewart. Taking the crime of pick-pocketing as an example, we see that he sentenced a miscreant who took an opium box[240] to twenty-one days with hard labour. Another who took money[241] received six weeks of the same. A third got six months for the same crime, but he had been in gaol before.[242] At present a pick-pocket can expect to receive a sentence of from twelve to fifteen months before any mitigating factors are considered. (This assumes he has pleaded not guilty. A guilty plea would bring a reduction of one third in the sentence.) Those who work in gangs can expect a starting point of two and a half years in gaol. An exception today to the comparative severity of modern sentencing is shoplifting theft. This is possibly because the perpetrators are usually women or because the crime is made temptingly easy by the open display of goods, a factor which probably was less common in Stewart's day. For shoplifting, there is no customary sentence nowadays, the sentences varying from fines and probation to short periods of imprisonment when there are aggravating circumstances.

It may be however that imprisonment is used less frequently now than in Stewart's day, and thus, when used, tends to be for longer periods. There are a number of reasons for this. One is that the range of sentencing options is more extended now and includes Probation, Community Service Orders and Training Centre Orders. Another is that one of the professed aims of imprisonment is rehabilitation. Although it would be wrong for a Court to increase a sentence so that the offender will receive the treatment he needs in prison, nevertheless it is clear that the longer the sentence the greater the chance of rehabilitation. Short sentences are not rehabilitative but purely retributive or deterrent in nature. Not that rehabilitation was absent from Stewart's mind. – One can see this from the case of the mendicant[243] when he ordered that she should "get one dollar from the poor box to pay for a licence and buy a stock of cakes so that she might hawk". – I wonder when the poor box ceased to have a function in Hong Kong? I have seen them in Magistrates' Courts in London, but only in the older buildings and I have a dim memory of a gentleman – it could have been a popular and rather old-fashioned magistrate called St. John Harmsworth – ordering cash to be given to a deserving case from it. Now our female mendicant would most likely be placed on probation so that a social worker would be empowered to oversee her.

Some things, however, still remain very similar.

The range of cases that Stewart tried would be broadly similar today: minor crimes of dishonesty – theft, handling stolen goods, and similar; minor assaults; a few dangerous drugs cases (these would now be more frequent as – prior to 1946 – dealing in and using opium, the then most popular dangerous drug, was not prohibited by law). Stewart would also try a quantity of what could be described as administrative offences – market offences, non-standard weights and the like. The latter category has grown immensely since the state has taken to regulating so much of our lives (the "New Despotism", a former Lord Chief Justice in England, Lord Hewart, called it). All magistracies in Hong Kong now have at least one court where a magistrate – usually a special magistrate (that is, not necessarily legally qualified) – hears cases on breaches of the myriad Regulations that control Hawkers, Food, Drugs and Buildings. To replace Stewart's cases involving rickshaw and sedan chair coolies, we have motoring offences.

It is estimated that ninety-eight percent of all criminal cases in England are heard in the Magistrates' Courts and the proportion is higher in Hong Kong.[244] The range of crimes heard in the Magistrates' Courts is also much larger than those heard in the District Court or the High Court (the latter including the Court of First Instance and the Court of Appeal), all of which, with the Court of Final Appeal, try or hear[245] the criminal cases in Hong Kong. In the High Court, the typical range covers homicide, serious assaults, drugs cases, serious thefts, robberies and burglaries, rapes and firearms cases. Other cases of course appear from time to time but – broadly speaking – the range above would cover ninety percent or so of all cases heard. The District Court, founded in Hong Kong in 1953 to take the less serious cases out of the High Court, and consisting of a judge sitting without a jury, tries a relatively narrow range of cases, the less serious of the assaults, drugs and dishonesty trials; and also (in place of the homicide and rape heard in the High Court) commercial crime, the hundreds of cases involving dishonesty in the business world which are a feature of Hong Kong jurisprudence.

Again, this list forms the bulk of the work, with a small proportion of other crimes. The range of the Magistracy is clearly much wider, and also calls for rather different skills from the Magistrate compared to a Judge. These necessary skills arise, amongst other causes, from the quite different style of trials in the High Court and the Magistracy.

In the High Court, all criminal proceedings are brought after committal proceedings in the Magistrates' Court. A typical example of such a committal for trial was reported from Stewart's Court on 12 October 1881.[246] Committal proceedings are an opportunity for the Magistrate to examine charges and witnesses to see whether there is sufficient evidence for the High Court to consider. It is therefore a "weeding-out" process: – those cases where the evidence is weak or the charge otherwise defective will be dismissed at the lower Court and obviate the time and expense of the higher Court doing the same. Before 1968 (when there was a change in the law), the Magistrate heard the witnesses in person and made or had made a note ("deposition") taken of their evidence.[247] Since that date the Magistrate has been able – if the accused is legally represented and consents – to commit him on the basis of the evidence contained in the police statements. That is, the statements themselves contain the evidence, without the need for witnesses to give it in Court. This of course results in a considerable saving of time, in those cases where there is a case to answer and the accused wishes to "reserve his defence" (not to disclose his defence until his trial). Occasionally – both before and after 1968 – the accused made "a statement"[248] (put forward his defence) if he thought there was no *prima facie* ("obvious at first view") case against him. If there was – and also in all cases where the accused wished to plead not guilty at trial – he would "put himself upon his country" for trial – an old-fashioned phrase which still occurs in the Criminal Procedure Ordinance (Section 50) – meaning that he wished to be tried by his countrymen, that is, the jury.

The High Court judge, then, will try criminal cases, which have already had some prior examination; and he will sit with a jury. The qualities he principally needs are *patience*, to deal with the sometimes slow proceedings, as witnesses are examined before laymen (the jury), and *clarity*, when it comes to sum up the case. His knowledge of the law need not be as extensive as the magistrate's, save in the comparatively narrow range of offences tried before him, and in relation to procedure and evidence; and the appropriate sentence (if the verdict is guilty) is usually a matter of setting the right number of years of imprisonment. The District Judge has a similar role, but with this exception: the absence of a jury means that the clarity which the High Court Judge requires to sum up to a jury the District Judge requires for his reasons for verdict instead, which are delivered in open Court. The Magistrate, on the other hand, does not face the onerous burden of providing detailed reasons for rulings or verdict (save later if they are required for appeal) but his patience must be as inexhaustible since, unlike the case of the High Court and District Court judges, parties appear more often unrepresented. In very few of the cases heard by Stewart does it seem that lawyers appeared. – The prosecutor was invariably a policeman,[249] as so it remained in at least one court in Hong Kong (North Kowloon) until quite recently.[250]

The need for patience in a magistrate makes one wonder whether Frederick Stewart possessed that quality – it is difficult to tell from these reports, most of which are purely factual. Colonial magistrates in Hong Kong have been castigated for their lack of this virtue by Jan Morris in her book *Hong Kong*.[251] This account was repeated, rather out of context, in Frank Welsh's *A History of Hong Kong*.[252] It describes a magistrate – "nationality immaterial", Jan Morris states – who, "sitting as he does alone upon his bench, hearing cases involving simple Chinese in a language he does not understand ... bullies defendants mercilessly ... bludgeons witnesses and testily proclaims his own importance ...". One is surprised to see a historian quoting uncritically from a one-sided account by a journalist/biographer/popular historian.[253] But Welsh's own limited insight is shown in the next paragraph of his book, where he compares the situation of the use of Chinese in official Hong Kong with that of the Welsh language in

Wales; and claims that (different from the situation of the Chinese language in Hong Kong) the Welsh language enjoys fully equal status to English in all aspects of government (he does not explicitly mention the courts). Of course it is not a fair comparison. – He is probably comparing 1970s Hong Kong with 1990s Wales. Taking into account the centuries that Wales has been linked with England, the use of Welsh in public official life is very recent. Even more important are the practicalities of language use. There was a huge difference between the ease of use of the Chinese and the English languages until very recently – and probably also between Chinese and difficult Welsh – and this lay in the technical areas of typewriting and printing. The complexity, rarity and sheer slowness of the Chinese typewriter made it previously virtually an unworkable written language for police and trial purposes, where the advantages of written English are obvious if speedy justice is to be effective. It is only very recently that computer programmes have evolved which make it possible for the necessary documents – charge sheet, bail form, witness statements – to be typed up, and copies made on the evening of a prisoner's arrest, so that he can be taken to Court the next morning, ready for trial. In the case of writing by hand, many Chinese judges tell me it is more expeditious to write their notes in English, even in a trial conducted in Chinese.

But I digress. It is not really the lack of use of the native language that is the gravamen of the charge, but the bullying and bludgeoning of witnesses by the magistrate. How common is this, and was it more or less common in Stewart's day? Did Stewart himself indulge in it, even if only occasionally? I see no hint of this from these reports. And I must point out the other side of the coin – the sheer dogged patience and perseverance that is needed when dealing with the ignorant, the mendacious and the unintelligent of all nationalities – descriptions that would cover probably the majority of witnesses and parties in magistrates' courts. Readers of *Myself a Mandarin* will be aware of the sheer opacity and self-centredness of many of the characters that the author, Austin Coates, had to deal with. Sometimes the problem is one of lack of imagination: – the witness cannot believe that the magistrate is ignorant of facts or problems which are central to the witness, and imagines him to be seized, without explanation, of the most arcane details of a dispute. Another problem is that of the witness who imagines that the intricacies of his job are so profound and exclusive that no layman could ever be expected to understand them, any more than he himself can understand the machinations of the law. And then of course there are the sheer perverse – the policemen who tell lie after lie because they think it will save a weak case, the witness who lies to protect a friend; both of them in fact unknowingly weakening their cause. The judge has to deal with them all, careful not to give the impression, by a flash of exasperation or impatience, that he has prejudged the case. On top of this, the magistrate of today – an experienced lawyer – will have to deal with the ineptitude of some of the lawyers and prosecutors before them, for the most part cutting their forensic teeth. Generally speaking, I would say that Jan Morris's criticism is unfair, both in the sense of not being true and also because it lacks comprehension of the magistrates' difficulties. Also, dare one say, it might be that the European magistrate has developed more moderation respecting a witness's failings than his Chinese colleagues, who can be more forthright in criticising prevarication. I knew one Chinese magistrate, always charming and imperturbable to myself when appearing before him, who was rumoured to have made even a traffic policeman cry! There are times when it would take a saint not to attempt the same.

I have said that the range of cases tried by Stewart in the 1880s would be broadly similar to those tried in Hong Kong in the 1990s. What are the differences? There were, of course, offences *then* which are no longer offences, or very rarely committed nowadays. Leaving an employment without notice,[254] giving a false report to the Lloyd's agent as to the arrival of a ship[255] – I have yet to come across these crimes myself – but the main difference strikes one as the naivety or lack of sophistication of the parties, which is rather amusing, but no ground for complacency – it is astonishing how gullible our immeasurably better-educated populace can be. The trick described in "All is not gold that glitters"[256] is still common, although company shares may well have replaced gilded bars of base metal as the tool for deception. Inflation has of course introduced another enormous change – Stewart rarely fined anyone above five dollars – a parking ticket costs three hundred and twenty dollars today. The laws themselves are very recognisable. Hong Kong Law in Stewart's day would have been about forty years old. At the founding of the colony, English Law was declared to apply as the law of Hong Kong, but from that date the Governor would add to it or amend it as was fit, first by Proclamation and later acting in Council with the Legislature; whilst law enacted in England after 26 January 1841 would not apply in Hong Kong. One would expect a growing divergence in the two systems subsequently, but in practice the Government – with the Legislative Council sitting once a week even in modern times – drafted laws that are very closely based on English statutes; and so the two systems today remain remarkably similar. The Government may not always have the resources to research and initiate laws, nor does the Hong Kong Legislative Council have the time and expertise to debate and amend them; nor is there the need, when adequate legislation has been tried and tested elsewhere. Of course there is a mass of legislation, which is unique or partly unique to Hong Kong, covering subjects from Immigration to Business Registration.

The mass of new legislation since Stewart's day has obviously contributed to the increase in the number of criminal prosecutions, but by a surprisingly small proportion – the vast majority of prosecutions today is for crimes that were crimes when the Ten Commandments were first drawn up – but there has been a more than proportional increase in the number of judges. In the 1880s there were two judges in Hong Kong – the Chief Justice, the puisne judge (a High Court judge below the rank of Chief Justice) – and two magistrates. In 1998 there were ten Court of Appeal judges, twenty-six High Court judges, thirty-four

District judges and seventy-five magistrates, besides other judicial officers such as registrars and coroners. There were also six hundred and eighty-three practising barristers. The number of barristers in Stewart's day is uncertain. We do know that, by 1882, thirty-three barristers only had been admitted in Hong Kong since 1844, and many of these practised in Shanghai and elsewhere. Of course, Hong Kong in the 1880s was far smaller in every way – the New Territories was not leased until 1898 – and the population was about two hundred and twenty thousand. But even so, the increase in criminal cases today is disproportionate. Every reader may have his or her own theory for this growth, but, after making every allowance for the increase in the number of crimes legislated against, most will agree that, in their lifetime, mankind has become both more criminal and more unpleasant.

The decline in agreeableness in one's fellow humans may be disputable, but certainly few of us seem to share the optimism about human nature that the Victorians had, and practice must have been clubbable for the handful of judges and lawyers a century ago. For instance, if a case was appealed from a judge, he himelf would sit with his brother in the Full Court – the precursor of the Court of Appeal – possibly co-opting the Attorney General if need be to hear the Appeal. The Attorney-General could also partake in private practice until 1890, when the policy changed and his salary increased to seven thousand eight hundred dollars a year in lieu.[257] Occasionally the Attorney General sat as a judge, but there seems never to have been an occasion to commission him, or any other lawyer, to sit in a criminal case, a practice that was common later and is still used, the title of "Commissioner" changing to "Recorder" in the 1970s. The clubbable nature of legal Hong Kong is shown by the congratulatory speeches, together with the gift of a pair of white gloves, which were given whenever there was a maiden sessions.[258]

A maiden sessions arose when the High Court, sitting in a session held once a month or so under commissions of oyer and terminer, gaol delivery and the peace (oyer and terminer – to hear and decide cases; gaol delivery – to empty the gaols of those remanded in custody for trial) had no crimes in the calendar (the list of cases) to try. In such a case it was customary in England, until the Assizes were abolished in 1971, to present the judge with white gloves and this custom also prevailed in Stewart's day in Hong Kong. It is unlikely that Stewart's court was ever empty. But in reading these reports one gets the feeling of Hong Kong having become a well-ordered (and no doubt well-regulated) society a mere forty years after its foundation. A golden age indeed.

The "Light and Pass" Rules

Unenlightened Law?

Gillian Bickley

Some of the laws and regulations that applied in Hong Kong in the 1880s appear now so strange that previous commentators have attributed them to some early perversion in Hong Kong society. The rule that no Chinese should be out after a certain time at night without a light or pass, or both a light and a pass[259] – an offence for which several people appeared in Stewart's court – is one of these.

In his essay, "In the Public Interest", in the present book, Tim Hamlett comments on this rule, which he describes as frequently cited as a negative example of British colonial administration. Crisswell and Watson draw the sting somewhat when they state that the rule originated at a time when the police could not cope with the very frequent burglaries committed by Chinese (who formed the majority of the population). The following survey of the relevant ordinances and some other relevant surviving records gives further information on this, and concludes by illustrating how these regulations were applied in Frederick Stewart's court. Crisswell and Watson explain that the light and pass rules first came into being in 1842, when Magistrate William Caine ordered that no Chinese except watchmen were to walk the streets after eleven at night. An 1843 amendment may be seen as some alleviation of this. All Chinese had to carry a lantern after eight in the evening and no-one was permitted to be on the streets after ten at night without a pass.[260]

One of the first westerners to comment unfavourably on this rule in print, in an attempt to change it (along with some other matters), was probably the Reverend George Smith, later the first Anglican Bishop of Victoria (Hong Kong). In October 1846, he returned to England from his "exploratory tour" of China (1844-1846) on behalf of the Church Missionary Society. Writing from Church

Missionary House, London, Smith sent a letter, dated 16 January 1847, to the British statesman, Earl Grey.

Reverend Smith begins by expressing his missionary presumption, "that the extension of the Colonial Empire of Britain involves responsibilities of the highest order, namely, of diffusing through the world the blessings of liberty, of civilization, and of Christianity". He then submits "specific measures as likely to exert a favourable influence towards these ends".

"My own observation," he continues, "leads me to fear that the present system of police injuriously affects the immigration of respectable Chinese and the consequent improvement of the Colony. For instance, no Chinese is permitted to move abroad in the street or public roads after a certain hour in the evening without bearing a lantern and a written note from his European employers. A respectable Chinese coming to Hong Kong and venturing in the public streets without such protection would be in danger of being apprehended by the Police, kept in custody during the night, and rendered liable to the humiliating disgrace of corporal punishment."[261]

Smith urged Earl Grey to follow the general principal "of adopting a more liberal policy towards our Chinese fellow subjects of the Island of Hong Kong, with a view of [262] encouraging more promising subjects for Christian instruction."

Smith does not hide the fact that there were reasons for the lantern and pass rules. – "It may be pleaded that such a precaution in the present social state of the Native population may be necessary". – But he insists on his point. "Such a régime as long as it is permitted to continue will seriously affect the well-being of the Colony and preclude every hope of securing any better class of immigrants than that which at present exists. Needy adventurers who have little of character or pecuniary means will be bribed to submit for a few months to this régime by high wages. But to the wealthy Native merchants, to the well educated native scholars, to the Chinese gentry, money will be an ineffectual inducement in leading them to submit to such invidious regulations."[263]

It seems likely that George Smith was particularly influenced to comment on Chinese objections to the lantern and pass rules by a conversation he had, when in China, with the Chinese Christian, Leang Afa, and his non-christian son, A-tuh. "Both of them spoke unfavourably of Hong Kong, as the resort of the worst classes, driven thither by destitution or crime," Smith wrote. "A-tuh especially spoke of the insolent treatment to which the Chinese residents were exposed from the police and the Europeans generally; and became much excited when he spoke of a recent indignity of treatment, which his father had suffered."[264]

However, George Smith himself indirectly records that the use of a lantern, and evidence of identity when out and about at night, was also a habit (if not a law) in China. When describing a visit to a Buddhist Monastery outside Ningpo, in company with a friend (nationality not given), in July 1845, Smith describes how, "At one point we were hailed by some soldiers at a watch-station, when our boy held up my companion's lantern, inscribed with his title and office, as proof of our respectability, and we were allowed to pass on."[265]

In response to Earl Grey's concern at what George Smith had reported, a Colonial Office official wrote the following in a report: "I have examined the ordinances and Police Regulations of Hong Kong, and I do not find that they corroborate the alleged practice. An Ordinance exists (Number 10 of 1844) under the authority of which Chinese offenders may be punished in the Colony according to the usages of China, but there is no law insisting upon persons of that nation carrying a lantern after a certain hour at night in the streets of the town of Victoria or that they should be provided with a certificate from their European Employer. If any such precaution is required it must be in virtue of some police regulation not communicated to this office."[266] Nevertheless, Earl Grey did receive corroborative evidence of George Smith's assertion and expressed his decision to call for an explanation from Governor Sir John Davis.[267]

According to Crisswell and Watson, the rules continued in force in Hong Kong until 1897.[268] However, this statement needs considerable elaboration. From time to time, during the total period of their existence, the "Light and Pass" regulations (which were, at times, simply "Pass" regulations, [269] and sometimes "Light *or* Pass" regulations) [270] were discussed, modified and variably enforced. Their vestiges were not finally removed from the Statute Book until 1930. [271]

The only reference to a "lamp or lanthorn" in Ordinance Number 14 of 1845 is the reference to the fine of a maximum of five pounds, for any person neglecting, "to affix to his house and keep alight during the night, such lamp or lanthorn as may be required and approved of by the Superintendent of Police". (Section III, division 4.) This repeats a similar reference in Ordinance Number 5 of 1844 (20 March 1844), entitled, "An Ordinance for the preservation of good order and cleanliness within the colony of Hong Kong and its dependencies", which it replaced.

This regulation and also the regulation that moored and anchored boats should be a certain distance (one hundred and fifty yards) from low water mark during the period from 9.00pm and "gunfire in the morning" (Section III, division 8) are plain indications that the community wanted to take measures for its protection during dark.

Frank Welsh takes the view that Security Ordinance Number Nine of 1857, passed on 15 July 1857, was introduced as a response to the Chinese attempt to kill the whole British population of Hong Kong by putting arsenic in their daily bread supply on 15 January 1857. [272]

Ordinance Number 9 of 1857, "An amended Ordinance for better Securing the Peace of the Colony", passed by the Legislative Council of Hong Kong on 15 July 1857, [273] provides that, "Any Chinaman found at large elsewhere than in his own Habitation between the hours of Eight in the Evening and Sunrise, and not having a Pass . . . shall be summarily punished by any Justice of the Peace for every such Offence, either by a fine not exceeding fifty dollars nor less than fifty cents, or by imprisonment and hard labour for a term not exceeding fourteen days nor less than one day, or by Public Whipping, and Public Exposure in the Stocks, yet so as that no such offender shall receive more than twenty blows, or be exposed for more than two hours, for any one offence."[274] The passes were to be issued by the superintendent of police to, "such of the occupiers of the several houses within Victoria, for use, as he shall find to be fit and proper persons to receive and use the same, and according to the wants of such occupiers: yet so as that no Chinese Occupiers shall receive or hold more than one such form at any one time."[275] The passes permitted the bearers to move to and from, "the house of [employer's name]".[276] It seems clear that anyone could receive a pass on application. What is not clear is what movements were permitted in the case of Chinese who were not employed or who were themselves employers, since the permitted movements were to and from the holder's employer's house. It was a misdemeanour for a Chinese man, not carrying a pass, to be carrying "any deadly weapon whatsoever" (XI). It is interesting that the same Ordinance amended Ordinance Number 14 of 1845 (Section III, division 8), *increasing* the required distance of moored and anchored boats from low water mark, during the night, from one hundred and fifty to three hundred yards. The danger, it seems, was very definitely perceived as being already on Hong Kong Island.

The Executive Council Minutes of a meeting held on 17 March 1858 report a reference to Security Ordinance Number Nine of 1857, and suggest putting back the hour restricting the Chinese from being out at night from eight to nine o'clock.[277] This may or may not have been done. However, referring to the "Chinese Gazette", where the notice had already appeared, the *Hong Kong Government Gazette* of 1 April 1865 published a notice, dated 29 March 1865, to the effect that Chinese must have a pass and light from 8pm to "morning gunfire".[278]

By 1870, the law had apparently become a dead letter. Ordinance Number 14 of 1870, published in the *Government Gazette* on 13 September 1870, aimed to "amend and consolidate" the Law "in relation to the issue of passes for Chinese, and to provide for the better security of the residents of the colony".[279] However, correspondence to the editor of the *Daily Press*, published in September 1870, shows that the existing regulations had been quite forgotten. Signing himself, "Fair Play", a correspondent refers to "the *new* law requiring every Chinese to have a pass and a lighted lantern",[280] and states, "I am at a loss to perceive how your correspondent could come to the belief that the regulation about the carrying of lamps was in force before, as I am not aware of any Ordinance to the effect."[281] The Editor's comment on this threw the responsibility for confirming the fact on the Hon. H. G. Gibb, who "stated at the Legislative Council that such was the fact,"[282] such an ordinance really did exist.

It is interesting that, in objecting to this law, "Fair Play" concedes "that in a Chinese town like Canton, where the streets are narrow and crooked, and where no lamps are provided, except some shops who[283] hang up a joss lantern after dark, which lasts no more than a hour or so, people generally go out with lamps". But he still objects to the law, "What necessity is there for lamps here, where the roads are wide and clean and lit with gas?"

One or more correspondents, signing as, "Poor Unfortunate Chinamen", wrote, arguing that, "lanterns do not add a bit more to the safety of the Colony, but rather the reverse; at the same time, the enactment will prove to be an unnecessary restriction on the Chinese, and be a source of continual annoyance and inconvenience to them." He or they conclude, "I am sure it is not the wish of the legislators to press the natives, and I hope, therefore, to see the repeal of that section of the Ordinance referring to lanterns".[284]

Some months later, the Minutes of an Executive Council meeting, held on 5 January 1871, record that, because of an increase of crimes against Europeans, Chinese should carry lanterns.[285]

Enforcement of the revised Ordinance now evidently continued. For on 29 January 1876, *The China Mail* asked whether the night-pass system could not be amended.[286] A year later, on 20 December 1877, *The China Mail* reported that "the *London and China Express* says it is able to state on authority that the question of night passes for Chinese in this Colony was dealt with in a despatch from Mr Hennessy which reached Downing Street about the middle of July [1876], and that in this despatch His Excellency reported that the general system of night passes in Hong Kong for the Chinese was a police regulation which had worked well, and which he saw no necessity for disturbing. This is a statement that will be received here with considerable satisfaction, because even up to the present moment many persons have not been altogether free from the apprehension that His Excellency would some day take advantage of a favourable opportunity for dealing a blow at the system. Whether His Excellency never contemplated any interference with the system, or whether further consideration of the subject and the lively discussion that ensued here upon it resulted in the withholding of his hand, are points which we are not in a position to decide. We only know that shortly after his arrival[287] Mr Hennessy expressed himself rather strongly with respect to one or two features of the system, and that somehow reports got abroad that His Excellency was contemplating some changes in regard to them."[288]

Evidently, the law remained. Yet its enforcement continued to be variable. For example, on 27 September 1878, the actor, Pat Amun, was charged with being out without a pass between one and two in the morning. As *The China Mail* reports, "Defendant admitted the charge, and His Worship said he felt bound to punish the defendant, as he (Mr Francis) was informed that the law had not been enforced for some months past, and that the Chinese generally were of opinion that the rule requiring them to carry a light and pass was repealed or in abeyance.[289] It would be much more satisfactory if a police notification were at once issued correcting this error."[290] In July 1879, two hawkers and a rice-pounder were convicted, "of being at large in the public streets without lights or passes and fined $50 each, or three months' imprisonment with hard labour. All three defendants were identified as old offenders."[291] In September 1881, Kwong Achu, servant to the European prostitute, Dolly Johnson, was very clear about the law. For, in bringing a case against his mistress, he stated that he had refused to go to a shop for more beer at one in the morning, because he had no pass.[292]

Nevertheless, the law was suspended at least once for special events. When "illuminations" were planned for two days in December 1881, "the exhibition of passes by the Chinese on the illumination nights was dispensed with", by Special Ordinance of Governor John Pope Hennessy.[293] Consistent with the outspoken opinion of English language China Coast newspapers at the time, this indulgence was taken as an opportunity to criticise the Governor's apparently liberal policy towards crime.

> An amusing story, the truth of which is asserted by the Chinese, is going the round of the native circles in Canton. On the night before the two[294] days' illumination at Hong Kong in honour of the Princes' visit, a meeting was convened in one of the back slums of the Colony, which the élite of the pickpocket and burglar fraternity were ordered by their King to attend. It will be remembered that by a Special Ordinance of the Governor, the exhibition of passes by the Chinese on the illumination nights was dispensed with, and this meeting was called to consider the best method of requiting the boundless compassion of His Excellency. After necessary preliminaries, one hoary-headed burglar, the decayed remains of what was once a literary graduate, got up and proceeded to "fetch"[295] his audience by excerpts from the Classics, among which were conspicuous the phrases, The master said, "without gratitude what is life?" – The master said, "verily the ungrateful man is even as the pigs of the gutter." The upshot of his peroration was a proposal that during the two illumination nights their usual operations should be suspended, in order to second His Excellency's benevolent designs and to draw his holy glance upon them, "which glance," added the speaker, "will certainly bring us luck in the future." The proposal was seconded by Tam Achuk, in thieves' slang, and being put to the meeting, was carried unanimously amidst rounds of

applause. The Governor must indeed be popular! Would it not be well if he could obtain the loan of the City Hall for them on the next occasion?[296]

The tone of this story suggests that the spate of crimes expected to result from suspending the law did not occur. And in fact, *The China Mail* reported little serious crime: "The procession, which so hugely delighted the Chinese onlookers, was certainly of a unique description. . . . The good humour of the vast crowds who moved among the street during the evening was most commendable, and we do not think that any European community of the same mixed class could have behaved in such an orderly and decent manner for such a length of time and similarly engaged. No case of crime of a serious nature is reported."[297] Yet four reports of Stewart's cases at this time refer to theft and pick-pocketing during the festive nights in question (23, 24 and 25 December 1881),[298] when both participants in the spectacles and spectators were victims. In two of the cases, victims had been watching a procession, and in another, the victim was a participant, helping to carry the dragon. In the remaining case, the victims – Lai Shun and his little daughter, carried in his arms, who had their caps snatched – had actually been watching the fireworks.[299] Surely, this is merely the tip of the iceberg?

Ordinance Number 13 of 1888, "The Regulation of Chinese Ordinance, 1888", dated 21 March 1888, contains several paragraphs on Night Passes. Paragraph 30 states, "No Chinese, without reasonable excuse, the proof of which shall lie upon him, shall be at large within the City of Victoria between 9pm and sunrise or between such hours of the night as may from time to time be fixed by any order of the Governor in Council without a valid pass under this Ordinance. This section is applicable to women as well as to men." [300] There was however less concern about the carrying of a lamp or lantern. "It shall be lawful for the Governor in Council by order to be published in the *Gazette* from time to time to direct that all or any Chinese, who may be out in or about the City of Victoria or any part thereof at night, shall, during the hours to be specified in such order, carry lamps or lanterns: Provided always that one lamp or lantern shall be sufficient for any number of persons, not exceeding twelve, who shall belong to the same party."[301]

Ordinance Number 6 of 1897, "Regulation of Chinese (Amendment)", dated 28 May 1897, amended Section 30 of Ordinance Number 13 of 1888, so that the requirement of a pass also was subject to an order, "to be published in the *Gazette*" "from time to time". Ordinance Number 6 of 1897 also defined "Night" as from 9pm to 5am.[302] Ordinance Number 13 of 1888 was subsequently to be referred to as the principal Ordinance. This was repealed by Ordinance Number 25 of 1930 dated 5 December 1930, one of several described as spent and no longer necessary.[303]

~~~~~

How did our magistrate, Frederick Stewart, respond to infringements of the Light and Pass Rules, during his 1881-1882 service as Police Magistrate? Fourteen cases, involving thirty-one men (no women) – all either working men or street sleepers – where the absence of both a light and a pass, or of a pass only, is mentioned, are reported in the period August 1881 to March 1882. An analysis of these gives us an answer.

An overview summary first. Six of these men had no accompanying offence at the time when they were found without a light and/or pass and they also had no prior convictions. In the case of eight of the men, there was some accompanying offence, of far greater seriousness, and in the case of six men, there was an infelicity in their manner or actions when responding to police enquiries. – A couple of men had no satisfactory answer when out after midnight, four pretended to be asleep, and another assaulted the policeman. – Eleven had previous convictions, of which seven are stated to have been prison sentences. The number of previous convictions between the eleven was forty-one, including two for house-breaking and four for larceny.

And now a case by case summary. On 8 August 1881, for a man (no occupation given), with two prior periods in gaol, found sleeping "on a mat" – presumably in the street – the sentence was three weeks' imprisonment with hard labour.[304] On 14 September, four men (no occupations given) who had been in prison for varying times before (two of them three times, one once and the fourth nine times) were sentenced to a fine of ten dollars each or three months' imprisonment. For the additional charge of being rogues and vagabonds, they were sentenced to three months (cumulative) with hard labour.[305] On 17 September, however, the sentences of all were amended, "in accordance with Section 11 of Ordinance 5 of 1850", to omit any reference to and any sentence for being rogues and vagabonds.[306] On 20 September, a coolie who was additionally in possession of a house-breaking implement, and who had previously been in gaol for six months for breaking into a dwelling house, was sentenced to three months' imprisonment with hard labour, under Ordinance 7 of 1865, Section 46.[307] On 22 September, two men (no occupation given) were charged. One was discharged. But the other, who had pushed the arresting policeman, was fined one dollar or four days' imprisonment, for assaulting the Police Constable.[308] On 10 October, three men (no occupation given) were fined two dollars or six days' imprisonment with hard labour.[309] On 12 October, two men – one, the chair coolie of the Hong Kong Legislative Council Member, the Hon. Mr Johnson – only one of whom had been in gaol before, were fined two dollars each or seven days' imprisonment.[310] On 20 October, a man (no occupation given), convicted six previous times, asked to be taken to the station because he had no place to sleep. His sentence was fifty dollars or three months' imprisonment with hard labour.[311] On 31 October, the main charges against a former tinsmith, now a brothel bully, were assault and possession of deadly weapons. The sentence was twelve months' imprisonment with hard labour.[312] On 11 November, with the additional offence of trying to bribe the arresting constable, a servant was fined fifty cents or two day's imprisonment, and confiscation of the bribe, which was placed in the Poor Box.[313] On 17 November, eight men were fined twenty-five cents or one day's imprisonment and their companion who was "somewhat saucy when apprehended" was sentenced double of each.[314] The group consisted of "cooks, chair coolies, etc." On 7 December 1881, one of two men (no occupation given) charged with fighting and creating a disturbance in the street was additionally armed with a deadly weapon and without a "night pass".[315] He had been found belabouring the other with a fighting iron. The victim admitted five previous convictions, four for larceny. Each was fined five dollars or fourteen days' imprisonment with hard labour, and additionally six hours' exposure in the stocks at the scene of the disturbance.[316] On 31 December 1881, two chair coolies were charged, the first for assaulting a third chair coolie, and the second for being armed with a deadly weapon and being *without a pass* the previous night (no *light* is mentioned). The former was fined two dollars, in default seven day's imprisonment with hard labour, and the second was fined five dollars, in default twenty-one days' imprisonment. The iron bar that the second had used was "forfeited to the Crown".[317] The far heavier sentence given to the second defendant (given that the first defendant's testimony was contradicted by the complainant's neighbour) seems to relate to the iron bar which the second was using to strike the complainant.

There seem to be no light and pass cases reported in January and March 1882.

On 3 February 1882, a hawker was charged with cutting and wounding another man, with being at large without a night pass (no mention is made of a light) and in possession of a dagger.[318] (As mentioned above, the possession of "any deadly weapon whatsoever", when not carrying a pass, was regarded as a "misdemeanour".) He had eight previous convictions for various crimes. The case was remanded until a week later, but was not reported in *The China Mail* court pages on that day, nor during the remainder of Stewart's time on the bench. On 15 February 1882 the main charge against a barber was possession of burglarious instruments (he had a gimlet down his stocking and a chisel nearby). He had two previous convictions, one of six months, for breaking into a house, and one of three months for being in possession of a chisel. He was sentenced to six months' imprisonment with hard labour, the first and last fortnights to be spent in solitary confinement.[319] [320]

Reading through these cases, it seems very clear from the sentences given, that being out without a light or pass, in itself, was not an offence that was punished by Frederick Stewart in the early 1880s. In the case of defendants with no prior convictions, and no accompanying charge (or only a relatively small matter), the sentences were either nil or very light. One man was discharged, even though his behaviour when questioned was inappropriate. His companion, who assaulted the policeman when arrested, was sentenced only to a one dollar fine or four days in prison. [321] A group of eight men were sentenced to twenty-five cents or one day in prison. The sentence of their companion, who was "somewhat saucy", when arrested, was double.[322] A man who tried to bribe the constable was sentenced to fifty cents or two days in prison, and the forty cent bribe he had offered was deposited in the Poor Box.[323] Three men were sentenced to a fine of two dollars or six days' hard labour[324] and two men to a fine of two dollars or seven days in prison (one of these had one prior conviction).[325]

Among these fourteen cases as a whole, there are some, where the accompanying offence involved being armed with a deadly weapon, fighting, creating a disturbance in the street, assault, or being in possession of house-breaking instruments. Comparing the higher sentences in all these cases with those discussed in the previous paragraph, it is clear that these relate to the accompanying offence or offences and that the absence of light or pass probably did not contribute at all to the sentence given, although it would have contributed to the conviction.

The highest sentence among all – twelve months' imprisonment with hard labour, with no option to pay a fine – went to a brothel bully, found guilty of assault and possession of deadly weapons. The deadly weapons in question were fighting-irons, commonly used by triad members.[326] Another, also found guilty of being armed with a deadly weapon, received only a fine of five dollars or twenty-one days in prison. But his "weapon" was an iron bar, and not therefore perhaps, associated to the same extent with triad membership.[327] The considerably higher sentence given in the one case suggests that the possibility of triad membership was taken into consideration when deciding the sentence.[328]

As for prior convictions, two cases are similar. One man found in possession of burglarious instruments had a previous sentence of six months in prison for breaking into a dwelling house and was sentenced to three months' imprisonment with hard labour.[329] Another man found in possession of house-breaking instruments, with a previous *six* months' sentence for breaking into a house, and a previous three months sentence for possession of a chisel, was sentenced to imprisonment with hard labour, the first and last fortnights to be in solitary confinement.[330]

It seems clear that the law was used by police, as requests to see a driving licence or an identity-card are, in Hong Kong today, to check up on people about whom the police have some suspicion because they were out late, or when there were other suspicious circumstances. The fact that so many of those arrested did have prior convictions, or were committing some other offence, or did behave in an incautious or disrespectful manner, tends to show that the law was beneficial in preserving law and order in Hong Kong at this time, and also, perhaps, in increasing awareness that law in general, not just this law in particular, was to be respected.

At first sight, two cases are puzzling, however. One man, found sleeping in the street – he had two prior convictions – was sentenced to three weeks in prison with hard labour.[331] A group of four men, with three, three, one and nine prior convictions, preparing to sleep in the street, were each sentenced to a fine of ten dollars or three months in prison with hard labour.[332] And a man, who asked to be taken to the police station because he had nowhere to sleep, was sentenced to a fine of fifty dollars or three months in prison with hard labour.[333] Should these men really have been given sentences, which in two cases almost equalled a sentence given for being in possession of a burglarious instrument?[334] Reflection shows that the sentence in each of these cases – and particularly in the last one – was a deliberate and probably humane way of providing shelter, food and work. (Work was considered essential to self-respect then, as well as now.)[335]

The last case confirms that contemporary newspapers were correct when they stated that some people deliberately courted confinement in prison. Men knew that infringing the Light and Pass rules was a way of appealing for assistance, and also knew – and accepted – that this assistance would take the form of imprisonment with hard labour. Homeless European sailors secured the same objective by deliberately "committing a nuisance" in the street.[336]

In the period following the establishment of Communist rule over Mainland China, all Hong Kong residents have been required to carry an identity card and to produce it on request, initially for the purpose of controlling illegal immigration to Hong Kong. No-one (except, presumably, illegal immigrants) particularly objects to this now. As for carrying a lamp, a few of the gas lamps, mentioned in 1870 as making a personal lamp or lantern unnecessary when out late at night, remain from the past. Otherwise, the streets in the urban areas are now very brightly lit, both by the authorities and by commercial premises. There is no onus on the individual pedestrian to provide his own light to prove his respectability and honest intentions. Only vehicles now are liable to a fine if at large on the streets and unlit at times when lights are required.

The discriminatory nature of the "Light and Pass" (more accutately, the "Light or Pass") rules in Nineteenth Century Hong Kong (it seems always to have applied only to Chinese)[337] was what gave rise to objections from Chinese and non-Chinese alike. It would have been more suitable – as now – if the rules had applied to all and been enforced in relation to all. Having said this, as we have seen, the enforcement of the law, as demonstrated by fifteen reports[338] of cases brought before Frederick Stewart's court in the early 1880s, could, in the right hands, be sensible and suitable. It could also be used and indeed was used as a concerned vehicle to provide for the welfare of street sleepers.

The Police Role
in Magistrate Frederick Stewart's Court

A Personal Commentary[339]

Geoffrey Roper

The seven hundred and twenty-two *China Mail* reports of Police Magistrate Stewart's court in 1881 and 1882 make fascinating reading, especially when read in depth and selectively studied, in my case for those showing police enforcement of the law. They offer a fresh insight into the policing of Hong Kong in the early 1880s, and in so doing, demonstrate police priorities and policies, as well as highlighting the pattern of activities, or seeming lack of activities, of both individual police officers and groups of officers.

For myself, this study also gained a broader historical dimension when I compared those years with my own early experiences after joining the Hong Kong Police in 1958, in particular my first working experience when based at Central Police Station between 1959 and 1960. (It was in the original Hong Kong Magistracy, within this same complex of Central Police Station buildings, that Stewart held his 1881-1882 court.) From this comparison a pattern emerges of political and social changes in the world, especially in China and Britain, eventually affecting Hong Kong and its police force. So, from the seemingly mundane hearings in a magistrate's court and the dross of a retired police officer's memory, there emerges the imprint of history, sometimes heavy, but sometimes light.

Hong Kong history is often a record of changed perceptions, sometimes to the point of rapid opposites, with, for example Left becoming Right in 1997 and the old Right becoming Wrong within a short space of time. Police Sergeant John Butlin could not be expected to realize this when he stated in court that the wearing of a false queue was evidence of a vagabond's lack of respectability.[340] For by 1911, with the fall of the Qing Dynasty of Imperial

China and the founding of the Chinese Republic, queues *per se* would be seen as a discarded Manchu imposition. In the meantime one rascally thief took advantage of history's measured step by impishly tying his absorbed victim's queue to his neighbour's before running off with his hat.[341]

Other, more weighty, early perceptions and values can be seen from reports on police raids by Inspectors Mathieson, Mackie, Corcoran, Perry, Thomson and Lindsay, as well as Sergeants Campbell and Rae, and Police Constables Forbes, Johnston and Smith.[342] Their targets were gambling divans, unlicensed opium divans and holders of unlicensed opium; in effect to protect the purchaser of the Government opium monopoly, the "Opium Farmer".

Other reports illustrate the work of Inspector John Lee, an expatriate police inspector seconded to the Registrar General as Inspector of Registered Brothels.[343] There were one hundred and three registered brothels for Chinese use alone.[344] (Lee's charging one brothel girl with Attempted Suicide was probably a way to get her psychiatric help.)[345] Activities within the brothels, registered or not, came frequently to the notice of the police.[346] Participants in one brothel fight rejoiced in the colourful names of Nocheum Greenstang[347] and Benjamin Flin.[348]

All these are a reminder – together with the all too frequent reports of drunken western seamen, and the robbing and defrauding of Chinese workers transiting Hong Kong on the way to and from the Chinese Mainland and other countries[349] – that, as late as the early 1880s, Hong Kong, despite many evidences of new-found respectability, retained many of the policing problems of a Nineteenth Century frontier seaport. . . . Real-life Charles Dickens, with a touch of Victor Hugo, Joseph Conrad and Sherlock Holmes.

The Years 1959-1960

In 1959-1960, I was myself raiding for opium, and its derivative, heroin, in Upper and Lower Lascar Rows and Square Street, also sometimes (as in 1881-1882)[350] entering through the roof. By then perceptions in Britain and internationally had changed. This had resulted in the closing of Hong Kong's licensed opium divans and dealers and the prohibition of opium and heroin as dangerous drugs. Under similar pressure from Britain, and after much procrastination, Hong Kong had made organizing prostitution a criminal offence and brothels illegal.[351]

This was not the only change for members of the world's oldest profession, Hong Kong Island chapter. During the Second World War, those near the Magistrates' Courts decamped to Wanchai, where prostitutes had been plying their trade almost from the beginning of Hong Kong's British administration,[352] leaving behind in Central only a few older members to cater for the needs of the Waterfront boarding house patrons. Ironically, in Wanchai they set up shop in streets named after such former colonial worthies as Frederick Stewart, our Magistrate, Tonnochy, Superintendent of Victoria Gaol, 1879-1882, and Lockhart, colonial administrator in both Hong Kong and Weihaiwei. All, no doubt, models of Victorian moral rectitude.

In case the irony of this situation was not enough, in 1959 the director of the film, *The World of Suzy Wong,* doubled the dose when he decided that the exteriors of the hotels and bars in Wanchai were not sufficiently obviously Chinese in appearance, for Miss Wong's reputed house. So Hollywood moved to Hollywood Road and the old tenement houses in Square Street served the purpose. As I witnessed in person, the camera was set up in the Man Mo Temple courtyard alongside the stone lions that were a re-opening gift from the Pork Merchants' Guild in 1851. In fact Square Street was, during the 1880s, the site of a notorious brothel[353] whose bouncer gang is described below in this essay, in connection with triad activity. The film director should have been awarded a special Oscar for his – albeit unwitting – sense of history.

Many of the road alignments of the Central and Western districts of the 1880s remain to this day, whilst in 1959 quite a number of the original tenement houses were still there. Quite a number were, however, jerrybuilt, and as one pounded up the wooden stairs with a party of colleagues during a police raid, often the whole building shook. It was a regular duty during the heavy summer rains, for police to cordon off collapsed tenements, while the Fire Brigade, no longer part of the Police Force, searched for survivors or bodies. According to the inspecting Public Works Department surveyors, these houses had been built with "too much sand in the mortar".

In 1959 the (Chinese) Recreation Ground, towards the western end of Hollywood Road, and the site of the queue-tying escapade referred to above,[354] was still in something close to its original state, although rather dilapidated. Only a few storytellers were there to tell the tales of old. Some of these were said to be salacious, but I would have been little use as a witness in any misconceived obscenity prosecution. For my knowledge of Cantonese in those days was based upon the vocabulary of Father Thomas O'Melia's *First Year Cantonese*, published by the Catholic Truth Society in 1938, which was required reading for the Hong Kong Government's Cantonese Examinations. This book has its merits and for many expatriates remains a treasured reminder of their early days in the public service; but it was written principally for priests – proclaiming on page forty-five that "building churches is better than building houses" – rather than for working police officers.

Standing in the Central Police Station compound in Hollywood Road in 1959, facing north, visitors from the 1880s would have found a number of familiar landmarks. The granite Barracks block, to the rear, built mostly in 1864, still dominated the scene (as it does today). The quarters blocks, built the same year – and to the right of the entrance ramp – also remained. In 1919 the Headquarters block replaced the temporary structures on the northern side of the compound. Post 1945, Central ceased to be the territory headquarters, except for Stores purposes. It remained, however, the Hong Kong Island Regional Headquarters, as it still was until the end of 2004; with its occupants proud of belonging to the most senior of the police regions and of the Antiquities order preserving their buildings, although they grumbled about the leaky old roofs.

Victoria Prison to the southwest of the Police buildings, also substantially built by 1864, was no longer the only prison, and had become the Victoria Reception

Centre. To the southeast, the Hong Kong Magistracy building, where Stewart held his court, was replaced in 1914 by the Central Magistracy building with the imposing Grecian frontage on Arbuthnot Road, that we see there today. By 1959 it had become one of a number of magistracies, its diminished role a further witness to the Territory's expansion.[355]

Motor vehicles and the role of the traffic police and courts would be a source of surprise to our imaginary visitors from the 1880s today, but in 1959 the occasional sedan chair still waited for hire outside the Liang Yu Barber Shop in D'Aguilar Street. Despite dwindling numbers, rickshaws were still a regular feature of the traffic scene in 1959, with pullers still disputing amongst themselves and with seamen and other passengers, as in 1881-1882.[356]

The biggest shock, however, for many of our visitors from the 1880s might well have been to see European police officers saluting Chinese police officers. In my case, the officer was Divisional Superintendent Fong Yik Fai, a widely respected gentleman, and much more understanding of the faults of young expatriate police inspectors than some senior expatriate officers in the Region.

In 1880s Hong Kong, much more attention was paid to race than today. The reports of the Captain Superintendent of Police categorised even offenders into three groups: Europeans and Americans, Indians and Chinese.[357] The police force itself was divided into three similar contingents, Europeans (Americans are not separately named), Indians, and Chinese. During the 1880s, only European – in effect British – officers were allowed to fill the two superintendent and twelve or thirteen inspector posts. They also held ninety or so (1880-1882) to about one hundred (1886-1889) rank and file posts. Out of a total Force strength averaging six hundred and twenty-one (1880-1882) or six hundred and eighty-seven (1886-1889), the Europeans held just *over* (1880-1882) or just *under* (1886-1889) seventeen percent of the posts, and the Indian contingent of Sikhs and Muslims just over twenty-seven per cent (1880-1882) or just over thirty-two percent

(1886-1889), leaving, as a matter of security policy, no more than just over fifty-four percent (1880-1882) or just over fifty percent (1886-1889) of the posts for Chinese officers.[358] Moreover in a public loss of face, Chinese policemen – the *lukongs* (green jackets) mentioned in some of the court case reports[359] – were generally not allowed to carry firearms, only short swords. All in a colony at least ninety-five percent Chinese, and with no real signs of attempts to attract a better standard of Chinese recruit.[360]

The court reports themselves[361] also illustrate how the European contingent dominated most aspects of the policing of the Colony (even after due allowance is given for *The China Mail* giving extra coverage to cater to its English language readership). For example, European officers – including, on occasion, police constables – led almost all of the vice raids.

Ironically, however, the restrictions on the size and official responsibilities of the Chinese contingent clearly played a part in the disproportionate, almost independent, unofficial power assumed by the group of about twenty Chinese on detective duties who appear in these reports. They seem to have been almost a force unto themselves. The police force needed a source of information on what was happening in the community, in particular the criminal underworld, and they played a key role in this regard.

Examples of the work of a few men support this point. The reports clearly show the independence of action of Police Sergeant 199, Pang Alui[362] and Police Constable 197, Wong Tsan[363] (both of whom we may assume to be detectives).[364] Additionally, on Thursday, 20 October 1881, the independent evidence of Police Constable 190 (probably also a detective) secured the conviction of a gambler, sentenced to twenty-one days' imprisonment with hard labour.[365] In another case,[366] the evidence of Police Constable 190, together with that of Sergeant Wong Ayau – probably another detective – led to the *complainant* being charged and the *defendant* discharged. Although more needs to be known about the background to this last case, the distinct impression is given that the two European inspectors involved were taken along on the related gambling raid by the detectives, rather than the reverse, and as a matter of formality only. Incidentally, Ng Choy, the defense barrister in this case, was the first Chinese member of the Legislative Council.

Similarly, the Chinese constable – clearly a detective – following his enquiries into the activities of the Square Street brothel bouncers, acted independently when he announced to the court the existence of a "gang of about one hundred men organised for the purpose of fighting".[367] This was to the obvious discomfort of the inspector in charge of the case, Inspector Fleming. Clearly there was much more to this case that what we read here.

This is reminiscent of my early days in the Force when even the most innocent young inspector soon realized that the staff sergeants, especially those in Criminal Investigation Department, held more *de facto* power than most of the inspectors at least. Charles Sutcliffe, a no-nonsense Commissioner, who abolished the rank soon after assuming office in 1969, ended this surreal situation.

The unusual way of using informers – in vice and counterfeit coin prosecutions – as seen in these reports,[368] may well have been necessitated in part also by the low numbers of Chinese police officers. One of the best known ways of gathering evidence is to infiltrate officers new to the district into the vice dens as paying customers. They then give evidence in court. This would have been difficult in 1881-1882 because of the low numbers of local officers and the lack of trust placed in them. So, it would seem, paid informers were used instead.[369] The informers, however, did not have the same protection from reprisals by vice den operators that officers of the law would have had, and they received payment only if those convicted paid up their fines rather than go to prison. In such a precarious situation, it is not surprising that some of them proved unreliable, as some of the reports show.[370]

A change in localization policy did not come in earnest until as late as 1946, as part of Britain's post-war urge to sweep with a new broom, both at home and in the Empire. Commissioner Pennefather-Evans' report on the reorganization of the police, drawn up in the Stanley

Internment Camp,[371] was implemented; and Hong Kong finally caught up with the tide of history and other British possessions, in having a police force where locals were in the majority. Expatriates were no longer recruited for posts below inspector.

Nevertheless, the word seemed not to have reached everyone, for when we patrolled the streets of Central in 1959, some passing old timers still addressed my expatriate colleagues and myself as sergeants. In contrast, and more pleasing to our youthful egos, some American tourists, confused by our Probationary Sub-Inspector single star badge of rank, commented that one star generals looked very young these days. Other visitors, confused by the fact that the tourist handbook clearly told them that English speaking officers wore red as backing to their shoulder numbers, and we did not, being numberless, regularly asked, in patient, slow tones, "Say, do you speak English?" Today, stars, red backing for English speakers and patrolling expatriate inspectors are no longer on the scene. Hopefully, the tourists are less confused.

The female searchers, mentioned in some of these reports,[372] were leaving the scene in 1959. A vanishing breed, mostly matronly ladies dressed in shapeless, simple uniforms, they acted merely as jailers and searchers of females in police custody and were being replaced by women police as part of the Force's post-war modernisation.

The Years 1881-1882

Viewing the 1881-1882 reports, a modern police commander would be struck by the very large number of preventive arrests for Unlawful Possession, being a Rogue and Vagabond, and for breaking the Night Pass Laws.[373] The first offence was still law in 1959 (but has since gone), whilst the other two offences were no longer on the statute book. Blunderbuss policing, aimed largely to improve the detection rate, would be a polite description of such tactics.

The charge of Unlawful Possession had some validity where the owner of the property was not known, but was best used with caution. As for the charge of being a Rogue and Vagabond, it seems that all that it was necessary for the police to prove was a criminal record and lack of settled accommodation, coupled with vague allegations that the defendant was living a bad life, to gain a conviction. Apart from the moral aspect of condemning offenders to a life of recidivism, similar experience shows that it would have had little effect on the more successful criminals. They would be left to go about their merry ways unheeded, while the beat constable wasted his time in court giving evidence of dragging some old lag, capable only of petty crime, from his cave on the hillside in the middle of the night.[374]

There is considerable evidence from these reports alone of a disturbing degree of serious crime. Outside the urban area, there is the murder at Stanley Village of Sikh Police Constable 693, Easur Singh, following an attack by armed robbers at Tai Tam[375] and a highway robbery at Pokfulam.[376]

Inside the urban area, the most threatening aspect is the influence of groups of violent criminals. One case reports the attempted intimidation of a bean-curd maker[377] and another of a shop accountant.[378] What was the fight between thirty or forty rice-pounders on Friday, 29 July 1881 in Battery Street,[379] and the fight with fighting irons between two men on Monday, 5 December 1881 in Centre Street,[380] really about? Most disturbing of all is the existence of the Square Street Brothel Bouncers gang. The case, reported as, "Assault with a Lethal Weapon", heard on

29 and again on 31 October 1881, when a brothel bouncer was prosecuted,[381] shows that the police – and Stewart's court – already knew of a gang in the area, four and a half months before the sensational testimony of the "native constable" mentioned above.[382]

Yet there are no reports of prosecutions for triad gang activity during this period, 26 July 1881 to 29 March 1882, despite legislation for that purpose being available since 1845. The explanation would seem to be the difficulty of securing criminal convictions in court, due to intimidation of witnesses and triad infiltration of the police force.[383] Another reason may be the fact that our reports cover a short period of eight months, and the work for such cases takes several years to complete. As for the lack of corruption charges against civil servants, including police officers, difficulty in securing convictions must certainly be the explanation here.[384] The best example of the latter can be seen in Captain Superintendent W. M. Deane's Annual Report for 1886,[385] where he reported the prosecution of fifty police officers for failing to take action against gambling houses on a certain day. This prosecution failed in court because of the bad character of the prosecution witness, and action against these officers for breaching Police Discipline Regulations was quashed on appeal. The same year, however, Deane – whose service as head of the Force from 1866 to 1892 is still the longest to date – managed to dismiss four Europeans, eight Indians and sixty-six Chinese policemen; and an Inquiry Board banished twelve triad gang leaders from the Colony. Work on this case may already have begun during the period of our court reports for 1881 to 1882.

It is all too easy to criticize, with the benefit of one hundred and twenty years' hindsight. Concepts of modern urban policing were still not fully accepted even in all British cities. And a considerable amount of good work was obviously being done by officers of all nationalities. The police force certainly came together for the prosecution of the Tai Tam murderers,[386] whilst the subduing of violent, drunken seamen – not always an easy task – was often achieved by officers from more than one contingent, working together.[387]

The reports on the vice raids seem genuine enough, with no evident signs of their being staged for show purposes only. If staged, why bother about rooftop entries to secure a few tame prisoners? The difficulty is that corruption brings with it a cloud of suspicion, even the most honest of actions being viewed as corruptly intended. In my experience, one of the great benefits of setting up the Independent Commission Against Corruption in 1974, was the eventual dispelling of this cloud around the Force.

Police forces have a lot to do apart from preventing and detecting crime, crowd control at major public functions being one of the most labour intensive duties. Several people appeared in Stewart's Court following the firework display, the butchers' guild dragon dance, the processions of fishmongers, butchers, coolies, and others, held over the Christmas weekend of 1881, to celebrate the visit of Queen Victoria's young sons, the Princes Albert and George.[388] My own first public duty in Hong Kong was during the 1959 visit of the Duke of Edinburgh, when officers under training at the Police Training School were called out to help line the royal route. This was one of the last royal visits where the route was lined in this way. But in neither 1881 nor 1959 were there computer-linked traffic-light control systems or elevated roads available, to help whisk VIPs about unhindered, as they do today.

The many Nineteenth Century graves of young police officers, servicemen, missionaries, and sometimes their families, bear witness to the health dangers and short life expectancies of those years. Just to the right of the main pathway in the Hong Kong Cemetery there stands a stone memorial to the police officers who died during the 1883 cholera epidemic. Among those listed is Police Constable 14, Frederick Cookson, who had given evidence on 12 December 1881 concerning the theft of his police blanket.[389] Cookson died on 11 August 1883, aged twenty-nine years. His wife had died two days previously; their infant daughter died two days later. Magistrate Stewart's own grave lies nearby.

Scottish tartans are woven deeply into the whole fabric of Hong Kong history, and no more so than in the history of the Hong Kong police, where there has been a strong representation, especially in the higher ranks. Many of the police witnesses in Stewart's court were fellow Scotsmen. In part this was because of recruitment from Scottish police forces[390] but also because of the long Scottish tradition of seeking employment abroad, which has a parallel among the Chinese.

Being something of an English nationalist, I was not enamoured in 1958 at being awoken at dawn in the Police Training School by the wailing of a Police Band bagpiper. This was the idea of the Police Training School Commandant, George Leys, who after police service in Scotland, had reached Hong Kong via the Shanghai and Tianjin municipal forces and internment by the Japanese. Despite his travels in so much of modern Chinese history, he had never forgotten where he came from . . . unfortunately, to my ears.

Gradually, however, after this rude awakening, I began to appreciate the pipes as being one of the Force's special traditions, to be heard at parades, weddings and the Force funerals of officers who had given their lives for Hong Kong. Indeed, a more happy, but still poignant, occasion came upon my retirement from the Force in April 1992, when I had the great privilege of taking the salute at a Beating of the Retreat held in the Central Police Station compound. As the pipes lamented and the drums closed the day, I felt an overwhelming sense of history, sure that Deane, Cookson and their colleagues were there, standing quietly in the darkening shadows beneath the trees. (It was not, however, until the year 2,000 that Mrs Catherine Roper Cheung Mei Ming, a much respected Senior Superintendent in the same Regional Headquarters, retired, invoking a wife's privilege of the last word, one might say.)

The Year 1999

The Hong Kong Special Administrative Region has good reason to be proud of its Police Force. The Force I joined in 1958 was a much better one than that of 1881-1882, whilst, in 1999, the Force – now almost fully localized – is far better than that of 1958. It is better led than ever before, whilst, after their humble beginnings in the Nineteenth Century, the junior police officers (as the rank and file are called today) have emerged as the very backbone of the Force. This position has been reached over many years through the cumulative efforts of all ranks and nationalities, and serves as a reminder that the imprints of history are indelible.

Reporting the Cases of Frederick Stewart

The Public Interest

Tim Hamlett

Looking at reports of Stewart's cases in *The China Mail* brings a surprisingly strong sense of déjà vu. People do not, of course, report court cases in this way now. But they did until quite recently. Like all reporting, writing court cases involves a complicated interaction with the material available and the technical circumstances in which it will be delivered to readers. *The China Mail*'s anonymous scribe (none of the stories are by-lined but the technique is quite consistent) worked under conditions strikingly similar to those, which prevailed when I started as a reporter in North Lancashire in the early 1970s. The undisputed star of our local court-reporting scene was a gentleman called Les Cully. He was a small and dapper man, who dressed more like a solicitor than a reporter. He could take shorthand faster than most people could talk, and his typewriting had the remorseless rhythm of a heavy machine-gun. Nobody else was allowed to use Les's typewriter, lest its delicate temperament be disturbed by the violent two-fisted typing style affected by most of my colleagues. Les's weekly moment of glory came on Tuesday, which was the day *The Morecambe Visitor* was put to bed, and also the day of the weekly performance at the local palace of justice where the Morecambe Magistrates sat. This coincidence meant that Les hared back to the office after the magistrates rose for lunch, and batted out a report covering everything more important than the parking fines, in time for it to be incorporated in a page that afternoon.

In those days of hot metal type-setting the court pages were not planned. The sub-editors gave each story a headline in the same typeface, the number of lines of headline ranging from one to four, roughly proportionate to the story's length. The stories might be typeset by several people – the headline, at least, required a different machine – and the results were assembled in the printing department on a table known as the random. The sub editor who was in charge of the page – known as the "stone sub" in honour of the marble-topped tables on which print was once assembled – would pick stories regardless of content or merits to fill the space available. The stories were "run on", which meant that if one arrived unfinished at the bottom of the page, it simply resumed at the top of the next column to the right. The stone sub traditionally carried a piece of grubby string with which to compare the length of the remaining offerings with the spaces available on the page. He had to avoid some awkward results, like headlines next to each other, or the headline at the bottom of a column with very little story underneath it, so he needed stories in a range of lengths. Very short ones were particularly welcome because they provided flexibility and could, if surplus to requirements, be used on other pages as "fillers", for which there was a constant demand.

For the reporter this meant that lengthy contemplation of news values or composition was not wanted, and would be wasted if supplied. Such luxuries would also conflict with the primary need, which was for speed.

It is not now clear precisely what the deadline structure of *The China Mail* may have been but clearly an English-language evening paper could not have been sold on the streets to homeward-bound commuters.[391] Most of the circulation must have comprised subscribers who had the paper delivered to their offices during working hours.[392] Given the technology of the time, this means the deadline for court copy to be with the printers can hardly have been later than 2pm. Magistrates no doubt expected, much as they do now, that the day's hearings would occupy most of the morning, with the court rising at about 12.30 or later. And no self-respecting journalist will willingly skip lunch.

The secret of achieving the necessary blinding speed is to follow a formula, which is applied to virtually every one of the *China Mail* reports of Stewart's cases if it is longer than one paragraph. The story starts with the name and often the occupation of the defendant and the offence with which he was charged. There is a summary of the prosecution evidence and some mention of the defence, if any. Then comes the verdict of the court and, if the verdict was guilty, the sentence.

A short example can be given in full:

> Leung Akam was charged with stealing sweet potato sprouts from a field belonging to Li Tai Shing, a fisherman living in To-kwa-wan.
> Complainant saw the defendant in the field cutting the sprouts, arrested him, and handed him over to a Police Constable.
> Defendant admitted having stolen the vegetables, but denied that they belonged to complainant. He had been in gaol three times previously.
> Sentenced to three months' imprisonment with hard labour.[393]

This remained pretty much the standard approach to hasty court reports for the next hundred years, right down to the occasional inclusion of legal words (defendant, complainant) and the breathless omission of occasional articles or even, as in the last sentence, verbs. The convenient feature of this conventional structure for the reporter is that it follows the natural order in which the material will usually arrive in his notebook. The name of the offender and nature of the offence can be copied from the court sheet before the trial starts; the prosecution and defence will present their cases and the court will then announce verdict and sentence. Putting the name of the accused at the beginning of the story made sense for local papers in England because the identity of the defendant was usually the strongest point in the story. For *The China Mail* there was no such incentive. Most of the defendants in Stewart's court were either Chinese coolies or transient foreign seamen. Their names would have meant nothing to *China Mail* readers, so the story structure is a matter of convention and convenience rather than news values.

Where the story is very short we get a basic version,

which comprises the name of the accused, the offence and the penalty. With luck these can be assembled in one sentence:

> Yip Akin admitted having stolen a blanket from Tuk Hing Shun and was sent to gaol for twenty-one days with hard labour.[394]

These short stories are eloquent testimony to the durability of functional plain English because many of them would still be perfectly at home in a modern newspaper. In fact the *Mail*'s nameless correspondent has only one habit which would now be considered quite unacceptable: the use of Latin words for nearby months – "*inst.*" for this month, "*ult.*" for last month and even occasionally "*proximo*" for next month.

There are surprisingly few misprints for a late page on an evening newspaper. This is a tribute to the care exercised by all concerned, because type-setting and composition were complicated technical exercises and the manual workers were probably not English-speakers at all, let alone native speakers. The copy would have been written in long-hand, in some haste. This would be edited and then passed to a type-setter. The assembled type would sit face-up in a metal trough called a galley and from this the production staff would make a proof copy. This is the origin of the phrase "galley proof". The proof, together with the original copy, would be passed to the proof-readers, who worked in pairs. One of them read the original copy while the other checked the type version. The resulting corrections would be passed to another type-setter, who would set the required new matter. This would then be sent to the composing room, where the compositor working on the court page was expected to insert the new words and remove the erroneous ones. Clearly there was quite a lot which could go wrong here. On newspapers in England the proof-readers, or "correctors of the press" were a mine of information about the finer points of English and the obscurer nooks of house style. In effect while checking the type-setting they also checked the editing. This was a luxury, not really appreciated until the arrival of direct input to computer terminals swept the whole system away. There is no technical objection to having proof-readers who do not speak the language of the copy. Modern Hong Kong printers often produce books in foreign languages which none of the production workers can speak. But you miss the extra check. I suppose the compositors also did not speak English, and this increased the risk of lines being misinserted, or the wrong lines being removed, producing sentences like "Fined $10 or suffer fourteen days' imprisonment with hard labour."[395] Other hazards lurked for stories assembled in haste. If deadlines were in jeopardy a page might be sent to the printers with some corrections simply omitted. Another danger was that the editorial representative (the stone sub), who also had a copy of the galley proof, might start sending out corrections of his own. These might not be compatible with the version of the story produced by the "official" corrections.

In some respects the *China Mail* court reporter enjoyed more freedom than his modern counterparts. He could jump to conclusions:

> One of the defendants had been somewhat saucy when apprehended, and was fined 50 cents, or two days' imprisonment; the others were each fined half that amount, or one day. . . .[396]

He could deploy ironic humour:

> Wong Asing, washerman, was found guilty of stealing a jacket. . . . Defendant said he had no employment and no regular fixed place to live in. . . . The magistrate, pitying the poor fellow's case, ordered that he should be fed and clothed and provided with a regular fixed place to live for the next 14 days.[397]

A man who stole an umbrella is described as being, "relieved of the necessity of having an umbrella by getting six weeks' imprisonment with hard labour",[398] and a man who damaged some trees by picking parts for medicinal purposes is said to have "suffered martyrdom to the extent of $5 or six weeks' hard labour".[399]

On busy mornings our writer could dispose of the great bulk of the proceedings like this:

> There were between 30 and 40 cases before the Magistrates today of the usual Monday-morning type ... but only the above were of any public interest.[400]

Faced with the aftermath of a large gambling raid the reporter's obligations to the defence could be discharged along lines eerily reminiscent of the famous last line in "Casablanca" ("Arrest the usual suspects!"):

> The defendants made the usual excuses. . . .[401]

Or in a later case:

> The excuses of the several defendants were of the usual varied character, playing for amusement, looking for friends, &c . . .[402]

This ability to be playful, to make judgements and to insert comments is actually due paradoxically to the absence of the legal protections later supplied to court reporting. At the beginning of the 1880s a court report was legally in exactly the same situation as any other story. But in 1888 the United Kingdom Parliament passed the Law of Libel Amendment Act, which conferred absolute privilege from libel suits on court reports, provided that they were fair, accurate and contemporaneous. In a sense this was a boon to newspapers. Previously anyone who was defamed during court proceedings – as you might easily be by a witness or the judge – could sue any newspaper which reported the remark, even though he could not sue the speaker because the court proceedings themselves were privileged. The amended law offered absolute protection as long as the story was a report. The result was pressure on court reporters to make it clear that the story they were producing was a report, and nothing but a report, of the court proceedings. This meant that every statement made in a court story had to be attributed to one of the actors in the proceedings. At worst, if in a hurry, one might wrap the attribution of a non-contentious item up in something like "the court was told". Anything, which was not part of the proceedings – comments, conclusions, jokes or other whimsical adornments – was rigorously excluded. The resulting stories were safe, though usually considerably less fun.

The danger of being sued seems to have sat lightly on *The China Mail*'s court desk. No doubt the sort of people who appeared in court – coolies, sailors and other humble folk – would have been even less likely to sue a newspaper than their modern counterparts are now. Certainly the newspaper had one curious habit, which would now be considered extremely dangerous – of stating the offence in the headline and merely referring to it as "the above offence"[403] or "this charge"[404] in the story. The danger of a headline attaching itself to the wrong story – and hence attributing a crime to the wrong defendant – ought to have been obvious.

The great attraction of magistrates' court reporting is that, along with a certain amount of tedium, you get a wonderful picture of how life is lived, especially among the less prosperous classes. The higher courts spend days dissecting one incident; but before a busy magistrate, life's rich pageant unrolls continuously. Court reports are a promising seam for the social historian, which historians of Hong Kong are only beginning to mine.[405] Our reporter preserves a certain ironic detachment from the parade of figures passing before him, and certainly offers nothing, which could be mistaken for a personal opinion. This is interesting in itself because Stewart's period on the bench coincided with the governorship of Sir John Pope Hennessy. Hennessy earned the resentment and contempt of his colonial contemporaries by introducing some humanitarian reforms into the Hong Kong penal system. He permanently abolished branding (tattooing) as a punishment (one of Stewart's defendants had been branded and deported for a previous offence) and suspended the use of flogging, which had hitherto been conducted publicly, with the victim tied to a post on the Central waterfront. Hong Kong western opinion had it that this was asking for trouble. Indeed as soon as Hennessy (and Stewart) had moved on, flogging – though not the public performances – was restored. [406] Stewart's brief judicial career in the 1880s (he had served on the Bench before) coincided with the period of controversial gentleness. The only exotic punishment applied to his defendants is the occasional use of the stocks. These seem to have been available in a mobile model, a cangue perhaps, as the sentence sometimes stipulates that the miscreant should be exhibited in them at the scene of the crime. [407]

The China Mail had strong views about the government's penal policies, but this editorial position was not allowed to influence the court coverage, which sticks closely to the business of the hour and the day. In retrospect the proceedings do not look grossly unfair considering the circumstances. Most of the defendants are Chinese, and in many cases it must have been literally true that the accused "had no idea why he was in court". But this seems to be more a matter of class bias than racial prejudice. There are enough foreigners accused, usually of offences involving drink.

Many of these are seamen, whose difficulties with rickshaw drivers inspired the *China Mail* reporter to a rare burst of social analysis:

The case was one of the ordinary cases of a
European from on board ship engaging a 'rickshaw
when he was more or less under the influence of
liquor, and when called upon to pay for it, not only
refusing to give the coolie his cents, but assaulting
him as well. . . .[408]

The court often faced the question "what shall we do with
the drunken sailor?" Matelots who had become separated
from warships could be classified as "stragglers" and
returned to their respective navies. Seamen who were still
employed might be discharged on condition that they went
straight to their ships. The unattached would probably see
the inside of a Hong Kong prison. One wonders what
happened to destitutes.[409] The Hong Kong of those days
would have been a dangerous place for a poor European
with no money and no connections.[410]

The other regular source of Europeans in trouble
with the law was the local garrison. This, in the early1880s,
comprised the Royal Inniskilling Fusiliers.[411] No doubt
they suffered the usual bane of peacetime soldiering –
boredom. Certainly they resorted with enthusiasm to the
usual antidote – drink.

The only legislation enforced at the time which was
clearly racist in its own terms was the Light and Pass rules,
which required Chinese persons, but not others, to carry a
pass obtainable from the police or a light if they were out at
night.[412] This was not a particularly serious matter. – In the
cases in our study, we find a fine of twenty-five cents or one
day in prison for a first offence with no aggravating
circumstances. When larger sentences were given, there was
often a previous conviction and suspicious circumstances. –
For example, a defendant, fined ten dollars with the
alternative of three months imprisonment with hard
labour,[413] was in possession of a house-breaking implement
and had a previous conviction for breaking into a dwelling
house. Often, however, being out without a light or a pass
also led to conviction for the even less specific and equally
indefensible offence of "being a rogue and a vagabond".
The Light and Pass rules[414] were to flourish for another ten

years: protests from Chinese residents mounted in 1895 to a crescendo, now cherished by historians as an early specimen of an indigenous social movement. The government refused to bow to pressure but quietly dropped the law two years later.[415]

In some of Stewart's cases the court was by modern standards surprisingly willing to enforce what were in effect merely contracts of employment. Servants are punished for leaving their masters without notice, or for disobeying instructions. The "Omnibus" Ordinance passed in 1845 made it among other things an offence to leave one's employer before he had time to engage a successor.[416] On the other hand this enthusiasm for the master-servant relationship could cut both ways. One owner of three cows was fined for allowing them to stray on Crown land, even though he was not present at the time and his servant, who was, had specific instructions to keep the cows under control.

Hong Kong was still at this time largely rural, of course. A surprising amount of legislation seems to have been devoted to keeping it that way. There is a small but steady stream of cases for what would now be described as "environmental" offences. You could be prosecuted for cutting trees, for dressing stone in the street, for cutting earth or for fouling a stream. The authorities were already embarked on the forlorn effort to stop people dropping rubbish in the harbour.

Apart from providing a steady stream of unsteady sailors the harbour features as a venue for crimes of its own. Theft of coal seems to have been a constant problem. No doubt with hundreds of coal-fired ships visiting there was a lot of it about. Occasional altercations on the ships themselves occur, but it seems from the magistrate's comment on one such case, that these could be, and usually were, dealt with by the Harbourmaster, who was also a magistrate in those days. One offence crops up twice, and is so redolent of a by-gone world that it is difficult to make out what the problem was. It seems that under the post office regulations some people were required by law to report the imminent departure of a ship. I suppose this was so that mail could be sent on board if necessary. One of these cases is quite short and can be given in full:

> U Wan Cho was charged by Mr Lister, Post-master General, with omitting to give notice of the departure of the steamer *China*. Several people had been put to serious inconvenience.
> Defendant admitted that he had not given notice, and was fined $25 or 21 days' imprisonment.[417]

The *China Mail* sub-editor made this case even more baffling by adding the headline "Dispatch of a steamer without woman".

Another similar case records the failure of Yau Chung Ping, shopkeeper of Fokien,[418] to give due warning of the departure of the steamer *Plainmeller* for Singapore on 20 January 1882. Defendant Yau, through counsel, humbly apologised and promised not to do it again. With this assurance the Postmaster agreed to withdraw his complaint. The magistrate said it was a serious matter because the Postmaster was "likely to be accused of negligence" if mail was delayed.[419] The comings and goings of the *Plainmeller* are recorded in the *China Mail* shipping section but there is no mention of Yau. He seems to have been a man of some substance because he was one of those rare defendants who employed a westerner to address the magistrate on their behalf. There is also a reference to "his ships". Perhaps the "shopkeeper" description does him less than justice.

Modern readers would be puzzled by the nineteenth century approach to drugs cases, in which the miscreant is invariably charged with possession "without a permit from the Opium Farmer". This reflects the legal position at the time, which was that drug use was regulated, not banned. The government had a legal monopoly of opium, which it "farmed" out for a fee. This system seems to have worked surprisingly well, at least in the sense of avoiding drug-related crime. None of the "usual excuses" involves a desperate need for ill-gotten gains to fuel a drug habit. In fact, even if you disregard Europeans, the drug which got most people into trouble was alcohol. We must not, though, imagine people getting sozzled on San Miguel, or some early version of beer. A fearsome variation on gin was the tipple of the lower classes. A story of drunkenness printed on 3 December 1881 is headed "TOO MUCH SAMSHU". Unfortunately there is no hint in the story of what samshu was[420] but the effect on Private P. Mackanery was quite dramatic. No doubt some of those defendants who said they could not remember a thing afterwards were speaking no more than the literal truth.

The *China Mail* court reports present an interesting challenge to journalism theory, which usually assumes that people read newspapers because they want practical information, or because they identify with the people in the stories. Clearly Hong Kong's English-speaking readers were not seeking the information they needed to participate effectively as citizens of a democratic society, because Hong Kong was not such a society. Even the desire to see that justice is being seen to be done must be attenuated by the knowledge that there is nothing whatsoever you can do about any flaws in the system. Some individuals did work strenuously and successfully for the redress of grievances and the reform of social ills, but they worked within an imperial and autocratic system.

No doubt readers jumped, as readers still do, to unwarranted conclusions on the basis of a few cases – "Far too many robberies these days, my dear" – but even the most insecure individuals can hardly have regarded Stewart's usual motley clientele as a threat to the foundations of social order. There are hints of significant violent triad activity but the discourse of the court or police page generally offers a hopeful view because cases do not appear unless they have been solved. In police courts the Mounties nearly always get their man.

Yet one can hardly imagine that readers identified closely either with the plight of defendants or their victims. The gulf – social, financial and racial – was just too great. *The China Mail* seems to have had a local circulation of about seven hundred at this time, which, applying the usual multiplier, would suggest a readership of about three thousand. They would have included the local British, other Europeans, Portuguese from Macau, Parsees, Indians and the most prosperous and Westernised of the Chinese. Their occupations would be either business or government, including military and naval. Other professionals – teachers, missionaries, lawyers and so on – made up the numbers. The stories are often moving enough if you take the trouble to imagine the reality behind them. But readers are not particularly encouraged to make the effort. The style is a long way from tear-jerking.

Some of the stories include individuals who were presumably well known in the small circle of Hong Kong's expatriate society. Others would perhaps have resonated with readers who had their own problems with servants, pilferage, or the sharp practices of rickshaw pullers. It may be – Hong Kong was a much smaller place in those days – that the circle of Chinese people Westerners were likely to encounter, even in menial capacities, was so small that there was a real practical utility in discovering who had been dismissed for inattention to his or her duties. Reading this seamy section of *The China Mail* perhaps offered hints for day-to-day survival in an exotic colony, an assurance that departures from Western norms of social behaviour were discouraged, a way of participating vicariously in that colourful life "below stairs" from which the upper classes were banished by linguistic ignorance, inhibitions and noblesse oblige. In the more thoughtful parts of the newspaper much space was devoted to a then-current expatriate preoccupation, the question whether the Chinese were being coopted to Western values and modes of behaviour – or as they would have put it then, "civilisation".

I suppose though that for most readers, this part of *The China Mail* was more a social ritual than anything else. Despite the strange offences, the curious names and the occasional intrusion of such exotic officials as the Opium Farmer and the Inspector of Brothels, the *Mail*'s remorseless and objective chronicling of the misdeeds of the lower classes brought back memories of Home.

The Hong Kong (Police) Magistrate in the 1880s & 1990s

A Flavour of the Times

Garry Tallentire

In writing this chapter I have drawn on three sources to contrast the Magistrate's Court of the early 1880s with that of today: – my own experience as a Magistrate of some eleven years in Hong Kong,[421] my own knowledge and impressions of conditions in a Victorian Colony, and a selection of reports from *The China Mail* of cases heard by magistrate Frederick Stewart from July 1881 to March 1882. As one would expect, much has changed. But what I do find, much to my surprise, is how much has not. The Magistrate's Court of today must by necessity operate at a level of sophistication and technical expertise, unimaginable to our brothers of the 1880s. That leads me to an obvious area of difference from today: – the Magistrate. In the 1880s the animal would be easily recognisable: – male, British and unqualified in the law. This contrasts with the Bench of today, which embraces Magistrates of local, British, Indian, Australian, New Zealand and Canadian origins. There are both male and female Magistrates, all of whom must be qualified as solicitors or barristers with a substantial number of years' experience, prior to sitting. From the newspaper reports, one can gather that the prosecutor in the 1880s would usually have been a police officer of British extraction and male, of course. Again, this contrasts with the court of today, where the prosecutor can be either male or female; and one of the following: – a trained but unqualified lay prosecutor, a counsel on fiat,[422] or a Government Counsel. It is now rare indeed to find police officers appearing for the prosecution.[423] This tends to happen only occasionally, when bail is being opposed on perhaps a Commercial Crime Bureau matter, and the investigating officer appears to explain the progress and complexity of the case. There are few references to defence lawyers in these Nineteenth Century reports, although clearly the "Worthies" of the colony, when prosecuted, would appear with the benefit of representation. Although there was a contemporary view that court interpreters offered defendants off-the-cuff advice sotto voce in their native language, in effect, the average miscreant in the 1880s stood alone before the Police Magistrate without the assistance of the comprehensive Duty Lawyer Scheme that is in place today. Now the vast majority of defendants charged with criminal offences appears either represented by courtesy of the Duty Lawyer Scheme, or – if they so choose – privately represented. Only the most trivial of matters are not covered by the Duty Lawyer Scheme. This is a fairly recent development, consequent to a large extent on the passage of the Bill of Rights in 1991. Prior to that, an earlier scheme – in operation from January 1979 – assisted only in a limited number of cases before the Magistrate's Court.

An examination of the charges before Stewart's court in the 1880s shows many which span the years – we find the thieves, the robbers, the gamblers, the drunks, the drug addicts and dealers and the violent men committing what were known then as assaults and batteries and which today are determined as one of four charges – common assaults, assaults occasioning actual bodily harm, wounding, or grievous bodily harm – according to the degree of injury and the intention of the defendants. I do note (with some surprise) that there seems to be no reference to vice crimes such as prostitution and related offences. Nowhere in these newspaper reports do I find references to the modern offences of soliciting or loitering in a public place for the purpose of prostitution, managing or assisting in the management of unlicensed massage parlours or vice establishments, or living on immoral earnings. In Eastern Court today, there are fifteen to twenty such cases a month. It is impossible to believe that a busy, albeit Victorian (or maybe especially a Victorian), international port city – a cross roads of the Orient (and the Occident) – would not be amply served by the "ladies of the night", and the "ladies of the day" for that matter. And of course it was. The difference was, that brothels were licensed then.[424]

This level of tolerance towards the reality of the "oldest profession", lacking today, apparently originated in a concern for the health of the British troops in Hong Kong.[425] Licensing made inspection for venereal diseases possible.[426] Additionally, the local police may for various reasons have turned the proverbial "blind eye" at unlicensed "sly brothels". Of course, no one pretended that no such trade existed. But prostitution was not designated as a crime.

Apart from the health benefits brought by brothel licensing (and the medical inspections that this made possible), perhaps – in the male dominated society, that Hong Kong was during this period – a "service" provided purely for the relief of males was additionally considered beneficial to good order. – Perhaps this topic would be worthy of further research (with the aid of a red light). Today, of course, there are also homosexual cases of a similar type to those listed above but committed by males, with additional matters such as buggery in a public place or acts of gross indecency.[427]

One striking aspect of Victorian crime is how simple the crimes were compared to some of the charges appearing in the list of the modern Magistrate's Court. Although uttering counterfeit coin and forged bank notes occurred then, as now, you do not find such offences as computer fraud, credit card and related offences, or money laundering in the Nineteenth Century.

Again, turning to a seamier side of life, I find no references to crimes involving pornography, though I think without doubt that a city like Hong Kong would not have been short of the odd "dirty postcard", or similar.[428] Also, obviously there was no publishing of pornography[429] via the internet, or video compact discs (VCDs) or video cassettes! Today, the offences of possession for the purpose of publication, or the actual publication, of pornographic materials are common. In Eastern Court – which covers the traditional red-light district of Wanchai – these cases average twenty to thirty a month, the usual sentence being a custodial one, depending on the age of the defendant. This reflects the modern world of technology and communication.

Neither do we find in these reports from the 1880s many of the various bribery offences[430] now investigated and prosecuted by the Independent Commission against Corruption (ICAC) under the Prevention of Bribery Ordinance, 1971. Although there are cases where defendants offered a bribe, no policeman was charged with accepting one. The reason for the imbalance is partly explained by Endacott in his *A History of Hong Kong*. In 1867, a police constable was accused of having accepted a bribe, but was acquitted on the ground that there was no ordinance under which he could properly be charged. As a result of this, bribery became rampant.[431] Not until 1898, did the Legislative Council pass a draft ordinance, "for the more effectual punishment of bribery and other misdemeanours", making it an offence to accept and offer bribes with a view to influencing the conduct of a public servant.[432] It would be more than seventy years before the ICAC was born (in 1974) as a response to widespread corruption, especially in the police.

It is interesting to note also, the offences involving rickshaws and the modern translation into taxis. It seems from the reports that there were as many problems (maybe more) with the rickshaw drivers of those days, as there are with the taxi drivers of today.

Although it is not entirely clear from the reports in *The China Mail*, the Magistrate of the 1880s, like today,[433] had the benefit of a court interpreter.[434] Additionally, those who were studying Cantonese had their language teachers with them in court.[435] Today the court interpreters provide quick and lucid translation into English from Cantonese and Putonghua and vice versa. Additionally we have access to interpreters of every major Chinese district and every major international language. (The Interpretation Office keeps lists of approved private interpreters. Usually the police advise in advance of the need for a special interpreter. Otherwise the court will adjourn for the necessary interpreter to be secured.) Occasionally (as has happened once in my own experience) we do fall down on some of the more exotic languages from Africa. These days it is not uncommon to call for a "signing" interpreter – lists are kept of these also – to assist the deaf and/or dumb person who occasionally appears.

In my opinion, the job of the interpreter is possibly the most difficult and demanding of all the officers of the court. I personally have relied heavily on my interpreters and court clerks to try to understand the local cultures and mores.[436] It seemed to me that I would be in error to try to impose pure Western values on the society of Hong Kong, which enjoys a multi-racial and multi-custom social order.

The sentencing options available to my predecessors the Magistrates of the 1880s were few. Basically these were fines, time in the stocks (or cangue) and imprisonment – with or without the "pleasure" of hard labour.[437] Indeed most fines had attached to them an alternative and specific period of imprisonment for those unable or unwilling to pay.

Interestingly, as witnessed by these reports, prison sentences in the early 1880s tended to be shorter than those imposed today;[438] but I think it is clear that the conditions were much harsher. Also, there would have been options of binding over to be of good behaviour[439] and to keep the peace,[440] and confinement to the lunatic asylum when the condition of the defendant so warranted.

Corporal punishment was also an option.[441] Indeed it is only recently that caning was removed as a sentencing option in Hong Kong. I would add it is a punishment I have never imposed.

Today the basic punishments are the same – fines or imprisonment. However today, the imprisonment may be immediate or suspended. For trivial or technical offences, the court can impose an absolute or conditional discharge. Both lead to a recordable criminal conviction and conditional discharge involves a pledge of a sum of money for a specified period, payable in the event of reoffending. In nature and effect, a conditional discharge is rather like a bind over,[442] which was available in the Nineteenth Century, as now. Unlike a bind over, however, a conditional discharge is a criminal conviction, which leads to a criminal record. A bind over is a civil order, which does not give a criminal record.[443]

In crime and punishment today, we see a move towards rehabilitation, especially in respect of the young and those with good records. More and more, we are coming to regard prison as a last resort and in some ways a failure of the system. Of course this does not apply to very serious offences, such as those involving violence or gross sexual misconduct, where there is no alternative.

The keystone of rehabilitation is of course the probation order. This is a most useful and effective sentence, which usually has conditions attached to address the offender's problems. Probation orders include curfews, residence in approved hostels, residential drug treatment programmes, psychiatric and psychological treatment. A more recent addition to our sentencing options is the Community Service Order, which is both punitive and rehabilitative and seen as a constructive alternative to imprisonment. This requires the offender to perform up to two hundred and forty hours of unpaid work under the supervision of the probation service within twelve months. A probation order can be up to three years. Breach of either order can lead to revocation and sentencing again for the offence.

For the many drug addicts who appear, we have the Drugs Addiction Treatment Centres (DATC). Whilst this is a formal custodial sentence, it is regarded as rehabilitative in that it seeks to break the addiction of the offender. The regime is one of "cold turkey" – with physical manifestation of drug withdrawal being treated – and counselling. The success rate is difficult to gauge definitively, but given the difficulty of treating profound drug addicts, the evidence is, not surprisingly, that it is on the low side.

Other custodial options available for young offenders are Detention Centres (for those fourteen to twenty-one years of age) known as the "short, sharp shock", and Training Centres (for those of fourteen to twenty years of age). Each is an indeterminate sentence, the length depending on the offender's progress in the institution. Sentences to Training Centres are longer and emphasise training rather than pure punishment. Each sentence incorporates statutory supervision after discharge and the possibility of recall in the event of reoffending.

Unlike the court of the early 1880s, we have a separate and distinct Juvenile Court to deal with those of fifteen years and under. The Magistrate must be the holder of a Juvenile Warrant. Rehabilitation and prevention of reoffenders are paramount considerations. In the early 1880s the defendants – irrespective of age – simply appeared before the Police Magistrate.[444]

Also, in the gathering of information and obtaining of advice on sentences, we are much better served than our colleagues of the early 1880s. The basic and most widely used report today is that of a probation officer, who will investigate the background of the defendant – including his domestic and personal circumstances and his reaction to the offence – and make recommendations based on his likely response to a probation order, or an order for community service.

Whilst the reports are always helpful and constructive, there are times when the terminology affords some amusement. For instance, I recall a social welfare report on a girl of fifteen, in which I was told, that "she had committed suicide on five separate occasions". Yet the plucky lass still managed to continue to offend. A recent probation report informed me that the young lady I had convicted of the theft of a bra from Marks and Spencers – because of defects in her personality – had "no bosom friends". – Obviously she lacked support! A psychiatric report read "mental examination of the defendant revealed a lady with long clean hair". I now realise why psychiatrists have such long and impressive lists of qualifications.

It would seem however that my brothers of the 1880s did have the benefit of the opinion of the superintendent of the local asylum, in suitable cases.

Today, in addition to psychiatric reports we can also call for psychological reports.

Other reports are available from the Director of Correctional Services, as to the suitability for the Drugs Addiction Treatment Centre, Detention Centre or Training

Centre. If we are in difficulties, sentencing persons under twenty-one, we can refer the case to the Young Offenders Assessment Panel for a report.

Those in need of psychological treatment can be made the subject of a Hospital Order, which involves a stay at Siu Lam Psychiatric Prison, or treatment, as a condition of a Probation Order. Psychological treatment is enforced via a Probation Order also.

One common feature, which is to be found in the courts of the 1880s and those of today, is the presence of the press. The press are free to report and comment on the cases, subject to a few limitations, which are there to ensure anonymity of juveniles and fair trials for adults. Indeed it is from the excellent and comprehensive press reports of the day that we gain our knowledge of the operation of the courts of the 1880s.

Perhaps one matter of note and regret is that the press in 1880 seem to have had as a priority the faithful, accurate and objective reporting of the cases. This is not always so today. On occasions the pursuit of sensationalism clearly overrides truth and fairness, and we see malpractices such as seeking off-the-cuff reactions on sentences from victims or the families of victims, and reporting of ill informed criticism of the court. Even more worrying is that, on occasion, the press will go to so-called "experts" – often of dubious qualifications – and seek comments on the proceedings. More often than not the so-called "experts" have not been in the court, have no direct knowledge of what transpired, and no understanding of legal constraints and procedures. Add to this, outrageous misquoting of the Magistrate, and even of the facts of the case on occasion. Having said this, I still do hold the opinion that, despite such aberrations, the freedom of the press is a principle to be adhered to, for all our sakes.

To assist us in our deliberations today, each court building has an extensive law library, and each Magistrate's chambers has a supply of the most widely used criminal law books. In addition, we have access to a wide database of decided cases via our personal computers. Thus we are able to access procedural legal points and tariff sentences. The latter is essential so as to ensure a consistent approach to various crimes. In the 1880s it is unlikely that anything other than the laws themselves would have been available to the Magistrate.[445] Nowadays[446] the court record is provided by digital recording of the proceedings, and each Magistrate has the ability to replay the whole or selected parts of court proceedings of any court sitting. I assume that in the 1880s the record was made via the scratch of a quill pen, or a brass nib on a good day and if the ship had docked.

The business of a Magistrate's Court is serious and often deeply sad, with reputations ruined, lives wrecked and freedom lost. Nevertheless, there are – and I am quite sure that this was so even in the 1880s – moments of comedy and light relief. Situations often emerge which cause me to smile (not to laugh, of course). Or inadvertent remarks inject humour into the proceedings. One proper and abiding rule is that humour should not be such as to belittle or insult parties before the court. Sarcasm has no place in a court. I hope all who sit on the bench always remember that. It is easy to become case hardened and overlook that, for the defendant and sometimes the witnesses, the appearance in court is a significant and often distressing experience. They have a right to courtesy and not to be held up to public ridicule.

Having pontificated, let me turn to a few of my happy memories.

The lady was in her late thirties. She pleaded guilty to an offence of soliciting for the purpose of prostitution. Her criminal record reveals that this was her eighth conviction for this type of offence within the last two years. I was intrigued as, prior to that, she had led a blameless life free from any convictions whatsoever. Through my interpreter I put the facts to her. Back came the reply that two years ago she was working in a Dai Pai Dong (street cafe/cooked food stall) and had been feeling unwell. Therefore she consulted her doctor and the advice was "to find a job where she was not on her feet so much". – Logical?

In the New Territories many years ago, I met a cantankerous octogenarian charged with failing to exercise proper control over his dog. The dog had bitten the victim, causing quite a serious injury. The defendant denied the charge. In his evidence, he claimed firstly that the dog was not his; secondly if the dog was his, it had not bitten the victim; and thirdly if the dog was his and it had bitten the victim, it was because the victim was attacking the dog and the dog was only protecting itself. I pointed out that he could not plead three separate and irreconcilable defences. He told me very firmly that I was paid to decide which one applied. I obliged by rejecting all three and finding that he did own the dog, the dog did bite the victim and that the victim had done nothing to cause the dog to bite her. He seemed somewhat displeased with his conviction.

Recently, I described a teenager who stole one hundred and twenty condoms as dishonest and optimistic.

Often an integral part of the case against a defendant is his own statement, in which admissions are made.[447] If it is to be used as evidence, the prosecution must prove it to be made voluntarily. This means it must not have been extracted by threats, inducements, or violence. The defence are required to outline objections when challenging the voluntariness of a statement. The oddest allegation I dealt with was a claim that the defendant had been taken to a police station in the New Territories, placed in a room, ordered to strip and stand with his legs apart on two stools. Thereafter a police constable, supervised by a sergeant, tickled his testicles with a feather duster until he agreed to confess. I admired his invention but disbelieved his assertions.

The last little cameo is a tale that could easily have taken place in the 1880s. The defendant, a young man of undistinguished character, had "taken a refreshment" in Wan Chai. He boarded the ferry to return to Cheung Chau. Unfortunately, due to his inebriation, he boarded the wrong ferry and duly disembarked at Lamma. By the time he had realised his mistake, the last ferry of the night had gone. He sat for a while on the public pier at Lamma and then, whilst trying to decide what to do, walked around. Unfortunately he lost his footing and fell into the sea. He managed to haul himself into a boat which was in fact a dragon boat. He sat there for a while and, feeling wet and chilly, decided to keep warm by paddling the boat. This led to the idea of paddling all the way cross to Cheung Chau; not a good idea you might think. Well, he managed to paddle out into the channel and soon it became clear that the task was beyond his strength and skill. Indeed he was very relieved to be rescued by a marine police officer. Before me he pleaded guilty to taking a conveyance without the owner's consent. I fined him one thousand dollars, which was the amount of his bail. However, the duty lawyer asked me not to take all his bail as he had no money to get back to Cheung Chau. Having a fearful vision of him going for another trip in a dragon boat, I took half his bail and gave him seven days to pay the balance.

I wonder if, in one hundred years, a Magistrate will scour the newspaper reports of today's courts to try to get a flavour of *our* times?

2. *Hong Kong Bund*

3. *View from Hong Kong Island across Hong Kong harbour to Stonecutters' Island and Kowloon.*

4. *General View of Hong Kong, Looking West. The Murray Barracks is in the middle foreground; the City Hall in the centre.*

5. *Victoria Harbour and Victoria Barracks.*

6. *Hong Kong Island & Harbour, with Kennedy Road on the right, the Royal Naval Dockyard, HMS 'Victor Emmanuel', North Barracks & Victoria Barracks.*

7. *"Hong Kong Parade Ground, Looking North. The Eastern Wing of the City Hall on one side and the quarters for married soldiers on the other, form the boundaries of the lower Parade and Cricket Ground, Queen's Road separating it from the upper, southern, half.   Her Majesty's Ships 'Princess Charlotte' and 'Meeanee' are visible in the harbour, backed by the hills of British Kowloon, themselves backed by the higher ones of the Sunon district" – Original 19th century caption.*

8. *"Chinese Town, West Point. The Chinese Hospital and the Chinese Theatre. The roof and belfry of the German Mission Church can be seen over the former, while just beyond the Church lies a large open space, enclosed as a native recreation ground. This part of the town is named Possession Point. The Chinese Theatre may be distinguished by the inscription on the nearest face,*

9. *The Royal Inniskillings Fusiliers on parade near St John's Cathedral.*

10. *Government Central School for Boys, seen above Queen's Road West.*
As first Headmaster, living in the school, Frederick Stewart was close to the Queen's Road bars where seamen spent leisure time.

11. *Hong Kong Island and Harbour showing Victoria Gaol.*

12. *Victoria Gaol and Magistracy and the quarters of the Superintendent of Police shown in this View of the Mid-Levels from the slopes above Lower Albert Road. This Magistracy Building is where Magistrate Frederick Stewart heard the court cases in this book.*

13. *Old Supreme Court, Hong Kong (right middleground). Also seen is St John's Cathedral (middleground far left).*

14. *Victoria Gaol seen from the east end of Chancery Lane.*

15. *Staff of Victoria Gaol, Hong Kong.*

16. *Police Headquarters with Chinese, European and Indian police on parade.*

17. *Hong Kong Police Officers at the Central Police Station.*

18. *Chinese and Indian Police at the Central Police Station.*

(L:) **19.** *Chinese Policeman.*
(R:) **20**. *Ng Choy, first Chinese Police Magistrate when a practising barrister in Hong Kong.*

21. *Court scene. Some earlier magistrates (not Frederick Stewart, a model of rectitude) hurried court proceedings on a Saturday, to get to the races on time. Note the exaggeratedly tall Sikh, western constable, western defendant and smiling other persons in the court.*

22. *Chinese prisoner in the stocks, guarded by Sikh constables, Chinese constables nearby. The conviction is stated on the board in front of the prisoner.*

23. *Members of the Hong Kong Fire Brigade.*

24. *Fire at Hong Kong.*

25. *Tung Wah Hospital officials provided an important element in the regulation of Hong Kong society.*

26. *Chinese, European and Indian police with Chinese village leaders.*

27. *Posing for a photograph, a popular leisure activity.*

28. *Dancing the hornpipe on board ship.*

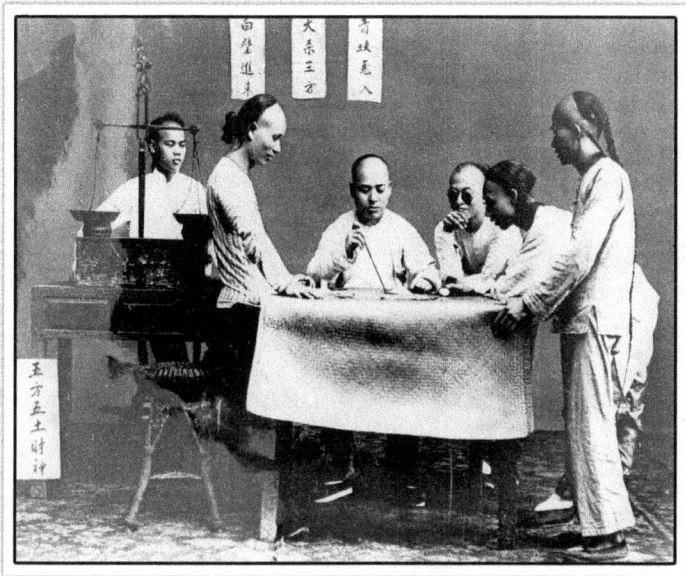

29. *Playing Fantan, reputed to be an ancient game, based on guessing the number of porcelain buttons placed under a cup. The Chinese characters indicate as follows:*
bottom left: "God of wealth of all directions and places"; top left: "Valuables coming in"; top centre: "Big win" or "Winning all sides"; top right: "Money flying in".

30. *Itinerant barber with stool, umbrella & water container.*

31. *European Travelling Circus at Hong Kong.*

32. *The Race Course, Hong Kong*
The Chinese love of gambling made horse racing immediately popular in
Hong Kong. Crowds gave opportunities for pickpockets.

33. *Chinese schoolmaster and pupils.*
Traditionally, the pupils sat with their backs to the teacher.

34. *Queen's College students taking an examination.*

35. *British and Chinese staff at Queen's College.*

36. *Queen's College (formerly The Central School) at Abedeen Street and Hollywood Road, w. masters and students.*

37. *Chinese girl in her best clothes.*　　**38.** *Chinese amah.*

39. *Hong Kong Chinese family in Ching Dynasty dress.*
Governor John Pope Hennessy (1877-1882) wished to encourage
respectable Chinese families to settle in Hong Kong.

A Magistrate's Court in 19th Century Hong Kong　　159

40. *Street children.*

41. *Chinese boys in the fields.*

42. *Man with a buffalow ploughing near a village,*
with a Fung Shui wood behind and distant mountains.

43. *Village Street Scene.*

44. *Houseboats.*

45. *Shroffs checking for counterfeit coins.*

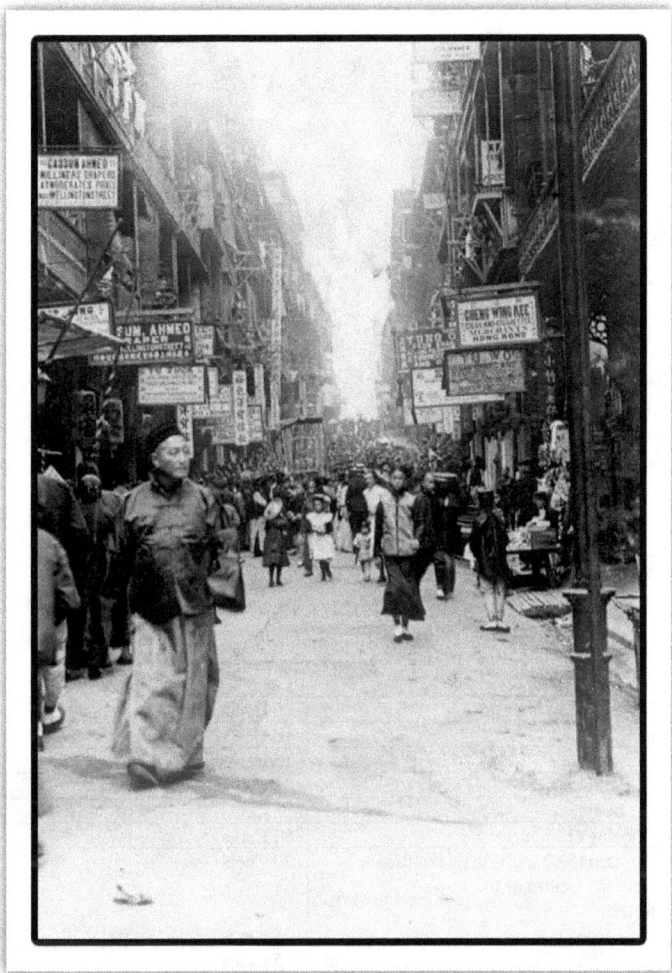

46. *Wellington Street, Central Hong Kong.*

47. *Young men in the Botanic Gardens.*

~~~~~

48. SCALE OF FARES FOR JINRICKSHAS WITH ONE COOLIE[448]

Quarter of an hour or less	5 Cents.
Half an hour	10 Cents.
One hour	15 Cents.
Three hours	25 Cents.
Six hours	35 Cents.
One day (12 hours)	50 Cents.
Per Trip to Shaukiwán or Pokfúlam, from the Centre of the Town Return	20 Cents. 35 Cents.
Per Trip to Aberdeen, from the Centre of the Town Return	25 Cents. 40 Cents.

If an Extra Coolie is employed, there will be an addition of half the above scale to pay. Nothing in this scale prevents private agreements.

J. RUSSELL,
Registrar General.

Approved by the Governor in Council, this 12th day of September, 1882.
ARATHOON SETH,
Clerk of Councils.

Without reference to nationality, all persons resident on British Territory are free agents. They cannot be under the restraint of others. If any of you, girls, have been kidnapped, purchased, seduced, deceived, or pledged for money, or have been compelled to swear before entering the brothels that you will act as prostitutes to which you object, you must understand that this is illegal, and you are at liberty to come personally to this office, or go to any police station, to report the matter at any time you please. Your grievance will be at once attended to. If you want to leave the brothel, and make up your mind to go to a protector, abandoning prostitution, the Government will certainly let you do what you please, and will not allow you to be detained against your will. You must be aware of this. Be not deceived by brothel keepers. Observe this notice.

Registrar-General's Department[449]

49. Translation of a Chinese document to be handed to each new brothel inmate, from 23 June 1882.
"The girl will not be able to read it,
but some of her visitors will read it to her."

The purchase of people for the purpose of prostitution is quite contrary to English law. Should you, brothel keepers, deceive or purchase ignorant women to force them to become prostitutes, or use other pretences to have power and control over them, they being thus in trouble can go at once to the officials, and report the matter, so that you can be punished according to the law. There can be no excuse for you whatsoever. Let each obey this tremblingly, and do not treat this as a slight matter.[450]

50. Translation of a Chinese notice to Brothel Keepers.

SCHEDULES to which this Ordinance refers.

A.

Weight.

120 Catties	{ Stone / Shik } 石	679·84 Grains Troy	{ Tael / Leang } 兩		
100 Catties or 133⅓ lbs.	{ Picul / Tam } 担	10 One Tael or 57·984 Grains	{ Mace / Tseen } 錢		
16 Taels or 1⅓ lb.	{ Catty / Kin } 斤	10 One Mace	{ Candareen / Fun } 分		

Measures of Length.

According to the Measure established by the Tariff, 141 English Inches, or 3⅔ Yard,...............	{ Four Yards / Cheung }	丈
14 1/12 English Inches, ...	{ Covid / Chek }	尺
About 1¼ English Inch, ...	{ Inch / Tsun }	寸
Ten Fun one Tsun, ...	{ Fun }	分
Ten Lip one Fun, ...	{ Line / Lip }	粒

Grain.

One Shik 3,160 Cubic Tsun (or Chinese Inches) 石

2 Hoh	斛	make one	石	Shik, or one Stone.	
5 Tow	斗	make one	斛	Hoh, or 1,580 Cubic Tsun.	
10 Shing	升	make one	斗	Tow, or 316	"
10 Koh	合	make one	升	Shing, or 31·6	"
2 Yob	侖	make one	合	Koh, or Gill.	
5 Choh	勺	make one	侖	Yob, or Cup.	
10 Chau	抄	make one	勺	Choh, or Ladle.	
10 Tsoh	撮	make one	抄	Chau, or Handful.	
10 Kwei	圭	make one	撮	Tsoh, or Pugil.	

本則例內所指格式第一

秤　碼

量　穀

一百二十斤即一石
一百斤或一百三十三磅
之三分一即一担
十六兩或一磅零三之一即
一斤

英冥藥材秤碼五百七十九
粒零粒百之八十四即一兩
英冥藥材秤碼五十七粒零
千之九百八十四即兩之
一錢
十分一即一錢
一分即一錢十分

遵照條約內所開之單
所定之法
英冥一百四十一寸或
三碼零十二分碼之十
一即一丈或曰四碼即
一丈
英冥十四寸零寸之十
分一即一尺
英冥一寸零寸之五分
即一寸
一分即寸之十分一
一粒即分之十分一

三千一百六十丁方寸即一石
二斛即一石
五斗或一千五百八十丁方寸
即一斛
十升即一斗或三百一十六丁方寸
十合即一升或三十一丁方寸零寸之
二侖即一合
五勺即一侖
十抄即一勺
十撮即一抄
十圭即一撮

51. *Schedules of Standard Weights and Measures referred to in Ordinance Number 22 of 1844, republished in October 1881, with a Chinese translation, as suggested by Frederick Stewart.*[451]

SCHEDULE.

(Forms of Passes referred to in Sections VII, and XI.)

No.   ANNUAL PASS,   No.
                       FOR 187 .

Granted to   of
No.   Victoria.

                                              Colonial Secretary.

This Pass is not Transferable.

REVERSE.

ANNUAL PASS, FOR 187 .

Same in Chinese.

Same in Ghuzeratee.

Same in Hindostanee, &c.

No.   SPECIAL PASS,   No.
                       FOR   , 187 .

Granted to
residing at

                                              Colonial Secretary.

This Pass is not Transferable.

REVERSE.

SPECIAL PASS, FOR   , 187 .

Same in Chinese.

Same in Ghuzeratee.

Same in Hindostanee, &c.

No.   QUARTERLY PASS.   Quarter of 187 .

Issued to A. B.
of No.   , for the Quarter specified at the Back hereof.

        , 187 .   Supt. of Police.

REVERSE.

This Pass is valid only for the   Quarter of 187 .

Same in Chinese.

Same in Ghuzeratee.

Same in Hindostanee, &c.

---

52. *Forms of Passes Referred to in Ordinance No. 14 of 1870, Sections VII and XI.*[452]

GOVERNMENT NOTIFICATION.—No. 427.

. His Excellency the Governor, having been pleased to grant permission for the erection of scaffolding for the display of various pictures, decorations, lanterns, &c., and for the exhibition of the same, on the nights of the 22nd, 23rd, and 24th December, 1881, has directed that the Police shall not require the production of passes under Ordinance 14 of 1870, from Chinese conducting themselves quietly until 2 A.M. of the 23rd, 24th, and 25th December, 1881.

By His Excellency's Command,

M. S. TONNOCHY,
Acting Colonial Secretary.

Colonial Secretary's Office,
Hongkong, 10th December, 1881.

號 七 十 二 百 四 第 報 憲

53. *Government notification temporarily suspending the requirement to produce night passes under Ordinance Number 14 of 1870.*[453]

GOVERNMENT NOTIFICATION.—No. 32.

Notice is hereby given that in view of the approaching Chinese New Year, the Captain Superintendent of Police has been authorized to give permission, under Ordinance 10 of 1872, for Crackers to be fired under the following restrictions :—

In the Districts West of the Cross Roads and of Shing Wong Street, the firing of Crackers will be permitted from 4 P.M. on the 17th until 4 P.M. on the 19th February.

In the Districts East of the Cross Roads and of Shing Wong Street, Crackers may be fired only between the hours of 4 P.M. of the 17th and 9 P.M. of the 18th February.

The Police will have strict orders to summon or arrest persons firing Crackers in contravention of the foregoing restrictions.

The firing of Bombs is strictly prohibited.

By His Excellency's Command,

M. S. TONNOCHY,
Acting Colonial Secretary.

Colonial Secretary's Office,
Hongkong, 28th January, 1882.

號 二 十 三 第 報 憲

54. *Ban against fire crackers modified for Chinese New Year, 1882.*[454]

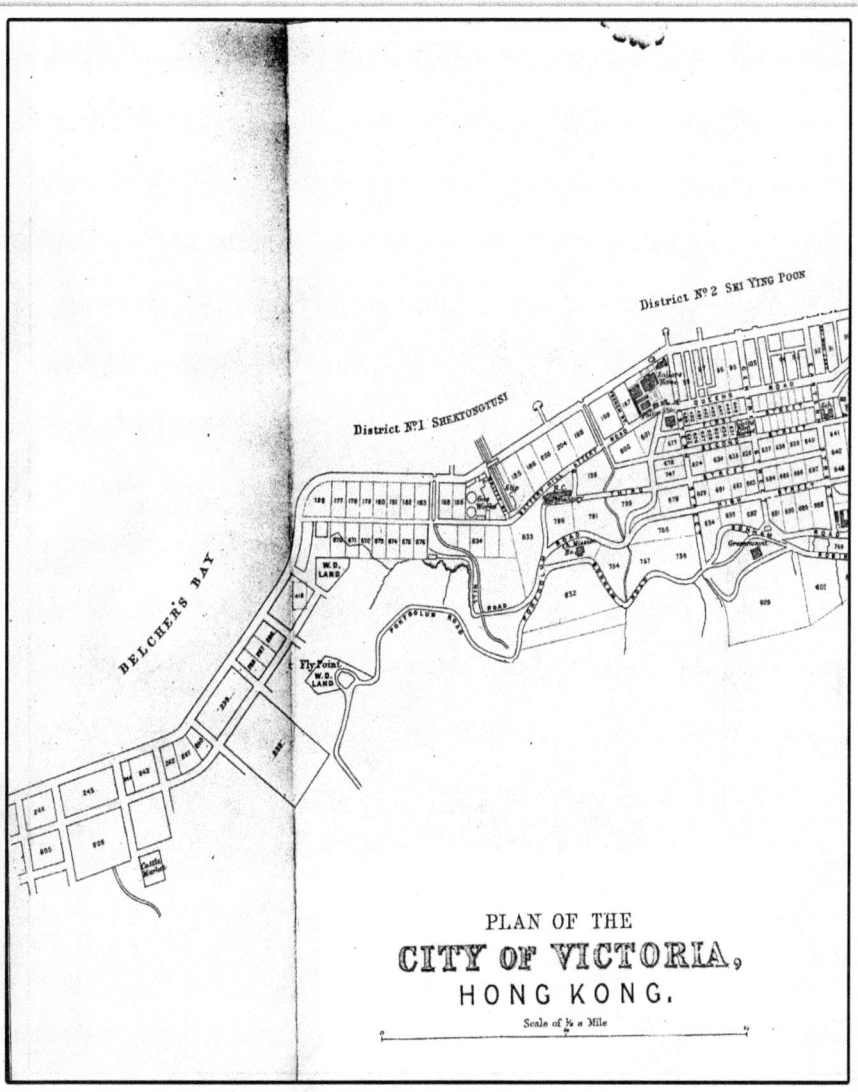

PLAN OF THE
CITY OF VICTORIA,
HONG KONG.
Scale of ½ a Mile

55a. *Plan of the City of Victoria, Hong Kong (western section).*[455]

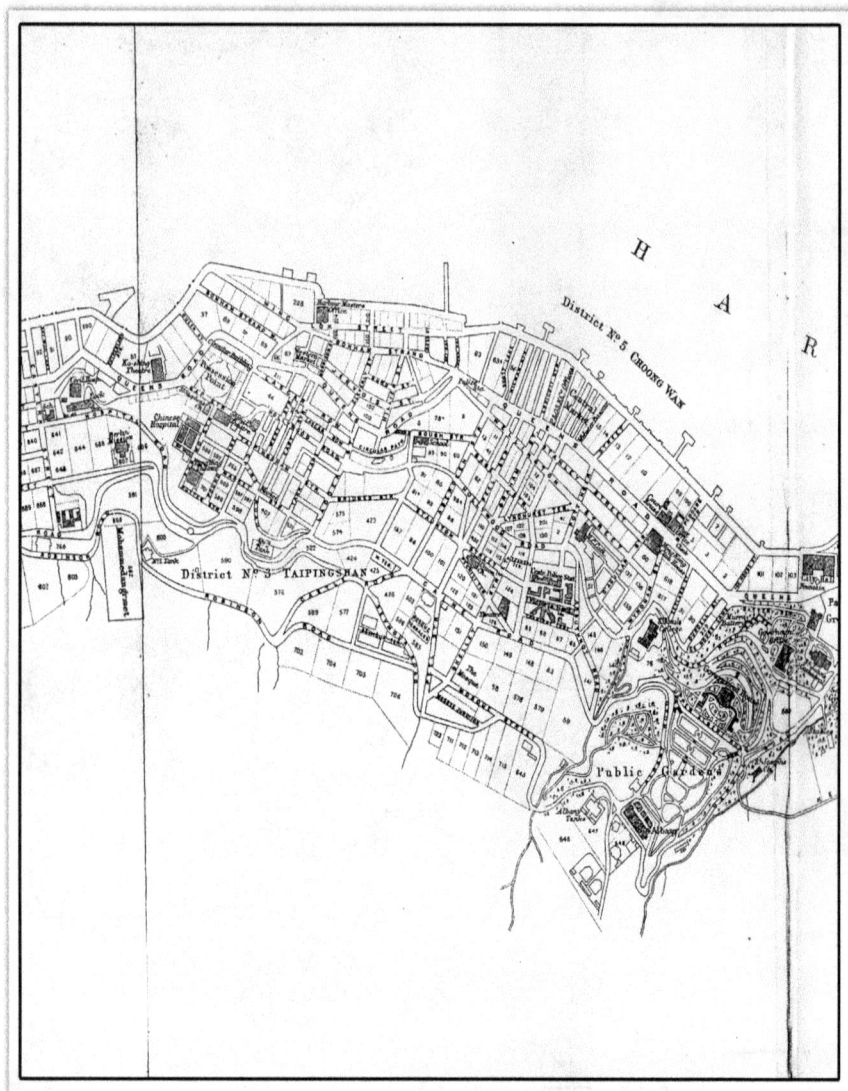

55b. *Plan of the City of Victoria, Hong Kong*
(western central section).

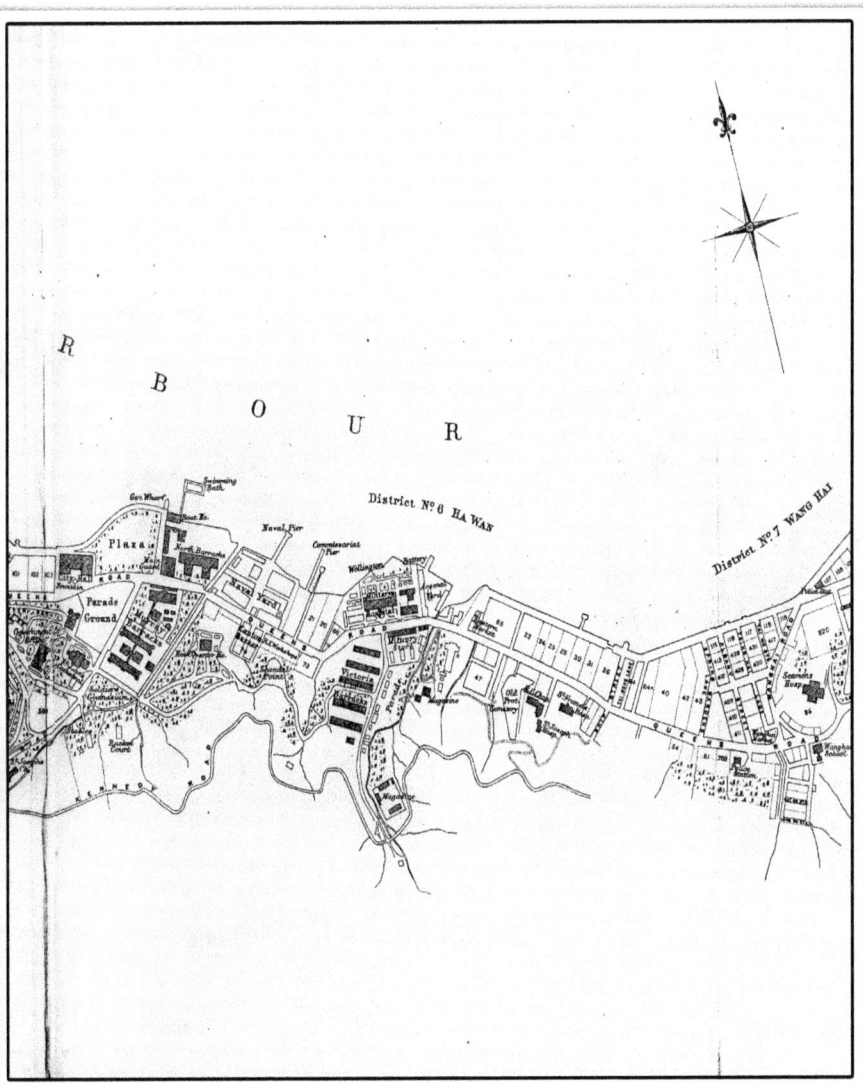

55c. Plan of the City of Victoria, Hong Kong (eastern central section).

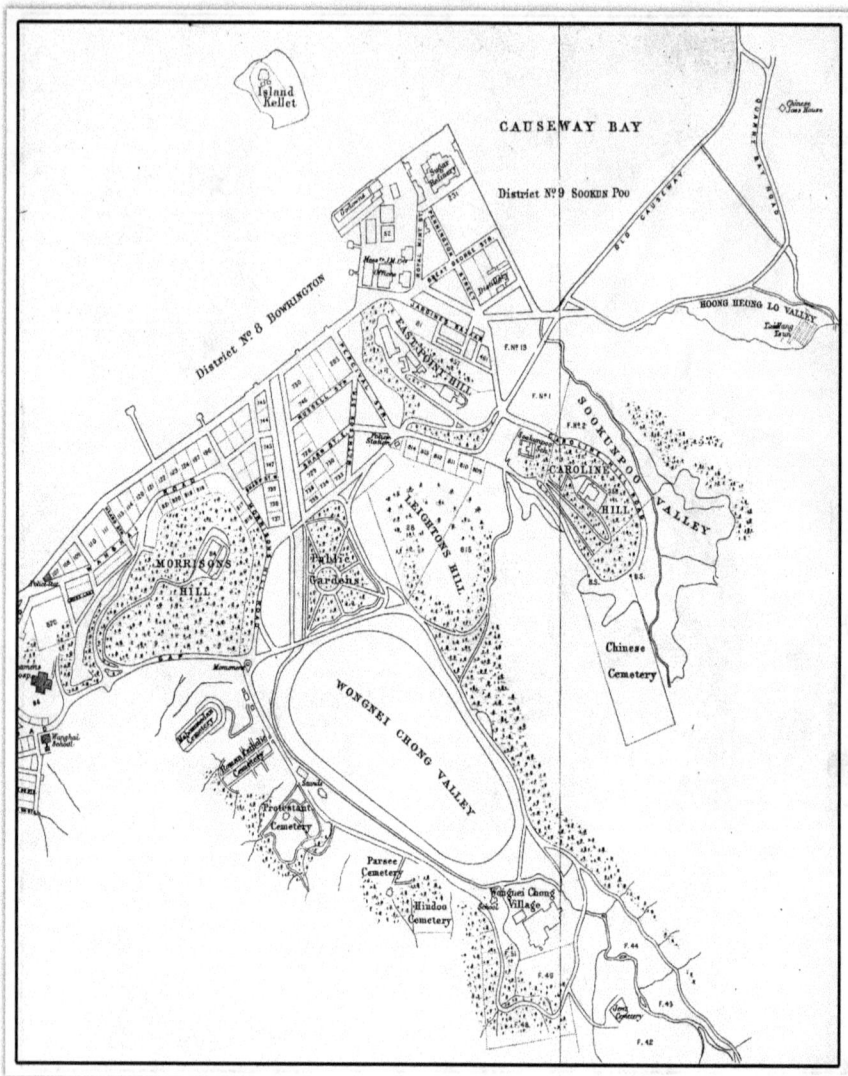

55d. *Plan of the City of Victoria, Hong Kong*
(eastern section).

SECTION TWO

Frederick Stewart's Cases as Reported in *The China Mail*: Background Essays with Selected Themed Transcripts

Introduction
The *China Mail* Court Reporter

In his essay, "Reporting the Cases of Frederick Stewart", above, Tim Hamlett claims that the reporting technique of these court reports, published in *The China Mail* between 26 July 1881 and 29 March 1882, clearly indicates a single writer. The style is certainly very different from reports of the same cases, published in the *Hong Kong Daily Press*, during the same period. But who was this *China Mail* court reporter? In October 1881, *The China Mail* records that there were "no less than four shorthand reporters" working for Hong Kong papers at this time.[456] Identifying one out of four should be simple.

A most useful, scholarly and detailed body of information about the newspapers of the China Coast was published as long ago as 1965.[457] But, while this includes a section, "Biographies of China-Coast Editors and Publishers", it does not list journalists, compositors, or other workers. James Joseph M'Breen, who worked for the *Hong Kong Daily Press* for a time, and who was one of the defendants in the "Alleged Assault" case, heard before Frederick Stewart on 17, 18 and 20 August 1881, is known to posterity from the present book alone. So is the out-of-work compositor, Capitulino Priamo Marçal, who was tried for disorderly conduct on 30 September 1881.[458]

Within the period of our reports, on 7 February 1882, there is an obituary notice about one of the "general reporters", Thomas Marr, "who for some years back has been engaged on the staff of more than one journal here in Hong Kong" and was "latterly attached to the *China Mail* as a general reporter".[459] The obituary comment additionally states that Thomas Marr "was on duty up to within a day or two of his death".[460] A comparison of the writing style up to some days before 7 February 1882 and after this date does not indicate a different hand, so this is not our man.

For the time being, at least, our reporter's identity must remain unknown.

Nevertheless, we certainly get a sense of the reporter's background and a strong sense of his personality. Verner Bickley, in his essay, "Differing Perceptions of Social Reality in Dr Stewart's Court", comments on the reporter's irony and flippancy and the insensitivity of his comments on some of the people who appeared in Stewart's court. Christopher Coghlan, in his essay, "White Gloves and Patience", also comments on the reporter's irony and humour, while admiring his clear, limpid and factual style.

In spite of the speed at which court reporters necessarily worked (which Tim Hamlett explains in his essay, "Reporting the Cases of Frederick Stewart", above), this court reporter took the time to indulge himself verbally now and again. Although his use of Latin was mainly for convenient brevity – "inst" and "ult" and "proximo" in connection with dates – he enjoyed his little Latin joke too, describing an unemployed seaman, charged with being "Drunk and Disorderly", as having had "quantum sufficit".[461]

Occasionally, the reporter lets slip what may be an indication of weariness, as much as a consciousness of the constraints of time. Reporting the "Assault and Robbery" case on 13 October 1881, he summarises most of the evidence, stating that it, "extended to great length".

THE PRESENT TEXT
Organisation and Sources of the Court Reports

Within each subject group, in Section Two, which follows, the reports quoted are presented in chronological order, according to the date of the first report of any particular case. Subsequent reports of the same case (or once, of a related case)[462] follow on immediately from the first report.

All reports are from *The China Mail*, where most were reported on the same day as the hearing. On the rare occasions when the report appeared on a later day, this is signalled in the quoted main text of *The China Mail* report.

In *The China Mail* at this time, the regular columns dealing with court cases are captioned, "Police Intelligence", and usually appear on page three – rarely, page two – of the newspaper. Since the date of the hearings is given in the main text of the present book, the endnotes do not repeat this information. On the one occasion where there is an error in the date given in the newspaper,[463] however, this is commented on.

Occasionally, a report from the Police Courts was given greater prominence, either in the "Local and General" columns (on page two, page three, or pages two to three of *The China Mail*), or by being given its own caption. With a very few exceptions, all the reports of cases reproduced in *Court in Time* are from the "Police Intelligence" section of *The China Mail*. Occasionally, a comment is included from a different part of the newspaper. These two types of content are distinguished as follows. For the former, the date is given in capital letters; in the latter, in both upper and lower case letters. For the latter reports only, endnotes with the full newspaper reference are given.

Modifications of the Original Text

In his essay, "Reporting the Cases of Frederick Stewart", above, Tim Hamlett explains how both the structure of the reports and the sprinkling of printing errors are a product of the pressures of time under which the reporter and then the type-setters, compositors and proof-readers worked. There are errors in syntax. There are the occasional implausible statements that the currency in which a fine was to be paid was sterling. There is the embedding of direct speech in reported speech with no use of quotation marks. Sometimes, complete lines are omitted. Errors in substance include phrases like, "Reserving his offence" for "reserving his defence",[464] and the use of the word, "deceased's", for "witness's".[465] These errors have been corrected in the text given here, but for those who are interested in this topic, they are preserved in endnotes.

In general, the body of the text of the original *China*

Mail reports is here reproduced exactly. Minor printing errors (for example, "u"s for "n"s, and similar) and some larger ones (for example, imperfect layout) are corrected silently. Frequently, in the originals, reported speech is not given in inverted commas; and on occasion, these have been supplied, sometimes with, sometimes without, indicating that this has been done. Additional punctuation may be indicated by square brackets. The names of ships are italicised, whether or not this is done in the original. On occasion, italics are added when the original reports dialogue as in a play script.

Abbreviations

Some abbreviations (for example "Geo." for "George", "Aug" for "August", "P. C." for "Police Constable", "Ins" for "Inspector", "P. S." for "Police Sergeant", "Co." for "Company", "No." for "Number", "cts" for "cents" are spelt out in full. Some numbers are given as words, rather than figures, and some money symbols are also given as words. When time is indicated, using the word, "o'clock", preceding figures are given in words. Some typographical features (for example, typeface, font, decorative lines) are modified. "Inst.", "Ult." and "Prox." are spelt out in full, and italicised.

Place and Personal Names

"Hongkong" is given as "Hong Kong". Otherwise, place names are given as in the originals, preserving the original variations. When a personal name is given in several versions, these variations also are preserved, and, after rechecking the often difficult originals for any misreading or misconception, if cross-identifications still seem inarguable, a note is given of all variations for each report or group of reports, when any one of the variations appears for the first time.

Comments on and Explanations of the Text

In addition to the comments and explanations given in the endnotes, some comments and explanations may be given in the main text, enclosed in square brackets. (These are always used in this book to indicate editorial intervention in those reports, which are reproduced, as well as within any other quotations.) On occasion, errors in the originals are corrected (as indicated by square brackets), and a note is given, stating how the original reads. For example, for one case, the main text is given as follows: "with [intent][466] to commit a felony on the 8th instant". And an endnote states, "The original reads "intend" [*sic* for "intent"]." Omissions or illegible portions of the originals may be supplied in square brackets, but with no further comment.

Conventions used in the Original Reports

Some of the conventions used in the original reports need comment. When information is given in response to a question, the reporter does not necessarily indicate this. Sometimes, in describing the dialogue in court, he writes, "By [so-and-so]", meaning, "in reply to a question from the particular person named". Sometimes the reporter simply provides the answer to such a question, leaving it to the reader, first to deduce that a question had been asked, and also to work out what the question had been. An example of this is the report of the "Assault" on 22 October 1881, where we read, "He did not know defendants and none of them were concerned in a case recently in which complainant was fined fifty cents".[467] Another is, "Public Obstruction", reported on 16 November 1881. Doubtless in response to a question or an implied accusation, the Police Constable is reported as saying, "He never at any time kicked defendant's empty baskets about."[468]

Hong Kong Life and Society in the 1880s

One hundred and twenty or so newspaper court case reports, and a handful of other commentary, have been edited[469] and are reproduced below. They relate to about one hundred cases, heard by Police Magistrate Frederick Stewart, during the period 26 July 1881 to 29 March 1882, and give a unique insight into Hong Kong life and society as a whole – rather than simply into the offences committed by residents – at this time. Grouped by the profession or situation of the defendant ("Sailors", "Soldiers", "Police", "Teachers and Men of the Cloth", "Prostitutes, their Associates and Clients", "Kidnappers and Traffickers in Human Beings", "Children and Students", "Gamblers and Informers"), they show us life's rich pageant. Grouped by location ("Urban Life", "Country Life"), or a combination of location and profession or situation ("The Domestic Scene. Wives and Husbands, Amahs and Cooks, Widows and Protected Women, Sons and Adopted Daughters. Burglars", "Pirates and Life at Sea"), they evoke domestic and street-life, varying life-styles, conditions and personalities.

The present writer's introductory essays to each section comment on the subjects of the section as well as on the reports that follow, often drawing on most interesting supporting material from additional contemporary sources and her own previous research, as well as from the work of other writers and scholars.

The notes acknowledge sources, comment on the text, and discuss ambiguities in the reports. They give considerable further background information on some of the events mentioned, and seek parallels in both the practice and attitudes of other countries, cultures and societies, as well as in creative literature. When possible, biographical notes on those named in the reports are given. When a case was committed to the Supreme Court, the sentence given there is noted, when available.

This is a rich resource, from which much can be learned.

Sailors

The *Band* Sergeant on Her Majesty's Ship *Iron Duke* had the appropriate name, Luigi *Libretto*. Most other sailors in this selection of cases from Frederick Stewart's court in the early 1880s have British-sounding names, and belong to British, Canadian[470] and American merchant ships; some to British naval vessels.

Why were they in court? – Often because of quarrels. Ordinary seamen had quarrelled with each other or their officers on their ships. They had quarrelled with the staff and the other residents where they stayed in Hong Kong. They had quarrelled with chair-coolies and shopmen in the town. Occasionally they had stolen from each other. Some were the victims of theft. One was guilty of impersonation and making a false report in the hope of cadging food and drink.

They had been drunk and incapable. – Many of their quarrels arose from drink, or were brought into the open by drink. A common question asked in court was whether a man who had been drinking still had his wits about him.

There was resentment of authority, a sense of grievance; both exacerbated by the conditions of their lives: – cramped, often boring, sometimes dangerous. Their ships were very small; the seas they sailed were only recently or incompletely charted; and the elements of wind and waves were violent, extreme, not always predictable. There was tale-bearing and resentment of tale-bearing.

Quarrels led to destruction of property, the flash of a knife, and in one case, to a death. The sailors' problems in the town were partly because they were not familiar with the place. They objected to the price of goods asked for; they could not make the chair-coolies understand them; they mistook one shop for another and perhaps mistakenly thought that others were trying to trick and deceive them.

There was a strange innocence about their lives, all the same. In town, they shopped for cigars, had their portraits painted, drank in the Welcome Tavern, engaged chair-coolies to go from place to place and slept in the

Seaman's Home or (ironically) the Temperance Hall. On one occasion they won the concern of *The China Mail* Editor, following a correspondent's report of "cruel and brutal treatment administered to drunken European sailors by Sikh policemen".[471]

In addition to ordinary sailors, these cases mention ship's firemen, a chief and third engineer, a mate and second mate and a boatswain. Even a chief officer and a captain had scuffled with each other. In one case only, we find a Chinese boatswain on a vessel with a Chinese name, accusing the western second officer with assaulting a young Chinese boat-boy.

Sailors on merchant ships worked under contract to the owners of a vessel for a particular voyage only, as part of a crew usually of fewer than one hundred men. The ship's captain and officers were themselves also often under contract for a particular voyage. The men on the Queen's ships had more security, serving under contracts of many years. In between ships, merchant seamen were free to sleep rough and starve.

In the public perception, there was a definite hierarchy. Although in 1881, both fleets participated in the Victoria Regatta that coincided with the visit of Queen Victoria's sons, merchant sailors seem to have been excluded, four years previously, in 1877, from the suggested, "bumper dinner at the City Hall", for "the Soldiers and Sailors in port."[472] This selection of reports from Stewart's court, however, suggests that there was little difference in the behaviour of the two groups when ashore.

There was also a third group. Often there were several merchant seamen in Hong Kong, waiting for employment – some from wrecked ships; a few deserters from American ships – often in penurious circumstances, and sometimes obliged to sell all but one suit of clothes to buy food. The drunkenness of these – *The China Mail* suggested – was the result of injudicious generosity by fellow sailors in port, offering gin when a solid meal would have been very much more welcome. From time to time, the Hong Kong foreign community cast a compassionate glance in their direction. On one occasion a square meal was served to all who would come; once – when there was a firework display – work was offered to a small number as extra firemen on stand-by duty, which they gratefully accepted.

On 2 December 1881, *The China Mail* printed a letter from "Junius", explaining the situation of these men and eliciting support for a hostel and donations of food. Their previous charitable facility had closed the day before. "Last night," as Junius reported, "the men called at the Central Police Station and solicited a night's shelter." On this occasion only they were allowed to rest in the waiting-room; and they did not know what to do for the future.

In January 1882, *The China Mail* took up their case, urging the community to take appropriate thought for "the waifs and strays that misfortune has cast upon our shores." As *The China Mail* stated; the Portuguese and the Chinese already had ways to prevent *their* poor from "arriving at such a low state of destitution as Europeans from the West", through the kind offices of the Catholic Clergy and the Tung Wah Hospital respectively. "Beyond the Consuls – and these are only for men whose papers are perfectly *en règle* – there has been a neglect of our destitutes not altogether creditable to us as a community." *The China Mail* took issue with the practice of sending such men to gaol "as a rogue and a vagabond", stating, "This more than anything else goes to degrade and demoralize men, who up to their present misfortune, were seamen earning their bread by honest sweat." *The China Mail* suggested that "the 'Sailors' Rest' should be developed into something of a House of Call, where the men by giving a certain amount of work instead of money could feel that they had paid for their lodgings and their breakfast, and that as long as they wished they were entitled to the advantages of the house until they were in a position to leave the Colony."[473]

Some of these destitutes however were judged simply as "loafers", not really wanting to work. These were disliked and sometimes feared by the non-Chinese residents of Hong Kong. Women in particular were alarmed when accosted for assistance in the street, or when men begged them for alms at the doors of their homes. Sometimes it was the demands of the Hong Kong Courts that brought a seaman into these sad straits. He might have been attacked and seriously injured on ship and hospitalized in Hong Kong. His evidence was wanted in court when he was well. Pending his recovery, his ship left without him, and the resulting loss of employment caused serious further injury to an innocent man.[474]

Sailors: Cases

FRIDAY 30 SEPTEMBER 1881
SERIOUS ASSAULT[475]

Charles Naylor,[476] second officer of the *Kang Chi*, was
charged with assaulting one Apo of the age of seventeen
years, so as to cause him to jump overboard in Victoria
Harbour on the 29th of September.

Ho Asing said he was boatswain on the *Kang Chi*.
On the 29th about 7.30 p.m., he was below on the 'tween
decks when he heard a noise on deck. He went up to see
what was the matter. He saw the boat boy jumping from the
deck to a cargo boat on the starboard side of the vessel.
Defendant went into the cargo boat after Apo, who jumped
into the water. Witness after some delay got a boat and
looked for him, but could find no trace of the lad. The other
Chinese on the vessel looked round the vessel with lamps.
Witness had not seen the boy since. He did not know why
defendant was following Apo. Witness made a report at 9
p.m. on the 29th. The steamer left for Haiphong this
morning. She was lying about 50 England[477] yards from the
shore. Witness did not know if the boy could swim. Before
Apo joined the steamer he was a boat boy.

By Mr. Wotton:[478] He had been once at Shanghai.
He did not know what the "Shanghai dodge"[479] was. The
boy was strong and had the use of all his limbs. He was an
active lad and in good health.

The case was adjourned to Tuesday first at half-past
two, and defendant was admitted to bail in one householder
of one thousand dollars, or two of five hundred dollars each.

SATURDAY 1 OCTOBER 1881
THE SERIOUS ASSAULT CASE

The case in which C. Taylor, second officer of the *Kang Chi*,
was charged with assaulting a Chinese boy and causing him
to jump overboard, was reduced this morning to very slight
dimensions. The boy who was said to be amissing, came up
to the Magistracy yesterday afternoon, and was examined
this morning. He had had no intention of reporting the

matter to the police. Defendant had challenged him for leaving the ship too soon with the boat for the purpose of bringing off the Captain. Defendant ordered him forward, and slapped him in the face. The boy said he got frightened and jumped into the cargo-boat. He was frightened to go back. He had no wish to press the charge.

Defendant was fined one dollar, or one day's imprisonment.~~~~~

FRIDAY 30 SEPTEMBER 1881
DRUNK[480]

George Cameron,[481] seaman, American ship *Twilight*, was convicted of being drunk and incapable.

Defendant said he was sorry. He had had a little too much.

Prisoner was fined twenty-five cents or one day's imprisonment.

TUESDAY 4 OCTOBER 1881
THE *BOLTON ABBEY* – FALSE REPORT

George Cannron, of the ship *Twilight*, was accused of being a rogue and vagabond.

Mr Maconachie said he was manager of the firm of Messrs. Gilman & Company; on the 27th ultimo he was informed that the British ship *Bolton Abbey*, had been spoken [to] by the *Twilight* about 300 miles from Hong Kong. On the afternoon of the 20th[482] defendant came to witness' office and represented himself as the boatswain of the *Bolton Abbey*. He told witness the ship had been anchored near the Cape D'Aguilar and Cape Collinson lights. Witness asked why he came instead of the Captain. He said the Captain and the Chief Officer were sick, and had been so, prisoner said, since the big typhoon. Defendant said he had been sent to report the ship's arrival. On the strength of the defendant's report, witness sent a telegram to Lloyd's[483] that the ship had arrived in Hong Kong Harbour. The defendant on finishing his story said he had been sent ashore without money or food. Witness told him that Lloyd's were not the people to provide him with such things. Witness had to send a telegram to Lloyd's contradicting his former one.

The prisoner made a statement in the graphic words appended: – I can't swear whether I did it or whether I did it not. I was drunk, and when drink is in wit is out. I was before you the other day and was fined twenty-five cents, and I have been drunk most every day since I came here by the *Twilight*. I know I passed the *Bolton Abbey*, and that is all I know about her.

The case was remanded till the 5th *instant*.

WEDNESDAY 5 OCTOBER 1881
THE *BOLTON ABBEY*

In this case, today; Captain Thomsett[484] gave evidence. He said defendant (Cannon) came to him and told him a rambling story about his ship[485] having passed a village on a river. Witness thought the ship had got among some islands; the ship according to defendant's story was dismasted, and the fall of the masts had carried away the deck house.

Defendant said he would rather go to Gaol than go back to his ship. As he had lost three wives, he had been driven to drink.

He was sentenced to three months' imprisonment with hard labour, as a rogue and vagabond.~~~~~

FRIDAY 14 OCTOBER 1881
THE STABBING CASE[486]

In this case H. Sewart,[487] Police Constable, applied for a remand, as complainant could not get out of hospital before the 17th *instant*. The case was remanded till the 17th accordingly.

Monday 17 October 1881
THE STABBING CASE[488]

The case in which a seaman named John Parry was charged with stabbing a fellow-sailor of the name of Thomas Finlay,[489] aged twenty-eight,[490] a native of Arklow, Ireland, on board the Canadian barque *Helen Marion*,[491] on the 13th last, has now assumed a serious aspect.[492] Today (17th), the wounded man's deposition was taken by Dr Stewart at the

Government Civil Hospital, where he now lies. The Captain and a boy on board gave evidence, as the ship is ready to sail. Finlay is in a very weak state, and it was considered advisable under the circumstances, to take the precaution of securing his deposition: –

Thomas Finlay said he was an able seaman serving on board the Canadian barque *Helen Marion*. About dinner time on Thursday the 13th *instant*, he went into the forecastle, when Powers[493] (a nickname for the defendant Parry),[494] came in after him and took a square-faced bottle of gin from the bunk. He held it in his hand for about a quarter of an hour and then broke it over witness's head. A portion of the broken glass remained in the prisoner's hand, and on witness trying to take it from him, he, the prisoner, drew a sheath knife from him and stabbed the witness in the right breast. There was no one else in the forecastle at the time. When he was stabbed he ran out on deck and saw the Captain. Witness then fell and recollected nothing further. On recovering consciousness he found himself under treatment in the hospital. There was no previous row or quarrel between the two men. Prisoner was sober at the time and was talking to himself, but witness took no notice of what he said. He believed Power wanted to stow away the bottle, and was waiting till witness left the forecastle. Witness was not sober at the time. After having been struck with the bottle he took it from Power so as to prevent him repeating the blow. (Shows a small wound on the head.) No conversation took place between us at the time. The knife produced was the one with which he was stabbed.

To prisoner – I still say that no words passed between us before I was struck with the bottle. I am sure I did not strike you before I was struck with the bottle. You had the knife in your hand when you stabbed me, but you took it from your belt. I did not see you cutting tobacco. You stood for a quarter of an hour with the bottle in your hand waiting for me to leave the forecastle before you stowed it away. You and I have been on friendly terms all the voyage, and have never had any words previous to this.

Captain R. J. Robinson, master of the *Helen Marion*, said that about half past one on the afternoon of the 13th *instant* he was in the hold. The boy Edward Jeavous came down and informed him that Thomas Finlay was cut. He immediately went on deck, and met Finlay who was wounded and bleeding from the right breast. He had the knife in his hand. Witness took it from him and dressed the wound, and then went to the *Victor Emanuel* for a doctor, who came on board, dressed the wound, and advised that the man be sent to hospital at once. Finlay was sent to hospital, and the case reported to the police authorities.

To the prisoner – You have behaved yourself on board to my satisfaction up to the time of this occurrence. You have been in trouble with others before this happened. You have been drunk on board ship in harbour before this.

To the Court. – Prisoner's general behaviour before coming to this harbour has been satisfactory. Had he not asked me I should not have thought it necessary to refer to his drinking.

Ed.[495] Jeavous, ordinary seaman on board the *Helen Marion*, said that about dinner time on the 13th *instant* he was in the forecastle. After supplying Finlay with some things he wanted he left the forecastle. At this time Finlay, Power (Parry), and Brislan were in the forecastle. He heard Finlay ask where the bottle was, and say that he wanted to give Power a drop. He also heard Finlay say that he would hit the prisoner with a cane if he did not go away from him. Power then said that he would either go to gaol or to hospital for him. Witness then again entered the forecastle and when in the doorway he heard the crash of a bottle, and two seconds afterwards he saw blood flowing from Finlay's breast, and heard him say that he had been stabbed. Witness then jumped down the after hatch and told the captain.

To the Court: – Finlay looked as if he had been drunk and was just recovering. Power and Finlay had a few words before the bottle was smashed, and it was then I heard Power say that he would go to gaol or hospital for him. By this I understood that he would do something to Finlay, or that Finlay would do something to him. I saw no blow given, but I saw blood running from Finlay's breast. I saw no knife. I have not noticed any particular bad feeling between Finlay and the prisoner more than between any others on board.

To the prisoner: – I could see you when in the forecastle, but I could not see what you were doing. I saw nothing in your hands. Had you been cutting a pipe of tobacco I could have seen you. I did not see you with any bottle, you had nothing in your hands when I was looking at you.

At this point the enquiry was remanded till tomorrow morning at eight o'clock at the Magistracy, for the production of another witness.

Tuesday 18 October 1881[496]

THE STABBING CASE

This morning the investigation into the circumstances attending the stabbing of seaman Thomas Finlay, by another sailor named John Parry (nicknamed Power) aboard the *Helen Marion*, was resumed at the Police Magistracy before Dr Stewart.

Philip Breslin said he was an able seaman on board the *Helen Marion*. He remembered Thursday, the 13th *instant*. About one o'clock witness was sitting outside the forecastle door; Thomas Finlay called him in to the forecastle, and asked witness if he knew anything about a bottle of grog. Witness said the bottle had been finished. Power had taken the last of it. When he said this defendant was present. A quarrel at once began between Power and Finlay concerning the bottle of whisky. Some very bad language passed between the two.

His Worship asked witness to tell him as nearly the exact words as possible as provocation might be an important element in the case.

Witness repeated some of the expressions used. Finlay gave Power a sort of shove and Power then said he would either go to gaol for him or make an hospital case of him. At this time Power deliberately put his hand on his sheath knife. After this they both sat down, but continued using dirty expressions. Finlay had been drunk up to eleven o'clock, but the mate had objected to his moving about the deck, and ordered him to go in and rest himself. This he did, and by the time of the affair witness would say he was sober or at least capable of doing his work. Power was sober. Witness had seen Power about eleven o'clock drink two glasses. After sitting some time still quarrelling, Finlay rose and stepped towards Power, and this time struck him; Power took up a large square-sided bottle and broke it on Finlay's skull. They continued pushing and struggling and witness heard Finlay say Power is holding a knife. Witness at once looked and saw the knife clenched in Powers's right hand and Finlay hanging on to his wrist. Finlay had been stabbed by this time. After Power struck with the bottle, witness was frightened, and did not look until he heard the man say he had been stabbed. Witness was sitting on a chest between them and about eight or ten feet separated them. Witness did not see the knife used. Witness on hearing him cry out ran to his assistance and helped him to clutch the knife. Finlay showing his wound exclaimed, "Oh Lord bless us all; look at me! This blow he has used me." On seeing the wound witness let go the knife, and ran out of the forecastle. Finlay came out after him with the knife in one hand, and, holding the other on the wound. He went towards the main hatch with the knife in his hand.

Defendant said he had no questions to ask. He did not believe the witness had exaggerated. He had spoken no doubt according to his lights. He was sure he would not tell a lie.

His Worship said the witness had given his evidence in a most honest and straightforward manner. It was the most clear and straightforward evidence he had heard for a long time.

John Kavanagh, able seaman on board the *Helen Marion*, said he was sitting outside the forecastle door. He heard Finlay asking for Power. In two or three minutes Power went in; witness heard Finlay ask him where the bottle was. Witness did not hear the answer; Finlay said if he had the bottle he would not give Power a nip out of it. They had then some bad language, to which witness did not pay much attention. Finlay said if Power did not get out of his sight he would hit him with a tin he had in his hand. Power said if he hit him with the salt tin he would make a hospital case of him. Some short time afterwards he heard something else, a crash of glass. And then he heard Finlay sing out "He has struck me." Finlay then came out with the knife in his hand, bleeding from the breast.

Defendant did not wish to ask any questions.[497]

Wednesday 16 November 1881[498]
STABBING CASE ON BOARD THE *HELEN MARION* COMMITTAL FOR MURDER

John Parry, a seaman on board the *Helen Marion*, charged with wounding Thomas Finlay, was again placed in the dock this morning – Dr Stewart on the bench – when the charge was altered from wounding to murder.

Dr Murray, Acting Superintendent of the Civil Hospital,[499] gave similar evidence to that tendered at the inquest some days ago namely, that deceased was admitted to hospital suffering from a wound which was in the right lung, and that death had resulted. The knife he had seen was such as would produce the wound.

In reply to defendant, witness said that in cases of phthisis people sometimes lived to a considerable period with one lung filled with tubercles, provided these were sewn up. Wounds in the lungs were not necessarily fatal, but were likely to prove so even when as in the case of the deceased no large blood vessel was damaged; if it had been, death would have rapidly followed. The fatal wound had healed some time before deceased died.

Police Constable Number 4, Herbert Servant deposed as to taking the deceased from a boat at Canton Wharf to the Government Civil Hospital. Deceased was wrapped in a large rug which was covered with blood. Witness afterwards went on board the *Helen Marion*, arrested the defendant, and received a knife from the Captain. Defendant was taken to the Police Station, where, after being cautioned by Inspector Mackie, he said, in answer to the charge, that "it was quite an accident."

He said he was in the forecastle on 13th of October cutting some tobacco, when Findlay came in with a bottle of whisky and said "You don't deserve any of this." Defendant answered that he did not wish any of it, upon which Findlay got up and struck him. He (defendant) told him to be quiet as he wanted no quarrel with him. Deceased then struck him several times with the bottle, upon which he (prisoner) picked up a bottle and struck deceased on the head with it thinking this might stop him, but it did not, for the deceased laid hold of him, and in struggling to get the bottle from deceased he accidentally stabbed deceased with the knife.

The prisoner was then cautioned that he need say nothing in answer to the charge unless he pleased. He reserved his defence, and waived his right of notice of trial, so he might be tried at the forthcoming Criminal Sessions.[500] ~~~~~

MONDAY 7 NOVEMBER 1881
DISORDERLY CONDUCT[501]

Edward Morris, seaman on board the American ship *Stonewall Jackson*, was charged with being drunk and disorderly, and damaging property on the 6th *instant*.

It appeared that defendant and some of his comrades went into a cigar and book-binder's shop in Queen's Road yesterday evening. He asked for two bundles of cigars, but declined to pay the proper price for them, upon which the shopman refused to let him have them. He thereupon took up a tray containing writing materials and threw it at one of the assistants in the shop, smashing a pane of glass in a show case, breaking the tray itself, and damaging some paper. His companions meanwhile drew their sheath knives and stuck them in the counter. A constable who witnessed the disturbance attempted to arrest the defendant, which resulted in a struggle taking place between them, and the other men who had their knives in their hands threatened to use them. Ultimately assistance was procured and defendant was locked up, his companions in the meanwhile decamping with the cigars without going through the formality of paying for them.

Defendant said he did not remember anything about it.

Fined ten dollars for disorderly behaviour, in default fourteen days' imprisonment with hard labour, and to pay one dollar amends to complainant, or two days' further imprisonment.~~~~~

WEDNESDAY 9 NOVEMBER 1881
JACK ASHORE[502]

George Hansen and Arthur Scott, firemen on board H.M.S. *Comus*, were charged with wilfully damaging paintings valued at twelve dollars, and also with assaulting the police, on the 8th *instant*.

Fong Chu Ching, photographer and painter, Queen's Road, said that the two defendants came to his shop at nine o'clock last night and wanted their portraits. He told them they had not had their portraits taken there, and they must have mistaken the shop, but they became very violent and smashed the four pictures produced. The assistance of the police was called for, but it took several men to take them to the station.

First defendant said he had given a photograph to complainant a fortnight ago to copy, and when he went for it last night it was refused. He denied having struck the complainant and had never seen the damaged pictures before.

Second defendant told a similar story, adding that there was not an angry word spoken in the shop.

Fined five dollars for the assault, or seven days' imprisonment with hard labour, and to pay six dollars each to complainant or suffer seven days' imprisonment.~~~~~

SATURDAY 26 NOVEMBER 1881
WILFULL DAMAGE ON BOARD SHIP[503]

James Allen, a mariner unemployed, was charged with committing wilfull damage on board the steamer *Crusader* on the 25th *instant*.

Mr W. Bryce, third engineer on board the *Crusader*, said he was speaking with defendant in the alley way, near the lamp-room on board, yesterday afternoon. Defendant was formerly second officer of the ship, but left yesterday. He complained of the Captain having stopped some of his wages, and threatened to take it out of him for so doing. Defendant then went into the lamp-room and smashed the lamp now in Court, which is generally used as the mast head light. Witness spoke to defendant about what he was doing, but he told witness to go to —, and mind his own business. The lamps did not belong to his department. Witness then looked for the chief officer, but as he could not find him, he locked the lamp-room door, but defendant asked for the key, saying he was not done in there yet. Witness refused to give him the key, but gave it to the chief officer. The side lights were smashed during the three or four minutes he was looking for the chief officer. Defendant was slightly intoxicated.

Mr T. Occkerill, chief officer of the *Crusader*, said he was in the cabin writing yesterday afternoon when he was told something by the chief engineer. He at once went on deck where he saw defendant and asked him if he had damaged the ship's lamps. Defendant said "No." He then looked in the lamp-room and found the mast head light and the two side lights in court broken, and the glass strewn about the floor. He estimated the damage at L6 sterling. The lamps were the property of Messrs Baird & Brown of Glasgow. Defendant had been drinking, but he had his wits about him when he spoke to him.

Defendant said he never had charge of the lamp-room key till yesterday morning when the chief officer ordered him to get it from the night watchman and with a padlock lock up the closet to keep the Chinese out. He did so and hung the key on a nail. A few minutes afterwards the chief officer bade him give it up for the purpose of issuing some oil to the coolies to clean brass work. He never saw it again till the third engineer had it. He met the captain ashore and was paid off. On going on board again he saw the third engineer in the alley way, and the lamp-room door was then open.

Sentence six weeks' imprisonment with hard labour.~~

WEDNESDAY 7 DECEMBER 1881
WILFULL DAMAGE[504]

Luigi Libretto, Band Sergeant, H.M.S. *Iron Duke*, appeared on a summons at the instance of one Mok Aping, a chair coolie, charged with that on the 5th *instant*, he did unlawfully, wilfully, and maliciously commit damage, injury, and spoil to a street chair to the extent of one dollar fifty cents.

Complainant said defendant hired his chair at seven o'clock on the evening of the 5th *instant*, to take him from Queen's Road to Number 7 Station. Instead of paying him his proper fare he, defendant, proceeded to strike him and afterwards smashed his chair doing damage to the extent of one dollar fifty cents. Defendant was not sober at the time.

Defendant said that he hired a chair on Monday evening, but not complainant's, to take him to the Central Station to visit a friend. Instead of bringing him here they took him over the hill, and on his asking them where they were taking him to they did not seem to understand him, but put him down and asked for their money. He told them they would not get any money until they took him to his proper destination. Defendant's coat was unbuttoned at this time and one of the chair coolies put his hand inside his jacket and took all his money. Complainant and his mate were not the men who carried him, but the chair outside the Court is the one he engaged. He admitted smashing the chair after he found he had been deprived of his money.

Complainant's partner was called and gave corroborative evidence to that given by first witness.

At this point the case was remanded till Friday morning, the 9th *instant*,[505] – defendant being admitted to bail in his personal security in ten dollars.~~~~~

TUESDAY 20 DECEMBER 1881
AN UNJUST ACCUSATION[506]

George H. Peters, seaman, accused George Oakes with stealing, along with another man, a bag containing nineteen dollars on the 16th *instant*.

George Henry Peters stated that on the 16th *instant*, he was in the Welcome Tavern, and was in the act of loaning a shipmate one dollar which he took from his bag, when someone snapped the bag from him. Turning round, he observed defendant making for the door with something in his hand. He gave chase and followed him as far as the Sailor's Home, where he lost sight of him. On the 18th *instant*, plaintiff went in search of defendant, and while walking along Queen's Road saw him going towards the Sailor's Home along with two others. Stepping up to him, Peters asked defendant to accompany him to the Police Office.

Defendant was then given into Sergeant Butlin's custody.

Sergeant Butlin gave evidence as to the apprehension of Oakes in Hollywood Road.

After several others had been examined Dr Stewart said that he was perfectly satisfied that defendant had nothing to do with the offence, and expressed sympathy with Oakes in his being placed in so hard a position. Dr Stewart also observed that the defendant left the court without a stain on his character, and thought that Peters had made a mistake and ought to apologise to Oakes for placing him in such a very hard position. The case was then dismissed.~~~~~

FRIDAY 6 JANUARY 1882
BLUE JACKETS ON THE WAR PATH[507]

James Caine, William Haines, and George Murphy, seamen of H.M.S. *Carysfort*, were placed in the dock to-day, and charged with disorderly conduct in the Temperance Hall at an early hour this morning.

Mr E. Shillibeer, Manager of the Hall, said that a complaint was made to him between one and two o'clock this morning by a boarder in the house. From what he was told he got up and went to one of the rooms which he found locked on the inside. He knocked at the door, but getting no reply he ultimately burst it open. In the room he found the three prisoners, two of whom were in bed, the other sitting up. They had no business there and he ordered them out, but they declined to go and abused him. One of them threw him down on the bed, another struck him on the head, and the third assaulted him in a dangerous part of the body, from which he had since suffered much pain. He called for assistance, and eight or ten of the boarders came and released him, and he gave defendants in charge of the police.

The first and second defendants expressed a desire to see any marks of assault which complainant bore, and they were shown accordingly.

Lo Ai, a coolie employed at the Hall, said the three prisoners came there about midnight and asked for some place in which to sleep. He told them the beds were all occupied, and they commenced to beat him with their fists. He ran away from them, and they went upstairs, after which he saw no more of them. The first prisoner was drunk, but the other two were sober.

John Glaholm, a mate unemployed, residing at the Temperance Hall, said that some time between midnight of last night and two o'clock this morning, the three prisoners came into his room there. He told them it was a private room and they could not be permitted to remain. They however evinced no intention of leaving and he went to last witness's room and roused him. Mr Shillibeer accompanied him back to his own room, which was then found locked inside. On last witness bursting open the door and going inside he heard a scuffling going on, but he did not see any assault. There was not much light in the alley-ways. The Manager sent for the police, but before a constable arrived the three prisoners had come out into the Hall. Several of the boarders came from their rooms, but he did not see them do anything, and he did not think Mr Shillibeer required any assistance.

Police Constable Number 5, George Rogers, said he was called to the Temperance Hall about two o'clock this morning, and the Manager asked him to take the three prisoners into custody on a charge of entering one of the rooms for an unlawful purpose. One of the men had a stick in his hand, which was said to have been taken from the room in question and was claimed by last witness. He refused to give up the stick to the man who claimed it, but gave it up to the constable. The men went quietly to the station, and there a charge of disorderly conduct and assault was preferred against them by Mr Shillibeer.

In defence, the first prisoner said that when they went to the Hall shortly after midnight they saw the Manager whom they asked for beds. He did not know whether there were any vacant, and told them they could go round the house and see for themselves. They did so and found an unoccupied bed in Room Number Ten.[508] Two of them turned in and the other lay down on the floor. The third witness occupied another bed in the same room and ordered them out, but they refused to go as they had been sent there by the Manager and had paid for a bed. When the Manager came to the room to turn them out, he struck him, first prisoner, over the arm with a stick in Court (shows swelling on arm).

The other two prisoners made a somewhat similar defence.

Complainant, recalled, denied having seen the defendants till he was called by the third witness. He went to bed at half-past eleven o'clock, and left no one in charge except some coolies to let in boarders who might be out late.

An officer from the ship gave the prisoners bad characters, and His Worship fined them three dollars each, in default, seven days' imprisonment with hard labour.~~~~~

SATURDAY 7 JANUARY 1882[509]
ROBBING A SHIPWRECKED SEAMAN

William Blood, a seaman unemployed, was charged with stealing an overcoat on the 6th *instant* from one William Lecky, a ship's boy.

William Lecky said he had been on board the British barque *Forward Ho*, which was recently wrecked, and he was now living at the Sailor's Home. The prisoner was also staying there but he was not acquainted with him.

He identified the overcoat in Court as his. It was worth four dollars. Yesterday afternoon he went out for a walk, leaving the coat under his bedclothes. On returning to his room about six o'clock he observed that the pillow of his bed was very low, and on making an examination he found that the coat was missing. Enquiries had been made at the Home without any result, and he afterwards asked several policemen if they had seen any sailors with a bundle of clothes. Amongst others he asked constable Servant who gave him certain information, and took him to a shop where he was shown the missing coat.

Police Constable Number 4, Herbert Servant said he apprehended the prisoner at the Sailor's Home this morning. When charged with stealing the coat he replied that he had nothing to say. Witness had seen the prisoner selling a coat in a shop in East Street yesterday evening, and on questioning him about it, he said it was his own property, that he had brought it here from Manila, and that he was obliged to part with his clothes as he was staying at the Sailor's Home and had no money. About half an hour afterwards he met the complainant from whom he heard about the missing coat.

Defendant admitted the charge, saying that he was very hard up. He had no tobacco and no soap.

Sentence – two months' imprisonment with hard labour.~~~~~

FRIDAY 10 FEBRUARY 1882
BREACH OF RECOGNIZANCE[510]

Charles Ring, seaman, who was allowed out on his own recognizance in the sum of five dollars last Saturday, by the Magistrate, was again brought up yesterday; he having failed to quit the Colony as he had distinctly avowed to do.

George Rogers, Police Constable said he had been to Messrs Butterfield & Swire's where the Captain of the *Ajax* had volunteered to give the defendant a passage home to England, on condition that he went to the Sailors' Home sober, to-day at eleven o'clock.

Defendant could not show cause why his recognizance should not be estreated and said he could offer no explanation of his non-appearance on Monday.

The Magistrate then remanded the case till to-day.

Police Constable Rogers volunteering to-day to convey the defendant to the Sailors' Home; and if necessary see him on board the vessel, he was discharged.~~~~~

SATURDAY 11 FEBRUARY 1882
ASSAULT BY A SHIP CAPTAIN[511]

A. Roper, Captain of the steamer *Anjer Head*,[512] at present lying in harbour, appeared on a summons charged with assaulting, on board that vessel, John Dare, chief officer, on the 10th *instant*.

John Dare, the complainant, said he went to the Harbour Master's Office yesterday morning regarding a claim he had on the ship, and returned to the ship about half past two in the afternoon, when the Captain asked him if he was going in the ship. He answered yes; and the Captain then got hold of him, shoved him against the cabin door sill, threw him into the cabin and locked the door. Witness opened the door with a key he had under his charge and said to the Captain that he had no right to imprison him. The Captain struck him on the shoulder, tore his coat and broke his watch chain, and by so doing made witness lose pendants to the value of sixty-five dollars. He was also struck with a bamboo by the Captain and ordered to leave the vessel.

In answer to the defendant the complainant said he was disappointed at Capt. Thomsett's decision, which was that he had no claim against the Captain. He denied shaking a key in the captain's face and saying that it was a master key.

The second mate of the vessel said he was at the gangway of the ship keeping order, and had heard the complainant and defendant talking together very loudly, but had seen no blows struck. He never heard anything of the watch chain being injured until he came to the Court. The witness had heard the parties have some angry words at the breakfast table about stowaways being on board, at which time the complainant laughed in the defendant's face, when he was checked for allowing the stowaways on board.

The defendant denied assaulting the complainant, but admitted taking a master key from the complainant as he did not care to have anyone on board his vessel in possession of such an article.

The Magistrate expressed his regret that the case had not been tried before the Harbour Master,[513] who would have been much more conversant with all the sides of the question. It was quite apparent to him that there had been a good deal of temper displayed and provocation given, on both sides, but the evidence showed him that some assault had been committed and he therefore ordered the defendant to pay a fine of five dollars, or, in default, to be imprisoned for two days. The fine was paid.~~~~~

Friday 17 February 1882[514]
[Cutting and Wounding]

A case of a peculiar nature was brought before Dr Stewart this morning, in which Samuel Simons, fireman on board the British steamer *Gleniffer*, was charged with cutting and wounding James Whitley Simson whilst the ship was lying at the Tanjong Pagar wharf at Singapore on the 5th *instant*. It seems from the evidence heard that the defendant, who had been working some time extra, had been asked by the chief engineer, the complainant, to turn to again, when defendant used some indecent language, with the result that complainant struck him on the mouth. Defendant had then struck complainant with a knife, and wounded him slightly on the shoulder. Defendant, in his statement, admitted having done so, but said he went ashore and intended to deliver himself up to the police, but as it was a holiday in Singapore, it was advised that the case should be brought on here and tried. The Captain of the *Gleniffer* said that on the way up he allowed the defendant, on a promise to behave properly, to return to his work, and he had conducted himself very well. The case was discharged through want of jurisdiction.~~~~~

MONDAY 27 FEBRUARY 1882
ALLEGED ATTEMPTED SHOOTING[515]

John Bryant, boatswain on board the steamship *Ashington*, at present in harbour, was charged[516] with assaulting Samuel Bryant, fireman, and also with firing a revolver at the complainant on the 26th *instant* on board that vessel.

The complainant said that while in the forecastle on the morning of the 26th, between eight and nine o'clock, along with another man, the defendant came along and asked the complainant and the other man to accompany him to the chief engineer's room to have a dispute settled. The dispute arose from the defendant accusing the complainant of taking sails. The second engineer, who was in the engineer's room, when appealed to, said he believed that the complainant's statements were true. The defendant then ordered the complainant away from the engineer's room, which order the latter complied with, followed by the defendant. The complainant, when they reached the alley way, told the defendant, that if he was again insulted he would have to speak to the Captain, whereupon the defendant struck the complainant a blow on the eye with his fist, which blow the complainant returned in self defence. Defendant then went to his berth and fired a revolver at the complainant from the door-way; how the shot missed, the complainant was unable to say.

James Bath, chief engineer, said he was present when the two parties came to the room, shortly after which he heard a pistol shot. He then went out of his room and asked defendant what he fired for, to which he received the reply "Oh, it's all right. I only did it to frighten him." Questioned by defendant, the witness was forced to confess that he, the defendant, was considerably intoxicated and excited at the time, although witness had said to the court that he was but slightly drunk.

Edwin Allison, Captain of the *Ashington*, said he heard a report at the time of the occurrence, but thought it was a Chinese cracker, until he was informed of the affair. He then sent for the Police. On Saturday he gave the defendant a half day's liberty, but this time was exceeded. In answer to the defendant, the Captain said that he did not think it possible that a shot fired from the defendant's berth could injure any person standing before the galley, and that defendant had been a steady, persevering man during the time he had been in witness' employ, eight or nine months.

The case was remanded till Wednesday, the 1st March.

WEDNESDAY 1 MARCH 1882
ATTEMPTED SHOOTING[517]

John Bryant, boatswain, on board the S.S. *Ashington*, was again charged with assaulting, and firing a revolver at, Samuel Bryant, fireman, on board that vessel on the 26th *ultimo*.

Mr Wotton, of Messrs Brereton and Wotton, appeared for the defendant.

John Stafford, the second engineer of the vessel, said he was in the chief engineer's berth when the defendant along with the complainant and a seaman, came to the berth and asked the witness to settle some dispute. The defendant asked witness if the complainant and the seaman had said the defendant carried tales. To this the witness replied that the complainant had said so. Defendant accused the complainant of this, whereupon a disturbance ensued. The chief engineer then turned the men out and locked the door. Witness then heard some disturbance going on forward and shortly afterwards heard a shot fired. The Chief opened the door and went forward. The witness followed and found the chief holding the boatswain by the hands. The chief told witness to go inside the boatswain's berth and get the revolver. He did this and found it at the inner end of the table. The chief engineer succeeded in persuading the boatswain to go to bed. Witness was of opinion that if the defendant had not been drunk, the revolver would not have been fired. In answer to Mr Wotton he stated that he along with others had made a search for the mark of a bullet all over the alley way and found none. He was of opinion that if there had been any marks they would have been discovered.

Some further evidence was taken of a similar character.

The constable who arrested the defendant said that

the revolver was loaded in five chambers, and that one was empty.

Mr Wotton in reserving the defendant's defence said that he did not think that there was any necessity for sending the case to the Supreme Court.

The Magistrate said he thought the question of the defendant's intention was one which he would like to be left to a jury, and he would endeavour to have the case brought up before a special sessions.[518] ~~~~~

MONDAY 20 MARCH 1882
BOTH MAGISTRATES SITTING
THEFT AT THE SAILORS' HOME[519]

James Howard, an unemployed English seaman, was charged with stealing six dollars from A. Anderson, seaman, on the 19th *instant*.

The complainant said he was a seaman on board the *Oneida*, and was at present residing at the Sailors' Home. Yesterday about eleven o'clock in the forenoon he went out with the defendant, who resided in the same room, and returned in about an hour, slightly the worse for liquor. He immediately went upstairs, leaving the defendant downstairs, and went to bed with all his clothes on. At that time he had six one-dollar notes in his trouser pocket for certain, but how much more he was unable to say. He awoke at four o'clock in the afternoon and found his money missing. The defendant, who knew of him having money in his possession, he had reason to think, had stolen the dollars.

Henry Grastin, who also occupied the same room, said he saw the defendant go to the complainant's bed and take some money out of the former's pocket, about half-past one yesterday afternoon. He did this without knowing that witness had seen him, and acted all through in a very suspicious manner. Witness did not mention the matter to the complainant because he thought the defendant had taken the money to look after it; the men being great friends.

William Blood, seaman, entered the room about half-past one on his bare feet, and just as he got inside he saw the defendant jump away from complainant's bed and put something in his pocket. At the time he did not suspect that anything was wrong.

The defendant when searched had in his possession one five-dollar note and some cents, and averred that the money had been given him by various men. He had got the note by changing four notes and one silver dollar for it at the Welcome Tavern.

Peter Joyce, seaman on board the *Glenelg*, said he knew that the defendant had money previous to the 19th *instant*, he having given to him five dollars some nine days ago. He also saw the defendant return thirty dollars, to James Dalton, a shipmate, on the same day. This money Dalton handed to the defendant to keep while the former was in a state of intoxication.

Another witness said he knew the defendant to have had money in his possession previous to the 19th.

The defendant said he went upstairs about dinner-time to awaken the complainant, but changed his mind thinking that Anderson was too drunk. He bought a looking-glass from the second witness who was lying in his bed, and then went downstairs again. He was just leaving the room when the third witness came in. He protested that he did not take the money, and pointed out that the third witness had just finished two months' imprisonment for larceny. He admitted having suffered four months' imprisonment for cutting the tackle of the P. & O. steamer, which he was discharged from about the middle of November last.

The Magistrates imposed a sentence of eighteen months' imprisonment with hard labour.~~~~~

Soldiers[520]

The British soldiers based in Hong Kong at this time were the Queen's men. They had sworn allegiance to the Queen of England, under a contract of long-term employment. Each belonged to a large, highly-disciplined unit, with its own character and traditions, and they were also part of the very much larger body of men, the army of the British Empire, on which the sun never set. The senior officer in Hong Kong at any time was a very senior member of the Hong Kong Community, one of the handful of members of the Executive Council.[521]

The soldiers played a distinct part in public life. When St John's Cathedral was being planned, financed and constructed as St John's Church, one of the concerns and constraints was to provide sufficient dedicated seating for the soldiers to attend services. Subsequently, church parade was a regular feature. Among its Religious Services announcements, *The China Mail* of 24 September 1881, for example, has a separate item, "Military Service. – Revd C. Gilbert Booth, B. A., Military Chaplain. Parade Service at 8 a.m. Holy Communion on the second and fourth Sundays at the conclusion of the Parade Service. [A Voluntary Service is held in the Garrison Theatre at 7.45 p.m.]" The Union Church also had a Soldiers' Service, at 6.45am.

On occasions, the streets were cleared to allow the soldiers to march by. The parade ground itself was in the centre of town, where the Hilton Hotel later stood; a site now graced by the Cheung Kong Centre, a large glass cube dedicated to office accommodation. For celebrations, such as the visits of royal personages and royal anniversaries, the soldiers fired a *feu de joie*.

The soldiers' assistance was valued in other areas also. A Public Subscription Ball was given to the Officers of the Detached Squadron (including Queen Victoria's young sons, Prince Albert Victor and Prince George) at the City Hall on 30 December 1881. Pioneer-Sergeant MacMillan, Royal Inniskilling Fusiliers, worked with Mr Milton, Boatswain of the ship *Victor Emmanuel*, to make the elaborate decorations, and the results were praised in the

Mail.[522]

The Garrison Theatre was already in existence;[523] their public performances were sometimes repeated "by request".[524] From time to time, the Regimental Band entertained the public at the Botanic Gardens. – On Friday, 23 September 1881, the advertised programme by the Band of the Royal Inniskilling Fusiliers at 5pm was: the March, "Silver Threads" by Riviere, the Overture to "La Dame Blanche" by Boildieu, the Gavotte, "Imperiale" by Faust, the Valse, "Unter den Linden" by Gungl, a Selection from "Mefistofele" by Boito and the Galop, "Ueber Stock und Stein" by Faust. The performance for Friday, 2 September 1881, was scheduled later in the day, 9pm to 11pm, and included a piece from Sullivan's "H.M.S. *Pinafore*" and the vocal March, "Let the Hills resound" by Richards. (Perhaps the high proportion of German names reflects the germanic origins of the reigning British Queen and her husband?) – At Christmas, the troops in Garrison kept open house.[525]

Army sporting activities were regularly reported in the Press: an inter-regimental shooting match on 12 September 1881;[526] a cricket match between "H" Company of the Royal Inniskilling Fusiliers and the Royal Artillery on 2 December;[527] a lawn tennis match in which Lieutenant J. G. Mayne partnered Mr A. N. Tomkins of Hong Kong against a Singapore double on 15 December.[528] At the time of the visit of the young Princes, several military and naval personnel stationed in the region converged on Hong Kong, and participated in a crowded programme of events with those based in Hong Kong.[529]

In the one case quoted here, the men accused belonged to the Royal Inniskilling Fusiliers. Their Regiment had been stationed at Hong Kong on garrison duty from 25 February 1879. It had arrived as "the 27th (Inniskilling) Regiment of Foot"; but with effect from 1 July 1881, together with the 108th (Madras Infantry) Regiment and their connected militia regiments, it became "The Royal Inniskilling Fusiliers".[530] During the Christmas open house in 1881, at the Sergeants' Mess, regrets were "pretty freely expressed at the change of title and the consequent loss of all individuality".[531]

The Inniskillings obviously contained difficult elements. On one occasion, the Band failed to appear, because part of it was on strike. *The China Mail* was severe in its response and concurred in the punishments given: "Military discipline calls such disobedience of the orders of those under whom they are placed and such breaking out of barracks as they were guilty of, by a very ugly name;[532] and the ill-advised members of the Band have already been dealt with in a manner considerably more severe than it is believed they expected. Some go back to their duty with a severe reprimand; others are fined in various sums according to the degree of their culpability, and others have received smart terms of imprisonment by order of the Commandant."[533]

In view of the Regiment's visibility and integration with the community (and in spite of a few hiccups), it is not surprising that, when it left the Colony, the Regiment was given a hearty farewell. They were replaced by the Buffs (who arrived on 11 March 1882).[534] His Excellency Lieutenant General Donovan (Major General China, Hong Kong and Straits Settlements), Captain Bury and a large number of the officials and civilians of the Colony went on board their ship, and "wished their departing friends bon voyage."[535] Soon however, the Buffs were as much a part of Hong Kong life as the Inniskillings had been. Only a couple of weeks later, the March 1882 report of the Hong Kong Civilian Amateur Athletic Sports, open to members and visitors of the Hong Kong Club, the Club Germania, Commissioned Naval and Military Officers, and to Members of the Hong Kong Cricket Club and those members of the Victoria Recreation Club, who had joined on or before 1 March 1882, names the official time-keeper as a Buffs officer, and several officers of the Buffs among the Stewards.[536]

As with the sailors found in Hong Kong, the soldiers' time in the Colony was an interval in a dangerous calling. The soldiers' battle with men was less routine, however, than the sailors' battle with the elements. It is true that, at an earlier period, when the troops were based in Happy Valley, which was then malarial, it was dangerous even to be stationed in Hong Kong. The extremely high mortality that the troops suffered then shocked and alarmed those who knew of it. (Measures were taken to *prevent* public knowledge.) This period was now over. The surplus energy of these mostly healthy men now made them subject to the careful watchfulness of their superiors.

There is no doubt that the community had come to take it for granted that *sailors* would commit offences when in Hong Kong and would regularly appear in court mainly for assault and drunkenness. But when *soldiers* made an appearance, as in the one case given here, this seems to have been thought exceptional, and the *Mail* gave considerable coverage.[537]

On each of 9 and 10 December 1881, *The China Mail* included a lengthy article, additional to the very lengthy reports from the Police Courts, on the "Two disgraceful attacks" made on the evening of Thursday, 8 December, when "a party of four men belonging to the regiment in Garrison" disturbed "gentlemen taking a quiet stroll on one of the most popular of the few roads in the colony available for walking exercise."[538] – One of these gentlemen, Mr D. R. Billia, was evidently a person of substance, as he was one of the jury of three at the Coroner's Inquest held on the body of the Sikh constable killed following the Tai-Tam armed attack on the night of 26 and 27 November 1881. – It is undeniable that the editorial tone is somewhat uneasy. Having expressed a standpoint by the one word "disgraceful", and indicating that any respectable walker might be similarly at risk, the *Mail*'s subsequent comments focus on the interest taken by the military authorities (who conducted their own investigation); the difficulty of identifying the men concerned; and concern that a rightful verdict should be reached. The opportunity for preaching a moral, taken when rickshaw men caused problems, when dealers in fish obstructed the pavements, and when policemen acted dishonestly, was ignored. After all, these were the men whose protection from foreign powers the Hong Kong community might call upon at any time.

It seems clear that the jurisdiction of the Magistrate

in this case was not clear-cut and that there was considerable pressure on Stewart behind the scenes. Although the men were brought before him on 10 December and formally charged, the investigation was remanded at the request of the Military authorities, and the prisoners were not at this stage handed over to the Civil Authority. As the *Mail* explained, "Colonel Geddes [Lieutenant Colonel Andrew David Geddes commanded the Royal Inniskillings][539] is instituting enquiries of the most stringent and searching nature into the whole of the circumstances of the case . . . and to enable him to do so with more facility the prisoners are permitted to be retained for the present in the Regimental Guard Room." [540] Continuing a careful balancing act, the *Mail* wrote soothingly: "while every effort is being made to bring the guilt home to the guilty parties, no one would wish that others should be unduly brought to punishment by injudicious hurry." [541] It further states, that "The Magistrate's investigation will . . . not be resumed until the Military authorities are thoroughly satisfied that they have the right men."[542]

The *Mail* may have somewhat misrepresented the situation. Two days after this was written, Stewart did hear the case. He himself pronounced the evidence insufficient to find any of the accused men guilty, although, he said, "There was no doubt soldiers had been there". Stewart did however state, in concluding, that he "would refrain from making any remarks on the case". It seems clear that there were several remarks that he would have liked to make.

Soldiers: Case

SATURDAY 10 DECEMBER 1881
ASSAULT WITH INTENT[543]

Francis Wyley and Robert Whitley, Privates in H. M.'s Royal Inniskilling Fusiliers, were arrested on a warrant and charged with unlawfully assaulting Mr D. Byramjee and others with [intent][544] to commit a felony on the 8th instant.

Lieutenant Davidson[545] applied on behalf of the Military Authorities for a remand, and the hearing of the case was accordingly adjourned till two o'clock on Monday afternoon; the prisoners in the mean time to remain in Military custody.

MONDAY 12 DECEMBER 1881
ALLEGED ASSAULT WITH INTENT[546]

The case in which Francis Wyley and Robert Whitley, Privates in H. M.'s Royal Inniskilling Fusiliers, were charged with unlawfully assaulting Mr D. Byramjee and others with intent to commit a felony on the 8th instant, again occupied the attention of the Court this afternoon.

Lieutenant Davidson was again present [to] watch the case on behalf of the Military Authorities.

Mr D. Byramjee said that on Thursday evening last, the 8th instant, about a quarter-past six when he was coming along the Kennedy Road[547] in company with Messrs Mehta[548] and Billia,[549] and when near the last seat above the Racket Court, he came upon four or five soldiers. Two or three of them were stretched on their backs on the sloping bank, and two others were crouching down by the side of the road. Some of them had great-coats on, the others their uniform. One of them had on [a] helmet. As witness and his friends approached, all the men with the exception of one, jumped up and stood in front of them. One man did not stand in front of them, but stood a little way off, and when asked for his assistance he stood perfectly passive. The first prisoner is that man, but I cannot say whether the second defendant was there or not. One man caught Mr Billia by the collar of his coat, but he could not say if it was either of the defendants. Another man caught witness by the sleeve, but he freed himself from his grasp, and he and Mr Mehta ran. When about ten yards off they stopped and called Mr Billia, to come to them. Mr Mehta's chair was following, but neither Mr Billia nor Mr Mehta's chair coolies would come along. It was at this time that they called on first defendant for his assistance, but he remained quite passive. Ultimately Mr Billia got clear, and two of the men then chased witness and his companions as far as the second bridge. They were then loudly crying out for police. Soon after Mr Horspool and Mr Maconnochie came to their assistance from the opposite direction. Mr Horspool then gave chase to the men, and witness and Mr Billia followed. They met two men in dark clothes and on being asked for their assistance they at once joined in pursuit. Near the third seat, above Head-Quarter House,[550] these two men passed the first defendant and asked him if he knew anything about the men who had attacked them, but he did not give any definite answer. The pursuit was continued till near the Magazine[551] behind Victoria Barracks,[552] when they met Mr Horspool[553] returning. While speaking to him the first defendant came slowly along and was stopped. Mr Horspool enquired of him if he knew the men they were looking for, and where they had gone to. He said he knew them, but when asked their names he either would not or could not tell. Mr Horspool then asked him to come down to the barracks with them. The first defendant smelt of liquor, but he was sober. The other men were all intoxicated, more or less. Witness did not know what had become of the other men. (Mr Byramjee here illustrated how he had been seized–by one of the men catching hold of him by the left sleeve of his coat–not by the arm). Nothing was said to him when he was seized, but he could not tell what he had been seized for. On going eastward, about 5.45 p.m. at the commencement of the walk, they passed a number of men on the Kennedy Road, near its junction with the path leading to Head-Quarter House. One man was separated from the others, and witness thought it was the first defendant. At this time witness and Mr Mehta were alone. Two of them tried to throw their arms round Mr Mehta, apparently in a drunken frolic. He pulled Mr Mehta by the arm to enable him to avoid them. The men did not follow, and it was on the return walk that the assault complained of took place. The first defendant kept by himself, and did not join in what the others were doing. He took no part whatever in the assault. Witness was unable to say whether the second defendant was present or not. He was unable to say whether the men were laughing at the time, or whether they were in a determined mood. They came upon them suddenly.

Mr D. R. Billia said that about a quarter past six on the 8th instant he was walking on the Kennedy Road where he saw Mr Mehta and Mr Byramjee occupying a seat. Before this he had passed four or five soldiers one of whom stood in front of him and held a stick over his head. Witness did not know whether it was in fun or whether he had any intent. The man did not speak and he did not know what he meant by it. Had he not ducked his head he would probably have been hit. He could not say whether it was a cane or a stick. Witness was unable to say whether either of the two defendants was one of the men he had seen on the Kennedy Road on the occasion. When he joined his friends he told them of what had occurred. On their way back he saw five or six soldiers, they were all in red coats, some of them were stretched on their backs on the bank, but he could not say if they were the same men that he had passed before. When the men jumped up one of them seized witness by the collar of the coat and said something which sounded like d—d fool. The button of witness's coat slipped from the button-hole and he stepped aside, while the man assumed a fighting attitude and attempted to stop him, but he avoided him and slipped by on the other side. Another of the men then tried to catch him and these two men collided and fell, and he then escaped. He could not say whether the men were drunk or sober. When they fell he escaped and joined his friends. The chair coolies gave no assistance. Taking all the circumstances into consideration, and looking at the thing calmly now that he had got over his fright, he could not say whether it was the result of a drunken frolic, or if with any malicious intent. He was unable to identify either of the two prisoners. It was dark and he only saw the men's white faces and that they were soldiers. He only noticed the first defendant when speaking to Mr Horspool afterwards, but he could not say that he saw the second defendant.

Mr D. M. Mehta said that on the evening in question when going out with Mr Byramjee a soldier jostled against him slightly. He had been drinking but was not drunk. Mr Billia joined them further on.

Witness then proceeded to detail what had occurred to him and his friends on returning from their walk, which was similar to that given by Mr Byramjee. He also corroborated Mr Billia's evidence as to two men trying to intercept that gentlemen. He heard nothing said by any of the men. He saw two of them come into collision and fall. They came against each other with great force, and would have fallen even if they had been sober.

Witness then left the witness box, and after closely inspecting the two men in the dock, said he could not recognise either of the two prisoners. It was very dark.

Mr. Hermann Aarons,[554] clerk at Messrs. Vogel & Company,[555] said that on the evening of the 8th inst. he was walking on the Kennedy Road at half-past six o'clock. When near the path leading to the barracks he met two soldiers. One of them was a tall stout man, and the other was short. The tall man rushed upon him in a violent manner and asked him who he was. Witness thought he was going to be robbed and defended himself by brandishing his stick to prevent him getting hold of him. Witness told him there was a policeman at hand, and he called out "Police," although he had no hopes of being heard. Witness walked quickly on till he met Inspector Horspool, but the men did not follow him. He told Mr Horspool what had occurred and warned him, and he said he had already heard of the men. Witness joined Inspector Horspool in pursuing the men and he saw the man who had attempted to seize him make his escape. When he met the soldiers they were not running but walking along quietly as if enjoying an evening stroll. Mr Horspool told the shorter man that he was a police officer and took him to the barracks.

Witness having carefully inspected the two men in the dock could not say if either of them was on the road that night.

To Mr Horspool: I think the man who rushed on me had a cap on.

Mr G. Horspool Acting Deputy Superintendent of Police, said that about 6.20 p.m., on the 8th instant, he was walking with a gentleman on the Kennedy Road, in plain clothes. He heard a cry[556] of "Police" at some distance on the road. He at once turned to the eastward and when he had gone about 150 yards he met the three first witnesses. They were calling "Police," they appeared very much frightened, and Mr Byramjee told him something in consequence of which he proceeded some 300 yards further on when he met the last witness. Mr Aarons called out to be careful, as there were some soldiers on the road who had attempted to stop him. He also said something about a policeman. Witness ran on till he came nearly to the path leading to Head-Quarter House where he came upon two soldiers. The first defendant was one of them. He was standing up with his belt on and properly dressed. The other man was sitting. He had no belt, and no hat, his coat was unbuttoned, and witness noticed he wore a dark shirt. Witness at this time heard sounds of two or three persons running down the footpath. He would say they were soldiers. He asked the two men what was the matter, and the one who was sitting got up and asked him what he meant. Witness told him he was a police officer, and that they would have to be careful of what they said. The four last witnesses came up directly afterwards, and when they got quite close the man who was sitting down made a bolt along the road. Witness left first defendant and followed the running man until he escaped down the hillside towards Victoria Barracks. Witness called out to an Artilleryman "Stop this blackguard," but they did not attend to him. On his, witness's, return he met the Artilleryman with the first defendant. Mr Byramjee, the first witness, then said, in the hearing of the first defendant, that he was with the party who had attacked him and his friends, but that he had taken no active part in the matter and had refused to render assistance when called upon. Witness then took the first defendant and handed him over to the Military authorities at the Victoria Barracks. The two Artillerymen and four witnesses came to the barracks. The Artillerymen said they thought witness had been only larking, or they would have paid attention to him. First prisoner was not sober. He said he did not know the other men's names, but they lived in Victoria Barracks. Witness could not swear that the second defendant was the man who escaped from him, but he corresponded with him in height and in build. He was tall and young, had a florid complexion, with dark hair, and taller than witness. He knew he was an Irishman by his voice.

Mr H. MacCallum, Apothecary and Analyst at the Government Hospital, said that shortly after six o'clock on the evening of the 8th instant he was walking along the Kennedy Road in company with a friend. When some little distance east of the first bridge they met a group of soldiers. They seemed to have been drinking, and were very merry. He heard one of them invite the others either to dinner or supper. Witness and his friend went as far as the Magazine,[557] when he turned. On the way back he met two men running. The last one[558] was shouting, "Stop that blackguard." Witness remarked to his friend that he thought they were soldiers amusing themselves. A little way further on they passed two soldiers who looked at them very intently, and from this he judged there was something wrong. Witness was unable to identify either of the two prisoners.

To Lieutenant Davidson:[559]–The soldiers I first passed were not sober.

Sergeant T. Noble said he was Regimental Provost-Sergeant in the Royal Inniskilling Fusiliers. On the evening of the 8th inst., between seven and eight o'clock, he was present in the Guard Room when Mr Horspool and Mr Byramjee came there. A report had been made to the Sergeant-Major[560] and he gave witness an order to get a lamp and search on the Kennedy Road for a cap that had been lost by one of the men. He got a lamp and searched the road, but did not find the cap. Two of the Regimental Police were left behind to see if any of the men might come to look for the cap, and to search for it themselves when the moon got up and it would be much lighter. They did so, and found the cap and brought it to the barracks. The cap was produced and bore the second defendant's regimental number.

T. Duffield, a private in the Regiment, said that on the evening of the 8th instant, about half-past seven o'clock, he was in his barrack room in Victoria Barracks. He saw second defendant come in without his cap. He was drunk and had his waistbelt under his serge jacket. His face was a little flushed with liquor but he did not seem to have been running. He came into the room, made down[561] his bed and took off his jacket. He took his rug and lay down half an hour in the verandah.[562] He was wearing a white cotton shirt. A corporal then came and took him to the guard room. Witness had no conversation with him, and he heard nothing to account for the loss of his cap.

First defendant said that on the evening of the 8th instant he was walking on the Kennedy Road for his own pleasure. He was alone and heard some one in front of him shouting for the police. He took no notice but walked on about his business, until he was apprehended by Mr Horspool. He asked defendant if he knew the men who had interfered with the gentlemen on the road, and he told him in reply that he did not. Defendant was then marched off to the Barracks and put in the guard room. He admitted having been drinking, but was not drunk. In reply to the bench: I heard no one ask me for assistance. Second defendant said that on the evening of the 8th instant, at twenty-five minutes to four o'clock he went to the Canteen, where he remained till five o'clock. He then went to his room, and as he had no braces on he put his belt beneath his serge. He returned to the canteen with another man, but left his cap lying on his bed. He remained in the Canteen till half past five but did not remember anything more until midnight, when he was woke up,[563] a prisoner in the Guard room, by the Sergeant-Major and Sergeant Noble, who asked him if he knew of anything that had happened on the Kennedy Road. He said he knew nothing at all about Kennedy Road, as he had been confined for being drunk. The Sergeant-Major then asked him his Regimental number and he told him. Defendant saw a cap in the Sergeant-Major's hand as he left the Guard room. The cap in court bore his Regimental number, and was his cap. He knew nothing more of this matter till he was brought up on Saturday. Any of the men who were about the room could see his cap on his bed. Any man could have taken his cap from the room. Defendant said he was very drunk, and did not remember being confined or anything that occurred that night.

W. J. McCormick, one of the Regimental Police, said that about eight o'clock on the evening of the 8th instant, he was ordered by Sergeant Noble to accompany him to Kennedy Road. After a time Sergeant Noble left him to continue the search, and he found it about half past eleven o'clock between the second and third bridges.

To the Bench:–Witness did not know that it was customary for one man to take another's cap. He had no doubt however that it often occurred, for instance if one man got the ribbons of his cap torn he might take another's.

Lieutenant C. J. L. Davidson, Royal Inniskilling Fusiliers, said he knew both defendants. The first prisoner bore a very good character; the second defendant also bore a very good character, and the charge against him of being drunk was the first against him in the service. He had served in the second battalion previous to his joining here twelve months ago.

To the Court: – I do not know that it is a customary thing for men to take each other's caps. No man is allowed to have another man's property, but I think it is a very likely thing to occur, that men may take the loan of each other's caps.

Mr Aarons, recalled, said that the prisoners resembled in size and general appearance the men who accosted him, but he could not swear to them. The tall man who tried to assault him most certainly wore a cap.

His Worship, addressing the men, said that under the circumstances there was nothing for it but for him to discharge them. He had gone into the case most fully both for the sake of the prisoners and of the public, and looking at it in every aspect as a jury would do, he saw nothing for it, but to dismiss the case. At one time things looked very seriously against the second defendant, but from the place where the cap was found and where the alleged assault was made on Mr Aarons, who swore the man wore his cap, the man must have run a considerable distance before he lost it. He must look at the case as a jury would look at it, and there certainly was not enough evidence for him to convict them. There was no doubt soldiers had been there, and he would refrain from making any remarks on the case, further than that they were now discharged.~~~~~

Police

Not surprisingly, the cumulative force of these police court reports results in a very clear impression of what police work was like in the early 1880s.[564] They also give some insight into the domestic and private lives of individual members of the force, including their marriages with Chinese women, their drinking habits, and their love of pets. [565] We learn something of their previous and subsequent work, their relationships with colleagues, and their social organisations.

Police work was dangerous. In this short period alone, two Police Constables lost their lives during the execution of their duty: a Sikh policeman was killed, investigating a burglary at the village of Tai-tam;[566] a British policeman died, assisting at a fire in the urban Central district.[567] These sad events called forth expressions of sympathy and solidarity from their colleagues. Detachments of European, Sikh and Chinese policemen accompanied Easur Singh's body to the grave.[568] Robert Anderson's body was drawn to the cemetery by the fire brigade. The vehicle which transported it was covered by a black cloth, topped by his helmet, belt and axe, and the nozzle of the hose he was managing at the time of his death.[569] Chinese policemen also had dangerous work, the detectives among them infiltrating triad and smuggling gangs.

There were dangers to health as well as to life itself. A young Scot, who joined from the Glasgow police force in October 1877, died in December 1881, aged 27, after catching "fever" – perhaps malaria – a year previously when posted at the village of Aberdeen.[570] In September 1885, a constable developed syphilitic symptoms, after his knuckles were cut by the teeth of the man he was arresting.[571] Another was severely hurt by falling debris, during another fire in Central.[572]

Police work was difficult, and it was difficult, in different ways, for each of the three groups of policemen – European ("the gentry in blue coats and silver buttons"),[573] Indian (in turbans) and Chinese (in green jackets); but in all cases their problems were compounded by differences of culture, language and expectations within both the force itself and Hong Kong society at large. The Hong Kong English language newspapers show that the English speaking public watched police behaviour closely, but tended to waste their good-citizenship when they wrote to the newspapers, with some concern or complaint. In September 1881, *The China Mail* suggested instead that members of the public should take note of a policeman's number and report him "respectfully" to the Captain Superintendent of Police, whenever they witnessed breaches of common humanity or "any flagrant offence in the way of exceeding his duty". [574] Sometimes a preference was expressed for one group of police, and sometimes for another. In January 1876, the bilingual language skills of the Chinese were recommended.[575] In October 1878, the behaviour of the Europeans and Indians, when experiencing danger, was preferred. [576] Doubtless, other groups of citizens also passed their own comments among themselves. Others showed their opinion by their behaviour. "The coolie and hawker classes are frequently to blame for the exasperating way in which they shower abuse upon and laugh at the Punjabees."[577]

Occasionally, remarks would be passed on police proficiency. "We are glad to know that the Police Force are about to make some effort to become acquainted with the use of the weapons with which they are armed. The records of their successes when called on to use their arms during the late attacks on Yau-ma Ti, Tai-tam, and Mong-kok Tsui,[578] have been anything but creditable. No one with a claim to Christian charity would rejoice at the death, or even the severe wounding of a fellow creature, simply as an evidence of his proficiency in shooting, but there are times when all charitableness of this description must be thrown aside, and matters must be dealt with on the hard and fast lines of stern duty and necessity."[579]

In general, there seems no doubt that most of the police force did the best they could, according to their lights. Not all in the main body of men were particularly well-educated. A decade earlier than this, when Stewart was

Coroner, he explained that the reason why a Sergeant, who worked as summoning officer to the Coroner's Court, could not be promoted to Inspector, in spite of long years in the Force, was because his handwriting was inadequate.[580] A Police School was set up for the benefit of such men. Those who needed it studied basic literacy and numerary. Chinese and Indians studied colloquial English. Europeans studied Chinese.

Other members of the force had distinguished themselves before joining the force. Some of the Indians had won war medals while in the Indian Army.[581] European Police Constable Foley, who retired in March 1882 after serving in the police service for more than twenty years, held the Canton medal for 1857, which he won when a private of the 59th Regiment.[582] Other good men among the Europeans had joined the force in Hong Kong, as discharged sailors.[583]

Similar to today, police work was not limited to enforcing the law. As already seen, they might be detailed to assist in case of fire. They helped when some major accidents threatened life. In September 1881, *The China Mail* reported that European and Sikh Police constables cleared away the debris where the wall of some buildings in course of demolition had collapsed, and people were feared buried in the rubble.[584]

In fact, in April 1881, *The China Mail* expressed the view that the morale of the force was the highest that it had ever been.[585]

Even in this period, however, it did happen that members and ex-members of the force themselves appeared as defendants in court. The three cases quoted below show three found guilty as charged: "a Malacca-man" (a dismissed policeman), a European member of the naval yard police, and a Chinese constable. The first and the last were cases of larceny, the second was an embezzlement case, compounded by desertion from duty. It is relevant to note that inadequate pay was a repeated complaint during this period. On the one hand, it made the police more likely to succumb to bribery. On the other hand, it deprived the force of men who could command a higher salary. When discussing the estimates for 1889, the Finance Committee, chaired by Frederick Stewart, commented on proposed increases in pay, which "had been seriously called for for a long time". Encouraged by the Hon. J. Bell-Irving's response, "Yes, I think the men were underpaid", Stewart continued, "There is no doubt that now we shall be able to get better men. Sometimes now we get very good men. . . . but with the improved salaries we shall be able to get better men all round."[586]

Of course court appearances such as those quoted below gave cause for comment. In the Embezzlement Case, Stewart expressed his regretful view of the matter from the bench. As for one of the Larceny cases, which occurred during a very severe typhoon, *The China Mail* made its view very clear in its narrative of the storm and related events. The typhoon had raged for several hours, sinking and breaking up an immense number of cargo-boats, junks, and sampans, and running a steam launch on the rocks.[587] It killed eleven Chinese.[588] Yet, while several European members of the Police Force were gallantly saving two hundred and fifty-seven Chinese lives from the sea, one constable joined the numerous other "rascals" on land who were seeking petty profit from the storm. "The most melancholy case of the lot was that of a Chinese policeman, Number 433, who was caught by an Indian Sergeant carrying away a bundle of newly made Chinese clothing which he had taken from a bale, landed quite close to the station, amongst other wreckage, a bale which there was every reason to believe this pretty limb of the law had cut open for his own theftuous[589] purpose. Of course this energetic gentleman, so valuable in the case of a typhoon, will not from today ornament the Force longer. . . . "[590]

As this report shows, the ever-present criticisms and complaints were more than balanced by a justly generous climate of public opinion. Good coverage was given when senior and long-serving members went on leave, retired,[591] or renewed their period of service.[592] Their sensitivities were respected. Welcoming the Governor's promise of additional street lights – "Upon the principle that a lamp is nearly as good as a policeman" – *The China Mail* took care to state that no disparagement was meant "to the stalwart members of the Force".[593] Helpful suggestions were made. One, that, as in Ceylon, they should be provided with that new invention, the bicycle.[594] Even more appreciated, doubtless, was the support *The China Mail* gave, in September 1881, to a pay increase among inspectors, "a well-tried, persevering and highly respected section of the establishment".[595]

In June 1886, four years after Stewart left the bench, there was a major exposure of triad activity among the police, and this was obviously brewing during Stewart's time. A police interpreter was sacked. The police constable, Li Afan,[596] who had appeared in Stewart's court to give evidence in November 1881, was now charged in the magistrate's court himself, for demanding money with menaces.[597] The additional rumour was that he was head of a Triad Society.

At the conclusion of the trial, Li was committed to appear at the Criminal Sessions of the Supreme Court. Bail was set at two thousand dollars – an enormous sum then. Doubtless, he was expected not to find it. But he seems to have done so easily, in effect proving the charge.

On the day of the trial, the number three typhoon signal was hoisted, and Li Afan did not appear. The money was forfeited.[598] He vanished from sight, and nothing was heard of him for two months,. Suddenly, the report of Li Fan's violent death appeared in *The China Mail*.

At least some Triad Societies in those days had as their objective the overthrow of the Chinese Manchu Empire, and now, after his death, the former extortionist and oppressor of poor working men was instantly rescripted a hero. In a quite astonishing account, the events of Li Fan's escape and death are coloured with revolutionary romance, ninety years before Hong Kong postcolonialism began.

A Chinese Mandarin watched the case when the former detective of the Hong Kong Force was being tried at the Supreme Court, and it was generally thought that if the Chinese authorities came across him in his native land they would make pretty short work of him. And this it seems has been the case. Li Fan first retired to the Lo Fau hills beyond Canton, which abound in nunneries and temples and within the sacred surroundings of which the Chinese soldiers did not seek to touch him. But the old leader of a secret society could not rest at ease in such a district and he hied him home to his native district of Tamsui some two days journey from Kowloon City, there to mature his plans and plots afresh. But the myrmidons of the Chinese powers were not long in finding out his retreat. They seemed determined to suffer neither him nor his followers to live in peace . . .. Li Fan, therefore, had not been long in his native village ere his house was surrounded by a hundred soldiers, who summoned him to surrender. This, notwithstanding the odds against him, the intrepid revolutionary refused to do, and for some time he held the place against the one hundred bravely. Finally he retreated to the upper chamber of the house and from there fired on the soldiers who had come to [arrest?] him, killing one and wounding seven. He was, however, disabled by two shots, one of which penetrated his right leg and another his left side. The soldiers then rushed into the room and one of them ran his sword through the abdomen of the helpless man. They then threw him on a plank and bore him off towards the barracks. But he never reached this destination and avoided perhaps a more dreadful death by succumbing to his wounds en route.[599]

In Hong Kong, many things are not what they seem. In the 1930s and 40s, a barber might have been a Japanese spy. In the 1970s, a bar attendant at the Hong Kong Cricket Club might have been a former Professor of Physics at a

Mainland China University. In the 1990s, your amah might have turned out to be your landlady, or your landlord's wife. In the 1880s, an extortionist might have been a Byronic hero filling his war-chest.

Again, events draw to long-term consequences. The month when Li Fan's death was reported, fifty-three Chinese policemen were charged with possibly associated corruption, collecting bribes from the owner of a gambling establishment.[600] Eleven years later, in a raid on the headquarters of a gambling syndicate, documents were discovered which revealed that a large number of police officers, Europeans as well as Chinese, had been receiving bribes for a considerable time.[601] Following investigation, the force was purged. Criminal proceedings were taken against one European police officer, forty-nine were dismissed, and a number of others were required to resign. Chinese and Indian officers were also dismissed, as well as civilian government employees – interpreters, for example – who were also involved. In 1912, F. H. May, the Captain Superintendent of Police who had led the investigation, returned to Hong Kong as Governor. As he was carried in a ceremonial sedan chair from Blake Pier, the son of a Chinese constable, dismissed in 1897, attempted to assassinate him.[602] Was this an act of personal revenge for lost face? Or was it a further act of revolutionary fervour, inspired by the death of former Chinese Police Constable, Li Fan?

There was however a second Police Force in Hong Kong, composed of the District Watchmen, and paid for, at least partly, by the Chinese community.[603] The later nickname given to this force – "The Chinese Executive Council" – and a discussion of the history of the District Watchmen by H. J. Lethbridge, both show how important this group ultimately became, as a nursery for the Chinese leadership of the majority Chinese section within Hong Kong society. In 1870, *The Daily Press* had expressed considerable concern about the District Watchmen, quoting the Chief Justice's recent remarks at the Legislative Council: "There are sixty odd men in Hong Kong who are constables; who are not under Mr Deane [the Captain Superintendent of Police], and who are responsible to nobody". Describing them as "dangerous and irresponsible men", *The Daily Press* asked, "by virtue of what power or ordinance is it that the Chinese are paying one-half of these men's salaries?"[604] The view we would form of the district watchmen from the whole group of reports of Frederick Stewart's court cases from 1881 to 1882, in which they appear four times as arresting officers, is, however, unexceptionable. Su Atai, in Circular Pathway, arrests a thief.[605] Chan Akok, in Webster's Bazaar, responds to a disturbance.[606] Chan Sing, on duty in Hollywood Road, arrests a pickpocket.[607] The fourth, unnamed, brings in a man for snatching.[608] The indignation and alarm expressed by *The Daily Press* in 1870 is an indication of the strong feeling of insecurity felt by some at least in the non-Chinese part of the Hong Kong community in that earlier period, and gives us a point of comparison from which to conclude that Hong Kong society in 1882 and 1883 had felt at least a degree more confident in those responsible for its policing.

Police: Cases

BEFORE FREDERICK STEWART, ESQ.
FRIDAY 2 SEPTEMBER 1881
THEFT OF A WATCH, ETC.[609]

Ahmed, a Malacca-man, twenty-five, a seaman, was charged with stealing a watch and chain, sixty cents in money, a knife, a handkerchief, and some beads, all of the value of twelve dollars twenty-five cents, on the 30th *ultimo*.

Ameer Khan deposed that he was formerly in the Police Force, from which he was dismissed. He had had no employment for a year. Saw the defendant for the first time in the Mahomedan[610] Cemetery. Went there, about 12.30 p.m. to pray. Defendant was in the compound at the time. Took off his long coat, in the pocket of which he had sixty cents in silver, a knife worth fifty cents, a handkerchief worth ten cents, and some beads worth ten cents. Also took off his belt, to which his silver watch and chain were attached. Went to a well to wash his hands and feet before saying his prayers. Left his coat and belt on the table in the Mosque. Was away about ten or fifteen minutes. When he came back he found the coat and belt there, but the other property described was amissing. Went out at once; but defendant was not to be seen. Went to Number 2 Station and reported the matter and gave the constable a description of the man. To-day, saw defendant in Lascar Row; when defendant saw him (witness) defendant ran away. Ran after him and the Constable stopped him. Had not recovered any of his property.

To the Court the complainant said the only other person within the gate was the gardener, who was at work. Witness, recalled later on in the case, stated that the watch and chain produced were his property.

Other evidence was given connecting the defendant with the pawning of the watch and chain thus identified.

Prisoner was sentenced to four weeks' imprisonment with hard labour.~~~~~

FRIDAY 7 OCTOBER 1881[611]
THE NAVAL YARD EMBEZZLEMENT CASE[612]

Cornelius Conner, charged with embezzling money belonging to the Naval Yard Canteen, was today committed for trial at the Criminal Sessions.

FRIDAY 14 OCTOBER 1881[613]
THE ALLEGED EMBEZZLEMENT CASE

This case, which was committed for trial at the Criminal Sessions, was to-day reopened.

William Lynsaght[614] said he was Inspector of Naval Police in H.M. Dockyards here. The members of the canteen comprise all the employees in the dockyard, workmen as well as police. The canteen was an association of a purely private character. As far as discipline went, witness was head of the canteen, but in other respects he was simply a member. The refreshments supplied to the canteen were got from the store and paid from the receipts at the end of the month. If any balance was over it was handed over to him for the benefit of the police mess. In return for this the police manage the canteen in turn. The police mess consisted of the unmarried members of the force, who stopped[615] in the Yard. This mess was entirely unconnected with the canteen except in so far as he had already stated. Each policeman managed the canteen for six months at a time, and in addition to his privilege as a member he got the proceeds of the sale of empty hogsheads or barrels. Defendant[616] was a member of the canteen. Arrangements had been made for paying the bills which defendant ought to have paid. An advance for that purpose had been obtained from witness. The canteen was thus in debt, and the surplus funds will go to clear off this advance. On 2nd instant defendant was absent from duty at noon, at which time he should have gone on.[617] When witness mustered the men at six o'clock, he found defendant still absent. He sent a Sergeant of the Police to look for defendant, but the Sergeant returned in about an hour without him. Latterly a reward was offered by the Commodore.[618] Defendant was captured on the 5th *instant* by the Police. He had been absent from duty for three days and a half.

Remanded till 15th at ten o'clock a.m.

SATURDAY 15 OCTOBER 1881
THE EMBEZZLEMENT CASE[619]

This case, which was reopened yesterday, again came before the Court to-day.

G. Northcote, Police Constable, gave evidence as to arresting Conner. The Police Constable was in plain clothes at the time.

His Worship expressed his regret to find a man of his character, having ten years good character in the Artillery and four in the Naval Yard police, in the position in which he was. A legal technicality had arisen which had prevented the Supreme Court from dealing with the charge of embezzlement. Had he been in England he would have been amenable to the law, but such law did not affect this Colony, although he hoped it would soon. Had prisoner returned within twenty-four hours, the charge of desertion would probably not have been made. Although the charge of embezzlement had been withdrawn he could not overlook the fact as an element in determining his punishment for the crime of desertion. He felt compelled to give him the full term of punishment laid down by the Ordinance, namely that he be imprisoned for six months.~~~~~

SATURDAY 15 OCTOBER 1881[620]
LARCENY BY A CONSTABLE

Number 433, Kong Asow, a Constable stationed at Yau-Mah-ti, was charged with the larceny of a quantity of clothing on the 14th instant.

Sultan Malak, Acting Sergeant of Police, said that he was on duty at half-past eleven o'clock last night on the Praya, Yau-ma-ti. He saw some one pass under a verandah, and as it was rather dark he threw the light of his lantern on him, when he saw the prisoner throw down a bundle and run. Constable Number 696, who was also present, pursued and apprehended the prisoner while witness picked up the bundle. On examination it was found to contain a number of jackets and other articles of clothing similar to a quantity which had been washed ashore from a wrecked junk.[621] When arrested the prisoner said he was a lukong and on duty. He was wearing an oilskin coat over his uniform and was walking in an easterly direction, away from the station, when first noticed.

No further evidence was taken, and the further investigation of the case was postponed till Monday morning, the 17th instant.[622] ~~~~~

Teachers and Men of the Cloth

The teachers and men of the cloth who appeared in Frederick Stewart's court show the variety of those occupying these professions in Hong Kong at the time.

Five are complainants. Brother Cyprian, a French national, belonging to the Christian Brothers, was Principal of the Roman Catholic St Joseph's College, a school mainly teaching Portuguese boys at this time. It is now a very prestigious secondary school, headed until the early 2000s by a Christian Brother – an Irishman noted for his fellow-feeling for the boys and energetic encouragement of football. The pupils and teachers today are mainly Chinese.

George Piercy, one-time tutor in Japan for the Jardine family, and briefly a master at the Hong Kong Government Central School for Boys (during Frederick Stewart's time as Headmaster), became head of the Diocesan Home and Orphanage. – This was originally established by Lydia Smith (wife of George Smith, the first Anglican Bishop of Victoria, Hong Kong) as the Diocesan Native Female Training School, admitting Chinese girls. The plan was to train them up to be suitable Christian wives for the former pupils of St Paul's College, of which the Bishop himself was the first Warden. Following the Smiths' departure for England, various events led to the Diocesan School's becoming a boarding institution mainly for Eurasian Boys. – Today, the school survives in two further embodiments. The Diocesan Girls' School and the Diocesan Boys' School – both very prestigious schools – today, like St Joseph's, admit mainly Chinese pupils.

Agha, a Chinese schoolmaster, probably had his own one-teacher school, where he taught the Confucian Classics. There are no schools in the mainstream of Hong Kong education today which confine themselves to this curriculum.

The different reasons for the appearance in court of these three educationists suggest considerable differences in life-style. George Piercy made two complaints: one about a domestic servant and the other about rotting rice bags left out to dry, producing a putrid smell, and Brother Cyprian complained about a former domestic servant. Agha, on the other hand, was the victim of a pickpocketing attempt.

The two other complainants – Roman Catholic priest Revd Marcus Leang and his friend, missionary Revd Chü Tak Mong – had had property stolen from a room in the "parsonage" in St Francis Street.

Three men appear as defendants. Former schoolmaster Chu Un Fuk, over-excited by his approaching ordeal as a candidate in the Civil Service Examinations of the Chinese Empire, soon to be held at Canton, was charged with disorderly behaviour. Revd Lechler, a missionary of the Basel Mission, appeared for the fault of the boy whom he employed to look after his cows. – It is astonishing, considering how densely-populated urban Hong Kong is today, to think that a private individual could then keep three cows in the Central District of Hong Kong, where they strayed into the Botanical Gardens! – James Robert Ransome, claiming to support himself by teaching English to some Indian soldiers belonging to the British Army, appeared for a range of charges: being a rogue and vagabond and also for being drunk and incapable. Present-day native English teachers of the mother-tongue in Hong Kong may be pleased to know that Ransome's claims to be among their number were considered false.

One teacher appeared as a witness. This was Soonderam Ramasammy, a master at the Wanchai Government School.

Teachers and Men of the Cloth: Cases

FRIDAY 14 OCTOBER 1881
SUSPICIOUS CHARACTER[623]

Francis Xavier Sardrean (Brother Cyprian), said he was principal of St. Joseph's College. Defendant was second cook at the College until some time ago. He was then dismissed and ordered never to return to the premises. This morning he found defendant (Ho Apui) in the kitchen with the servants. Witness gave defendant into custody.

Prisoner was ordered to find two sureties in twenty-five dollars each to be of good behaviour for six weeks, in default to be committed.~~~~~

THURSDAY 20 OCTOBER 1881
NUISANCE[624]

Leung Ahong was accused of leaving a number of stinking rice bags on the hillside, near High Street.

Inspector Cleaver said he had received a letter from Mr Piercy[625] of the Diocesan Home complaining of the stench. Witness visited the spot and found a number of bags containing damaged rice, which had been laid there to dry. He reported the matter to Dr Ayres, who told him to take out a summons. The bags were on a vacant piece of Crown land.

Prisoner was fined ten dollars, or seven days in gaol.

~~~~~

SATURDAY 12 NOVEMBER 1881
DISORDERLY CONDUCT ON BOARD A STEAMER[626]

Chu Un Fuk, a clerk, was charged at the instance of Sergeant Campbell with disorderly conduct on board the steamer Powan on the 11th instant.

It appears that yesterday evening defendant went on board as a passenger bound for Canton.

He placed his mat in such a position that it was in the way of the Chief Officer, and when asked by him and the complainant to remove it, he worked himself into a high state of excitement. Sergeant Campbell, who was in plain clothes, told him through his interpreter[627] who he was, and desired him to go to another part of the ship and be quiet.

This seemed to wound his celestial[628] dignity in a vulnerable point, and he proceeded to array himself in a long silk gown, adorned his face with a pair of spectacles as large as saucers, and stretching himself to his full height literally roared in the Sergeant's face. He explained, through the interpreter in the most grandiloquent language, that he did not care if witness was the Governor, and that he should not even open his eyes to look upon such a mighty man as he (defendant) was. He continued in this strain for some time, using defiant and abusive language, and attracting crowds round him, until it was found necessary to place him in restraint.

Defendant said he had been a schoolmaster, but was now employed as a clerk. He had been in the colony for six or seven years, and was on his way to Canton to attend the examinations now going on there. He was sorry for what he had done, and promised to behave himself in Canton.

Cautioned and discharged.~~~~~

TUESDAY 13 DECEMBER 1881
STRAYING CATTLE[629]

The Reverend R. Lechler, of the Basel Mission House,[630] appeared on a summons at the instance of Mr Ford, Superintendent of the Government Gardens, charged with unlawfully permitting three cows to stray on Crown lands and destroy young trees planted there.

Mr Lechler said his cow-boy had allowed the cows to stray while he was taking his breakfast. He should not have done so, as he had been told to be careful not to allow the cows to touch the young trees.

Fined two dollars, in default one day's imprisonment.

~~~~~

SATURDAY 24 DECEMBER 1881
ATTEMPTING TO STEAL A GOLD BANGLE[631]

Ho Apak was brought up on a charge of stealing a gold bangle, value $35, from Ip Apak, on the 23rd inst. in Wing-lok Street.

Ip Apak, a fishmonger, said that while he was

taking part in carrying the dragon in the fishmongers' procession[632] some one attempted to snatch the bangle from his arm but was prevented from doing this by it being attached to his arm by a string. He could not swear defendant was the person.

Soonderam Ramasammy, a master at the Wanchai Government School, while looking at the procession heard a cry of "stealing a bangle." He ran to the spot and seized a man whom some person pointed out. Defendant was not the man he handed over to a European Police Constable, but witness had seen defendant before this time snatch at the bangle in Court.

Donald McDonald, Police Constable 84, apprehended defendant, whom he found in the custody of some Chinese, belonging to the procession, and who were using him roughly.

Defendant said he went to witness the procession and saw some people fighting with complainant's party, when some one seized him and he fell down. He had no employment at present.

Sentence of four months' imprisonment with hard labour was imposed.~~~~~

TUESDAY 10 JANUARY 1882
A CHAIR COOLIE IN LIQUOR[633]

Lai Asu, a chair coolie, was charged with being drunk and unfit for duty on the 9th instant.

Mr George Piercy, head schoolmaster of the Diocesan Home and Orphanage, said that defendant was ordered to take his wife's chair to West Terrace about five o'clock yesterday evening. He had been on leave at three o'clock, but returned to duty at the proper time, but he was so drunk that his wife was compelled to leave the chair.

Defendant admitted the charge and said he had taken a little samshoo.
Fined one dollar, in default four days' imprisonment with hard labour; and to forfeit what wages were due.~~~~~

THURSDAY 19 JANUARY 1882
VAGABONDS AND INCAPABLES[634]

James Robert Ransome, unemployed telegraph operator, and Wyra Boory, an unemployed steward belonging to Penang, were charged with being rogues and vagabonds, and also with being drunk and incapable on the 17th instant.

Police Sergeant[635] Butlin said he found the two defendants lying drunk in East Street yesterday. Neither defendant had any visible means of subsistence and they were without any place of abode. The first defendant had been once previously convicted as a rogue and vagabond.

The first defendant said he lived in Francis Street, Wanchai, and made his living by teaching some Gun Lascars[636] the English language. He was put in gaol before as a matter of charity.

Police Sergeant Butlin said he had made enquiries about the truth of this statement and found it to be untrue.

Second defendant admitted the charge.

Each sentenced to fourteen days' imprisonment with hard labour. ~~~~~

FRIDAY 17 MARCH 1882
ROBBERY[637]

Chu Azing, Wong Awing and Chiu Apo were charged with receiving two pieces of bark and a large leather box, knowing the same to have been stolen, on the 7th inst. the property of the Reverend Marcus Leang,[638] part of articles stolen to the value of over two hundred dollars.

Reverend Marcus Leang said he was a Roman Catholic Priest and lived in the parsonage in St. Francis Street. On the 7th of February he went to the chapel about ten minutes to six, leaving the large box in Court in his room near his bed. The box which was locked, was the property of a friend, the Reverend Chü Tak Mong, and had been in his for two months and a half. He was not aware of the contents nor their exact value, but he knew the two pieces of cinnamon were part of the contents. The small teak box in Court was part of his own property, and was left unlocked, at the same time as he left his friend's box, and contained a quantity of valuable books. He missed the articles on his return from the chapel, but next morning found his own box and some of the small books on the hill side.

The defendants were arrested by Inspector Corcoran, and each of them was proved to have been implicated in the affair.

Reverend Chü Tak Mong, missionary, identified the brown leather box, a tin of medicine, the empty tin, two pieces of cinnamon, two show-cases and some valuable books as belonging to him, which he valued at four hundred dollars.

The second defendant admitted being concerned in the robbery, and the third defendant was proved to have pawned several of the articles. The second defendant has one previous conviction against him, and the third five previous convictions.

After being cautioned the prisoners were committed for trial at the April Criminal Sessions.[639] ~~~~~

TUESDAY 21 MARCH 1882
A NEEDY HAWKER[640]

Hou Asze admitted attempting to steal eighteen dollars from the pocket of Agha, schoolmaster, on the 20th instant. He had no money, he said, to purchase articles to trade in and tried to pick complainant's pocket for that reason. Four previous convictions were also admitted. Sentenced to six months' imprisonment with hard labour, first and last fortnight in solitary confinement. ~~~~~

The Domestic Scene. Wives & Husbands, Amahs & Cooks, Widows & Protected Women, Sons & Adopted Daughters, Burglars.

These police court cases give a sad view of domesticity. This would not be surprising anywhere. However, it is frequently stated even today that Hong Kong exerts unusual strain on personal relationships, with predictable results.

The first case given here concerns a former Hong Kong policeman and former *Daily Press* reporter, Irishman James M'Breen, now a clerk, and his very recent and unhappy marriage.[641] His wife Jane M'Breen is identified – from her use of pigeon English at least – as Chinese. Nevertheless, she seems to have been previously married to another westerner, buried (as at the time of the trial) in the Hong Kong Happy Valley cemetery, and she had a couple of young children from the marriage. She owned or managed a bar. She represented herself as having married M'Breen when he was out of work. He however claimed that she asked him to resign from the Police Force to help her manage the bar, and that she offered him a financial inducement to do so.

The second case focuses on two members of a Chinese household in the Central Chinese neighbourhood, Tai-ping-shan: a woman polygamously married to a marine hawker, and her little adopted daughter, living in the household as her son's future wife. This was a common arrangement in Chinese families during this period. As also seems to have been unfortunately common, the child was treated as a servant and ill-used. The child's attempted suicide and even the method of the attempt (jumping into a well) were also not unusual.

In the M'Breen family disturbance, neighbours played an active part. In this second case, the neighbours played an even more active part, urging the policeman to arrest the woman; and several appeared as witnesses in court.

The domestic disturbance described in another report, "An Old Man's Troubles", also took place in Tai-ping-shan and arose because father and son had different ideas about the son's responsibilities. His father stated that his son spent the father's money on gambling and "other bad practices". To prevent him doing so in this instance, the father's cousin and two nephews tied the son up. As a long-term measure, the father planned to send his son to school in their native country. The son, who was unemployed, had threatened his father, a shopkeeper, to emigrate. Who will keep me in my old age? the father worries. Such apparently odd behaviour still occurs. On 11 July 1999, the Hong Kong newspaper, *Sunday Morning Post*, carried a front-page story, "Boy, 13, chained, padlocked by father". The boy in the 1882 case alleged that the reason was that his father did not want him to go out to "play". Reportedly, the boy in 1999 was chained after asking if he could go out at 10pm on a Friday night.

The burglary at Bellevue case gives a glimpse of a middle-class household. Mr Scott was a banker. He had a bedroom with a verandah that faced the harbour,[642] servants (including a "house-coolie"), and a dog. The items that were stolen from him and his wife were luxury items – a gold watch, a pencil-case, and a travelling clock; also the key to their cash box. The tracing of the property to a pawn-shop and the incrimination of a Chinese woman with two missing front teeth show a contrasting segment of Hong Kong life.

Another middle-class establishment was that of Mr and Mrs Whitehead. They had a cook to send to market daily to procure fresh food to eat. (Even into the early 2000s, many Chinese families like to go to market twice a day to get fresh food for meals.)

Mr Whitehead was a government servant, the chief inspector of brothels. When he was at work one day, his wife was involved in a dispute with the cook, who left without cooking dinner. – In his official capacity, Mr Whitehead had an interpreter whose duty it was to accompany him on official duties (including the regular visiting of brothels). Hungrily, he sent his interpreter to the cook's house, and the man came back with the far-fetched story that the cook said he had no wood to cook dinner with. (Although gas was introduced into Hong Kong in the 1860s, wood was what was used in Hong Kong during the

Japanese Occupation of December 1941 to August 1945 when it was in very short supply.)

It is difficult to believe – as the cook alleged – that Mrs Whitehead suggested to the cook that he should take planks from a fence to fuel his fire. It is less difficult to believe that she was fussy about the food he brought home to cook for the Whiteheads' dinner that day.

It is intrinsic to the relationship that employers and domestic servants come from different backgrounds. The disparity is inevitably greater when one or other of the parties is in a foreign country, and when there are language difficulties. If, in addition, the servants live in the employer's household and either employer or servant has pressures in another area of life, conflict is likely to arise. Mrs Whitehead may well have had a difficult personal situation. Her husband's official occupation laid him open to considerable and varied temptations. Only a year or so after this case, Frederick Stewart was to come across Mr Whitehead in another capacity. In 1883, seven months into his appointment as Registrar General and Protector of Chinese, which made him responsible (among many other matters) for brothels, Frederick Stewart submitted a letter dealing with the relationship between Mr Whitehead, chief inspector of brothels and "a woman called Rich or Anderson". This led to a Commission of Enquiry, followed by the resignation of Whitehead and changes in the organisational structure and conditions of employment of inspectors of brothels.[643] Given a relationship between Mr Whitehead and "the woman named Rich or Anderson", it is not surprising that Mrs Whitehead's alleged domestic behaviour indicates considerable stress.

The Driscolls' was also a middle-class household. Mr Driscoll was a tailor and outfitter, whose establishment was in the main non-Chinese shopping area of Queen's Road Central, and he lived at 3 West Terrace.[644] Mention is made in the court report of various employees: an amah or female servant, "boys" or male servants, and coolies (labourers). The Driscolls had a little girl and at least one other child (one of them a baby). Both (or all) of these, it seems, the amah looked after. The immediate cause of this domestic quarrel seems to have been that the little girl said something to the amah that made her take offence. The affair escalated. In court, different stories were told by the amah and her fellow servant, and by Mr Driscoll and Mrs Driscoll. From the report of the case brought before Frederick Stewart, Mr Driscoll appears as a reasonable man, careful to train his children to be polite to their amah and concerned to let the amah see that he did do this. What the amah says about Mrs Driscoll and what the coolie says about both his employers is difficult to credit. Later events suggest that what the Driscolls stated in court about their amah – that she screamed and made trouble – was accurate. For the Driscoll's amah was in court again two days later, appearing before the other Police Magistrate of the time, Mr Wodehouse. (To flesh out the picture, this report also is given below. It is the only case in *Court in Time*, not heard "before Frederick Stewart, Esq.") The amah seems to have made a similar impression on each of the two magistrates.

Both the Driscoll and Whitehead cases are interesting for the light they throw on the employment of domestic helpers in Hong Kong at that time. Threats to dismiss a servant and threats to resign form part of the evidence in both cases. This helps to explain why resignation from a job, without giving time for employers to find a substitute, was made an offence in Hong Kong, as early as 1845.[645] There were several occasions in Hong Kong's early history as a British colony when Chinese working for foreign residents flocked in thousands back to China on the sudden edict of Chinese mandarins on the Mainland, seeking to exert political pressure on western powers. The habit extended also to Government servants. Cheong Alam, Porter at the Gaol offices since September 1843, and one other were the only Chinese who refused to desert the Queen's Service at the dictation of the Canton Authorities in 1856.[646] And there was always in mind the memory of the occasion in 1857, when all the bread prepared for foreigners in Hong Kong one morning was poisoned with arsenic, and Chinese inhabitants were advised in advance not to taste the bread themselves.[647]

It may be as a tradition from the past that some

Chinese amahs today, when leaving an employment, offer to find a replacement or actually do introduce a designated successor whom they themselves have chosen on their own initiative. Today also, in the case of long-term amahs, the crumpled testimonials – bearing testimony to reliability, honesty, good health, English language skills, initiative, being good with children, cooking skills – are a treasured possession.

The registration ticket[648] that the Driscolls' amah speaks of resembles the contract that foreign maids and drivers (from the Philippines, Sri Lanka, Thailand) need, to work in Hong Kong today. Local Chinese amahs have the Identity Card, which all Hong Kong residents are obliged to have.

Finally, the household described in the Cutting and Wounding case introduces another domestic situation which was probably also not unusual. A Chinese widow living with another woman, described as her sister, was "under the protection" of a Chinese man. – Often, the term, "protected woman", is understood by writers about Hong Kong (for example, Revd Carl Smith) to mean a mistress.[649] Here, however, the fact that the man in question asked for money and stabbed the woman, the day after she refused to give him any, suggests that he may rather have been her pimp.

Apart from such court reports, other records survive of various Hong Kong domestic scenes. – Diaries tell of missionaries and their associates, and describe church services, missionary teas and extempore prayer. Others speak of businessmen and their wives, and picnics and social visits. Yet, although the worlds of missionary and leading businessman were culturally separate from those of lesser "European" residents, there was much less geographical separation than there is between similar groups today. In the 1850s, the Bishop's wife and her missionary friend, Miss Harriet Baxter, visited the soldiers' wives living in the lanes down the hill from the Bishop's home, St Paul's College. In the early 1880s, many of the small population of non-Chinese lived in or close to the Central District, some above shops or in schools. Similarly, although there was a notional line between the European

Central area and the Chinese area of Taipingshan, drawn perpendicularly towards the harbour, round about Aberdeen Street, in practice each group infiltrated the other. Customs and culture, language and the generation gap, personality and personal circumstances, these were the main dividers and also the greatest cause of conflict, not class or racial difference.

The Domestic Scene.
Wives & Husbands, Amahs & Cooks, Widows & Protected Women, Sons & Adopted Daughters, Burglars: Cases

WEDNESDAY 17 AUGUST 1881
ALLEGED ASSAULT[650]

James Joseph M'Breen, a clerk, belonging to Ireland, and George Blake, staff sergeant were charged with assaulting Jane M'Breen, wife of the first defendant.

Mr Mossop, who appeared for the complainant, asked that the summons against the second prisoner might be amended to aiding and abetting, and he produced a letter from first defendant to complainant. Mr Mossop requested that the summons might be withdrawn against the first defendant if he would consent to return her clothes, jewellery and money and agree to separation.

Remanded till to-morrow at 2 p.m. to see if the parties could come to some arrangement.

THURSDAY 18 AUGUST 1881
ALLEGED ASSAULT[651]

The case in which James Joseph M'Breen, a clerk, and George Blake, staff sergeant, were charged with assaulting the wife of the first defendant, was resumed this afternoon.

Mr Mossop, who appeared on behalf of the complainant, said that his client was Mrs. James M'Breen, wife of the first defendant. About nine months ago the two had been married, and since then they had lived most unhappily together. The first defendant at the time of the marriage was out of employment, and was for some time entirely supported by complainant; about four months ago he obtained employment in the Commissariat,[652] as a clerk, and from the time of his securing this clerkship up to now, he had ceased to live with the complainant, and ceased to allow her anything for her support, but had lived with the second defendant.[653] Complainant had requested her husband to live with her, but this he refused to do while in the house she then occupied. Accordingly rooms were taken at the Blue Buildings.[654] Defendant when asked to pay the rent by complainant, said he had not got the money. The two had gone to some Chinese friend and borrowed the money. Defendant however had not used this money to pay the rent, and on the evening of Sunday, the 7th, complainant had bitterly reproached him for appropriating the money to his own uses. On the evening of that day defendant had attacked her fiercely, struck her, knocked her down and jumped upon her, leaving some very severe marks on her body. She left the house in Blue Buildings and returned to the one she had formerly occupied,[655] to which place first defendant had gone and taken away a box containing personal clothing, jewellery, and money, by force. As his Worship had suggested yesterday with a view to an arrangement, the box had been opened in the presence of Mr Parker,[656] when it was found that not only the money and jewellery, but also some of the personal clothing, had been removed.

Complainant then went into the box.

Jane Francis M'Breen said she was the wife of the first defendant.[657] She was married to him nine months ago. When witness married him, she was living in No. 208, Queen's Road Central. First defendant, after marrying witness, left the police force, where he had been, and came and lived with witness. For four or five months witness entirely supported the first defendant. He got employment about four months ago in the Commissariat Department. The first day he got employment there he stopped in the Sergeants' Mess.[658] Since he had got work he had never given her any money. First day he got paid he had given her thirty dollars, but the next day he took them back. The second moon[659] he gave her eleven dollars and took away five dollars. Every evening he came up to see witness, she had to pay his 'rickshaw and give him cigar money. The third month he gave witness twenty dollars, but he asked her to take the gold ring out of pawn. For this she paid about five dollars for the redemption. The ring, for which she had paid, costs[660] about ten dollars. This was all the money she had received. In the latter part of July he asked witness to take lodgings so that they might live together. He took rooms next door to the American Consulate.[661]

Witness moved with her private effects. First defendant sometimes came and lived with her there. She asked him when rent was due to pay it. This was the week before last. He told her he had no money. First defendant asked witness to go to a friend's house and borrow the money for him. She and her husband went and borrowed the money from Mrs Aku, who handed the money to him. He did not pay the rent with this money. On the 7th *instant* the first defendant came to her house, when she asked him to pay twenty dollars of house rent, but he said he had spent the money. First defendant came there about 9 p.m. that evening, and as witness described it he was proper drunk. He gave her a slap in the face, knocked her down and jumped upon her. Witness called out for her cook to come and save her life.[662] The cook came and pulled the first defendant away from her. Her arms and legs were bruised. After this the first defendant went away. On the 14th of August the two defendants came to 208 Queen's Road, where she was then living. The first defendant said he must have a large box, which witness said belonged to her; she was quite agreeable to let him have a smaller one, but first defendant said he would take anything he liked; he was "boss" of the house. Four or five coolies came upstairs, but witness dismissed them, and then sent for an Indian Police Constable First defendant said witness had stolen the boxes. The whole party then went to the Central Station. The Inspector said he had nothing to say in the matter. They went down into Pottinger Street, when Sergeant Blake said to the husband "You take hold of her hands and I'll take the box." Her husband held her hands behind her back, and she cried out for police. A constable came from the charge room, and then her husband let her go. She and the two defendants proceeded as far as the Naval yard; two coolies carried the boxes – second defendant following. At this place witness got out of the chair and took hold of her own box. Her husband again held her hands, while the second defendant helped the coolies to put the box into a jinrickshaw. Afterwards she saw the second defendant take the box from the vehicle and put it into his house. In the box were one gold watch, value thirty-five dollars; one silver watch, ten dollars; one gold chain, thirty dollars; one neck chain, fifteen dollars; one pair earrings, five dollars thirty cents; one brooch, four dollars; two twenty-five dollar notes; thirty mexican dollars; and a quantity of clothes, value about one hundred and twenty dollars. There were two shirts which had been left with her for redemption for three dollars. There was nothing of her husband's in the box. The box was opened in the Magistracy office yesterday, and witness examined it. All her clothes were not there, and the jewellery and the money were gone.

Neither of the defendants wished to ask any questions at present.

Mr Mossop said they had no right to cross-examine the witness at a later stage, unless his Worship gave special permission.

His Worship agreed with this view.

First defendant wished to know from witness how he came to leave the police, and witness answered that she wished to employ him to manage the tavern, and requested him to leave the police force. She did not offer him two or three hundred dollars to leave. Defendant asked if he gave her any money while employed in the *Daily Press*. Witness said, Yes, but that he had got it all back. Witness knew nothing about a stipulation by the Commissary General that on getting the appointment in the Ordnance Store he should leave Queen's Road.[663] During the week they stopped in the Blue Buildings, first defendant came home every night. The cook boy complained of want of food, after witness left the house. She did not strike him with a chair on the Sunday night. The gentleman and lady living on the second floor asked defendant, not witness, whether the latter had been beaten. Witness did tear his shirt, but did not force him from the house. He did furnish a house for her, and she did leave it. She took away a number of things.

Re-examined: – The things she took away were witness's own property. She took away three chairs which her husband had bought. The only furnishing her husband provided consisted of five chairs. When first defendant could not pay for things he would have liked her to do so.

By the second defendant, on the 4th of August,

when the boxes were taken to the Central Station witness had no wish to go, but the policeman made her. The Police Constable did not tell second defendant to fetch the coolies, the second defendant told the Constable to do so. She did not hear her husband tell the Constable to call the coolies. Witness did not hear her husband ask the second defendant to help him to carry the box. Second defendant asked the Constable to carry the box. She did not push the box while being taken downstairs – she pulled it. It was her husband who told the coolies to put the box in the 'rickshaw. Witness was close to the 'rickshaw when her husband took hold of her hands.

Chan Asan, cook to the plaintiff, gave evidence as to the assault committed on the evening of the 7th *instant*.

Joseph Ramsay, Constable of the Naval Yard Police, said he was on duty at the gate in the 14th. He saw the first defendant holding complainant by the arms. She was shouting police. This was on the side-path about thirty yards from the gate. Witness did not see second defendant there.

By the second defendant: – Witness did not see two boxes being put into a rickshaw.

Re-examined: – Second defendant might have been there, but he did not see him.

The case was adjourned till half-past two on Saturday.

SATURDAY 20 AUGUST 1881
ALLEGED ASSAULT[664]

The case in which Joseph James M'Breen, clerk, and George Blake, staff sergeant, were charged, the former with assaulting his wife, and the latter with aiding and abetting therein, was finished this afternoon.

Mr Mossop, who again appeared for the complainant, applied that all witnesses leave the Court.

His Worship drew attention to the fact that the second defendant had nothing to do with the assault said to be made on 7th *instant*.

First defendant stated that the boxes were his property, and the Magistrate said that as he was the husband of plaintiff he could not deny that,[665] whereupon Mr

Mossop observed that if the boxes were not returned the case would not end in this Court.

Further evidence was then called.

C.A. Paterson, Police Constable 20, said he went down to Pottinger Street having heard a noise there. He saw the complainant get out of a chair and try to prevent the coolies from taking the boxes away. First defendant took hold of complainant's arms. Witness told him to let go and he did so. First defendant seemed to be stopping her from preventing the coolies taking the boxes.

By second defendant: – Witness did not hear him say anything to the first defendant.

This closed the case for the prosecution.

The first defendant wished to call Mr Parker to explain about the means he took to come to an arrangement.

Mr Mossop said he would object to that. Carl Siemund[666] said he saw first defendant and his wife on the night of the 7th about nine o'clock. He heard a dreadful noise as though somebody's throat had been cut. He went half way down stairs. The noise was simply disgraceful. The voice was a woman's. The woman was howling like a maniac. The first defendant was sitting as quiet as could be smoking his pipe. Witness asked him what was the matter, and whether she was drunk. He said no. The screaming was something about twenty-five dollars. First defendant said there had been no fighting whatever. The noise was most disgraceful, and latterly he went to the Police Station to see if he could get a policeman. She tried to incite him to strike her.

Mr Mossop: – Be careful.

Witness: There is no careful about it. She said "You likee flog me." Witness is quite certain about the words. When he went downstairs he found a European constable looking in at the window; he sent to the Station. Witness said first defendant was as drunk now as he was then (meaning that he was sober). Complainant had a couple of youngsters sitting howling in company with her, and the noise was dreadful. On the morning of the 8th, the yelling by complainant commenced again. Witness did not see complainant throw anything at first defendant.

By Mr Mossop: – Complainant did try to incite defendant to flog her. The words were "You wanchee flog my; You likee flog my."

Inspector Adams said he was in first defendant's house on the evening of the 7th August. On that day he was in first defendant's house. He was there seeing him and his wife. She was pulling and hauling about. It seemed to him that it was in earnest. It was about twenty-five dollars. This witness did not understand. Witness then left in disgust, as he did not think such conduct proper.

Mr Mossop objected to any evidence of anything that took place before the affair.

The Magistrate admitted the evidence.

Witness: – About eleven o'clock that night – he stopping next door to first defendant, – heard Mrs M'Breen calling her husband very filthy names. (Witness, at Mr Mossop's request, repeated one or two of them.) He heard first defendant say keep quiet. This continued for two or three minutes.

By Mr Mossop: – Witness would not give his opinion as to whether it was surprising, that if complainant had been assaulted at nine o'clock, she should have been abusing him at eleven o'clock.

Mr Mossop: I think you said something about them walking away.

Witness: I think you have made a mistake.

Mr Mossop: Perhaps I have; you may correct it.

Witness: No I won't.

Mr Mossop: Be careful; you are in a Court of Justice.

Witness: I think you had better be careful.

Mr Mossop again cautioned witness, who thanked him for his advice.

The Magistrate said Mr Mossop had a very delicate duty to perform, and Mr Adams should answer the question properly.

This witness then did.

Subject to Mr Mossop's objection, complainant was examined by her husband.

Mrs M'Breen, on being shown a ring, said it did not belong to her husband. It was the ring she had taken out of pawn.

First defendant then made a statement in defence. Complainant on the afternoon of the day in question asked him to go to Happy Valley. They went there; and when there complainant threw herself down upon a grave. He remained there for two hours, but she would not come away.

The Magistrate: Was the deceased any relative?

First defendant said he did not know. She said it was her late husband. Directly she came home she assaulted him violently, and kept up such a disagreeable row that he left and that night slept in the house of a friend. With regard to the taking of the box, his wife, when she left him, had taken away all the articles of furniture, food, and clothing, all his wearing apparel, and some of his linen, as also some articles he had got from Mr Cassumbhoy, also two or three pairs of white trousers. She had afterwards gone and taken away the small box. He was rather doubtful of going to the house himself, and so he asked if second defendant would kindly go with him. Prior to this he had asked the Captain Superintendent of Police to send a policeman with him for his protection, but he said he could not do this. When first defendant arrived there he wished to remove the small box, but she sat down on the top of it and began screaming. He said if she did not be quiet he would not only take the small box but the large one. An Indian Constable came, and first defendant asked him to get coolies to remove the boxes. The boxes ultimately were taken to the Central Station. The Inspector there would have nothing to do with the matter. In Pottinger Street he asked the second defendant to take charge of the boxes. He held his wife, who was screaming police.[667] When the constable came he let go[668] and walked by the side of her chair as far as the Hotel de l'Univers. He next saw her beyond the Dock-yard gate, where she was violently abusing the second defendant. The boxes were taken away solely under his superintendence.

The second defendant said he would like to say a few words about an assertion made by Mr Mossop in his opening speech, which seriously affected his character as a military man. He referred to the statement that the first defendant had lived with him.[669] As he had only one room, and he was a married man, this would not have been decent, and beside he was not allowed to keep lodgers.

The Magistrate said he was sure that Mr Blake[670] would do nothing which was not proper. Of course Mr Mossop was acting under instructions, which was quite a different thing from what Mr Mossop might do individually. It was a delicate matter, and he was bound to say that Mr Mossop had conducted the case very properly.

Mr Mossop said that he did not think that the complainant meant to infer[671] that first defendant lived in the same room with the Sergeant.[672]

Mr Mossop then addressed his Worship on the case. He thought it was a most imprudent thing on the part of a Staff Sergeant – a man who ought to have known better – to go into his client's private room and aid in taking away these boxes. He had no hesitation in saying that the evidence of the complainant did not support the assertion that first defendant had lived with the Sergeant.[673]

The Magistrate said as far as the Sergeant[674] was concerned the summons was dismissed. His Worship was sorry he had got into this disagreeable affair. If he had known then what he knew now, probably he would never have been mixed up in it. With regard to the assault on the 7th, the evidence given today had put a very different complexion upon it. Besides, the corrections made upon her own evidence had led him to doubt the complainant's truthfulness. Although there was much in the case which should not have been, yet he could not say that the assault had been proved against the first defendant. Mr Seimund had said that, though complainant was screaming like a maniac,[675] the husband was calmly smoking his pipe.

Altogether he could not convict the first defendant of the assault; and therefore the summons would be discharged.~~~~~

TUESDAY 20 SEPTEMBER 1881
HABITUALLY ILL-TREATING A LITTLE GIRL[676]

Li Achoy, fifty-six, of Shanghai, wife of Fung Awai, was charged with assaulting and ill-treating a female named An Asam, at different times during the last seven days.

An Kam Yan, Police Constable 311, said that today about 10 a.m., he saw defendant beat the little girl she was charged with ill-treating. She slapped the girl's face very severely. The girl cried and some of the neighbours made witness arrest the defendant, as she had beaten the girl before. Did not know defendant. The girl is betrothed to defendant's son. Defendant lives in Tank Lane.

Lam Yun, broom maker, Tanner Lane, Tai-ping-shan, about 7 a.m. saw the girl jump into a well in the Lane; ran to her and took her out; she said – "I don't want to be taken out, I want go home,[677] I rather die here." The girl's clothes were all wet. Took her home and saw defendant there; defendant slapped her face.

I Azs, wife of Ching Agan, living in the second floor of the house, the second of which is occupied by the defendant though the one enters from Caine Road and the other from Tank Lane, said the defendant often beat the little girl. Witness often heard her crying bitterly. Saw the girl fished out of the well and taken home. Defendant is a wife of a marine hawker.[678]

Leung Kam Yew, widow living in Tank Lane, said that this morning she saw the little girl jump into the well, and saw first witness run out and save her. Witness said it was the common talk of the neighbourhood that the defendant habitually ill treats the little girl.

Li Along, coolie, living in San Lane, off Caine Road, next door to defendant said he often saw the defendant beating the girl. Had seen defendant beat the girl unmercifully with firewood. The girl often cried bitterly. Defendant sometimes beat her as often as four or five times a day. Last saw the girl beaten four or five days ago, when a bamboo was used.

The girl herself, An Asam, said she was fifteen years of age. Her mother was dead. Her father gave her to the defendant to be her adopted daughter, about six years ago. She cut her lips when she accidentally fell into the well this morning.

The case was adjourned, without the girl's evidence being further gone into until the 27th *instant*, the defendant being admitted to bail in fifty dollars, two householders in twenty-five dollars each.

TUESDAY 27 SEPTEMBER 1881
HABITUALLY ILL TREATING A LITTLE GIRL[679]

Li Achoy, fifty-six, of Shanghai, wife of one Fung Awai, was charged with assaulting and ill-treating a female named An Asam, at different times during the last seven days.

The case was last before the court on the 20th, when it was fully reported in our columns.

An Asam's evidence was now continued. She said: Defendant treats me very badly; she sometimes beats me with firewood. I jumped into the well, because I was hungry, because I do not get enough to eat. Sometimes I get no food, but I had had a meal early that morning. Whenever I take anything to eat, defendant beats me. Defendant slapped my face when I was taken out of the well.

To defendant: – No one taught me what to say here.

Defendant said: The people above let dirty water run down into my room, and I scolded them for this. They have, for revenge, taught the girl to accuse me. I thanked the man who took the girl from the well, and gave him two hundred cash as tea money. I do not know why the girl jumped into the well. I was not out of bed when it happened. I slap the girl when she is naughty.

The Magistrate sentenced the woman to fourteen days' imprisonment with hard labour.~~~~~

THE BURGLARY AT BELLEVUE[680]

Ng Aking, thirty-three, wife of one Wong Fuk, was charged yesterday, with the unlawful possession of a gold watch value forty dollars, burglariously stolen from the residence (Bellevue) of Mr George Scott, manager of the Overseas Banking Corporation, on the 20th July last.

Inspector Perry formally charged the defendant on the 16th *instant*, when a remand was granted to enable him to find the defendant's husband.

Mr Scott's evidence was now taken. He identified the watch as his wife's and stated: On 7th July, between two and three o'clock a.m. a travelling clock worth about forty-five dollars, a pencil case worth twenty-five or thirty dollars, and the watch in court worth about fifty dollars, were taken from his bed-room. Attached to the watch by a ribbon were a key and the pencil case; the key was a Chubb's one and belonged to a cash box. His bedroom opened on to the verandah facing the harbour. All the doors were open. Any person entering must have come from the cook-house roof. He was disturbed by the barking of a dog in his room. At ten minutes past two o'clock the clock was in its place; he knew this because his wife got up then to look at the time. At 3.15 the clock was gone; he knew this because he got up then to look at the time. It was between these two times that the barking of the dog took place. At 3.15 he missed the watch and its appendages, as well as the clock. He went into the verandah in consequence of the barking of the dog. Saw nothing there; it was when he came in again that he missed the clock, watch, &c.; went down stairs and roused the servants. The house-coolie brought up a light and he found the mark of a bare foot on the balustrade of the verandah just above the roof of the cook-house, which was easily accessible from the ground at the back. Did not know the defendant.

Ting Apik, accountant in the Ki Hing pawn-shop at the corner of Queen's Road and Wing On Lane, said that on July 20th, about noon, defendant brought the watch in court to witness; asked her to whom it belonged. Defendant said it belonged to a woman named Asam who asked her to bring it to the pawn-shop. The defendant said she wanted a loan on it of ten dollars. He gave her the money and pawn-ticket Number 5,037; defendant gave the name of Ng Ting residing in Number seventy-five Fung Man Lane. Told one of his men to follow the defendant when she left the shop, and he did so. Never saw defendant before. About eleven or twelve days ago the police came to his shop looking for a watch. Showed them the one in Court; was asked who pawned it. He told them the name and the address the woman had given. The Inspector said there was no such number as seventy-five there. Witness said he did not know the number but knew the house; went there and found Asam, who said she knew who pawned the watch, but denied that it belonged to her. Had no doubt whatever that the defendant was the woman who pawned the watch. Was taken into the gaol about a week ago, and picked out the defendant from amongst six or seven women who were prisoners.

I Awan, coolie in the same pawnshop, said that on the 20th *ulto.*, after the defendant had pawned the watch now in Court, or one very like it, receiving eight taels, he followed her by order of the last witness and found that she went into a house in Tung-Man-Lane which he could point out; went back and told last witness that on the ground floor of the house this woman went into was the Kwong Sun Lung shop. Last witness wrote that on the paper in which the watch was wrapped up. Was positively certain that the defendant pawned a gold watch on the date he had mentioned; was taken into the gaol about a week ago and picked out the defendant from among six or seven women.

The case was remanded till the 1st *proximo*.[681]

SATURDAY 1 OCTOBER 1881
THE ROBBERY FROM BELLEVUE[682]

The case in which a Chinese woman named Ng Aking was charged with being in unlawful possession of a gold watch belonging to Mr George O. Scott, was resumed today.

Inspector Perry was recalled and detailed the circumstances of the finding of the watch, and the arrest of the prisoner.

Defendant said that on the 11th *ultimo* she met Police Sergeant Pang Loi in the street. He asked her if she had become rich, and asked her for the loan of a few dollars. She said she was too poor to do so. The Sergeant said "all right" and went away. On the 15th the Sergeant returned and arrested her in Tai Wai Street. She was put in gaol, and in a line with several others. Before doing this Sergeant Pang Loi told the witness that the woman who had lost two front teeth was the person wanted.[683] In this way, the witness pointed her out. She had nothing more to say.

Prisoner was fined ten dollars,[684] in default three months in gaol with hard labour.

THURSDAY 10 NOVEMBER 1881
A REFRACTORY SERVANT[685]

Fung Akai, a cook, was charged yesterday with leaving his employer's service on the 7th *instant*, without giving reasonable notice.[686]

Inspector Whitehead said the defendant was in his employ. About half-past one on the afternoon of the 7th he was sent to market to procure some fish for dinner, but nothing more was seen of him till half-past eleven on the forenoon of the next day. Witness sent his interpreter to the prisoner's house to make enquiries respecting him, and he returned with a message that defendant had left because Mrs Whitehead would not let him have any firewood.

Defendant said that when he asked his mistress for firewood she ordered him to take some rails from the fence, but he said if the police saw him he would be arrested. She beat him and turned him away.

At this point the case was remanded till this morning for the attendance of Mrs Whitehead, who now said she had sent the defendant to the market for fish and fowl. He returned without the fish and she declined to take the fowl which he brought. She then told him to send the coolie back to the market with the fowl, but he need not go himself. He then went away, and she saw nothing more of him till next day. She did not beat him, nor did she dismiss him from her service.

Fined one pound sterling,[687] or seven days' imprisonment with hard labour.~~~~~

FRIDAY 30 DECEMBER 1881
CUTTING AND WOUNDING[688]

Ngau was charged with cutting and wounding Chu Atam, a woman under his protection, on the 8th November.

Chu Atam said she was a widow, living under the defendant's protection in Number thirty-three, Upper Lascar Row. On the 8th November the defendant asked her for some money but was refused, he then went out and did not return that day. On the following night defendant returned and she opened the door to him, and while proceeding upstairs before him, felt a stab in the right shoulder. The wound bled very much, but she was able to go and make a report at the Station, whence she was taken to the Civil Hospital, where she remained twenty-seven days. Defendant ran away after stabbing the complainant, and she only discovered his return to the Colony on the 28th when he was taken in charge.

Chü Apin, sister of the complainant, said she lived with her sister and witnessed defendant strike her but thought it was with his hand and not with a knife. On hearing her sister's cries she ran downstairs and went to the door, but defendant was gone.

Dr. Marques, Assistant Superintendent at the Civil Hospital, gave evidence as to admitting Chü Atam on the 8th November suffering from an incised wound, one inch deep and one inch in length, and said the wound had probably been inflicted with a knife or some sharp instrument.

Defendant denied the charge but had no witnesses to call.

Sentenced to six months' imprisonment with hard labour.~~~~~

FRIDAY 3 MARCH 1882
AN OLD MAN'S TROUBLES[689]

Liu Him, Liu Hing, and Liu Luk were charged with assaulting Liu Fuk on the 2nd *inst.*

Liu Fuk stated that he was unemployed. Between five and six p.m. while he was walking in Centre Street the third defendant, an uncle of his, seized him and took him to his father's shop. There his legs and hands were tied up by the three defendants. A Police Constable seeing this entered the house and arrested them, though the witness was not calling out. His father and mother were in the house at the time. These measures were taken to prevent him going out to play, which his father would not give him permission to do.

Liu Hip-kat said the complainant was his son, the first defendant his cousin, the second and third nephews. His son was a very bad youth, spending witness's money in gambling and other bad practices. His intention was to send the son to his native country to school, and thereby remove him from temptation. The witness cried bitterly while giving his evidence and stated that he would be without hope in his old age if the son emigrated as he threatened to do. The defendants had used no unnecessary violence.

The Magistrate cautioned and discharged the defendants.~~~~~

MONDAY 27 MARCH 1882
A DISORDERLY AMAH[690]

Yau Akan, an amah, was charged with leaving her employment without leave,[691] and also with creating a disturbance in her employer's house on the 23rd *instant*.

The case was adjourned from Saturday, on which occasion the following evidence was given:

T. N. Driscoll, tailor and outfitter, Queen's Road Central, said that defendant was told to go and get her dinner about six o'clock on the evening of the 23rd. Shortly after, his little girl seemed to have told the defendant to make haste, at which the defendant had become angry, made some disturbance, and used very bad language. Witness went downstairs to know the cause of the disturbance, when the defendant abused him and wanted to know why the child was sent down to tell her to make haste. He corrected the child before the defendant, told her to finish her food and go upstairs. A few minutes after this the defendant went upstairs and commenced to yell. Witness put her in her room, but several times she renewed the disturbance. When wanted to put the children to bed she could not be found in the house.

The defendant said she wanted her dinner, the boys and coolies were busy and she could not get it, and her mistress wanted her to take the child. Witness went for her dinner, and when she returned her mistress checked her, slapped her face, and kicked her. Witness then asked her wages, and said she would leave, but these were refused. After the children were bedded she told her master, mistress, and all the servants that she intended to leave. Her master seized hold of her and would not let her go. She afterwards reported the matter at the station, and had come to Court next day to take out a summons, but instead she received a letter to take to her master's, where she was given into custody.

The case was resumed this morning when Mrs Driscoll said she returned from a walk about six o'clock, asked the defendant if she had had dinner, told her, after being answered in the negative, to go and get it. Witness gave the child no orders to the amah; defendant became angry, and made use of abusive language. Witness said defendant was very noisy and abusive for some time and tried to get on to the verandah to scream and attract the attention of neighbours.

Kwok Akau, coolie, said he saw the last witness slap defendant on both sides of the face, while the latter held the baby. The master then took the baby from defendant and then the mistress kicked defendant, who fell down.

James Parker, first clerk at the Magistracy, said the defendant came to the Court on the 23rd or 24th *instant* and applied for a summons against Mrs Driscoll. As the Court was closed he bade the defendant return next day. She came back next day and renewed her application, adding that she would be content to let the matter drop if her clothes, registration ticket, wages and testimonials were given her. Witness reported the matter to Dr Stewart (the Sitting Magistrate), who asked witness to write Mr Driscoll to see whether the matter could be amicably arranged. He wrote, and soon afterwards Mr Driscoll came to the office and said he had given the defendant into custody.

The Magistrate found the charge proved and fined the defendant two dollars, with the option of two days' imprisonment.

Wednesday 29 March 1882
MR DRISCOLL'S AMAH AGAIN[692]
Before H. E. Wodehouse[693]

Mr T. N. Driscoll charged Kun Ayan with disorderly conduct in his house on the 28th *instant*. He stated that he went from his store to his house, 3 West Terrace, with the intention of partaking of luncheon. At the entrance to the Terrace he saw a crowd of several coolies and the defendant, who was talking very loudly and was very excited. On noticing the complainant the defendant ran up the hill in the direction of Robinson Road. From what he afterwards learned, he took out a summons against the defendant. He also stated that Mrs Driscoll was ill and unable to appear.

Leung Alai, house-boy to Mr Driscoll, said the defendant was an amah with his master until the other day, when she was fined two dollars by the Magistrate for leaving service without notice. Yesterday she came to the house and applied for a pair of stockings, a tin of tea, and a small bamboo, which things she had left behind. Witness admitted her, and she followed upstairs to his mistress's room, where her mistress told the defendant the articles were not in the house. The latter persisted that they were in the house. His mistress told the defendant to leave, and dragged her downstairs. The defendant on this called out "save life" and made a considerable noise.

After the defendant stating that what she really wanted was her wages, and that she had gone there at that hour because she knew her late master had luncheon at that time, the magistrate discharged her. ~~~~~

Prostitutes, their Associates and Clients

Although times change, Hong Kong has been known as a society separated into groups, communicating little, if at all, with each other. On the surface, at least, this seems true even of the brothels, or perhaps *especially* of the brothels, in the Nineteenth Century. There were brothels for non-Chinese clients and there were brothels for Chinese clients.[694] But a second glance shows a different picture. For who were the prostitutes in most of these brothels? – mainly Chinese. Unlike the French, British Empire-builders did not take their own prostitutes with them.[695] The handful of Caucasian prostitutes in Nineteenth Century Hong Kong probably never exceeded twenty at any one time. Given the well-documented enthusiasm of British soldiers and sailors in patronising the Hong Kong brothels, it follows that there was a great deal of contact between Chinese and non-Chinese in these premises at least. Indeed, when, in 1880-1882, there was reduced enforcement of the Contagious Diseases Ordinance of 1867, the Garrison of Hong Kong fast regained "that notoriety it has previously had as to the magnitude of its sick list",[696] a delicate way of reporting a huge increase in venereal disease among the British troops.

An Ordinance of 1845 had made brothels illegal in Hong Kong, although no action could be taken unless a complaint was made. It was also an offence for females, but not males, to solicit in public places.[697] Prostitution itself was not illegal. There was a large number of single men in the Colony (both Chinese and non-Chinese) and both the government and the police turned a blind eye to the innumerable brothels that there were. Still known as such today, Wanchai was a red light district almost from the first and five brothels for the garrison were opened by the military in the 1850s.[698]

It was concern for the health of the British garrison troops in Hong Kong, which had led to the contentious 1857 Ordinance for checking the spread of Venereal Disease. After similar concern led to the passing in the United Kingdom[699] of the Contagious Diseases Ordinance of 1867, the 1857 Hong Kong Ordinance was replaced with the Hong Kong Contagious Diseases Ordinance of 1867.

Under the latter, Miners writes, based on a document dated 1879 and describing the situation in 1878, "all prostitutes were required to attend for a weekly inspection at the Lock Hospital and were then issued with a certificate of good health which could be shown to their clients, and those found to be diseased were detained at the hospital until cured." However, Miners continues, using the same source, "Chinese prostitutes catering for Chinese clients . . . objected vigorously to being examined internally by a European doctor, and would prefer to suffer any punishment rather than submit to such an indignity. So compulsory medical inspections were imposed only on the inmates of brothels catering for the European population, principally servicemen and seamen. The Registrar General had the legal power to compel other prostitutes to be medically examined, but if they became diseased they normally made their own arrangements with Chinese doctors or herbalists or were sent back to Canton by the brothel-keepers."[700]

By the time of Stewart's court, July 1881 to March 1882, the situation may have changed. Certainly, the few Caucasian prostitutes in Hong Kong in the 1880s were treated somewhat differently than Miners describes. Probably because they did not deal with the troops, they were not required to submit to examination. However, very sensibly, they attended voluntarily. Thus, the minutes of an Executive Council meeting, held on 2 July 1884, report that the Colonial Surgeon had suggested that European women, voluntarily submitting to medical examination under the Contagious Diseases Ordinance Number 10 of 1867, should be required to pay a registration fee of five Hong Kong dollars. But it was advised that there was no legal power to enforce this payment.[701]

It seems, certainly as of June 1884, that there was also no power to require "European" prostitutes to live in specific locations. The minutes of an Executive Council meeting, held on 5 June 1884 – a couple of years only after Stewart held his court – refer to correspondence about their living separately. It was noted, however, that the Government had no power to interfere. "But they should be warned that if their houses become a nuisance they will be proceeded against according to law . . .".[702] Similarly, women kept by foreigners could not be confined to any particular area under the Ordinance.[703]

Priests, missionaries and like-minded people among Caucasians opposed the licensing of brothels and considered the trade and its customers shameful and immoral (as well as an obstacle to the work of converting the Chinese). Writing as late as 1896, the second headmaster of the Government Central School for Boys (by now named Queen's College) spoke of "the immoral reputation of the immediate neighbourhood" of the school, "it being a matter of common knowledge that brothels and secret gambling dens abound, which prove a source of ruin to several of our scholars".[704] For a number of years, there was a Roman Catholic church in Wellington Street, an area where a number of women kept by foreigners lived. Wellington Street was a main thoroughfare at that time, and Roman Catholic women and children – three quarters of the foreign population of the island – saw these women daily. In 1877, Roman Catholic Bishop Raimondi complained about the possible worsening of the situation when new buildings came into use; and unknown "respectable residents" complained to the Governor about women who had "beckoned" priests. An article critical of the Registrar General's Department for permitting the nuisance was published in the *Catholic Register*.[705] At least one member of the Hong Kong public took a dim view of the complaint. "Peeping Tom" wrote to *The China Mail*, "Allow me to suggest that in order to compel the Governor's attention to the next issue of the *Catholic Register* [– Hennessy had said that he had not read the article –] the name of that publication be changed to *The Wanchai Mirror*.[706] Records survive that show clearly that at least some members of civil society seem to have regarded visiting brothels almost as a fashionable habit.[707]

As for the majority Chinese population, this was heavily skewed in favour of males. Families of "respectable" men were only just beginning to be brought to Hong Kong; [708] and the working men were mainly unmarried. It is not surprising that brothels had so many Chinese clients.

The period of reduced enforcement of the Contagious Diseases Ordinance, already mentioned, included the entire period during which Stewart heard the cases reported in this book. It is not as surprising as it would otherwise be, therefore, that none of the reports of the twenty hearings quoted in the following section show brothels where servicemen clients met Chinese prostitutes. (It appears that, in these *China Mail* court cases, the terms, "inmate of a brothel" and "brothel" always refer to Chinese prostitutes, and that the term, "single woman" is a pointer to a Caucasian prostitute.) Presumably the absence of such cases is an accurate reflection of the fact that relatively few offences against the Contagious Diseases Ordinance were brought to court at this time. At the end of this period, *The China Mail* states, looking back: "Occasionally a case has been brought up and the offenders punished, but no energetic attempt to grapple with this crying evil has been made."[709]

Eighteen of the nineteen cases quoted below [710] substantiate and put additional flesh on the little that has already been written about three other prostitution situations in Nineteenth Century Hong Kong, where the garrison was *not* involved: – one, brothels in the Taipingshan area, where both prostitutes and clients were Chinese; another, Caucasian prostitutes, living and working in the Central district (in this case, in Gage Street), who presumably received Caucasian clients;[711] and the third (represented by only one of these cases), [712] a brothel with Chinese prostitutes and non-Chinese clients. Three men with non-Chinese names appear in this last case. But one (the complainant) was a merchant. And the two brothel clients who appeared as *defendants* in Stewart's court are not stated as members of the garrison. In none of these situations, therefore, would we, in fact, expect any case to be brought under the Contagious Diseases Ordinance, even when it was being vigorously enforced, because (as already mentioned), the Ordinance was applied mainly or entirely in relation to brothels the garrison patronised.

In these nineteen cases, the locations of from two to four brothels are mentioned: Square Street (mentioned five times), Caine Road (no street number is given), 44 Caine Road, and (presumably) 25 East Street.[713] All are in either the Central or the Taipingshan areas. (An area within the former was assigned to Caucasian prostitutes, and an area in the latter was assigned to brothels for Chinese clients.) None are in Wanchai, where, apparently,[714] the brothels for the garrison were confined.

What do these nineteen cases show? All but four of the people reported as appearing before the court are Chinese. Among the Chinese mentioned, sixteen are prostitutes, four are brothel mistresses and one is a male brothel manager. (The names are generally not given, so double-counting is possible, although this is not in fact suggested by the material.)[715] One only of the nineteen cases mentions a European prostitute (although the woman friend, whose lack of money and indisposition caused the event complained of, is evidently also a prostitute and certainly also European). One case (not the one involving Caucasian prostitutes) mentions three Caucasian clients at one brothel.

In eight cases, the *complainants* are described as an "inmate of a brothel", or the "mistress of a brothel". Of the complaints which were sustained, there were two cases of the theft of clothes and/or jewelry, one theft of a clock and two smoking pipes (presumably for opium), one of damaging a blanket and other articles by throwing strong sulphuric acid over them, one of assault and creating a disturbance, two of disorderly conduct (one consisting of making a noise and damaging the roof, presumably of a brothel, and one consisting of throwing lighted crackers into a brothel). In a ninth case, a male employed as a cook at a brothel complained of another Chinese male stealing a ham.

In one of these cases, a charge of earring snatching was brought against a fireman, but when it was discovered that the complainant kept a brothel, where the defendant had been, the result (as reported) was somewhat puzzling.

The *defendant* was *discharged*, and *the complainant* was *charged* – with giving false evidence, as the caption and not the story claims.

A similar turning of the tables occurred in another case, in which a Chinese man brought a charge against a Chinese coolie. When the defendant stated that the complainant was the keeper of a "sly" (or unlicensed) brothel, the *coolie* was discharged, and the *complainant himself* was charged with bringing a malicious charge.

In only two of these cases were prostitutes themselves brought to court under a charge. In one of them, nine prostitutes (including the madam) were up for disorderly conduct; for making a noise in the street. The other involved a brothel inmate (stated to be from Canton), who seems to have been possessed of a quite different character. She was charged with attempted suicide by swallowing opium dross, after an argument about money. When her mother appeared in court, asking for the girl's release and stating that she would look after her, the girl was cautioned and discharged.

Prostitutes did not only appear as complainants and defendants, however. They also appeared as witnesses; and their evidence was given the same weight, case by case, as that of any other witness. In the case where a clock and two smoking pipes were allegedly stolen from her brothel, the brothel mistress gave evidence. The defendant was ordered to find five dollars security from each of two householders to be of good behaviour for six weeks. If the security was not forthcoming, he was to be committed. In the case where a member of a Chinese gang was charged with creating a row in a brothel in Square Street, an inmate of a brothel was a witness. This case is mentioned in an editorial, which omits to report the sentence. What it does report – and this is the reason for the editorial – is the rumour that there was a gang of about a hundred men in the area, armed with fighting weapons, a clear sign, as Geoffrey Roper glancingly indicates, of triad activity. There is no doubt that the prostitute's corroboration, of what the "native constable" said, was given considerable weight, both by magistrate Stewart and *The China Mail*.[716]

Similarly, the sentences given when Chinese and non-Chinese prostitutes were complainants show that offences against them that were proved were taken as seriously as those against any other members of the community. (In this group of nineteen of Stewart's 1881/1882 court cases in general, it seems to be true that the sentence was most severe for assaults with aggravating circumstances, less severe for thefts, false evidence and malicious charges, and less severe again for unaggravated assaults and disturbances.) One of the sentences for theft from a prostitute was three month's imprisonment with hard labour; another, four month's imprisonment with hard labour. On the other hand, as we have seen, in two cases, brothel managers who brought charges were themselves charged, one with giving false evidence and the other for bringing a malicious charge. Again, a case against one prostitute was dismissed, presumably because it was trivial, or because it seemed there was fault on both sides. All other magistrates may have been equally even-handed. However, it is worth noting that, in 1893, Stewart was remembered as insisting that girls rescued from prostitution, and whose marriages had been arranged by the Po Leung Kuk (the "Protect the Innocent Society"), should be given the same marriage ceremonies as every other Chinese woman. "He would not allow them to be treated in any way different from respectable women. . . . he intended to show his respect for them as much as he would for his own daughter had he one."[717]

The only difference in the treatment of prostitutes in court, compared with anyone else, seems to be that their names tended not to be stated in court, or perhaps, not reported in this newspaper.[718]

In one case, it was a man, working at a brothel, who was charged. A former tinsmith, now a "brothel bully" (what we call a "bouncer" today), was charged with assault, possession of a deadly weapon, and being out at night without a light or pass.

In several cases, as already mentioned, a brothel was the *scene* of an alleged offence. Other cases involved *clients* of brothels. A Chinese male, with no occupation, in

Hong Kong for the previous five months to visit a friend, accused a Chinese man, stated to be a tailor, with assaulting him with an iron bar at a brothel in Square Street. A Chinese member of a gang was himself charged with creating a row also in a brothel in Square Street.

In another case, an emigrant, returning from the goldfields of America with pockets full after twenty-five years, seems to have made up the story that he had been enticed to a brothel, where he was robbed; for, when asked to do so, he failed to identify the brothel. A brothel was mentioned, it seems, because the man considered a brothel a plausible location for such an occurrence, and thought that mentioning one would support his story.

Two cases show interesting points of view, about brothels and about life. As part of his evidence, doubtless intending to show that he was making serious attempts to earn an honest living, a Chinese man, recently arrived in Hong Kong, and accused of pickpocketing, stated that he had sent his wife to a brothel while he was planning to set up as a hawker. In another, a Chinese who said he had arrived from Shek Loong two days previously and was on the way to Foochow, defended himself against the charge of theft from a brothel, and was obscurely reported as stating that he thought it was Chinese custom to go anywhere one wanted in a brothel, but that when he had wanted to settle himself down to smoke a pipe of opium, the prostitute complainant had tried to turn him out.

In these cases as a whole, the clients of Chinese brothels, who are mentioned, are a tailor, a Hong Kong visitor of no occupation, a money-changer, a boatman, a fireman, and the former servant for nine years of Sir John Smale (the Chief Justice), now employed in a soda water factory.

As for the two cases involving Caucasians, in one, both complainant and defendants were Caucasians; and in the other, the complainant was Chinese and the defendant Caucasian.

In the first, a Hong Kong merchant, living in Pottinger Street, accused two other European men of assaulting him in a brothel. Their sentence was two dollars each or four days in gaol with hard labour. Stewart was evidently even-handed also, as between Chinese and non-Chinese. For this sentence was similar to the one he gave to two Chinese men, charged with assaulting the inmate of a licensed brothel, creating a disturbance and smashing crockery and other things. They were fined a dollar each, or, if they failed to pay, four days in prison; and additionally, twenty cents for damages, or two additional days in prison.

In the second case where Caucasians were involved, a Chinese tailor charged a European woman with pulling his ear when he pressed her friend (presumably, as said above, a prostitute) for money she owed. The *defendant* is explicitly stated (in the way used at the time) to be a prostitute (a "single woman"). Christini[719] Brown, "of Germany", gave opposing evidence that, when the tailor continued to clamour for instant payment of a debt from her friend, she (Christini) took him by the collar of his coat. She was showing him the door, when the complainant slapped her face. She threatened to summons him for assault, but he beat her to it. – The case was dismissed.

The reason for the reduced enforcement, during 1880-1882, of the Contagious Diseases Ordinance of 1867 was apparently the interest taken in the subject by Governor John Pope Hennessy,[720] who had arrived in Hong Kong in April 1877, and who left in March 1882. Cynics in Hong Kong and London argued that Hennessy wished to look good before the House of Commons;[721] that he would and did argue that the absence of prosecutions proved a reduction of offences, and hence, the success of his own various law enforcement policies.[722] But in reality, this inaction had led to, "an enormous increase of unlicensed brothels."[723] Once Hennessy left Hong Kong, it was hoped that matters would return to the status quo.[724]

When Hennessy left, Dr Stewart was invited by the incoming administration to occupy a higher post in the civil service, and there are thus no consequences to evaluate in Stewart's magistrate's court. The Contagious Diseases Ordinance continued in force until 1894, however, and when it was repealed, under pressure from London, the results were such that a similar system was introduced extra-legally in 1900, continuing up to 1932. Crisswell and Watson state that when brothels were officially closed by the police in 1932,[725] this led to a great increase in the number of so-called "sly" brothels and street-walkers, as had happened previously, during the period 1894-1900. Subsequently, in the 1960s and 1970s, Wanchai was a popular area for American sailors on "Rest and Recreation" visits to Hong Kong. Richard Mason's novel, *The World of Susie Wong*, published in 1957, draws the scene very clearly. And so does Arthur Hacker's *Wanchai*, published much more recently, in 1997. In his essay, "A Flavour of the Times", in the present book, Garry Tallentire, writing in 1999, reports that he hears about fifteen to twenty vice-related offences a month in *his* magistrate's court today.

Within the period of Stewart's court, *The China Mail* quoted Sir John Smale, in turn quoting Hong Kong barrister, J. J. Francis, as stating that he had calculated from official figures that there were over 18,000 prostitutes and only about 6,000 respectable Chinese women in Hong Kong.[726] Our handful of cases, therefore, may be taken, to some extent, as illuminating the lives of the majority of Chinese women in Hong Kong at this time.

Asian newspapers today occasionally condemn what is presented as modern-day sex tourism, focussing on Caucasians who travel to their countries on short visits. But the topic of prostitutes and their associates and clients in Nineteenth Century Hong Kong shows that the exploitation of women in this way (little is said about males) was a part of two systems at least, existing in almost monstrous proportions in both the Caucasian and the Chinese worlds. It illustrates also the widening divergence between public opinion in England and Hong Kong, which some might put down to cultural adaptation or consider perhaps as sensitivity to other customs and cultures.

~~~~~

THE CONTAGIOUS DISEASES ORDINANCE, 1867.

It is hereby notified that the part of the house hereinafter mentioned, that is to say, First Floor of No. 3, Aberdeen Street, was on the 29th day of September, 1882, pursuant to Section 23 of the above Ordinance, declared by me under my Hand and Seal of Office to be an Unlicensed Brothel.

J. Russell
Registrar General[727]

THE CONTAGIOUS DISEASES ORDINANCE, 1867.

It is hereby notified that the part of the house hereinafter mentioned, that is to say, First Floor of No. 1D, Aberdeen Street, was on the 21st day of September, 1882, pursuant to Section 23 of the above Ordinance, declared by me under my Hand and Seal of Office to be an Unlicensed Brothel.

J. Russell
Registrar General[728]

58. *Unlicensed Brothels: originally bilingual notices published in "The Hong Kong Government Gazette" of 30 September 1882.*

Prostitutes, their Associates and Clients
Cases

MONDAY 8 AUGUST 1881
ASSAULT[729]
Two Chinamen charged with assaulting an inmate of a
licensed brothel, creating a disturbance, and smashing
crockery ware, &c., were sentenced to pay a fine of one
dollar each or four days' imprisonment, and ordered to pay
twenty cents for damage, or two days' additional
imprisonment.~~~~~

TUESDAY 30 AUGUST 1881
[LARCENY][730]
Lan Aping, 29, boatman, was sentenced to three months'
imprisonment with hard labour for stealing clothing and
jewellery to the value of twenty-two dollars and fifty cents
from the inmate of a brothel.~~~~~

WEDNESDAY 13 [*sic* for 14], SEPTEMBER 1881[731]
LARCENY OF JEWELLERY[732]
Sun Yeung Mun was charged by the inmate of a brothel
with stealing a quantity of jewellery.

    After evidence had been heard defendant was
sent to gaol for four months with hard labour.~~~~~

FRIDAY 16 SEPTEMBER 1881
ASSAULT[733]
Nocheum Greenstang and Benjamin Flin were charged by
Joseph Greenberg with assaulting him.

    Complainant said he was a merchant residing in
Pottinger Street. He had gone into a brothel where the
defendants were. They set upon him and beat him, and the
first defendant also beat him on the left hand. After calling
"Police"[734] two constables came to his assistance. After
some more evidence had been heard both defendants were
fined two dollars each or four days in gaol with hard
labour.~~~~~

MONDAY 19 SEPTEMBER 1881
THEFT OF HAM[735]

Un Afuk was charged by Chan Alam with stealing a piece of ham from him on the 17th inst.

Complainant said he was a cook in a brothel. He saw defendant put his hand in at the window and lift the ham. Witness ran out and found him in the custody of a Police Constable.

Sentenced to fourteen days in gaol with hard labour.~

SATURDAY 24 SEPTEMBER 1881
DISORDERLY CONDUCT[736]

Four Chinamen were charged with disorderly conduct and damaging the roof of a house. It appeared that defendants had been for one or two nights past sleeping on the roof of No. 25, East Street, had got to skylarking and displaced some of the mortar from the tiles. The complainant, mistress of a brothel, complained of the noise, and the defendants were arrested.

They were each fined two dollars or seven days' in gaol with hard labour.~~~~~

WEDNESDAY 12 OCTOBER 1881
DISORDERLY CONDUCT[737]

Nine inmates of a brothel were convicted of making a noise on the street, and were sentenced – the mistress of the brothel, who formed one of the party, to be fined five dollars or seven days' imprisonment; and the other defendants fifty cents or two days' imprisonment each.~~~~~

WEDNESDAY 12 OCTOBER 1881
FALSE EVIDENCE[738]

Shu Ahi, a fireman, was charged by Ho Ayau, a Chinese female, with snatching her earrings, but after evidence had been heard, it turned out that complainant kept a brothel, where defendant had been. She was put in the box and fined twenty-five dollars or two months in gaol. Shu Ahi was discharged.~~~~~

TUESDAY 18 OCTOBER 1881
THE TABLES TURNED[739]

Li Ayau, a coolie, was charged with stealing a jacket from one Cheung Yu Ming, this morning.

From the evidence of complainant it appeared that on his return from his ordinary employment yesterday evening he found prisoner and another man, who both occasionally visited him, sitting in an empty room in his house. When witness left home in the morning he placed a jacket he was not using in the cock loft, and on his return in the evening he missed it and accused defendant of having taken it. This was denied, but about five o'clock this morning he saw him come out of an adjoining house with the missing garment in his hand.

A watchman gave corroborative evidence as to prisoner having been seen with the jacket in his hand at an early hour this morning.

In defence, prisoner said complainant owed him half a dollar and gave him the jacket in payment. He also said complainant keeps a sly brothel, and he went to his house on invitation. He took the jacket to another house after it had been given to him, and when leaving there he was arrested. When he received the jacket complainant asked him to assist in removing some of his things as he was going to a fortune teller's house in Queen's Road. After carrying a few things he struck work and declined to carry any more.

Prisoner was then discharged, and complainant placed in the dock instead.

On being charged with preferring a malicious charge against the last defendant, he said that when he saw him with his jacket he thought it would be returned to him, and consequently did not give an alarm of thief. He also admitted having allowed him to sleep in his house.

Fined twenty-five dollars, in default three months' imprisonment with hard labour.~~~~~

FRIDAY 21 OCTOBER 1881
A DARING OFFENCE[740]

Li Afuk was charged with damaging a blanket and some other articles belonging to the inmate of a brothel on the 17th inst., by throwing sulphuric acid over them.

Mr McCallum, public analyst, said he had examined the contents of the bottle, and found them to be strong sulphuric acid.

Defendant admitted throwing the liquid on the blanket. He said he had been a servant to Sir John Smale for nine years. He was employed in the Soda Water manufactory.

Prisoner was fined twenty-five dollars, and five dollars compensation for the damage, in default two months' imprisonment with hard labour.~~~~~

FRIDAY 29 OCTOBER 1881[741]
ASSAULT WITH A LETHAL WEAPON[742]

Wong Acheuk, a tinsmith, was charged, first, with assault; second, with being in possession of a deadly weapon, to wit, two fighting irons, on the 28th inst., he not being in possession of a night pass.

Tam Atang, a carpenter, said he was passing along Square Street yesterday evening when the defendant knocked against him, and on being remonstrated with he drew a dagger and stabbed him in the hand. Complainant at once seized hold of him when he passed the weapon to another man. He could identify the man to whom the dagger was handed if he were to see him. On the prisoner being searched two fighting irons were found concealed upon his person. Complainant was alone at the time, but there was a number of other men with the prisoner.

Defendant said that he knocked against complainant accidentally and he at once began to beat him. He pulled out an iron bar and cut complainant's finger.

Remanded till Monday the 31st instant.

MONDAY 31 OCTOBER 1881
ASSAULT[743]

The case in which Wong Acheuk, a tinsmith, was charged on Saturday last with assault, and with being in possession of deadly weapons without a light or pass, was again[744] called to-day, when Sergeant Ip Nam said that he had since ascertained that this disturbance and assault on complainant arose out of a brothel row. The prisoner, he said, was once employed in a tinsmith's shop in Square Street, but was now a brothel bully and frequently mixed up with brothel rows.

Sentence twelve months' imprisonment with hard labour.~~~~~

THURSDAY 10 NOVEMBER 1881
DISORDERLY CONDUCT[745]

Li Asui, a hawker, was charged with disorderly conduct, throwing crackers into a brothel, on the 9th instant.

The mistress of the brothel, a house in Square Street,[746] said some one threw a lighted cracker into her house yesterday evening, and it exploded with a loud noise. She did not see who threw it. Two Sikh constables, however, were able [to] give evidence on this point and identified the defendant as the perpetrator of the pyrotechnic display. Defendant of course denied the charge.

Fined five dollars, in default fourteen days' imprisonment with hard labour.~~~~~

MONDAY 12 DECEMBER 1881
LARCENY[747]

Ng Anam, a money changer, was charged with stealing a clock and two smoking pipes on the 10th instant.

Lai Su Lin, an inmate of a brothel in the Caine Road, said that on the evening of Saturday her attention was called to her room, and on looking to see what was the matter she found defendant there. He wanted to go away, but she would not allow him to do so until he had been searched. He then dropped from under his jacket the clock and two pipes in Court. She claimed them as her property, and valued them at five dollars.

Defendant said he thought it was Chinese custom to

enter any room in a brothel, so he went in and wanted to have a pipe of opium. Complainant came in and wanted to turn him out, but he refused to go. He only came here two days ago from Shek Loong, and was now on his way to Foochow.

The mistress of the brothel corroborated the evidence given by the first witness, and defendant was ordered to find security of two householders in the sum of five dollars each to be of good behaviour for six weeks, in default to be committed.~~~~~

WEDNESDAY 21 DECEMBER 1881
A PICKPOCKET[748]

Lan Aching, a hawker, was charged with picking the pocket of one Tam Awai, on the 20th instant.

Defendant was caught about eight o'clock yesterday evening in the Recreation Ground plying his trade on Tam Awai. He inserted his hand into complainant's pocket and succeeded in abstracting a handkerchief containing two one dollar notes.

Defendant said he was standing near complainant when the cry of "thief"[749] was raised and he was arrested. He did not pick the man's pocket but he believed some one else did. He only came here a short time ago intending to become a hawker, but he had not yet commenced business in that line. In the meantime he had sent his wife to a brothel.

Three months' imprisonment with hard labour.~~~~~

SATURDAY 21 JANUARY 1882
ROBBERY[750]

Cheong Yak Fong and Tsung Yang Kiu,[751] doctors, were charged with being concerned, with others not in custody, in robbing Chow Young Chan of two hundred and five dollars on the 9th instant.[752]

This case was again brought up on remand from the 17th inst.[753] The complainant stated on that date that he had been a gold-miner in Portland for twenty-five years and had returned from San Francisco on the 7th inst. He took his abode at the I-wai-kü Lodging house on the Praya. He handed over his property to the master of the house to take care of. On the day of his arrival he met the second defendant, who accosted him and offered to get a person to cure a sore eye, which had been bad for sometime. At that time the second defendant, after enquiring where he came from, said he belonged to a village close to the complainant's and they agreed to go home together by the Canton steamer. On the 11th instant he packed up his traps, and along with the second defendant proceeded to go to the steamer, but on the way he was enticed to go to a brothel by him. A man whom the second defendant knew asked some money from complainant, but being refused they seized him, along with some others, and abstracted his gold from his pocket, where it was concealed. He then returned to the Lodging house and afterwards reported the matter.

Tung Chung Man, the master of the Lodging house, stated that the complainant had given him a bag to keep, said to contain some gold coins, but after living four days with him, complainant received the bag and other property as he said he was going to live with a clansman of his. Complainant did not mention to him his intention of going to Canton. Three or four days after he had left witness's house he came back and said some men had cheated him. He said nothing about gambling nor of his having been enticed into a brothel and robbed. Judging by the weight of the bag, witness imagined there would be about two hundred dollars worth in it.

A constable gave evidence as to apprehending the second defendant in his own home in Po-yan Street; and the first in Hollywood Road. Both were pointed out to him by the complainant as being concerned in the robbery. He heard some of the crowd, who were at the door say, "They have promised to give him back eighty,"[754] but he could not say who "They" referred to. He knew the second defendant to be the first defendant's apprentice, and they both practised in the Recreation Grounds.

Tsui Yat Ko, a dentist, residing in the same house as the two defendants, said he heard complainant accusing them of stealing two hundred dollars.

The case was again remanded till Monday, 23rd January.[755]

WEDNESDAY 1 FEBRUARY 1882
ROBBERY[756]

Cheong Tak-fong and Tsung Yang-kin, doctors, who were charged with being concerned in robbing Chow Yang Chan of two hundred and five dollars were to-day discharged. The case had been remanded to allow of the inmates of the brothel in which the complainant said he had been robbed to appear as witnesses, but the complainant had been unable to point out the house to the police. The defendants acknowledged supplying him with some medicine for a sore eye on the 9th December, but knew nothing further about his actions until he came to the second defendant and said he had been cheated of the two hundred and five dollars.~~~~~

WEDNESDAY 1 FEBRUARY 1882
ASSAULT[757]

Ho Achi, a tailor, was charged with assaulting Chan Ayan.

The complainant said that he had no occupation and had been here five months on a visit to a friend. On the 31st ult. he was in a brothel in Square Street, when the defendant along with some others commenced to beat him and drove him out. The defendant struck him on the head and arm with an iron bar. The wounds bled freely and he had to visit the Hospital to have his head dressed.

The constable who apprehended the defendant said he saw him beating the complainant with his fists, but did not observe any others assisting him.

Defendant said he was on the way to his shop, when he saw the complainant fighting. The complainant seized hold of him thinking he was one of his assailants.

He was fined one dollar, or suffer[758] four days' imprisonment with hard labour, and required to give personal security in the sum of ten dollars to keep the peace for two months.~~~~~

WEDNESDAY 15 FEBRUARY 1882
AN UNHAPPY INMATE OF A BROTHEL[759]

Lo Chun, of Canton, was charged with attempting to commit suicide on the 12th instant.

John Lee, Inspector of Brothels, said he went at the instance of the keeper, to the brothel No. 44, Caine Road, and there found Lo Chun sitting on a bed, in one of the rooms, vomiting. In reply to him she said she had taken opium dross.[760] He took her to the Government Civil Hospital, where Dr. Marques, in the witness' presence, gave her an emetic.

Defendant stated that she had had a quarrel about some money and took the opium dross, but did not state her object in doing so.

The defendant's mother appearing and asking for her release, in order to take care of her, the Magistrate cautioned and discharged her.~~~~~

Thursday 9 March 1882
LOCAL AND GENERAL[761]

A somewhat alarming disclosure was made in the course of a case which came before Dr Stewart this morning. A native constable who had been told off to make inquiries into a row which occurred in a brothel in Square Street yesterday, stated that the defendant in the case, who when arrested was armed with a chopper of the class used by butchers and carpenters, belonged to a gang numbering about one hundred men, organised for the purpose of fighting. Inspector Fleming, who was in charge of the case, said the statement was merely founded on rumour. This may be so, but as Dr. Stewart remarked it is a rumour which should be most carefully inquired into, as the existence of gangs such as this is a danger to the peace of the Colony. One of the inmates of the brothel admitted, in reply to the Magistrate, that she had heard of the existence of such a combination.~~~~~

WEDNESDAY 15 MARCH 1882
ALLEGED ASSAULT[762]

Christini[763] Brown, of Germany, single woman residing at

22, Gage Street, was charged with unlawfully assaulting Luk Achü, tailor, on the 14th instant.

The complainant said he went to 15, Gage Street in the forenoon yesterday to ask for payment of a one hundred dollars, which a woman was due him.[764] The defendant was present in this house; after making his request to the woman, who said she had no funds and who promised to pay him next month, he protested that he was in urgent need of the money. The defendant then pulled his ear, called him a thief, and said he had cheated her friend. The complainant warded off her blows, and took to his heels.

The defendant asserted that while on a visit to her friend, who was lying on a couch indisposed, the complainant entered the house and asked for payment, which her friend promised in a few days. The complainant, however, persisted on[765] having immediate payment, and said "You must pay me money just now, what for you keep me? You wantee things, you must pay money!" Witness [*sic* for "defendant"] then interfered, and asked him why he made such a noise, when he commenced to abuse her, necessitating her taking him by the collar of the coat and showing him the door. Complainant slapped her in the face; she then took hold of him, and threatened to summons him for assault, but he had anticipated her.

The Magistrate dismissed the summons.~~~~~

Kidnappers and Traffickers in Human Beings

The previous chapter, "Prostitutes, their Associates and Clients", shows cases in which prostitutes and brothels are mentioned or involved. It mentions the segregation of brothels and their authorised locations. It describes the operations of the Contagious Diseases Ordinance of 1867, particularly the weekly medical examination of prostitutes.

Clearly, the Ordinance aimed to control the spread of venereal disease, particularly among the soldiers and sailors of the British garrison. But it also sought to prevent the exploitation of Chinese women as prostitutes in conditions, which often amounted to virtual servitude.[766]

As stated by Mr Courtney in a debate in the British House of Commons, an 1875 Hong Kong Ordinance enacted, "that the sale or purchase of a woman or child for the purpose of prostitution, or the harbouring of any woman or child for that purposes, should be a misdemeanour".[767]

The cases quoted below show how Stewart's Court worked with both the Registrar General's Department and the Voluntary Social Welfare Organisation, the Po Leung Kuk,[768] to protect women and children from offences and crimes associated with their enslavement.[769] Prominent among these crimes were their sale and purchase for the purposes of domestic servitude[770] and prostitution. The licensing of brothels under the Contagious Diseases Ordinance provided necessary legal machinery and a context within which part of this work could be done.

Reporting to the Governor in 1884, the Assistant Registrar General, J. Stewart Lockhart, gave the background to the Po Leung Kuk and its work. "In 1878 a considerable amount of attention was drawn by Sir John Smale, who was then Chief Justice, to 'Slavery'; or what was more commonly called 'domestic servitude', in Hong Kong."[771] Following this, a group of Chinese established the Po Leung Kuk, "for the purpose of suppressing kidnapping, domestic servitude, and the purchase of females for prostitution".[772]

According to Stewart Lockhart, "to a great extent it may be said to have fulfilled those objects." He writes, "The assistance it gives in detecting cases of kidnapping and brothel slavery cannot be too highly estimated. It not only houses and feeds unfortunates and those who have been kidnapped, but also defrays the expense of the passage home of those who have been brought to the Colony under false pretences. It helps young girls who have been decoyed away from their homes for the purposes of prostitution to obtain husbands and become respectably settled in life, and finds employment for youths who have been rescued from slavery."[773]

The reports of the four cases given below show the selling or attempted selling of children and of women. The voices of the victims and their exploiters are loud and clear. So are the voices of those who worked together to rescue them: informers, two Po Leung Kuk detectives, a Detective Police Sergeant, an Inspector of Police, a Chinese Police Constable, an Assistant Inspector of brothels and his Chinese interpreter. Although muted, the voices of the court interpreter and *The China Mail* court reporter are also distinct. The intervention of the (Acting) Registrar General is reported. The coverage is comprehensive and detailed.

In three of the four cases, the children and women had been brought into Hong Kong from the Chinese Mainland by other Chinese. A reason given for setting up the Po Leung Kuk (the Society for the Protection of Women and Children or – literally – the "Protect the Innocent Society") in 1878, with the legal authority specifically to protect women and children from kidnapping, was, "that the number of kidnapping cases had increased with the recent alternating flood and drought in China, which had led to poverty and crime."[774] One of the four cases heard in Stewart's court, July 1881-March 1882, and quoted below – "Wholesale [Decoying] of Boys and Girls" – mentions floods as contemporary with the hearing, and these natural disasters could certainly therefore still be a factor, perhaps giving a generally atypical impression of the relative number of cases Frederick Stewart heard, relating to offences originating in the Chinese Mainland. The first and the fourth cases quoted (the former concerning a boy, and the latter concerning a woman) show that, while such cases were before the court, alleged victims were housed at the Tung Wah Hospital,[775] a social welfare institution, senior to the Po Leung Kuk, and with which the Po Leung Kuk worked closely.

Other causes for kidnapping allegedly arose within Hong Kong itself. In late 1879, the Chief Justice, John Smale, stated his belief that, "mothers have even kept their daughters from going to school for fear of their being kidnapped".[776] Writing in early 1883, E. J. Eitel attributed the fact that some girls attended Hong Kong schools, dressed as boys, to the parents' fear that, if dressed as girls, their daughters could be kidnapped on their way to and from school. – Eitel writes of "a curious illustration of the continued prevalence of kidnapping practices in Hong Kong". "I noticed in 1882 several cases in which Chinese girls, living at a great distance from school and having to traverse on their way to and from school the most crowded portion of the town, were dressed like boys and attended, all through the year, girls' schools in boys' dress."[777] At one period at least, it was popularly argued that the kidnapping of girls, within Hong Kong itself, originated in the need to pay gambling debts, incurred in the Colony. A recent article, pubished in the *South China Morning Post*, Hong Kong, describes the significant number of child kidnapping cases on the Chinese Mainland, in present times.[778]

Such cases were viewed seriously under Hong Kong law. In two of the four cases quoted, where adult women were the victims, the defendants were committed for trial to the Supreme Court. Although in the first of these, the Supreme Court found the defendants not guilty, and the outcome of the second is not shown, similar cases were committed for trial at the Supreme Court and sentenced during a similar period, and these show what the sentences for such cases were. In the December 1880 Criminal Sessions, Fung A-sai was found guilty of "Unlawfully by fraudulent means bringing into the Colony a woman named Wong Lea Kwai for the purpose of emigration"; and of "Unlawfully bringing into the Colony the same woman, knowing that she had been purchased for the purpose of prostitution".[779] He was given two years' imprisonment with hard labour. In the April 1881 Criminal Sessions, Leung A-kam was sentenced to four years' penal servitude and Chan Yau Mui to two years' imprisonment for firstly, "Unlawfully and by force detaining against her will a girl named Ki A-mui, with intent to cause her the said Ki A-mui to be carnally known"; and secondly, of "Unlawfully purchasing the said Ki A-mui for the purpose of prostitution."[780]

Of the two cases involving children, quoted below, one was committed for trial at the Supreme Court,[781] and it was certainly expected that the other also would be.[782] The reports quoted below do not show how these cases ended. However, sentence was passed in other similar cases during this period, and the punishment was similar to that when women were victims. In the August 1881 Criminal Sessions, two years' imprisonment with hard labour was given for two counts, firstly, "Unlawfully and by force detaining within this Colony a certain female child named Tong Tai Tai, for the purpose of selling her" and secondly, "Receiving stolen goods".[783] The same sentence was given at the December 1881 sessions for "Feloniously and by force detaining one Chun Kwai Lan, a child, under the age of 14 years, with intent to deprive one Yeong A-leong with the possession of the said child,"[784] and also for, "Unlawfully by fraudulent means enticing into the Colony a boy named Cheung A-wa for the purpose of selling him".[785]

Nevertheless, Chief Justice John Smale considered the allowable sentence for some of these crimes insufficient. In March 1881, sentencing Lam A-chun to two years' imprisonment with hard labour, for "Unlawfully, and by fraud enticing away from this Colony a woman named Li Shan-ho for the purposes of prostitution", he made the following remarks: "I purpose to refer to this and like cases in a separate letter. The extreme penalty by Ordinance for this crime is inadequate to the injury."[786]

The story of the first of the cases quoted below, "Detaining a Boy", is as follows. As of 14 July 1881, according to "a woman" in the house, one of five children then detained at 4 Cheung Lane, Sai-ying-pun, had been there for two months, the others about ten days. On 12 July, a certain Kwan Atsu informed a doctor, Kwong Kwok Tai, about the children, and on 13 July, in turn, Kwong Kwok Tai informed Wong Man Yu, a Po Leung Kuk detective. On 14 July, Wong Man Yu went with Kwong Kwok Tai to the house to investigate, saw the children, and then laid "an information" at the court. The same day, Wong Man Yu, Detective Police Sergeant Fisher and Chinese Police Constable Number 192 (Kwong A Cheung) went to the house and saw the five children, the defendants (marine hawker, Tong Achi, aged forty-two, and Wong Ang "of Samshui", aged fifty-two, wife of Li Au), and "a woman" there. After some questions and answers, the warrant for the arrest of the first two was shown, and they and the children were taken to the Central Police Station.

At the first hearing on 15 July, the case was remanded and continued to be remanded or adjourned, week by week, until 1 October, when it was remanded again until 8 October.[787] At the first two court hearings, Mr Tonnochy was on the bench. All the following hearings were before Dr Stewart. The reason for the weekly adjournments was that strenuous attempts were being made to find the parents or relatives of the children. The Police were in communication with the Po Leung Kuk, who were "taking the usual steps in the matter". Four men were sent "to make enquiries in the neighbouring province" (Canton Province). As of 19 August, they had not yet returned. The case to date was summarised in *The China Mail* on 30 September, the day before the writer (wrongly) expected it to be resolved. By this time, several people had come to see the children. (This in itself is evidence that many children were missing.) One was the uncle of one of the boys, Chan Hing, who had been missed as long ago as June.[788] After finding the boy, his uncle went to fetch the boy's mother from Lo Fan, Sam Shui District, a journey of about three days. He seems not to have returned by the day of the report.[789] By 1 October, Wong Man Yu, the Po Leung Kok detective who had conducted the original investigation, had gone to the Mainland. His colleague, another Po Leung Kuk detective, reported in court that he had gone to Tung Kin to make further enquiries about the parents, presumably of the other four children.

This case has remarkable features. As already mentioned, the Po Leung Kuk was recently founded, in 1878. Yet this case shows that the Po Leung Kuk had a key role in a very well-established system, involving informers, investigation both in Hong Kong and on the Chinese Mainland, care of the victims and prosecution of the accused. It also shows good co-operation among the Police, the Magistrate and his staff, the Po Leung Kuk and the Tung Wah Hospital.

Whereas the first case quoted shows what happened after the abduction of children to Hong Kong, the second case additionally shows how a child came to be brought to Hong Kong to be offered for sale. The eleven-year-old boy told his own clear story. [790] (Presumably the children abducted in the first case were younger, and either unable or considered not old enough to give evidence.)

The boy stated that he had no parents, and lived with an uncle. Another uncle (his mother's brother) had taken him to a relative's at Whampoa, from where, after fifteen days, he was made to leave with the two defendants (widows aged fifty and sixty respectively), who brought him to Hong Kong, and sold him for forty-two dollars. It seems clear that the boy's uncle had in fact arranged for him to be brought to Hong Kong to be sold.

In May 1882, writing only of Chinese girls in Hong Kong, E. J. Eitel testified to the existence of a very large number of them, who, "are not living with their own parents, but are purchased servant girls, though of tender age, and live under a sort of servitude".[791]

In a dissertation, submitted for the degree of MA by Mr Chan Man Kam to Shung Kyun Kwan University in 1975, he states that the reason why Chinese people sold their children was in order to change the child's luck.[792] Frank Welsh states that, "The custom of adoption, of both boys and girls, by which poor families transferred their rights in their children for a cash payment, was long established, and the forms clearly defined in the Confucian volumes of Domestic Rites".[793]

Within Hong Kong society, as Verner Bickley hints

above, in "Differing Perceptions of Social Reality in Dr Stewart's Court", there was considerable ambivalence on this topic; so much so that, even today, women still live, whose lives have been spent as *mui-tsai*, purchased female servants. Although many were regarded as part of the family (and in the past decade one could sometimes see a *mui-tsai* having tea at the Mandarin Hotel with the family), during the Nineteenth Century, there were serious abuses of the system, which the first two cases quoted below partly indicate.

The victims in both the third and fourth cases quoted were adults,[794] and they recount both how they came to be in Hong Kong and what happened to them after they arrived.

In the first of these, a woman gave evidence that she was travelling voluntarily from the Chinese Mainland, to join her husband in Singapore. However, on the ship, she came under the influence of a man, claiming to be a clansman or distant relative, who settled her in Ship Street in Hong Kong's Wanchai, persuaded her to give him her money for safe-keeping, spent it, and then proposed to raise more funds by selling her in marriage.

The charge in the fourth and last of the cases quoted was, bringing a woman into Hong Kong for the purposes of prostitution. Chan Nui described her situation in life very clearly, how she lived with her father-in-law in a Mainland village, and was visited by her husband, a coolie, working in Canton, during Chinese festivals. She was enticed away from her home, first to a boat, then to Hong Kong, where she was taken to a brothel, given a new dress, and told to make herself agreeable to visitors. Fortunately, her husband came looking for her, and as a result of his petition for her release, the case came before the court.

This last case in particular shows clearly the workings of the Contagious Diseases Ordinance, and also some of the ways by which its work was frustrated. Whenever new prostitutes entered employment in Hong Kong, the brothel mistress had to take them before the Registrar General, who asked them questions, "to ensure that they were entering the profession of their own free will and had not been kidnapped or otherwise forced into servitude."[795] Brothels had to keep a list on display in the brothel of the prostitutes living there,[796] and to supply up-to-date lists to the Registrar General.[797]

Although, according to Miners, the police and medical authorities could inspect brothels at any time, these court reports suggest that it was the Inspector(s) of Brothels, who had this right.[798]

In this fourth case quoted, Stewart's magistrate's court was told about two visits to a brothel by the (Assistant) Inspector of Brothels, together with his interpreter. The first was a routine visit. The second was a visit made, under instruction by the Acting Registrar General, to investigate a complaint.

On the first occasion, as stated by the Assistant Inspector of Brothels, he made a roll call of the list of names, and someone answered to each name. (We learn later, that, under instructions from the brothel mistress, the complainant, Chan Nui, answered when the name "Kwok Ching-kam" was read out.) The inspector also asked the women as a group, whether they were all there as voluntary prostitutes, but – as he reports – none of them answered.

Probably the western Inspector, speaking in English, had read the roll and asked the question, being interpreted into Chinese by his interpreter. For at a later hearing, cross-examined by counsel for the defence, the complainant was evidently asked whether she had heard the *interpreter's* question (not the *inspector's*, which of course she could not understand). She replied that she had *not* heard the interpreter's question. The interpreter was called, and insisted that he did ask the question and the complainant had answered in the affirmative.

It is clear that having an Inspector of Brothels who did not speak or understand Chinese was an obstacle to the efficient functioning of the system in the interests of those it was intended to protect. It is also clear what power this gave to the inspector's interpreter.

It was evidently a regular trick to ask a new inmate, who had not been interviewed by the Registrar General as required, and whose name was not on the brothel's list of prostitutes, to answer to an assumed name, during the inspector's visit. For, during the second visit, when the complainant was asked her name, another woman called out the assumed name, which Chan Nui had previously been asked to answer to.

A simple means of addressing this problem – using photographs (an innovation introduced at about the same time to combat similar abuses in connection with Chinese Emigration)[799] – was discussed in 1882, when James Russell, the Acting Registrar General, wrote to Frederick Stewart, now Acting Colonial Secretary, to tell him, "I have this day sent out notices to the registered keepers that all fresh applicants for enrolment must fetch two unmounted photographs, one for record here and one to be kept by the applicant herself."[800] The rule was to apply to all women, "whether those belonging to the native or foreign Brothels".

Afraid of a negative response to his suggested innovation, Russell had nevertheless consulted the Committee of the Po Leung Kuk and Tung Wa Hospital, who had – to his surprise, as it seems – approved the plans. At the same time, Russell had prepared two Chinese documents. One was to be handed to each girl, telling her that she need not live as a prostitute unless she wished to do so.[801] The other was to serve as a heading to the list of women hung up in each brothel, warning the brothel keepers to keep the law.[802]

On 13 September 1882, the Po Leung Kuk addressed a letter to the Hong Kong Government, giving it as their opinion that, since the adoption of this system, "the number of young people who are inveigled into, or bought for the purpose of being prostitutes has gradually decreased,"[803] and commenting favourably on "the manner in which British Officials put an end to abuses and the love they have for the people."[804] Registrar General James Russell sent an English translation of this to Frederick Stewart, Acting Colonial Secretary. Stewart brought it to the attention of Administrator Marsh. And Marsh brought it to the attention of the Secretary of State for the Colonies (which is how the information has survived).

A year after the last of these court cases – and

perhaps partly as a tribute to his patience and sympathy in dealing with them – Frederick Stewart was appointed Registrar General.[805] He now had complete responsibility for the Contagious Diseases Ordinance and the superintendence of the working of the Ordinance.[806]

As always after Stewart took up a new position, the statistics that emerge after his first year of office are very useful. Those for the period 26th March 1883 to 26th March 1884, covering his first complete year as Registrar General, show the numbers of those helped by the Po Leung Kuk for that one year. Were they the tip of the iceberg?

The table, "Number of persons taken care of by the Po Leung Kuk during the last twelve months, with a statement of their ultimate disposal", shows, for <u>Males</u>, the following details: sent back to their native place, fourteen; handed over to their parents, two; died, one; sent to the Reformatory at West Point, three – a total of twenty. For <u>Females</u>, the details were as follows: sent back to their native place, twenty-nine; sent to convents in Hong Kong, seven; adopted, six; handed over to their parents, twelve; married, twenty-three; returned to their guardians, two; sent home through the Oi Yuk Tong, Canton, six; failures to reclaim from prostitution, seventeen; security found [for] proper up-bringing, thirty-two; restored to their husbands, eight; employment found for, one; provided for, by Government, at Yaumati, three; Leper, sent to Canton, one – a total of one hundred and sixty-seven".[807]

Although Chan Nui, the lady in the fourth quoted case, showed little resourcefulness and a degree of passivity in not taking measures to rescue herself from an increasingly bad situation, particularly by not making a complaint to the inspector during his first visit, she was certainly an unwilling victim. Her apparently inconsistent behaviour was however consistent with the obedience and selflessness to which Chinese women at the time where apparently trained.

Other Nineteenth Century materials show that some women willingly allowed themselves to be sold – even into prostitution – to assist their families. And once sold, they took it that their rights as individuals were forfeit. Given this attitude in adult women, it is not surprising that girl children, sold away from their families, mainly on the Chinese Mainland,[808] did not know that they were free. Writing in early 1880, the then Inspector of Schools, E. J. Eitel, expressed his view that the Government should "make sure that such girls know, or at least have an opportunity of learning [through education], that they are free".[809]

It seems that such behaviour is not unknown today. On 11 June 2000, The *Sunday Morning Post* reported the story of how, "a well-educated woman with good prospects," turned to prostitution to finance the necessary medical treatment of her step-brother. A story Garry Tallentire tells in his essay, "A Flavour of the Times", above, shows a very practical attitude to the profession, unclouded by any moral or social concerns.

Kidnappers and Traffickers in Human Beings: Cases[810]

FRIDAY 29 JULY 1881
DETAINING A BOY[811]

Tong Achi,[812] forty-two, a marine hawker, and Wong Ang,[813] fifty-two, wife of one Li Au, were charged with forcibly detaining two boys and three girls for an unlawful purpose on the 7th inst.[814] They were first before the Court on the 15th, when they were simply remanded for a week, and again on the 22nd when they were remanded till today. Mr. Tonnochy was then on the Bench.[815]

Dr. Stewart now proceeded with the case.

Police Sergeant Fisher spoke to having gone to Number Four, Cheng On Lane, Sai Ying Pun, on the 14th in company with a Chinese constable Number 192 and an informer[816] named Wong Way Fu[817] who pointed out the defendant and the three children whom he would produce. He told the informer that he wanted two more children. Found two more children. He asked for a remand, as the police were in communication with the Po Leung Kuk (Society for the Protection of Women and Children) who were taking the usual steps in the matter.

Remanded till August 5th.[818]

FRIDAY 19 AUGUST 1881
TRAFFIC IN CHILDREN[819]

The case in which Tong Achi and Wong a Ng were charged with forcibly detaining two boys and three girls for an unlawful purpose, was again called, but Detective[820] Sergeant Fisher having stated that the four men sent to make enquiries regarding the children in the neighbouring province not having yet returned, it was further remanded till the 26th inst.[821]

FRIDAY 30 SEPTEMBER 1881
WHOLESALE [DECOYING] OF BOYS AND GIRLS[822]

A case comes before the Court tomorrow, on remand, which, although it has already been before the Court several times has not yet been noticed in either of the papers.[823] As it will probably be finally disposed of tomorrow,[824] so far as the Magistrate's concern with it goes,[825] it may very properly be briefly stated here: –

Tong Achi, forty-two, of Nam-hoi, marine hawker, and Wong Ang, fifty-two, of Samshui, wife of Li Aü were charged with forcibly detaining two boys and three girls for an unlawful purpose on July 7th.[826] This case has been before the Court since July 15th. The following is a summary of the evidence, up to the present stage in the case.

Detective Sergeant Fisher stated that on July 14th, by virtue of two warrants, he went to Number Four, Cheung Lane, Sai-ying-pun, in company with Chinese Police Constable Number 192, and an informer[827] named Wong Man Yu, who pointed out the two defendants to him and the three children he would produce at a subsequent stage of the proceedings. Told the informer, a[828] Chinese and in presence of the defendants, he wanted three more children. The informer said there were *five*[829] but he could not find the other two. Searched the other rooms and in them found two more children. The informer told him these were the children he was in search of; and he took the defendants and the children to the Station. The Po Leung Kuk had taken the usual steps in the case and endeavoured first to find out and communicate with the parents. Every effort had been made, but nothing could be discovered about these five children, although the case had been adjourned from July 15,[830] week by week, till August 12th, to give ample opportunity for everything being done. Several people had come but no one had yet claimed them. On account of the floods in the neighbouring province about that time people were prevented from coming to see the children. Then another week's remand was granted. Four men were sent out to make enquiries regarding the children and every effort was made to obtain some information concerning them. The case was remanded from week to week, awaiting the return of these men, until the 3rd September when,[831]

Wong Man Yu detective of the Po Leung Kuk,[832] gave evidence. On the 13th July, he[833] received certain information from one Fung Kwok Tai,[834] in consequence of which he went with his informant[835] to Number Four, Cheung On Lane where he saw the five children concerned in this case. Defendants and several other persons were in the house. Asked second defendant "Have you got boys for sale?" She said "Yes," and pointed out the boy Amui,[836] for whom she wanted sixty-five dollars and Ahing for whom she wanted fifty-five dollars. First defendant said, – "At that price they are cheap." Second defendant then said, – "These three girls (pointing to Amui, Asan and Aut) are also for sale." Did not ask the price of these three, but said he would see about it and come back again. He then left. Next day he came to the Magistracy and laid an information (information put in and acknowledged).

In reply to the first defendant, the witness[837] said he was quite sure he saw him in the house on the 13th July last. To the second defendant he said he did not know anyone called Tan Afau or Tsoi Acheong.

Kwong Kwok Tai, a doctor,[838] living in Tai Kwai Lane, deposed to having, on certain information received from one Kwan Atsu,[839] went [*sic* for "gone"] with that man to house Number Four, Cheung On Lane where he saw second defendant and some other women and the five children now in Court. Said to her – "Are these children for sale?" She said "Yes." He asked the price of the two boys Ahing and Amui. She said "The younger (Amui) in sixty-five dollars and Ahing is fifty-five dollars." He said "very well"; my master may want to buy them. He and the man with whom he had gone to the house[840] then left. Next day he gave information to the last witness[841] and went with him to the house.

To first defendant witness[842] said he was quite sure he was in the house.

To second defendant, witness denied that he had gone to her house on the 8th July just to borrow money, one Afau[843] being with him at the time. Did not return with

Afau on the 10th July. Did not threaten that if the second defendant did not give him money he would give her trouble. Did not go to her house with Afau on the 14th, and demand ten taels.

Kwong Acheung, Police Constable 192, said he went with Sergeant Fisher to Number Four, Cheung On Lane on the 14th July about 4.30 p.m., and saw the defendants and the children there. Asked the first defendant where the children came from, and he said he did not know. Witness[844] said – "You live here and do not know?" Defendant said "I go out every day to collect old wares".[845] Then asked second defendant, and she looked very much afraid and gave no answer. In another room were two of the children and a woman. This woman also said she did not know where the children were from. This woman further said in the hearing of both defendants that one of the children had been in the house two months, and the other[846] about ten days. Showed the defendants his warrant for arresting them, and they both said they knew nothing about it. He took the defendants and the children to the Central Station.

Wong Man Yu, recalled, said a man from Sam Shui came to the Tung Wa Hospital and identified one of the boys, Chan Hing, as his nephew who had been missed as far back as June last. That man had gone away to get the boy's mother. He had said he had to go to Lo Fan,[847] in the Sam Shui District; he would take about three days to go to the place. At the last date, this uncle of the boy Chan Hing had not returned, and the case is now down for tomorrow, when if he is forthcoming, his evidence will be taken.

SATURDAY 1 OCTOBER 1881
THE ABDUCTION CASE[848]

The case in which Fong Achi and Wong Ang were charged with the abduction of five children, was resumed today, when[849]

Mok Kai, detective in the employment of the Po Leung Kok,[850] said that Wong Man In, the other detective, had gone to Tung Kin to make further inquiries regarding the parents of the children. He was not sure when he would return.

Remanded till 8th instant.[851] [852]~~~~~

TUESDAY 2 AUGUST 1881
KIDNAPPING[853]

Chan Ang, fifty, a widow and Asam, sixty-one, also a widow, were charged with bringing into the Colony one Tang Tung Yau, a boy aged eleven years, with intent to sell him, on the 26th inst.

Wang Mun Yu,[854] a detective of the Po Leung Kuk,[855] gave evidence of the boy having been offered to him for sale, and subsequently to a friend, who agreed to pay forty-two dollars for him. The two women in the dock were trying to sell the child, who they said had been given to them by his uncle for sale. He sent them away to get a bill of sale,[856] and meanwhile went for a constable to whom he gave them in charge on their return.

To-day the first witness was the boy whose sale was the subject of the charge. He said he was twelve[857] years of age. Had no parents. Had lived with his uncle at the Man Kong village, Pun U District.[858] Some day last month – he forgot the exact day – his maternal uncle came to the house of the uncle with whom he resided and said to his uncle that he wanted to take the boy to Whampoa to get employment as a servant boy. His uncle said "very good." His maternal uncle took him to Whampoa and to the house of a relative there, where there were some women. He remained in the house for some fifteen days. His uncle then went away leaving him there. At the end of the fifteen days the woman with whom he was living called in the two defendants and made him go along with them to get employment. Defendants on the 25th of last month brought him down to Hong Kong, and took him to a house where he remained about ten days, during which he heard the defendants trying to sell him to various people. One day defendants took him to witness' house and tried to sell him. The second defendant asked fifty dollars for him. He was then sold for forty-two dollars. First witness[859] then said to come to the station and get the money.[860] Then we all went to the Central Station.[861] Was now living in the Tung Wah

Hospital.[862]

      The Police Constable who apprehended the women gave evidence corroborating that of the first witness. He said that he also heard the woman say in the Central Police Station that they had brought the boy for sale. They were cautioned by Inspector Mathieson,[863] but repeated that it was true. They also said they had paid thirty-six dollars for him, and only made six dollars for their trouble. The bill of sale was put in, and the defendants were duly committed to take their trial at the Supreme Court,[864] reserving their defence.~~~~~

FRIDAY 4 NOVEMBER 1881
ALLEGED TRAFFICKING IN HUMAN BEINGS[865]

Ng Sam Mui, and Li Akwai, two elderly women, and Wong Awa, Kum Asam, and Lau Asam, coolies, were charged with having unlawfully detained one Pun Afung on the 1st instant, for the purpose of selling her.

      This case has occupied the attention of the Court for several days,[866] when evidence of the most conflicting nature has been adduced.

      According to the complainant's story her husband, named Lau Ain, left her three years ago for Singapore, since which time she had resided in her native village Ka Ying-chau. He had recently sent her the sum of fifteen dollars to pay her passage to Singapore, and with that purpose she left her home by passage-boat. On this boat she met and became acquainted with a man named Wong Awa, the third prisoner, who represented himself as a clansman or distant relation. In due time (9th October), they reached Hong Kong, and on the recommendation of her pseudo friend she went to a house in the respectable locality of Ship Street[867] to live until such time as an opportunity should offer of continuing her journey to Singapore. Wong Awa had discovered the fact that she was in possession of a few dollars, and she was induced to give them up to him for safe keeping. On the 31st ultimo, becoming suspicious at the delay in obtaining conveyance to the Straits she asked for the return of her money, when her friend coolly informed her that he had spent the whole of it, and he further intimated that she would have to pay for her board and lodgings, which had now covered a period of over three weeks. She then expressed her willingness to pay the sum of five dollars, provided he would refund her the money she had entrusted to his care. This, however, he was unable to do, again telling her that he had spent the whole of it. Shortly afterwards, on the same day, the two female prisoners appeared on the scene, and in their presence and hearing, Wong Awa intimated his intention of disposing of her person by sale. To this she objected, and expressed her determination to go to Singapore to join her husband. Some disturbance was then raised about payment for her board and lodging, and during the afternoon her brother-in-law, who described himself as a fortune teller and necromancer, happened accidentally to pass, and he at once recognised her as his brother's wife. She then related to him the circumstances in which she was placed and he took her from the house. This caused a further dispute, as Wong Awa and the two women had been negotiating with a widower for the woman's purchase with a view to matrimony, and if the brother-in-law were allowed to interfere and spoil the interesting arrangement, they foresaw that they would be deprived of their commission as go-betweens. His Worship had occasion to remark yesterday, during the hearing of the case, that complainant had varied her after-statements very considerably from the story she told on the day of the first inquiry. He said her first tale was remarkably clear and explicit and appeared to be a truthful one, and remarkably well told for an ignorant country woman as she appeared to be. The case, however, was of too much importance for him to dismiss on account of any prevarications on her part, and after a tangled mass of evidence, which more or less implicated the whole of the prisoners, he decided to send the case to the next Criminal Sessions of the Supreme Court.[868] ~~~~~

Pang Asun[871] and Chan Acheung,[872] aged 21 and 22, married women belonging to Canton, were charged, on remand from yesterday, with bringing Chan Nui into this colony for the purposes of prostitution.

Chan Nui, the complainant, said she was the wife of Chung Tai-fuk, a coolie working in a chandler's shop in Canton, and who used to visit her in the village of Lo-kong,[873] where she lived with her father-in-law, on Chinese Festivals. On the 23rd September an old woman, who lived in the same village but whose name she did not know, came to her father-in-law's house and asked her to accompany her to Canton, which she did in the expectation of meeting her husband. The old woman said the object of her visit to Canton was to make some purchases. When they arrived in Canton the old woman placed her on board a small boat, and told her to remain there until she returned. This boat was occupied by two women, and she remained there until the 28th September, but still her friend did not return. On that date the first defendant came on board the boat and asked the boatwomen if they had a woman for sale, to which they replied in the affirmative and pointed to the complainant. After some disputing the bargain money was settled as two hundred and forty-five dollars, and this woman left in the boatwomen's hands three gold rings, and the gold earring as earnest money. This woman did not come back to the boat, but on the 4th October an old woman, which [s]he now knew to be the first defendant's mother-in-law, came and paid the money in silver dollars. Complainant at first refused to proceed with the first defendant's mother-in-law, but on her promising to find her husband she consented. She was then brought to Hong Kong and taken to the Kiu-lan[874] brothel,[875] where she was furnished with a new dress, and told to make herself agreeable to visitors. The second defendant, who is a servant, she did not see until she was taken to the brothel. The mother-in-law went back to Canton a few days ago. Her husband came to the brothel on the 23rd inst., with a friend in search of her. He stayed all night, went out early in the morning and returned at noon alone, and told her that he intended to petition the Court for her release. On the 25th[876] instant her husband, in company with Inspector Lee,[877] removed her from the brothel and took her to the Tung Wa Hospital.

In answer to the Magistrate she said she had not been brought by physical force, but had been deluded and deceived. She had not communicated with her relations, as she had no means of doing so.

The case was then remanded till the 31st instant.

TUESDAY 31 JANUARY 1882
ALLEGED KIDNAPPING[878]

Pang Asun, and Chun Acheung, married women belonging to Canton, were charged, on remand, with bringing to this Colony and detaining one Chan Nui for the purposes of prostitution.

In the previous examination the complainant declared that the first defendant had paid two hundred and forty-five dollars to some boatwomen at Canton, into whose keeping she had been decoyed by an old woman belonging to her native village, on the 23rd September. She was brought to Hong Kong by the first defendant's mother-in-law and detained in a brothel until the 23rd of this month.

To-day Inspector Lee[879] said that on the 25th instant, a man named Chung Tai Fuk[880] came to his house with a petition and instructions from the Acting Registrar General[881] to investigate the grievance of which he complained. He went to the brothel, called Mui Lan, Number Thirty-two, West Street, of which the second defendant was the registered keeper, and entered a room on the ground floor, where he saw the complainant and the first defendant. The latter[882] ran towards him, fell on her knees, and protested vigorously that she and her children would be ruined. Complainant was weeping, and after he[883] had called the keeper and demanded the list of inmates, he asked what was her name, which she said was Chan Nui.

Mr Holmes, of Messrs Stephens & Holmes, at this

point appeared for the two defendants.[884]

Inspector Lee, continuing, said that on examining the list he found no name corresponding to complainant's. He then asked her how her name did not appear, to which she made no reply, but some one in the room cried out that Kwok Ching-kam was her name. This complainant denied, but said her mistress had told her to answer to that name when the Inspector came. On the previous evening he made an official visit to the brothel and read out the names on the list, to each of which an answer was made by one of the inmates. The number of names on the list corresponded with the number of inmates. He asked them in a body if they were all there as voluntary prostitutes, to which no answer was made.[885]

The case was again adjourned till the 4th February, – Bail being allowed in the sum of one hundred dollars each.

SATURDAY 4 FEBRUARY 1882[886]
ALLEGED KIDNAPPING[887]

Pang Asum and Chun Acheung, married women, were charged, on remand from Tuesday, with bringing one Chan Niu into this colony for the purposes of prostitution, and also with detaining her.

Mr Holmes, of Messrs Stephens & Holmes, appeared for the defendants.

The complainant after changing hands several times had at last been brought to Hong Kong from her native village on the 5th October, and since that time had been detained by the defendants.

Mr Holmes examined the complainant this morning, and in answer to him, she said that though her husband did not send money regularly, she was not in need of it at the time she left her village in the expectation of seeing her husband. Although there had never been any violence used in bringing her here, yet they always deceived her by promising to find her husband. She never heard the Chinese Interpreter,[888] who accompanied the Inspector, ask her if she were willing to stay in the brothel.

The Interpreter was called, and in answer to Mr

Holmes said that he positively asked the complainant whether she was a willing inmate of the brothel or not, and that she answered him in the affirmative.[889]

The case was again remanded till the 11th of February.

SATURDAY 11 FEBRUARY 1882
ALLEGED KIDNAPPING[890]

Pang Asum and Chun Acheung, married women, the first, the keeper of the Mui Lan Brothel, Thirty-two, West Street, and the second an assistant, were charged on remand from the 4th instant, with bringing into and detaining in this Colony one Chan Niu for the purposes of prostitution.

Mr Holmes, of Messrs Stephen & Holmes, appeared for the defendants; and Mr Sharp, of Messrs Sharp, Toller & Johnson, the Crown Solicitor, appeared to prosecute.

Some of the witnesses were re-examined, but no further facts were elicited. The defendants were then Committed for trial at the Criminal Sessions of the Supreme Court, Mr Holmes reserving their defence.

The complainant had been decoyed from her native village, Lukong, by an old woman, who resided in the same place, to Canton, where the complainant expected to see her husband, who was then working there. On arrival at Canton[891] she was kept in close confinement in a small boat until the first defendant came and bargained, with the proprietors of the boat, for her purchase. The complainant saw the purchase money paid by the first defendant's mother-in-law, who conveyed her to Hong Kong, where she was taken to Mui Lan Brothel and detained until her husband discovered her on the 25th January. It was stated in evidence by the complainant that no violence had been used and that she had not made any complaint to the Inspector of Brothels, when he visited the place.

The case will come up on Saturday, the 18th instant.[892] ~~~~~

59. *As well as being brought to Hong Kong to be prostituted and sold, women and children were trans-shipped through Hong Kong for sale and prostitution elsewhere. The following notice (originally published bilingually) shows one measure introduced in Hong Kong, in 1882, to protect women and children.*

NOTICE

The Emigration Officer gives notice that for the better protection of Emigrants, it is hereby notified that on and after the 1st proximo women and children who are taken before him for the purpose of emigrating should be provided with one photograph each.

    If the woman or child is passed, the photograph will be stamped and given back to the Emigrant. The Emigrant will show this photograph to the proper Officer on board the vessel before departure, and again to the Protector of Chinese or proper Officer on the Emigrant's arrival at Port of destination.

H. G. THOMSETT, R.N.
Emigration Officer, &c.

Hongkong 21st August, 1882.[893]

Children and Returned Students as Defendants, Victims, Accomplices and Witnesses

Thirteen children and two returned students – all Chinese – appear in this group of reports. The two returned students and six of the children appear as defendants. Six children are complainants or victims. One is a witness.[894]

In two reports, reference is made to other children who share the same world as adult defendants. In one, the defendant tried to use a blind child as a cover for his theft. In another, the defendant's practice was to use children as accomplices. – He allowed them to win repeatedly at a game played publicly. He then invited gullible adults to play the same game. Impelled by greed, the adults played, he won, and they lost their money.

The number of cases is small, but they show a great deal.

One represents in little many of the concerns felt – by Chinese and westerners alike – about Chinese young people at this early stage in the opening up of China to the West.

The two returned students in one of these cases had previously studied in America and were dressed in European style. One spoke English fluently with an American accent. Both were accused of theft by a Chinese gentleman, living in Yokohama.

Hong Kong newspapers indicate that there was a general watchfulness, in the 1860s, 1870s and 1880s at least, as to the effects of a western education and contact with westerners on Chinese people. Many westerners were concerned lest the mere contact with another culture and resulting erosion of the mother-culture would itself lead to moral degeneration. Some – including Frederick Stewart – shared to some extent the Chinese concern that children should not move away from their own culture in proportion as they became acquainted with another.

The appearance in court as a defendant of any Chinese who had attended a school managed by westerners or who had had contact with missionaries was thus a regular cause for comment. The returned students' case was news, even before it came to court. And the treatment in China of the group of returning students, to which the two who were charged may have belonged, was observed and commented on for a further couple of months.[895]

Another long-standing concern was the large number of children in Hong Kong who did not attend school at all. The 1881 Census suggests that, at the time of these hearings (July 1881 to March 1882) the number of children who did not attend school was slightly more than fifty-four percent of the school age population, a total of eight thousand.[896]

When Inspector of Schools, from 1862 to 1878, Stewart had written several times about the numbers of uneducated children on the streets, and shown concern for the children's welfare, but using the general concern for public order and safety as a means of focusing readers' attention. In 1867, he wrote: "It is painful to see the number of children in the Colony who seem to spend their whole time in the streets, generally at play, frequently at mischief, always watching for opportunities to pilfer, and thus commencing a career of idleness and crime. Could these children be *made* to attend school, the opportunity at least *of doing evil* would, so far, be removed. It were much better that they should be confined for the greater portion of the day in school, than that they should spend, as it is to be feared many of them do, the best part of their days in prison."[897] In 1872, he wrote: "That our criminal classes are largely recruited from the ranks of the ignorant and idle is beyond a doubt. The boat-boys on the Praya commence their career with pricking rice bags, follow that up with picking pockets, and end their days as pirates."[898]

As we see in the group of cases given below, it was children like this who, in the early 1880s, appeared as defendants in Stewart's Court. None of the young defendants was attending school. On the other hand, one of the young *witnesses* – honest, responsible and helpful – *was* attending school, thus doubly showing his greater conformity to the expectations of a more modern, urban society.

In the annual educational reports, written by

Frederick Stewart and his successor, E. J. Eitel, fear of kidnapping is stated as one of the reasons given by the Chinese for not sending their children to school.[899] The court reports quoted below show that kidnapping was not the only concern. Children could be victims of all sorts of street crime and abuse. One little girl sent out shopping was enticed "up the hill" and deprived of her silver bangle, silver anklet and set of silver buttons. Two school-boys had their pockets picked, one of a knife, another of a silk handkerchief and a one-dollar note. A girl-child had her bangle stolen as she was carried on her elder sister's back, and another child also had its bangle stolen. A boy of nine, who kicked sand at a boatman, was thrown in the harbour by the man. Taking steps to resist attempted theft was itself dangerous. The school-boy, whose silk handkerchief and one-dollar note were taken, felt the thief at work and held him, but let him go when the thief bit his finger.

In some cases, adults took the initiative to complain on the children's behalf. But some children were active in seeing justice done. The girl who lost her silver jewellery pointed out the thief eight days later to a policeman in the street. A nine-year old boy appeared to testify to the assault made on him, promising to speak the truth.

This last touch evokes very clearly how Stewart dealt with the little boy, showing how his wide, continuous and tender experience of Hong Kong's young people made him an ideal person for such cases. The child obviously trusted Stewart. His account of what happened gives a vivid picture of the small and innocent entertainment he found for himself, jauntily smoking a paper cigar as he roamed the streets, neglected. The punishment Stewart gave to his abuser – three months' imprisonment with hard labour – is a strong indication of Stewart's views. The offence itself – throwing a child into the harbour – seems to echo (with a difference) the biblical warning: "Whoever causes one of these little ones who believe in Me to sin, it would be better for him if a millstone were hung around his neck, and he were drowned in the depth of the sea".[900] The man who enticed the little girl and stole her silver jewellery, and the hawker who picked the school-boy's pocket (and who also had three previous convictions) also got three months' imprisonment with hard labour. But the hawker who stole a child's bangle (there were no aggravating circumstances) was sentenced to the lesser punishment of twenty-one day's imprisonment with hard labour.

What had those children who were defendants done? A group of three little boys – two aged fourteen, one eleven – had stolen a jacket worth seventy cents. In two other cases, the defendants had victimised other children: – it was an eleven-year-old boy who picked the knife from the school-boy's pocket; and the coolie who stole the silver bangle from the baby girl, carried on her sister's back, was fourteen. A fifteen-year-old shop-boy, "liked very much as a servant", had succumbed to the temptation presented by an open till and a twenty-five dollar note.

There was evidently no law against naming children in court, whatever the capacity in which they were involved, and the omission of names is purely arbitrary. We are told the name of one eleven-year-old defendant, and not of another. We are given the names of all child victims but two; and in one of these two cases, we are told the name of the child's father.

It seems that the punishments given to the children took account of their age and circumstances, their offence, the value of what they had stolen (if that was their offence), and their means. The group of three (two of them aged fourteen, one aged eleven) was sentenced to seven days' solitary confinement. – The prisons at this time did not have the "separate system". All prisoners were accommodated together. And it was clearly for the protection of these children and young persons that solitary confinement was specified in so many of these cases.

The eleven-year-old pickpocket was given seven days' imprisonment, six of them in solitary confinement. The fourteen-year-old pickpocket was ordered to pay fifty cents to the complainant (as a coolie, he was earning money); but if he did not pay, he was to go to prison for three days, two of them in solitary confinement. (The mother of the fourteen-year-old boy had appeared in court to speak for him, saying that he had never stolen anything before. Evidently prompted by Stewart, she promised to look after the boy in future. – No other parent or relative appeared to speak for any of the other defendants; and her presence was clearly a factor in her son's favour.) The fifteen-year-old shop-boy (who had breached a three years' trust) was given four months' imprisonment with hard labour.[901]

But were there any societal attempts to reclaim young people who appeared as defendants in the courts? On 29 March 1882 – coincidentally the day when Stewart appeared in Court for the last time as magistrate – a Chinese boy, fourteen years of age, was sentenced to one year's imprisonment with hard labour, to receive, once, twelve strokes with the rattan, and to spend the last week of his imprisonment in solitary confinement. – He had been remanded to the Supreme Court by Stewart's colleague, Mr Wodehouse, not by Stewart himself. – In sentencing him, the Hon. F. Snowden, Puisne Judge, remarked, "that he had already been found guilty of picking pockets, and that it was quite clear that he was under the control of a set of men, who sent him to commit the crimes, and then obstructed any attempts that were made to arrest him."[902] (In other words, the boy was an Oliver Twist or an Artful Dodger, manipulated by some Hong Kong Fagin.) "Fortunately for him, perhaps," Judge Snowden continued, "he was not over sixteen years of age else his punishment would have been heavier; but as it was, a severe sentence would have to be imposed in order to teach him to reform his ways."[903]

At the conclusion of this case, the Crown Solicitor remarked that it was a pity there was no penitentiary to which criminals of such a class could be relegated.[904] The Judge replied that he had considered that point with regard to this case, and regretted very much that no such institution existed in the Colony.[905]

This statement may be surprising to those who know of the "West Point Reformatory", which had opened as early as 1863.[906] Initiated by Bishop Raimondi, who obtained a grant of land from the Government and liberal subscriptions from the foreign Community, this Reformatory had continuously taken in a small number of boys, some recommended by the Police Magistrates, who supported them out of their Poor Box; and the boys were taught carpentry, shoemaking and tailoring.[907] According to Police Magistrate John Whyte, writing in 1866, the boys sent by the magistrates up to that time had varied in age from six to twelve, and had come to the notice of the magistrates in two ways. Either they had been charged with the commission of a minor offence, or they had been found by the Police, apparently deserted, straying in the street. If no parents or other interested parties were found, they were then sent to the Reformatory to be looked after.

Only a few years later, writing on 12 February 1866, Stewart wrote in support of a *Government* Reformatory: "when one thinks of the number of children in our streets and on the Praya, who are growing up in ignorance and bidding fair to surpass their predecessors in the practice of violence and theft, the suggestion of a member of the late Board of Education that the Colony should possess a Government Reformatory on an extensive scale must, sooner or later, claim to itself that consideration which it seems to demand."[908] Nothing seems to have come of this view at this time.

In November 1866, however, the existing arrangements at the West Point Reformatory were put on a more accountable footing; and again in 1868. The average number of boys, recorded as being at the Reformatory, ranged from twelve in 1863 to sixty-four in 1877. The situation in 1882 was evidently similar to that in 1877, for, in an Editorial, responding to the sentencing of the fourteen-year-old boy on 29 March 1882, *The China Mail* commented that – in spite of Governor Hennessy's frequent talk on various subjects related to penal reform – nothing had changed in some areas over the past five years:

"After the sentence was passed, the Crown Solicitor observed that there was no penitentiary in Hong Kong, which might be utilised for prisoners such as this youth appears to be. The Puisne judge remarked that it was a pity there was no institution to which the young offender could be consigned. This is a consideration which may by and by receive the careful attention of the Executive. In the meantime, there is no reason why the Gaol should not be so arranged that special accommodation be given to such offenders; and had the separate system been carried out, or some other means been adopted by which the hardened criminals had been dealt with and disposed of, there would have been ample room for providing special cells for this class of offenders. As it is, all the talk in favour of separate systems and reformatories, and against more forcible repressive measures, has ended in nothing [as] the Gaol is now full, the separate system has not been carried out, and reformatory accommodation is exactly where it was five years ago."[909]

Slightly more than four years later than when these remarks were made, the Reformatory Schools Ordinance (Number 19 of 1886) is dated 21 May 1886.[910] By this, provision was made for both the certification of Reformatories and the withdrawal of certification by the Superintendent of Victoria Gaol. The intention seems to have been to make such Reformatories a regular part of the penal system. And on 31 August 1886, *The China Mail* quoted the suggestion, made in the report of a commission set up to enquire into overcrowding in the Hong Kong Gaol, "that early arrangements be made with the West Point Reformatory to receive all the Juvenile Offenders."[911]

However, as late as 1894, E. J. Eitel, writing in his Annual Report on Education for the year 1893, states that arrangements had been made during 1893, "to enable the only Industrial School of the Colony, the so-called West-Point Reformatory, a Roman Catholic Asylum, to come, in the course of time, under the provision of the Reformatory Schools Ordinance (Number 19 of 1886), which has hitherto remained a dead letter."[912]

In their essays in the present book, both Christopher Coghlan and Garry Tallentire comment on the considerable machinery, which now exists to reclaim young people who have made early mistakes.

Children and Returned Students as Defendants, Victims, Accomplices and Witnesses: Cases.

SATURDAY 10 SEPTEMBER 1881
LARCENY FROM THE PERSON[913]

Chan Akan was charged with stealing from the person of Leung Mi Chenn, a Chinese girl, jewellery of the value of two dollars seventy cents.

Complainant said that on the morning of the first *instant*, she went to a shop to get cucumber. She met defendant in the street and he offered to take her up the hill to get bamboo shoots. She went up the hill with defendant, and then he took away her silver bangle and a set of silver buttons, and a silver anklet. He then ran away. Witness was crying and a Police Constable took her to the station. On the 9th *instant* she saw defendant in First Street and told a Police Constable to arrest him.

Defendant denied the charge, but was sentenced to three months' imprisonment with hard labour.~~~~~

TUESDAY 20 SEPTEMBER 1881
TWENTY ONE DAYS SEVENTY CENTS[914]

Three Chinese boys, two fourteen years old, one little customer aged eleven, were each sentenced to seven days' solitary confinement[915] for stealing a jacket value seventy cents.~~~~~

FRIDAY 30 SEPTEMBER 1881
UNLAWFUL POSSESSION[916]

Wong Ayeung was charged by Police Constable 197 with being in unlawful possession of two jackets and one blanket on the 29th *instant*.

Police Constable 197 said that this morning just after midnight he got information about a man taking two bundles to an opium divan in Square Street. Witness went to the house and found defendant on a bed with the blanket in court for a pillow. Witness asked him where the other bundle was, and he answered under the bed. It contained two jackets. On being asked to whom the articles belonged defendant pointed to a blind boy, but this person denied the ownership. Defendant was often seen prowling about the streets.

Defendant, who had been in gaol three times before, was sent to that place again for a period of thirty days with hard labour, with the option of fifteen shillings[917] of a fine.~~

Thursday, 6 October 1881[918]
[Students returned from America][919]

Before Dr Stewart today there began a case which promises to develop some interesting features. Two Chinamen, said to be students returned from America, dressed in European style, were placed in the dock, accused by one Wong Yuen Woi Chuen, in Yokohama, and who it is said is the employer of the first prisoner, with stealing a travelling box, containing over two thousand dollars of bank drafts; Chinese documents; blankets and a watch and clock. Mr Horspool gave evidence as to receiving from Her Majesty's Consul at Nagasaki concerning the prisoners as mentioned above, and under Mr Horspool's directions Inspector Perry arrested the prisoners.[920] The Government had been communicated with, and assistance was asked for.[921] The first prisoner, who could talk English fluently with a American accent, said he had no questions until the arrival of the plaintiff, but he would ask whether they would be let out on bail or not. Dr Stewart said it was a very serious charge, and until he heard from the Government he could not take the responsibility upon himself. The first prisoner said it was a charge without proof, and thought if the law were properly enforced that bail would be allowed. "We," he said, "are placed in your hands." His Worship assured them if he could grant them bail he would, but that in the circumstances he did not consider himself justified in doing so. As far as he was concerned he would endeavour to see the case pushed through as soon as possible. The case was remanded until tomorrow, and if any communication was received from the Government, the application for bail would be decided on.

Friday, 7 October 1881[922]

[Students returned from America]
The case, in which two Chinamen were arrested on board the *City of Peking*, came again before Dr Stewart today. Mr Horspool (recalled) said he had no further evidence to produce. His Worship said he had been considering the case, and his opinion had been confirmed that he had no jurisdiction in the matter. The defendants were then discharged.~~~~~

THURSDAY 10 NOVEMBER 1881
THEFT OF PUBLIC DOCUMENTS[923]

Un Ying Cheung, a jinricksha coolie, charged yesterday with stealing Summary Jurisdiction Summonses,[924] was again placed in the dock this morning.

Mr. Leon,[925] Sheriff's Officer, now detailed the documents missed, as also the value of the stamps they bore. He went to a school behind Number 7 Station,[926] this morning, where some of the papers were given up to him by a boy. He was then taken to a shop near by where[927] he had other missing papers given up to him. A boy attending the school said he picked up a number of papers scattered about in the middle of the street and gave them to the shop people.

A constable residing at Number 7 Station said he was sitting in one of the windows playing chess when he heard a noise outside, and both complainant and defendant came inside; the latter pointing to him said he had taken the papers. He had not been outside the station.

In defence the prisoner said he just turned away his head and he saw the lukong come behind him and go to his machine,[928] but he did not see what he did.

Ordered to find security in two householders in ten dollars each for his good behaviour for six weeks, in default to be committed.~~~~~

TUESDAY 13 DECEMBER 1881
ASSAULT[929]

Chun Awai, a boatman, was charged with assaulting a child about nine years of age on the 12th instant.

The boy, after promising to speak the truth,[930] said he was walking along the Praya smoking a paper cigar when defendant slapped him so that he fell. On getting up he beat him again and threw him into the water.

Defendant said the boy threw sand at him, and he retaliated with orange peel. The lad fell into the water, and defendant at once stripped to take him out.

A Chinese constable said he saw defendant and the boy playing together on the Praya. The boy threw sand about him, and defendant threw the boy into the water. Some one jumped into the water and brought the boy out. When defendant was arrested he threw off his jacket to jump in also.

Sentence – Three months' imprisonment with hard labour.~~~~~

THURSDAY 26 JANUARY 1882
Larceny[931]

Ly Aying, a lad of fifteen, employed as a shop boy by Messrs Kelly and Walsh,[932] Queen's Road, was charged with the theft of a twenty-five dollar note on the 25th instant.

Mr. C. Grant, Manager of the business in Hong Kong, said that yesterday afternoon he put a twenty-five dollar note in the till. A short time afterwards he sent the prisoner to clear away a quantity of waste paper from behind the counter in which the till had been placed. Later on Mr Davidson, one of the assistants, had occasion to go to the till for change, and after getting what he required he omitted to lock the drawer. About five o'clock when the cash was balanced it was found that the twenty-five dollar note in question was missing, and on the boys in the shop being searched, it was found in the prisoner's purse, on his person.

Defendant said he picked the note up from the floor. He did not know why he had not given it to his master.

Mr Grant, recalled, said the defendant had been in his service for three years. He bore a good character and was liked very much as a servant.

Sentence – Four months' imprisonment with hard labour.~~~~~

SATURDAY 11 FEBRUARY 1882
A YOUTHFUL PICKPOCKET[933]

Tse Afuk, eleven years old, was convicted of picking a knife from the pocket of U Fuk, school boy. The complainant had been looking at some tricks being performed in the Recreation Ground, when the defendant had picked his pocket, actuated most likely by a desire to learn the profession he was looking at. He was ordered to be imprisoned for seven days, six of these to be in solitary confinement.~~~~~

MONDAY 20 FEBRUARY 1882
PICKPOCKET[934]

Luk Akun, a hawker, was charged with picking from the pocket of Wong Chung Kan, school boy, a silk handkerchief and a one-dollar note on the 19th instant.

Last night on the Praya West the defendant had been grasped in the act of putting his hand into the complainant's pocket, who held on to him until his finger was bitten. The defendant then ran off, but complainant followed and got a constable to arrest him. During the struggle the handkerchief and bank note had been handed over by the defendant to a confederate. Three previous convictions are standing against him.

The Magistrate sentenced him to three months' imprisonment with hard labour.~~~~~

MONDAY 20 FEBRUARY 1882
A JUVENILE THIEF[935]

Leong Asing, coolie, was charged with stealing a silver bangle from Ip Fung Yeung, a child, on the 19th instant.

The defendant, a lad of fourteen years of age, stole the bangle from the child, which was being carried on her elder sister's back. His mother appeared and stated that he had never committed any theft before and begged the Magistrate to release him, and promised to look after him in future.

The Magistrate ordered him to pay fifty cents to the complainant, in default to suffer three days' imprisonment, two of them to be in solitary confinement.~~~~~

TUESDAY 21 FEBRUARY 1882
ATTEMPTED LARCENY FROM THE PERSON[936]

Tse Atai, cook, was charged with attempting to pick the pocket of Chun Tim, hawker, on the 20th instant.

The evidence given proved that the defendant had made an attempt to steal something from the complainant, who was standing looking at some persons boxing on the Recreation Ground. The defendant when seized by the complainant struck out with his fists and made great endeavours to get off, but was unsuccessful. His character was not good, and he was known to be a notorious gambler. He has been frequently noticed playing with boys and allowing them to win, and by this ruse inducing grown up persons to take up the game, when they were generally cheated by the rascal.

He was sentenced to six weeks' imprisonment with hard labour.~~~~~

FRIDAY 17 MARCH 1882
BANGLE STEALING[937]

Lui Ahoi, hawker, and Chun Tak, money-changer, were sentenced – the first, to twenty-one days' imprisonment with hard labour for stealing a bangle from the child of Lai Akum, on the 15th instant, in Ng Kwai Lane; and the second to one month's imprisonment with hard labour for receiving the same, knowing it to be stolen property.~~~~~

Gamblers and Informers

It is notorious that gambling is a passion among the Chinese. However, when the British colony of Hong Kong was established, it took with it English Law and its variety of gambling legislation, permitting some forms of gambling, but forbidding others. Developed over centuries, the English laws relating to gambling tended to discriminate along class lines. Forms of gambling that were considered the occupation of gentlemen in England were legal (horse-racing – "the sport of kings" – and cards), whereas gambling on cock-fighting, for example, considered a working-class occupation, was illegal.[938] Similarly, betting in private clubs – the prerogative of the rich – was legal, but resorting to common gaming houses and gambling in the streets – the options open to the poor – were illegal.[939]

In an editorial, evidently intended to support legalisation of public gaming houses in Hong Kong, *The China Mail* called attention to this inconsistency, in its application to Hong Kong. "It is monstrous folly to regard as a crime in a Chinaman an act which is not looked upon even with disfavour when practised by others; for if the wretched little games Chinamen play with cash are to be stigmatised as gambling so also must be called the conduct of every man in this colony who sits down to play for quarter dollar points after dinner or joins a 'pool' in a billiard room. If whist and billiards are innocent enjoyment then also is the Chinaman's cash game innocent enjoyment." [940] But in Britain, Victorian morality – supported by the needs of industrialisation and the conditions of the urban poor – was concerned to protect the poor, in particular, from temptation, and to discourage ideas that luck rather than individual hard work could lead to success in life: it did not object to this double standard, considered as discriminating between classes.[941]

In Hong Kong, the situation presented a serious problem. The majority of the population in the early years of British Hong Kong were from the working, not the privileged classes, and they were also Chinese. English law in Hong Kong, therefore, criminalised a traditional habit of the majority. As early as February 1841, when the British took possession of Hong Kong, the *Canton Register* took the view that "gambling houses will soon spread".[942] This expectation was abundantly fulfilled, giving rise to police corruption in response to bribes offered to turn a blind eye to the constant illegal gambling which inevitably took place.

At the time of writing, gambling and other games of chance are still both highly popular and heavily controlled in Hong Kong. Raffles at private functions, when tickets are sold only to those attending, are popular, common and permitted, but any lottery open to the public must obtain a prior government license. As for public gambling, only one institution is permitted to operate it, the (formerly Royal) Hong Kong Jockey Club.

The "Jockey Club" was founded in 1884; but horse racing was in existence from the beginning, transferred from the early Portuguese colony of Macau,[943] where British China traders had previously lived. Early drawings and photographs show clearly that Chinese as well as westerners patronised the Hong Kong races at Hong Kong's Happy Valley racecourse. However, these events took place then only once a year.[944] Today, hundreds of thousands patronise each race meeting, which now occur, at one of two alternate locations, twice a week in the season.

The social histories of Hong Kong seem to include no discussion of gambling – legal or illegal – on the outcome of these early annual races, but it must have occurred.[945] Some nineteenth century illustrations show an inward facing small group of Chinese, evidently agreeing bets. This once a year opportunity, however, was entirely inadequate to slake the Chinese thirst for gambling. Even today, the legal opportunities to gamble that Hong Kong now provides are not enough. Chinese residents still flock daily to neighbouring Macau, where legal casinos offer the games they love – one of them, fantan, often mentioned in Stewart's nineteenth century court. As of 18 June 2000 – before the end of the Hong Kong racing season – Hong Kong had provided the greatest volume of business for British bookmakers, taking bets on the Euro 2000 football match.[946] At the time of writing, on-line gambling is now very popular, and a cause of much concern for the Jockey Club, which is losing revenue as a result. It is not surprising, that, in spite of an annual horse-racing event, we find the question raised, as late as 1867, "What are we to do with the Chinese passion for play?"[947]

Of course the legalising of gambling was considered by early Governors, but no measure was passed until the arrival in Hong Kong of Governor Sir Richard MacDonnell in 1866. Eleven licensed public gambling houses were opened in Hong Kong in September 1867 (later increased to sixteen) and a "Special Fund" created to receive the license fees.

In recent times, the takings of the (Royal) Hong Kong Jockey Club have enabled it not only to be rich and powerful but to contribute towards the welfare of the community. A Government Tax is paid on all bets and the Jockey Club donates considerable sums to community projects, large and small – at the one extreme, small local clinics, for example; at the other extreme, an example is the stunning building for the prestigious Academy for Performing Arts. In the 1860s also, the so-called "Special Fund", containing the license-money from legal gambling, grew rapidly.

The owners of the licensed gaming establishments paid Richard Caldwell (former Police Magistrate and considerable linguist) a salary almost as high as the Governor's to organise a detective force for them, to ensure that they obeyed strictly the conditions of the license and thus ran no risk of losing it. As a result, crime in Hong Kong dropped dramatically and several wanted criminals were arrested at the tables.

But the strict English morality of the time took a dim view of what the British Government saw as tainted money. The Colonial Office in London forbade Governor MacDonnell to use the funds except for a few specific items of police expenditure. Locally, missionaries had protested against the legalising of gaming establishments immediately after this legislation was passed. They then launched a campaign against the gaming establishments and manipulated public opinion in Britain so successfully, that the licensing system was withdrawn and all gambling recriminalised in 1871.[948] Matters soon returned to their previous state, and continued for decades. In 1895, the former missionary, E. J. Eitel, speaking as the first historian or chronicler of Hong Kong, wrote that, after the licensing system was withdrawn, gambling and police corruption had continued unchecked up to date.[949]

In an earlier period of service as acting magistrate, in 1876, Frederick Stewart heard at least one gambling case.[950] The report of this hearing and of the later cases which he heard as substantive Police Magistrate from July 1881 to March 1882 show how well organised illegal gambling was. The gaming places had cashiers, accountants and armed watchmen. They had look-outs employed to warn players and organisers to escape if a police raid occurred. If caught, participants were ready (as Tim Hamlett comments) with "the usual excuses".[951] The 1867 and 1880/1881 sentences are consistent in punishing organisers very much more severely than players.

The three reports given here show how recriminalised gambling was policed in Hong Kong at the time. Obviously, very similarly to how it was done before legalisation. "The police . . . on suspicion that gambling is being carried on in a given house, and with no legal instrument beyond a warrant issued by the Superintendent on information received by him, surround and break into the premises, invade those of the neighbours so as to prevent the escape of the unlucky gamesters, arrest as many persons as they can, and carry them off to prison . . .."[952] Geoffrey Roper's testimony suggests a continuing tradition. [953] Seventy years later than Stewart's court, he participated in police *opium* raids in the same location, Tai Ping Shan. The group he led in the 1950s sometimes entered buildings through the roof, as Police Sergeant Rae had done on 10 September 1881.

In June 1881, when criticising the current slack enforcement of the Contagious Diseases Ordinance, *The China Mail* conceded that the previous use of informers in connection with this law had been an abuse.[954] The second and third gambling-related court cases reports quoted below

(19 December 1881) show at firsthand the poor calibre of some of the informers whom the police used at this time to enforce the *gambling* laws, rewarding them from any fines obtained from successful prosecutions.

Although two of the four informers in this case had helped the police for a year previously, all three who appeared in court were sentenced. They had laid false information, and wasted police time. One allegedly stole items from the house while the police were raiding it, and another – who disappeared during the hearing of the case – may also have stolen some articles. One informer seems also to have accused the man he allegedly stole things from of seeking to frame him, and he also accused a police inspector of collusion in this falsehood. All three who appeared in court (a seaman, a coppersmith and a coolie) were sentenced to six months' imprisonment with hard labour.

It is not surprising that these events led Magistrate Stewart to give one of his rare remarks about a case. He regretted the necessity the police had of employing informers of this quality; and he advised that the police should be even more careful in future when handling both the informers and the information they provided.

Five years later, in August 1886, there was a major police scandal, in relation to illegal gambling. Following information received, police witnessed fifty-three Chinese policemen ("lukwongs") collecting bribes from the owner of a gambling establishment. The informer was Cho Aluk, a packer. He stated that his son had been beaten by Police Constable 207 for refusing to give him money. Evidently illiterate, he then had a fortune teller write a petition for him, dated 16 July, and he took the petition to the Registrar General (our present magistrate, Frederick Stewart) two or three days later. "I told the fortune teller to say the Police at Taipingshan received forty cents three times a day. After I saw the money paid I told the fortune teller to write the petition. The men off duty received three cents and the men on duty one dollar, forty cents. My son refused to pay Number 207 and he took him to the Police office, charged him with assaulting him and had him fined fifty dollars."[955]

Three of the lukwongs absconded before trial.

The China Mail editorial on Chinese gambling, published in April 1867, had advocated greater cultural relativity in approaching the topic, suggesting that a Hong Kong governor might act in a way that was practically independent of "the Home Government". "It is impossible that the Home Government can have the local knowledge which would enable it to give very minute directions as to the line of conduct which in the details of administration the Governor was required to follow out."[956] When, on moral grounds, the Hong Kong Governor was not permitted to continue a policy, sensibly adapted to Hong Kong conditions, apparently this created conditions which, regrettably, stimulated behaviour and attitudes, even more broadly reprehensible.

Gamblers and Informers: Cases

SATURDAY 10 SEPTEMBER 1881
PUBLIC GAMBLING[957]

Twenty-two Chinamen were charged with public gambling on the 9th instant.

G. Rae, Police Sergeant Number 69,[958] said that about noon on the 9th he went with a party of police to Number 11 Centre Street. He found the house secured. He entered from the roof. He saw third defendant sitting on a stool near the landing with a fan-dagger beside him. Witness jumped through a hole in the roof, and then opened the trap-door, which was a strong one with a spring lock. He unlocked it to allow the constables to come up. He arrested all the defendants with the exception of the 8th defendant who was now in hospital. In the house he found a table and mat, four stools, ten dollars scattered on the floor, a quantity of cash-cards, dice, counting-stick, pen and ink cups, square, scales, three daggers, one sword, one strong door with spring lock, two ladders, and two fighting irons. The game being played was fantan.[959]

A couple of informers gave evidence as to playing in the house in question, and as to the first defendant counting the cash, the second receiving and paying the money, and the third being watchman with a dagger in his hand.

First, second, and third defendants [were][960] fined one hundred dollars or four months' imprisonment with hard labour; the remainder were fined twenty dollars or six weeks' imprisonment with hard labour. All gambling implements to be forfeited. Informers to receive ten dollars each from fines.

Eighth prisoner remanded.[961] ~~~~~

MONDAY 19 DECEMBER 1881[962]
AN UNFOUNDED CHARGE

Lau Aluk, a shopkeeper, was charged with being the keeper of a public gambling house on the 18th instant.

Inspector Thomson said he went to defendant's house yesterday evening to search for gamblers. The house had all the appearance of a respectable house, and on asking the informer where the gambling was going on, after some hesitation, he told him ["]upstairs["]. Witness went upstairs and found on a table the blanket produced, with dominoes, two trays, and two dice, but no fan-tan implements. While examining the house a cry of ["]thief["] was raised. There were seven or eight women in the place where the dominoes &c., were found. They had just finished a meal.

The witness believed the charge to be unfounded and His Worship dismissed the case.

MONDAY 19 DECEMBER 1881
GAMBLING INFORMERS[963]

Lum Afuk, seaman, Wong Atai, coppersmith, and Tse Acheung, coolie, were charged, the first prisoner with stealing an opium pipe and two brass smoking pipes, valued at five dollars, on the 18th instant; and the other two with being concerned in the same larceny.

Lau Aluk,[964] defendant in last case,[965] a shopkeeper on the Praya West, said[, that][966] yesterday evening the three prisoners came up into his house, to the top floor, and thinking they were customers he invited them to sit down and take a cup of tea. Shortly afterwards Inspectors Lindsay and Perry came in, accompanied by a party of police. As witness knew the two Inspectors he invited them also, to have a cup of a tea, but they refused and said they had come to search for gamblers. He told them they could search and see whether any gambling was going on there and they went up to the top floor. His family house was on the top floor, and in addition to his own family, there were also his wife's relations there, who had come from Macao for the Royal visit.[967] The blanket and dominoes in court were used by the women for their amusement. While the police were searching the house witness saw the first defendant pick up the opium pipe in court and put it up the sleeve of his coat when Inspector Thomson, who was also present, arrested him.[968] The pipe was then dropped to the floor. Two other pipes were afterwards missed, one of which was in court, the other had not since been found.

Sergeant Rae gave evidence to the effect that he accompanied Inspector Thomson to complainant's house where they were met, according to appointment, by four informers. The police were led to expect that gambling was carried on and they had gone to the house armed with a search warrant. They found no one gambling, but while making the search a cry was raised that the first prisoner had stolen an opium pipe, and he was arrested by Mr Thomson. One of the four informers had since disappeared. The brass smoking pipe in court was found in a pawnbroker's shop in Queen's Road West.

Inspector Thomson said he went to the house to search for gamblers. He spoke to arresting the first prisoner when the cry of thief was raised, and he saw the opium pipe drop on the floor from his sleeve. He had known the second and third defendants as gambling informers for the past twelve months, but he did not know the first prisoner.

Lo Asam, an accountant in a pawnbroker's shop proved the brass smoking pipe having been pledged by first prisoner. He knew the man well, as he often passed the shop.

Sergeant Rae, recalled, said the information of gambling in this house had been given by second prisoner. He,[969] and the second prisoner, and the man who had disappeared came to the station at six o'clock to conduct the police to the house. They[970] went on a little in front and when the party[971] arrived they found the three prisoners and the other man there.

First defendant said the house was a gambling house, he had lost eight dollars there. The opium pipe was thrown out into the street by the first witness.[972] The inspector saw him do it.

Second defendant said he went to the house on Friday night where he played fan-tan, and lost one dollar. He gave information against the house to the police.

Third defendant said he accompanied the second prisoner to the house to arrest gamblers. He admitted a previous conviction for larceny in May of last year.

His Worship in sentencing the prisoners to six months' imprisonment each, with hard labour, said that the police were compelled to employ such men as defendants,[973] but if they[974] had been careful before, it would be necessary for them to be doubly careful in future.~~~~~

Urban Life

Particular groups of individuals have already been highlighted in this book: – Sailors and Soldiers, the Police, Teachers and Men of the Cloth, Wives and Husbands, Amahs and Cooks, Widows and Protected Women, Sons and Adopted Daughters, Boys, Coolies and Burglars, Prostitutes, Prostitutes' Associates and Clients, Kidnappers and Traffickers in Human Beings, Children and Returned Students, Gamblers and Informers. Most of the cases in which they are involved arise from and illuminate urban life.

The focus here is different. The vivid thumbnail sketches of individuals and individual behaviour that follow illustrate the perils of city life, and – occasionally – the support that is also out there on the streets, in the shops, and on the cross-harbour vessels.

Some goods offered for sale are not what one thinks. There is counterfeit coin. Deceitful stories can suck you in. If you buy gold on the street, it may be silvered copper. If you buy jade, it may be coloured, imitating the highest valued jade, which fetches a higher price. If you put your things down to do some business, or to have a drink of sugared water at a stall, you may look down shortly after, and find your possessions gone. Your jewellery may be snatched; your pocket picked. The cloth you buy may be falsely measured. If you return goods, which you now consider not worth the price, the buyer may return you less than you paid him. If you are with friends or acquaintances, you may become involved in a gambling quarrel. If you intervene as a peace-maker, you may suffer abuse and violent assault for your pains. If you are a collector of coins, you may be accused of passing off counterfeit articles as real. If you are a policeman, you may be offered a bribe to ignore an offence, or to share the proceeds of a theft.

Cony-catchers and their dupes are familiar to those who know Ben Jonson's play *Bartholomew Fair* and fellow Elizabethan, Thomas Nashe's prose pictures of late sixteenth and early seventeenth century London. As for the urban innocent – ignorant of his surroundings and the rules of the game – who committed a nuisance[975] in a place of all places where law-abiding behaviour might be advisable (behind the Police Station),[976] he is at home anywhere.

The urban offences of obstruction and snatching are still common in Hong Kong. Businesses – small and medium – still typically consider the pavement space outside their door theirs to occupy at will. Pedestrians accept as a matter of course that they should walk in crocodile, or risk their lives by stepping off obstructed pavements onto the busy streets. As for jewellery snatching, every now and then a sudden increase, a different target, a different technique, gives cause for comment and alarm. Similarly, construction (and deconstruction) work is still done, with little thought of the landslips and subsidence they might set off.

But there are always helpful people: the person who sees your pocket picked, and tells you; the policeman who investigates your complaint. Many of us have our own story of some valuable we left in a public place – a taxi, a mini-bus – and the great lengths some disinterested finder has gone to, in returning it to us.

The urban space described by the reports quoted below, where these many events took place, is still with us today, changed and changed again, but still bearing the same names. Queen's Road, Wellington Street, Hollywood Road and Graham Street, Tank Lane, Station Street and Square Street, Second Street, West Street and Caine Road, Western Market, Saiyingpun, Wanchai and Yaumati. The former Central Police Station building remains, and the later Supreme Court Building, though it now houses the Legislative Council of Hong Kong.

There have been other changes of course. Gone are the Gas Works and the P & O godowns on the Praya, and the Praya itself is gone too. Number One Police Station in Percival Street, Happy Valley and Number Seven Police Station at the junction of Queen's Road and Pokfulam Road are no more. The Government Civil Hospital and Crosby's Store have gone. So have the opium divans, Central Market, Ha Wan Market and the theatre and guardhouse nearby.

Along with much that is new, we can still find the

same shops:– hardware shops and chandlers, goldsmith's shops and pawnshops, sugar-water stalls; and the same occupations:– barbers, tailors and cooks, hawkers (of second-hand clothes and everything else), dealers in curios, watchmen, boatmen and junk-masters, road-diggers and servants. Rice-pounders and brick-layers may not be familiar in the still-crowded streets of today, but there are still rows of fish-packers' establishments at Connaught Road West and some still remember the marine hawkers at the typhoon shelter at Causeway Bay.

We still see people sleeping on the street, although they no longer have the light and pass rules to usher them to a bed in prison. We still come across the occasional harmless person, suffering from delusion.

Some of us may not understand the words when people shout out, "Police", "Thief" or "Robbery" in the city today, but we can all interpret what is happening when we see some man or woman volubly addressing passers-by in tones of complaint.

Sedan-chairs are no longer a familiar mode of coneyance, but we still take water transport across the harbour to Kowloon, and to the nearby former Portuguese colony, Macau.

Unlike the 1880s, however, Indian and British policemen are rare sights on the street today, although Chinese policemen are of course everywhere. Happily, the good relationships overcoming cultural differences, shown on the street by the cooperative effort of a Chinese police constable and an Indian sergeant in November 1881, are now almost commonplace.

In their essays in this book, Magistrate Garry Tallentire and Barrister Christopher Coghlan both observe that the crime scene in Hong Kong today is very much more sophisticated than it was in the 1880s. So is the veneer of today's Hong Kong. But beneath this surface, the people and their early city ways still persevere.

Some colourful customs – irritating and a nuisance to people in the 1880s – are now rare and regretted. Street cries are an example. Tradesmen – knife-sharpeners, seasonal lychee-sellers – seldom call out for business now in residential areas, as in the 1880s and still in the 1970s.[977] But one habit could happily be eroded even further: the tendency to put ourselves at centre, ignoring our neighbours' feelings, convenience and the law. Happily, the media no longer remark so perkily and insensitively on disadvantaged groups. Happily also, the desire for an ordered society is more widely shared and so perhaps is sympathy and protection for those in trouble or in need.

Urban Life: Cases

TUESDAY 6 SEPTEMBER 1881
ALL IS NOT GOLD THAT GLITTERS[978]

Chan Asai, trader, was charged with obtaining twenty-one
dollars and sixty cents, one pair ear-rings, and one gold
hair-pin, valued at thirty-seven dollars and sixty cents, by
false pretences, on the 3rd instant.

Mr. Wotton appeared for the defendant.

Chung Atong, widow, said that on the 3rd instant,
about noon, while in the Queen's Road, near the Central
Market, a man, apparently a bricklayer, came to her and
asked the way to Wanchai. She told him to go eastward. He
then went up to another man and they spoke together.
Afterwards defendant came up to her and said "That man
has taken gold from Wanchai; don't tell anybody."
Defendant asked her to follow him, and they went to the
lane between Crosby's store and the Supreme Court. The
bricklayer them took out five pieces of yellow metal and
showed them to her and the defendant. Defendant said she
had better buy some, and she retorted that he had better buy
some himself. He said he had no money. The bricklayer
said they were five dollars a-piece. Defendant then took her
aside and said "he does not know they are good; you had
better buy some." He got them at Wanchai while building a
house. He does not know the value of them. They are worth
thirty dollars a-piece. You had better offer him four dollars.
She had twenty-one dollars in notes, and handed them to the
defendant, who gave them to the bricklayer. In return she
got five pieces of the metal produced. Four more pieces
were produced, and she having no more money, took her
earrings and gold hair-pin and handed them to the defendant,
who passed them to the bricklayer. She gave defendant six
ten-cent pieces, which went to the same receptacle.
Defendant asked her if she had got a handkerchief. She gave
him one, and he wrapped up the nine pieces of metal in it,
and told her not to let people see them. He told her to take
some of them to a goldsmith's shop, and exchange them for
eighty dollars. By this means she would be able to get

money, which she could give to the bricklayer, and then he would give her back her earrings and hair-pin. She must get silver dollars, as the bricklayer did not want bank notes. Defendant said "I will stop and watch the bricklayer; you hurry up and get back soon." She went to a money changer's stall and asked if he wanted gold. He said "Yes." She then produced a few of her pieces; but the money changer said he did not want such gold as that. She went back to the lane, but the defendant and the bricklayer had disappeared. She showed the pieces to a large number of people. The police them came, and she went to the Police Court and made a report. She afterwards went to the Macao steamer and saw defendant there. She said to him "Now I have changed the gold for money; come along with me." But defendant denied all connection and said she must be mistaken. A constable then arrested him.

Mr. Wotton cross-examined.

Several witnesses were examined for the defence.

The prisoner having reserved his defence[979] was committed for trial at the Criminal Sessions.[980]

Bail in two sureties of two hundred dollars each.~~~~

FRIDAY 30 SEPTEMBER 1881
THEFT[981]

Chiu Ayau was charged on remand, with having stolen an umbrella the property of Cheung Akwai, cook.

On the 17th instant, complainant had been buying some sugar water, and while doing so put his umbrella against the hawker's stall. When finished drinking, he found the umbrella gone. He saw defendant running off with it in his hand. Complainant called out "Police" when defendant dropped the umbrella. A constable arrested him.

Defendant had been four times previously convicted. He was cautioned, reserved his defence, and was committed for trial at the Criminal Sessions.[982]~~~~~

FRIDAY 30 SEPTEMBER 1881
LARCENY FROM THE PERSON[983]

Lum Amui was charged by Lo Aping with stealing a bundle of clothing.

Complainant, a dealer in second-hand clothes had gone to Station Street to hawk clothes. His bundles were put on the ground, while he was bargaining with a customer. He missed a bundle, and made a report at Number Seven Police Station.[984] Afterwards he was sent for, and went to the station, where defendant was in custody. He went with a police constable to a pawnshop in Yau-mah-ti, where he found the articles amissing.[985]

Leung Ching, servant to the first witness, said he saw defendant pick up the bundle and run. Witness went to Kowloon, and saw defendant pawning some of the clothing. Defendant got away, but afterwards he saw him in Hong Kong, and asked him to deliver up the pawn-tickets which he did.

Defendant, who had been three times previously convicted, was cautioned, reserved his defence, and was committed for trial at the Criminal Sessions.[986]~~~~~

THEFT OF A HAIR PIN[987]

Au Apo was charged at the instance of Mok Awa, a boatman in the employ of the Harbour Department,[988] with stealing a silver hair pin from Chan Mui, a widow living in Square Street. It seemed that on the 29th about 3pm, while she was on the Praya, a man snatched her silver hair pin. She turned and saw defendant running away.

She called out thief, and defendant was stopped by one of the Harbour Office[989] boatmen. She was sure defendant was the man. Her son was there.

Mok Awang said he was twelve years of age. On the day in question, he was a little behind his mother on the Praya when he saw defendant pass him and snatch his mother's hair pin. Witness called out "robbery," and defendant ran. He was stopped by a boatman.

Mok Awa said he was a boatman in the Harbour Department. On the 29th he was on the Praya, when he heard a cry of "robbery." He saw defendant running towards him with the last witness after him. Witness stopped the defendant; no hair pin was found on him.

Prisoner denied the theft, but was sentenced to twenty-one days' imprisonment with hard labour.~~~~~

THURSDAY 13 OCTOBER 1881
CUTTING EARTH WITHOUT A LICENSE[990]

Tong Achi was charged by H. Gustave with cutting earth without a license.

Complainant said that he was a scholar at St. Joseph's College.[991] On the 11th instant defendant and several others began to cut earth close to his house. Some of the earth fell and struck some of the diggers. They came next day, when complainant gave them in charge. The foundation of the garden wall was left bare.

William Watts, an overseer in the Survey Department, said he inspected the cuttings which were to the extent of fifteen feet by twenty feet. The retaining wall of Inland Lot Four hundred and twenty[992] was undermined and caused damage to the extent of twenty dollars.

Fined five dollars or fourteen days' imprisonment with hard labour and six hours in the stocks at the place.[993]~~

THURSDAY 13 OCTOBER 1881[994]
FALSE MEASURE

Lul Singh, Police Constable 530, said that on the 8th instant he went to Li Kwo Ching shop, 11 Jervois Street, and bought four yards of flannel. When he went to a tailor's he was told that the cloth did not measure four yards.

Inspector Orley said he was examiner of weights, and measures. The cloth was four yards and two inches over. The measure was half an inch short. Some of the inch marks were too short, and some too long.

Defendant said he had applied for a new measure on the 6th. He had heard of the translation of the order,[995] but had been absent.

Prisoner was fined one dollar or two days' imprisonment for having an insufficient yard measure. A moiety of the fine, if paid, to go [to] the examiner.[996]~~~~~

THURSDAY 13 OCTOBER 1881
ASSAULT AND ROBBERY[997]

Yep Ahing was charged, with two others not in custody, by Chiu Ayuk, with assaulting and robbing him of some money.

Complainant said he was a cook unemployed.[998] He came here ten days ago, and had been stopping[999] at Wanchai. On the 12th instant on his way to the theatre, and when near the guard house opposite Ha Wan Market, he met defendant and five others. Two of the defendants seized complainant by the arms, and defendant put his hand into complainant's pocket, and took out a parcel containing money. Defendant struck him on the back of the hand with a stick. Complainant called out "robbery," and when a police constable came the men ran. Defendant went into a house and locked the door. Defendant was arrested. Complainant was walking with another man Li Atsai, but was in some doubt as to the whereabouts of this personage, when the assault and robbery was committed.

Li Atsai corroborated.

Police Constable 133 gave evidence as to the arrest of the defendant.

Another Chinese Constable deposed as to seeing a number of men fighting, who ran when he approached. He chased but missed them. When he went to the original place of the fight he still saw some men fighting; they also ran; heard no word of robbery.

The rest of the evidence, which extended to great length went to show that the whole affair had originated in a gambling quarrel and a fight had taken place in which complainant had got a smack across the fingers. The complainant and Li Atsai had added the robbery to the story.

Defendant fined one dollar, or four days' hard labour, for assault; complainant fined twenty-five dollars, or two months' hard labour, for preferring a malicious charge;[1000] and Li Atsai fined five dollars, or twenty-one days' imprisonment with hard labour, for giving false testimony.~~

THURSDAY 20 OCTOBER 1881
AN OLD OFFENDER[1001]

Kwok Chut Sing was found by Police Constable 273 in Queen's Road this morning without a light or pass.[1002] Prisoner asked the Constable to take him to the station as he had no place to sleep. He had been six times previously convicted.

Sentence fifty dollars or three months' imprisonment with hard labour.~~~~~

SATURDAY 22 OCTOBER 1881
ASSAULT[1003]

Tsang Ayui, Chu Aping, and Tse Akum were charged with assaulting one Li Asing, a tailor.

Complainant said he was a tailor in Sai-ying-pun. On the 21st instant in the forenoon he was in Caine Road. While passing an opium divan he saw defendants fighting with a fellow tradesman inside. Complainant went in and tried to separate them. Third defendant threw an earthenware pot at complainant and broke two of his front teeth; second defendant threw a pillow and cut his chin; third defendant broke his head with a bamboo. Complainant then thought it was high time to get a constable, and he gave the defendants into custody. He did not know defendants and none of them were concerned in a case recently in which complainant was fined fifty cents.

Chan Cheung[1004] said he was a fellow workman of the complainant. The quarrel in the divan arose about a pair of shoes. Complainant came to his rescue and got hurt.

A Police Constable gave evidence as to the arrest of the defendants.

According to the statements of the defendants some one in the divan had accused the second witness[1005] of stealing a pair of shoes. He[1006] left the divan and returned, accompanied with complainant[1007] and nine or ten others. A general fight ensued and the things in the house were broken. The third defendant[1008] had been in gaol for three months as a rogue and vagabond, and on the 18th of July last entered into a bond[1009] to be of good behaviour for eight months.

Chan Ahoi said he was a cook in Tank Lane. On the 21st he saw the three defendants pursue the complainant and second witness[1010] into the street. He saw complainant struck with an earthenware pillow.

First defendant[1011] was fined five dollars or fourteen days' hard labour, and in addition to find security, two householders,[1012] in ten dollars each to keep the peace for two months, in default to be committed; second defendant[1013] fined five dollars or fourteen days' hard labour, and to find the same security as the first[1014] for the same period; third defendant[1015] had his bond[1016] estreated, in default of payment of one hundred and fifty dollars to be imprisoned for three months; fourth defendant (Chan Ahoi)[1017] was fined twenty-five dollars or two months' imprisonment for giving false testimony. Complainant[1018] and his witness (Chan Acheung)[1019] to give personal security in twenty-five dollars each to keep the peace for three months.~~~~~

FRIDAY 11 NOVEMBER 1881
BRIBING A CONSTABLE[1020]

Wong Akwon, a servant, was charged with being at large in the streets at an early hour this morning without a light or pass,[1021] and also with attempting to bribe the constable who arrested him.

Defendant was arrested at half-past two o'clock this morning in Hollywood Road. He said he was going to a brothel; on the way to the station he slipped forty cents into the constable's hand.

Fined fifty cents or two days' imprisonment, the forty cents bribe to be placed in the Poor Box.[1022]~~~~~

WEDNESDAY 16 NOVEMBER 1881
PUBLIC OBSTRUCTION[1023]

Kong Him, of the U-Lung salt fish lan, appeared on a summons at the instance of Police Constable Number 306, charged with "that he, unlawfully and to the obstruction of passengers, did set out and leave one hundred and thirty baskets and fifty casks of salt fish on a public foot-path on Praya Central, on the 11th instant, in contravention of Clause Eleven, of Section Two, of Ordinance Fourteen of 1845."[1024]

The case was opened yesterday, when the constable, Lo Ayau, said the baskets and casks complained of were placed, some on the water side of the Praya, a number in the middle of the roadway, and others on the foot-path. There was room for one chair[1025] only to pass, two could not. The obstruction continued from ten o'clock in the morning till two o'clock in the afternoon. Defendant had been fined twice during the present year for a similar offence, and on the day now charged he told witness he was not afraid of any summons as he had plenty of money to pay any fine. Two other constables also saw the obstruction.

To-day, on the case being again brought before the Magistrate, Mr J.J. Francis appeared for the defence.

Lo Ayau, recalled, said he had been five years and four months in the Police Force. He was on duty on the Praya between the Peninsula and Oriental Company's Godowns and the Gas Works from 10 a.m. to 2 p.m. on the 11th, and had been on the same beat for ten days previously. There are about twenty fish lans on that part of the Praya and all the fish boats come there daily to discharge their cargoes. The baskets and casks of fish complained of were in front of defendant's fish-lan only, and not in front of the others. The same baskets were there all the time. It was not a succession of baskets, and there were from ten to twenty men at work at them. None of them were empty. Witness was over his beat eight times. He told defendant to take away his fish, but he said, "Oh no; the Governor knows we always put some fish there." There were also fish there on the days when he was on duty prior to the 11th. He never at any time kicked defendant's empty baskets about.[1026]

Sergeant Nund Singh said he was on patrol on the Praya West at one o'clock in the afternoon of the 11th, and saw about one hundred baskets of fish on the foot-path and the main road. They occupied the whole of the path and about one-third of the street. He gave last witness[1027] instructions to take out a summons.

By Mr Francis: – He did not see fish taken from a boat, but from the fish-lan. A number of men were packing the fish in the baskets. There were a number of empty baskets on either side. All the baskets were in front of defendant's premises. He was on duty there from 7am till 9am, and went on again at noon.

The following witnesses were called by Mr Francis for the defence.

Lo Awai said he was accountant in a chandler's shop next door to defendant's. He was in his shop all day on the 11th, and at eight o'clock that morning he saw about ten baskets of fish in front of defendant's lan, next the Praya wall. There were no baskets there between ten and eleven o'clock that morning. He had been five years in his present shop, and he had no complaint to make of any obstruction; people could pass in and out of his shop. The baskets he saw only remained a few minutes.

Tam Acheung, accountant in a hardware shop, gave similar evidence. He was in his shop all day on the 11th, but did not see any obstruction caused by defendant's baskets of fish, and he did not see his men[1028] packing fish on the Praya. There were not one hundred and thirty baskets and fifty casks on the Praya that day. If they had been there he must have seen them. Fish are generally landed before nine o'clock, and they only remain a few minutes, when they are carried into the fish-lan.

E. J. Gomes, a watchman, also gave evidence to the effect that the baskets only remained a short time on the Praya, and that the men packed the fish in the doorway, and not on the road.

Sun Amui, defendant's head coolie, said there were not a hundred baskets of fish on the Praya on the morning of the 11th. He had eight men at work in the shop, not in the street. About eighty or ninety baskets were landed that morning between five and six o'clock, and they were carried into the lan. About one hundred baskets were sold that day. The purchaser sends his own coolies, and his master has nothing to do with them after they are sold.

The accountant in defendant's firm also gave evidence. He said business to the extent of one thousand dollars was done that day, in exports and imports. The fish was packed inside the lan before being sent out, and there were not a hundred baskets on the Praya. There were about ten men at work.

Mr Francis addressed the Court, and submitted that it had not been proved that any obstruction had occurred, and if there had, it was after the fish had been sold when his client was not responsible.

His Worship however held the charge proved, and fined defendant ten dollars, in default two days' imprisonment.~~~~~

THURSDAY 17 NOVEMBER 1881
LARCENY OF CLOTHING[1029]

Kwong Akwong, a rice-pounder, was charged with stealing a pair of trousers from a house in Graham Street on the 16th instant.

It appeared that the trousers were hanging on a bamboo outside the door when defendant in passing appropriated them. A cry of "thief" was raised and the prisoner was captured with the trousers in his possession.

Defendant said a man brought him here to sell him and send him off to Singapore,[1030] but he refused to go. He had nothing to eat, so he stole the trousers to raise money to take him back to Canton.[1031]

Six weeks' imprisonment with hard labour.~~~~~

SATURDAY 26 NOVEMBER 1881
OBTAINING MONEY UNDER FALSE PRETENCES[1032]

Leong Achun, a hawker, was charged with obtaining the sum of one dollar and ten cents under false pretences on the 24th instant.

Wong Asam, a widow, said she lived in West Street. She met defendant on Thursday afternoon while on her way to the Western Market. He offered her two jade-stone drops for one dollar and sixty cents, but afterwards agreed to take one dollar and ten cents for them. Sometime afterwards she saw defendant in custody of a constable who called her and she produced the two drops she had purchased from the prisoner.

Li Atoi, an accountant in a shop in Wellington Street, said the jade stones were artificially coloured, and were only worth a few cents. If they had been real jade as he represented they would be worth about four dollars.

Ho Amang, a dealer in curios, said the stones were coloured to represent the best quality of jade. Real stones such as these professed to be would be worth ten dollars, but they were only worth about twenty-five cents.

Police Constable 197, Wang Tsau, said he saw defendant offer the stones to several women for sale. He arrested him after a sale had been effected to the first witness, and he then offered to divide the money with the constable.

Defendant admitted having sold the drops to complainant, but denied having cheated her. She was willing to buy and he was willing to sell.

Six weeks' imprisonment with hard labour as a rogue and vagabond.~~~~~

THURSDAY 15 DECEMBER 1881
A PICKPOCKET[1033]

Wong Achai, a barber, was charged with stealing three dollars and some broken silver from the person of a junk master on the 14th instant.

Ngan Aming said that he was a passenger yesterday afternoon on board a steam-launch going from Victoria to Yau-ma Ti.[1034] When they arrived at the wharf he waited till the crowd of passengers had dispersed. A man belonging to the launch[1035] asked him if he had lost any money, and on his examining his purse he found the money gone. Defendant was arrested with the money in his possession, and witness identified it as his from the characters that were written on the wrapper.[1036]

Leung Anam, a seaman on the steam-launch, said that he saw the defendant with his hand under last witness's jacket while they were both on board as passengers.

Defendant said he saw the complainant take out his purse when he paid his passage money. He put the purse down beside him, and the last witness took it up. Last witness went ashore, and defendant followed him and asked him for a share, and as he would not divide the spoil he took it from him with the intention of returning it to complainant. He admitted a previous conviction of larceny in March last.

Sentence – six months' imprisonment with hard labour, the first and last fortnights to be in solitary confinement.~~~~~

FRIDAY 6 JANUARY 1882[1037]
COUNTERFEIT COIN[1038]

Kan Akut, marine hawker, was charged with selling two pieces of counterfeit coin and also with being in possession of twenty-six other pieces.

Inspector Perry said on the 3rd January he met Ng Ahoi who gave him information, which led him to give this person a one-dollar note, which he returned the following day with the two counterfeit coins in Court. From the same informant's statement, he went accompanied by other officers to Number Ninety-five, Second Street, where after search he discovered all the other coins produced resembling dollars; fourteen of which were new, and the remainder old and chopped. He also found thirty copper coins which when silvered would look like Japanese twenty-cent pieces. In a table in the room, which had a false bottom,[1039] were found a packet of powder, and four steel chops. Defendant said to the witness while engaged doing this that he was a collector of coins.

Ng Ahoi, a tailor, said on the 28th December he,

along with an acquaintance, went to Number Ninety-five, Second Street, where his friend gave defendant twelve dollars, and received in return twenty-four coins resembling dollars. On the same occasion witness himself gave defendant fifty cents and received one of those coins in return, but going home and piercing it, he found it was not good and took it back to the house and said so to the defendant, who only returned him forty cents, instead of fifty as he had paid. He then did as Inspector Perry related.

In answer to defendant witness admitted that he had been told the coins were copper.

Leung Atsau, shroff, employed at the Magistracy,[1040] said he had examined the coins and valued some of the dollars at thirty-five cents, some at ten cents, and others at less. The powder presented was used for the purpose of giving copper coins the appearance of silver.

Bedell Lee Yun, interpreter[1041] at the Magistracy, said the wooden label[1042] in Court was that used by persons who collect old silver ornaments and bad dollars, and the words on it meant "I collect silver taels;" that is, adulterated silver.

The case was then remanded till the 9th instant.

MONDAY 9 JANUARY 1882[1043]
COUNTERFEIT COIN

The case in which Kan Akut, a marine hawker, was charged with dealing in counterfeit coin on the 5th instant, again occupied the attention of the Court to-day.

Mr H. McCallum, analyst at the Government Civil Hospital, said that he had examined a small parcel of a powder which he received from Inspector Perry, and found it to be finely divided tin. A similar powder is used in India for burnishing ornaments and it gives them a silvery appearance. He then produced a small piece of copper which he had burnished with the powder in question, and which had all the appearance of silver.

Defendant having been duly cautioned reserved his defence, and he was committed for trial at the next Criminal Sessions of the Supreme Court.[1044]~~~~~

SATURDAY 28 JANUARY 1882[1045]
COMMITTAL OF NUISANCE[1046]

Kong Ayuk was convicted of committing a nuisance at the back of Number One Police Station[1047] to-day and was fined twenty-five cents or two days' imprisonment.~~~~~

Friday 17 March 1882[1048]
[Disturbance at the Supreme Court]

Wong Leong-Tak, an old man of sixty-five years, and who is known by many in the Colony as the "King of Siam", and who is the possessor of a medal for distinguished services in some unheard-of warlike encounters, was this morning brought before Dr Stewart, charged with disorderly conduct at the Supreme Court, a place which he constantly haunts, and is frequently a considerable annoyance to those conducting the business. This morning he was turned away by a constable, but with his usual cunning he effected an entrance by the other passage; this led to the old man being ejected a second time, during which he raised a considerable row. It was stated before Dr Stewart that his passage had been frequently paid to Swatow from the Poor's[1049] Box, but he always retraces his steps to the Queen's Dominions. His object in visiting the Supreme Court this morning was to receive payment of the modest sum of one thousand dollars, which, he said, the Judge had promised him. Dr Stewart remanded the case till tomorrow, to allow of some means being devised to relegate the King to some quarter where his claims to distinction will be more fully recognised.

Country Life

Many visitors to Hong Kong today – and many residents – have no idea that there is still a great deal of open and green space even on Hong Kong Island itself. In the 1880s, there was, of course, much more. The two cases given here provide a glimpse of life in the Hong Kong countryside over a hundred years ago. One case concerns a commercial vegetable and flower garden, which also husbanded pigs, goats and fowl, in Tsim-sha-tsui. (Certainly, there is none there today hidden among the high-rise buildings and shopping arcades!) The other is an armed robbery at the village of Tai-tam (or Tai-tam-tuk), near Stanley on Hong Kong Island.

The first case has already been mentioned in Verner Bickley's essay, "Differing Perceptions of Social Reality in Dr Stewart's Court", above. The case is interesting for its details about the garden, as well as for the defendant's reported feelings of jealousy and rivalry towards the other Chinese man who had taken his job. Combined with his apparent dependence on his mother, and the fact that the Chinese doctor who appeared as his character witness was not really of much help to him, there is perhaps a suggestion that the defendant was simple. The case was remanded to the Supreme Court. (There, the jury of seven reached the unanimous verdict of guilty. The jurors' names suggest their owners were of English, French, Macau Portuguese and possibly German origins.) The defendant was subsequently sentenced to six calendar months' imprisonment with hard labour.

The second case was described by the Honourable Francis Snowden, Acting Chief Justice, as "one of the worst burglaries that had ever taken place in the Colony".[1050] In his chapter, "The Police Role in Magistrate Frederick Stewart's Court", above, Geoffrey Roper comments that the case shows men of different national origins within the Hong Kong Police Force working well together.[1051]

The case is also interesting for other details about police work: – the fact that Indian and European police constables were assigned to what was then such a remote area, on the south side of the Island; the problems of communication between the different national groups among the Police themselves; the use of a telegram to communicate from the Central Police Station to the Police Station at Pokfulam; the preparation of a plan by a clerk in the Police Department to show the house that had been attacked and the nearby roads. Also, the fact that one of the police constable witnesses was in the habit of searching the bundles of grass carried by grass-cutters, to see whether they had also cut any young branches, hidden inside.

There are also provocative details about the house that was attacked – its Ancestral Hall, and the dim light given by a Chinese lamp in the doorway. A vivid picture is conjured up. A small community, looking out at night, sees by the light of torches the home of one of their number surrounded and attacked by a well-organised and large gang of armed men. European and Indian policemen make a desperate journey over the hills, transporting their wounded colleague on an "ambulance", seeking to save his life. He bleeds profusely from both sides of his body, experiencing much pain. He cannot bear to be touched. He calls out for water frequently. After three hours' agonising jolting, he dies, and it is a corpse they deliver to hospital at a quarter past seven in the morning after all their efforts.

Not surprisingly, the case was given considerable coverage in *The China Mail*, which carried an initial news item and lengthy reports of both the inquest and the Supreme Court hearings, as well as regular Police Court reports.

In its first coverage, *The China Mail* expressed the view that "attacks of this kind must raise an uneasy feeling in the minds of residents in the Colony", and suggested that a reward be offered for the capture of the robbers. After the verdict of guilty had been pronounced at the Supreme Court trial, and before sentence was passed, *The China Mail* reported that W. M. Deane, Captain Superintendent of Police, had said that the previous night, "one of the Inspectors had been very nearly killed in a case very much similar to the present; that these gangs of burglars were very frequently met with, and were most dangerous in their attacks on the Colony."[1052]

This material, taken as a whole, identifies the house that was burgled as the family house of Mr Chan Afuk, second clerk in the Magistracy itself.[1053] He was not however at home at the time. His brother, described as master of an opium shop in Stanley Village, was the only man at home. Seeing thirty or forty armed men, he advisedly set aside his six-chambered revolver, and opened the door to them, "wisely thinking that against such odds resistance would be worse than useless."[1054] Also in the house were Chan Afoo's daughter, aged eight, his niece aged eleven, two servant girls aged about seventeen or eighteen and "an old woman who looks after the children". The thieves "did not hurt witness's child, but took two silver bangles from her." One of the servants ran and hid in the cow house, a small building outside the main building. One of the others caught up the little girl, who was sleeping in the same room with her, and ran into the bathroom. She stayed there a long time, and did not know when the thieves left. Chan Afoo's wife, Shing Ayee, was in Central the night of the robbery, visiting her brother-in-law Chan Afook.[1055]

Three men only were charged in the Supreme Court, and with burglary only. It was explained that, although circumstances suggested that a charge of murder would be appropriate, there was insufficient evidence; and the jury was advised not to allow the question of the murder of the policeman, "to weigh too much on their minds". Without retiring, the jury of seven returned a verdict of guilty of burglary. (The names of the members of the jury suggest English, Scandinavian, German and Macau-Portuguese origins in the proportions one, two, two and two.)

Before sentence was passed the following day, the first prisoner asked the judge, "to disbelieve the accusations made against them and allow him to go home and support his aged mother"; and the second requested, "to be allowed to go home to spend the New Year in his native town, as he had had no connection with the matter".[1056]
The Judge however said that he thought the prisoners had been found guilty on satisfactory evidence. "In the middle of the night, they with a large number of others had attacked

a peaceful household." Each of them was sentenced to twelve years' penal servitude.[1057]

Country Life: Cases.

SATURDAY 5 NOVEMBER 1881
WILFULL DAMAGE TO A GARDEN[1058]

Chang Apo, a gardener, was charged with wilfully damaging vegetables and flowers to the value of forty dollars, on the 4th instant.

Mr T. H. Smith, partner in the firm of Messrs Blockhead[1059] and Company, said that defendant had been in his employment but was dismissed in September last. Yesterday morning from information he received from his present gardener, he went to Tsim-sha tsui, where his garden is situated, and there found that the whole of the vegetables and flowers had been pulled up and thrown about, and the garden rendered a complete wreck. The garden is about an acre and a half in extent and he estimated the value of the flowers and vegetables destroyed at forty dollars.

Ng Alau, a gardener employed by Mr Smith, said he knew the prisoner, and when he was dismissed he said in witness's hearing "Well, I'll see who takes my place. I will beat him," and "If he plants any flowers or vegetables I will destroy them." Defendant said this when they were at work. He has had no employment since his dismissal from Mr Smith's service, and has lived with his mother at Yau-ma-Ti, about fifteen minutes' walk off. Witness said he lived in a house in his master's garden, and on getting up yesterday morning at six o'clock he found the door of the pig and fowl house broken. Nothing had happened to the pig[1060] or fowls. He then noticed that a large quantity of vegetables and flower seedings had been pulled up and destroyed. The whole of the young seedings had been destroyed, and the seedlings in about two hundred flower pots had been scooped out. Witness was sure the damage had been done by human hands, and not by fowls or pigs. The pigs and fowls were all safe in their shed, and there were the marks of human feet all over the flower beds. He went to bed the previous evening at nine o'clock, and everything in the garden was properly fenced and no animals could get in from outside, and the fence was not disturbed as of yesterday morning. After further evidence of a similar nature had been given by another employé of Mr Smith's,[1061] the case was remanded till Tuesday next the 8th instant.

WEDNESDAY 9 NOVEMBER 1881
WILFUL DAMAGE TO A GARDEN[1062]

The case in which Chang Apo, a gardener was charged with destroying his late employer's garden, was again before the Court yesterday,[1063] when some further evidence was heard.

Chan Anang, an apprentice fitter at Hung Ham[1064] Dock, said he had known defendant for some years. During a conversation which he had with defendant some days ago he told witness that a Punti man had taken his situation, but remarked that he would not keep the job, as when he planted his flowers defendant would destroy them, and this would be the cause of the punti man getting a thrashing from his master.

Lan Shui, P.S. 250, gave evidence as to complainant making a report at Yau-mah-ti Station, when Inspector Cameron sent witness to see the garden. He found that over one hundred pots of flower seedlings had been destroyed, as also several beds of vegetables. Damage had also been done to the door of the house in which the goats, pigs, and fowls were kept. On being arrested on the Praya at Yau-mah-ti, defendant, when informed why he was apprehended, said, "Oh that's a small matter. Let me go home; I want to consult with my mother about it."

Defendant wished to call some witnesses; but none of them knew anything about the case although they could speak as to his general conduct.

The case was then again remanded till the 9th inst.

On the case being called again to-day, Wang Wi Shi, a medical practitioner, said he had known defendant for about five years, but he knew nothing of the charge now preferred against him.

Two other witnesses were called upon by defendant, but they could not be found by the police.

Prisoner after having been duly cautioned, elected

to defer his defence, and was duly committed for trial at the next Criminal Sessions of the Supreme Court.[1065]~~~~~

MONDAY 28 NOVEMBER 1881
THE ARMED ATTACK AT TAI TAM[1066]

Eight men, one of whom is described as a farmer, the others as coolies, were placed in the dock this morning, charged, first, with being concerned, with others not in custody, in an armed attack on the dwelling house of one Chang Au Fuk[1067] at Tai-tam village, and stealing therefrom property to the value of one hundred and twenty-eight dollars; second, unlawfully wounding and killing an Indian Constable named Easur Singh,[1068] No. 693, on the 27th instant, at Stanley in this Colony.

Sergeant J. C. Grant deposed: – I am a Sergeant of Police in charge of Pokfulum[1069] Police Station. On the 27th instant, at three in the morning, I received a telegram from the Central Station. I took the European and Indian Constables in the Station with me and searched the roads and by-paths. About five twenty in the morning, while coming up the Aberdeen Road near Number Ten Bridge, I saw first and second defendants coming from the seaside towards the road. Soon afterwards I saw third, fourth, and fifth defendants coming in the same direction, but a little way behind the other two. I overtook these five men as they got on the Aberdeen Road near a place known as Kai-lung Wan. I asked them where they came from, and they said Aberdeen. I knew that was not correct as I had been on the road for two and a half hours; and besides, they did not come from the direction of Aberdeen. I searched the first defendant, and in the blue bag in court, which he had over his shoulder, I found the five charges of powder, two leaden bullets, percussion cap, slug shot, blue cotton trousers, black cotton trousers, and purse I now produce. I arrested the men, the first five prisoners, and took them to the station. On the morning of the 27th instant, about two o'clock, there was an armed attack at a small village called Tai-tam, near Stanley. An Indian constable was shot, and an inquest is now being held on his body. I apply for a remand to enable me to produce further evidence, as I charge the first five prisoners with being concerned in the attack at Tai-tam.

Inspector Perry said – I charge sixth, seventh, and eighth defendants with being concerned in the armed attack at Tai-tam on the morning of the 27th instant, and I apply for a remand pending the inquest on the body of the Indian constable who was then shot, and pending further enquiries.

The case at this point was consequently remanded till the 5th proximo.

Monday, 28 November 1881[1070]

Armed Attack at Tai-tam-tuk

A Sikh Constable Killed

About two o'clock on Sunday morning (27th) an armed attack of a most desperate character, and which has resulted in the death of an Indian constable, was made on the family house of Mr Chan Afuk, second clerk in the Magistracy, situated in the village of Tai Tam Tuk, near Stanley. The operations of the thieves prove that some of them must have been intimately acquainted with the interior of the house. At the back part of the building is a large piece of vacant ground. From this, by means of a ladder formed of lashed bamboos, they got on to the roof of an adjoining building, and from that to the roof of Mr Chan Afuk's.

Immediately above the owner's room they lifted the tiles, cut a purlin,[1071] and then a means of access having been secured, threw lighted torches into the room. Just under the place where they lifted the roof was a cupboard, by which an easy descent was made into the room by from twenty-five to thirty men. They ransacked the whole place, and probably being disappointed at the small value of their plunder the robbers made for the room in which Mr Chan Afuk's brother was. Here there is an outside door at the end of an alley, and this the desperadoes at once set about demolishing. The occupant had a six-chambered revolver; but wisely thinking that against such odds resistance would be worse than useless, he threw the weapon away, and shouted that he would open the door to them. This he did and at once stood aside, and it was well for him he did so, as a man rushed straight in with a long spear. The moment they saw him, one man who is now in custody pointed a spear at him, and another, who was a rather young man, held a revolver to his head. A third robber said, "You must not hurt this man." The man thus threatened now says he would be able to identify these three men. After ransacking the house thoroughly and taking away what they thought worth the trouble, the band decamped. The value of the property stolen is about $150. Such was the glare from the torches that some of the neighbours looked out, and they saw parties, of two and three each, guarding the different approaches to the house. It was with one of these parties that the unfortunate Indian constable had come in contact, and at whose hands he suffered death. Whether the constable or the robbers had fired the first shot is not known, but in all some six or seven shots were fired. On hearing the shots two European constables at once made for the place whence the sound came. The constable was found stretched on the road with his rifle lying beside him. He had received a bullet wound in the centre of the belly, one in the right and another in the left side, while a fourth bullet had lodged in his hip. Some of the men had fired pellets, as three were extracted from his body in hospital, on the way to which he died. As soon as Mr Chan Afuk's brother could manage it, he started for the Police Station, but half way he met the police, who went in pursuit of the robbers, but must have taken the wrong road, as they found no trace of the thieves. Sergeant Grant, stationed at Pok-fu Lam,[1072] received from the Central Station a telegram communicating the news of the affair about two in the morning, and he at once proceeded with a force of men to search the roads. After doing so for about two hours and a half he succeeded in capturing five men, in whose possession were found a bag containing several charges of powder, leaden balls and slugs. Three others were captured this morning by Inspector Perry at Sai-ying-pun. From the fact that the police have in their possession a woollen quilt with a bullet hole in it, and stained with blood, it is surmised that one of the robbers must either have been killed or badly wounded. An inquest was opened on the body of the Indian Constable (Easur Singh, Police Constable 693),[1073] today but no evidence was taken, and it was adjourned to the Magistracy till tomorrow at ten o'clock. The body was buried at Happy Valley in the afternoon, a detachment of European, Sikh and Chinese policemen, under Inspectors Grey and Mathieson, accompanying it to the grave. An outrage such as the above discloses an alarming state of affairs, and justice must in this case be administered to the utmost rigour of the law. We do not wish to be alarmists, but certainly attacks of this kind must raise an uneasy feeling in the minds of residents in the Colony. We think it might lead to the more speedy capture of the villains if the Government were to offer a reward for their apprehension.

MONDAY 5 DECEMBER 1881
THE ATTACK AT TAI-TAM[1074]

The prisoners in this case were again brought up this morning, when Inspector Perry applied for a further remand till the 8th instant, as the witnesses were required at the inquest on the body of the Sikh constable still pending.

WEDNESDAY 14 DECEMBER 1881
THE TAI TAM ATTACK[1075]

This case again occupied a considerable portion of the time of the Court to-day. Most of the evidence given was precisely the same as that given at the inquest. The following two witnesses had not been previously examined: –

Sawan Singh, Police Constable 584, said that on the 27th ult. the deceased and witness went on duty at midnight. Deceased's beat was Number Two and that of deceased was Number One.[1076] About two o'clock in the morning Police Constable Hill, who was on patrol duty, met witness and had some conversation with him, and then proceeded towards the village. About five minutes afterwards witness heard two musket shots, coming from the direction of the village. Witness ran in the direction of the sound, and while running he heard some eight or ten more shots. When near the junction of the footpath with the road witness saw Police Constable Hill standing there, and blowing his whistle. The deceased constable was lying near him. He ordered witness to remain there while he went and made a report. While standing there witness heard a noise in the bushes, and fired his carbine. The noise stopped but he saw no one. Witness spoke to the wounded man and asked him what was the matter. Deceased said four men fired at him and that he had fired in return. They had run towards Tai-tam village. Deceased said he was in much pain and that he was dying. Witness afterwards in company with Inspector Fleming and a party searched the roads leading to Victoria and Aberdeen. He afterwards returned to his beat. The sound which came from the bushes was "Tsau Tsau," ("run, run")[1077] – There were two or three distinct voices.

Kaiham Khan, Police Constable 562, said that on the morning of the 27th while in his own house in Stanley, he heard two musket shots. He ran out and went in the direction of the sound, and at the junction of the roads came upon a wounded man. It was the deceased. Last witness was standing beside him. He spoke to deceased. After some search on the road leading to Victoria, he returned to the station, and then searched in company with Chan Afoo,[1078] the road leading to Aberdeen. They found a bed quilt on the road. It was lying as if it had been thrown down. There was fresh blood on it. About twenty yards further on they found another quilt. About forty yards further on still there were found a pair of trousers, a jacket, a handkerchief, and a child's headdress. They continued the search for another two miles, but finding nothing else they returned to the station. From where the blood-stained blanket was found for a distance of about a mile witness observed blood-stains, of about the size of a cent, and separated from each other by about a yard. About half-past one witness returned to the Aberdeen Road, and near the stone bridge found a hair pin. Witness knew two of the defendants (first and fifth) to be grass cutters at a place called Tsing Shui Wan (Shallow Water Bay) between Stanley and Aberdeen.

By Mr Holmes: – Witness had seen first defendant three times. Witness did not know where he lived. He had searched bundles of grass cut by the first and fifth defendants to see if there was any young branches.

A plan of the roads about Tai Tam, and of the house attacked, prepared by Mr G. J. King, Clerk in the Police

Department, was then put in.

The case was adjourned till Saturday next at eleven o'clock.

SATURDAY 17 DECEMBER 1881
THE TAI-TAM ATTACK[1079]

The seven men charged with the armed attack on a house in the village of Tai-tam were again placed in the dock this morning.

Mr Holmes, of the firm of Stephens and Holmes, again appeared on behalf of the prisoners.

Chan Afoo,[1080] recalled at Mr Holmes' request, said he did not recognise many of these prisoners. He remembered the night of attack. The thieves remained in the house about five minutes. There was great confusion, but witness was not frightened. He was standing in a side room (witness here pointed out the room on the plan produced).

By Dr Stewart: – He knew the room.

By Mr Holmes: – He was standing there when the thieves entered. The door of the ancestral hall was opened by him and the prisoners had not come in in a rush, but one by one. The seventh prisoner attempted to stab him. There was a dim light given by a Chinese lamp in the doorway. He remained standing in the hall until the prisoners had left, and during that time was not frightened. Had never seen the seventh prisoner previous to that occasion nor any person like him. Saw the seventh prisoner again with the police on the 27th November. Had not seen any of the others at any time.

Mr Holmes then said he did not propose to examine the police and supposed that His Worship would probably remit the case, on the evidence given, to the Supreme Court. He reserved the prisoner's defence until then.

Police Constable Duncan, twenty-one,[1081] then corroborated Sergeant Grant's evidence as to the apprehension of five of the prisoners.

His Worship afterwards remanded the case till Tuesday next.

TUESDAY 20 DECEMBER 1881
THE TAI TAM CASE[1082]

This was again brought before the Magistrate, and some slight cross examination was made by Mr Holmes on recalled witnesses.

His Worship then committed prisoners for trial at the January Criminal Sessions,[1083] and Mr Holmes reserved their defence.~~~~~

Pirates and Life at Sea

The name has an old-fashioned ring, but sea-piracy is a major factor even for large ships today, moving from Singapore down through the Malacca Straits. One morning in 1992, on board the P and O ship, *Canberra*, the present writer heard the loud-speaker announce that pirates were successfully repelled in the night. On entering the Straits, at dusk, nets were put on the decks to make boarding difficult, and merciful water-cannon used to repel the pirates who nevertheless did attempt to board. As long ago as the appearance of steamships, steam hose proved so effective against pirates, as to influence a major change in the nature of piracy on the China Coast.[1084]

Pirates are recorded in the Hong Kong region as early as 1710.[1085] Later, in the 1840s and 1850s, when Hong Kong was still young as a British colony, the Hong Kong authorities and the British naval forces at their disposal were continually worried by their operations, often in extremely large fleets.[1086] The pirate fleets frequently obstructed trade along the China coast, and even blockaded Hong Kong harbour.[1087] Hong Kong itself was believed to be a pirate headquarters at this time.[1088] As late as 1865, piracy was as common as ever,[1089] a matter of almost weekly occurrence, interfering with the native junk trade and small European coasting vessels, and frequently also causing the loss of many lives.[1090]

The local population were the usual victims.[1091] Relief, therefore, may have been one factor in drawing the crowds, when, at one public hanging of three pirates in July 1866, one hundred and fifty police were needed to keep order.[1092] Relief is certainly expressed by the name of the *then* Chinese area in Central (now *all* areas are Chinese), "Taipingshan", meaning "Quiet Mountain"; reputedly adopted after the removal of a pirate gang made life there, thankfully peaceful.[1093]

In spite of many successful prosecutions, however, during the period 1859-1864, only 157 out of 224 people charged with piracy were convicted. Governor Sir Hercules Robinson blamed this on loopholes in the British Judicial system, and consequently sought – but failed –to put in place legislation, enabling the Hong Kong authorities to hand all suspected pirates over to the Chinese for summary execution. In 1865, Robinson did however have an Ordinance passed,[1094] in accordance with the Treaty of Tienstsin (1858), which legalized handing over suspects, charged with offences outside Hong Kong waters,[1095] as well as suspects in piracy cases not involving British ships, to the Chinese authorities.[1096] (Under Chinese law, it was easier to find suspects guilty.) Guarantees were however obtained from the Chinese that torture would not be used against suspects. In the one case quoted below, heard in Frederick Stewart's court from December 1881 to January 1882, the Chinese authorities' application to have the prisoners handed over to them was rejected.[1097] Perhaps it was felt (correctly) that the prosecution could not fail, even under English Law.

Governor Sir Richard MacDonnell (1866-1872) is still remembered for his vigorous and very effective action against pirates at the beginning of his term in Hong Kong, which Revd James Legge early praised in a talk he gave at the Hong Kong City Hall in 1872. Legge also considered that, even more effective, were, "the organisation of the armed cruisers in the Chinese Customs' service, and a greater energy which has of late years been manifested by the Chinese Government itself."[1098] Measures taken by Hong Kong itself to reduce piracy at this time included the combination of Harbour Office and Police Office duties, in the case of the Police Inspectors at Yaumati, Aberdeen, Stanley, Shaukiwan and East Point (Whitfield Station).[1099] Controlling legislation for the registration of native craft was enacted in the late 1860s.[1100] Measures following from the 1872 Police Commission also had an impact. Piracy cases dropped from twenty-six in 1866 to five in 1876.[1101] By the 1880s, Hong Kong harbour was nearly under control, although piracy was still rife on the sea-lanes south of Lantau Island because of the pirate base on Cheung Chau.[1102] Bucking the trend, in 1890, the infamous piracy on the Douglas steamship liner, *Namoa*, on her regular route from Hong Kong to Swatow, took place. The pirates, who had boarded pretending to be passengers, rushed the bridge and killed the Commander and his Chief Officer.[1103]

Two suspected leaders of this attack were arrested in Hong Kong, but released for lack of evidence. Later, they came under the jurisdiction of the Mandarin in charge of Kowloon City. He arrested them, along with seventeen other suspected pirates and ordered their execution.[1104] The unpleasant before and after photographs of the pirates with and then without their heads are frequently republished in books featuring the photographic record of Hong Kong and its neighbourhood.

The amount stolen from the *Namoa* was worth $55,000.[1105] However, the value of the usual amounts stolen by pirates may have been very much less, as is true in the incidents described below. This suggests that it may indeed be that, during some periods at least, piracy was a way of life, necessary for survival in the area.[1106] This might explain why the men charged in the case quoted below considered it worthwhile to risk their lives for such small likely returns. However, the people the pirates preyed on may also generally have been poor, as the four charges quoted below – three involving others who made an *honest* living from the sea – clearly suggest.

This one case refers to four separate acts of piracy, three on 28 November 1881, one on 30 November, two of them with a very similar opus operandi.[1107]

The first act involved a widow who plied a small boat for hire,[1108] and was attacked by pirates on her way home after ferrying a client from Tai O to Mah Wan.

In the second act of piracy, two cattle dealers and a crew of three were robbed by five men, armed with swords. The complainant, one of the cattle dealers, was robbed of his purse, a small sum of money, his bag, shoes, hood, blanket and other articles. The pirates disabled the boat and took all the food of those aboard.

In the third act of piracy, the master of a junk – his work was the transport of stone – his wife, daughter and crew of seven were asleep on board, when, at midnight, three men with swords entered the cabin, with others outside. The pirates stole twenty-four articles of clothing of small monetary value (but valued by their owners), four guns, domestic and cooking utensils, a pillow, and various ship's items. They cut one junk master's wife's wrist by snatching a jade bangle from it.

In the fourth act, the master of another stone junk, his wife, daughter and crew were all asleep, when at about ten o'clock at night, four men threatened him, two holding daggers to his chest. They took away thirty-three pieces of family clothing, quilts, and jewelry, pans, opium pipe and lamp, and a bag. The clothing included two silk jackets, each with a set of silver buttons, a man's jacket with a hole at the front and twenty pieces of black calico. They also stole an umbrella.

None of the defendants was defended, but the questions some of them asked two of the complainants suggest some familiarity with court proceedings.[1109] They understood the principle of seeking to cast doubt on the complainants' evidence; but, not surprisingly, they were not skilful enough to avoid serious errors.

As reported, the defendants seem most concerned about the evidence of the two junk masters, particularly the second. Although the widow identified some of the prisoners in the dock, they asked her no questions. The cattle-dealer had bad eyesight, and did not pretend to recognise any of them. Perhaps because of this, they also ignored the opportunity to question him. However, the first junk master gave definite evidence that the number of men with swords who entered his cabin was three. Although this junk master had stated he was unable to identify any of the prisoners, the fifth defendant obviously felt he should call this evidence into question. "Why did not you and your men resist the thieves?" he asked.

The second junk master bravely insisted that the fourth and sixth prisoners had been the ones who had held the daggers to his chest, and also stated that the fourth prisoner had been wearing his (the junk-master's) coat, when seen in gaol. The first, fourth and sixth prisoners all questioned him. "How do you make up the value of thirty-five dollars for the clothes you lost?" "Do you call an umbrella an article of clothing?" "How do you know there were ten men on board your junk?" "What was the size of my boat?" "How did you identify as yours the jacket I was wearing in gaol?" "Why did you not report this matter to the mandarin at Ping Chow?"

The question, "How big was my boat?", was obviously a mistake, since the form of words the defendant had used constituted an admission that he had been there. Stewart very fairly pointed this out, offering the man the opportunity to put the question again, "How big was *the* boat?" Not understanding, perhaps, the defendant let the original question stand.

Ten days later, when the case was heard again, the second junk master, Li Pak Shing (also referred to as "Puk Sing"), testified to having, a week previously,[1110] identified the boat by which he was attacked, and also to finding some of his property on board. The boat belonged to the defendants. The men appeared in Stewart's court for the last time on 4 January 1882, when the case was remanded to the Supreme Court.

A report of the Criminal Court proceedings, heard before the Honourable F. Snowden, Acting Chief Justice, sitting with a jury of seven, was published on Wednesday, 18 January 1882.[1111] The jury consisted of: Messrs A. F. Ribeiro, C. O. Heerman, H. B. Polishwalla, R. Schultz, S. Corvet, W. A. F. Schmidt, and W. Poate. The Attorney General (the Hon. E. L. O'Malley) prosecuted. There seems still to have been no counsel for the defence. The second and third of the four charges which Stewart had heard in his magistrate's court were not proceeded with, and the first and fourth only were brought.

Wong Afuk (the owner of the junk) and five others were charged with "piratically attacking and seizing a junk, belonging to Toat-Shing, a widow, and with being in unlawful possession of certain property belonging to Toat Shing". The second of these charges was brought, "under a special Ordinance". The evidence here was supplied by the police, "who searched the boat, at Shau Ki Wan on the 2nd December, and discovered a large quantity of goods, which the prisoners were in unlawful possession of." The widow's evidence is more or less the same as reported in Stewart's magistrate's court, and she additionally describes her property. The police evidence also is additional. Inspector Swanston stated that he searched the prisoners' boat, finding a large quantity of fighting implements and ammunition. There were some fishing nets and other appliances – all in a disused condition – but the arms had recently been used. No defence from the prisoners is reported.

The second charge (the fourth in the magistrate's court) was, "piratically attacking a boat belonging to Li Pak Shing, on the 13th November, at Ping Chow, and with stealing a large quantity of clothing and other articles from him." Again, the victim's evidence of the piracy is similar to that in the magistrate's court. Additionally, it is stated that, "He had also identified the prisoners' boat, when at Shau-ki Wan, as being the boat, which had attacked his." In court,[1112] he pointed out several articles as belonging to him. In this case, the defendants did speak up. "The whole of the prisoners denied having any connection with the attack, and said that the clothing and other articles were their property."

The Judge's directions to the jury were similar for each case. In the first, he pointed out, "that only the second and sixth prisoners, whom the woman had identified, could be charged with the attack, while they along with others, were charged with unlawful possession." In the second, he said, "that though they all might be convicted on the first count, it would be better, in order to prevent any injustice being done, to confine any conviction on this count to the prisoners identified as having taken part in the attack." Finding the prisoners guilty in both cases, the jury distinguished among them, as directed.

At the Supreme Court, the prisoners came up for sentence on 23 January. All of them again pleaded innocence; and (following what was evidently a standard formula, but which may also have reflected their true circumstances) requested release to return home and support their poverty-stricken parents. In giving sentence, the judge responded to this, saying, "If they had been honest traders, as they held themselves out to be, they could easily have satisfied the Court and jury of their innocence."[1113]

Prior to sentencing, the judge stated the jury's

finding, and reflected society's attitude towards the prisoners' offence: "they had all been found guilty in various degrees of piracy and assault; and . . . it was necessary to put down piracy, as being the curse of these seas."[1114]

The sentences given reflect the men's varying convictions. Allowing for concurrent sentences, the heaviest sentence to be served was twelve years' penal servitude, and the lightest, eight years' penal servitude.

This case gives a very clear picture of what must have been the regular run of piracy cases in and around Hong Kong at this time, and of how they were dealt with in the Hong Kong courts. Two of the four incidents described give also a strong impression of what life was like for the tens of thousands of people, counted in the Hong Kong censuses of the time, who lived on boats. We do not see only the ever-present danger from pirates to which they were exposed, and the muskets they kept for protection from them; but we see their domesticity. The sleeping arrangements of family and crew. The daughter on one junk, and the seven children on the other. The jade bracelet, worn by one of the wives. The silver bracelet and two pairs of earrings on the other junk. The rattan pillow and quilts, the opium-smoking equipment, the rice bucket and rice bag, the brass ladle, the clothes and the valued silver buttons.[1115] These were the families, here today and gone tomorrow, whose children attended various Hong Kong village schools in a necessarily interrupted manner, and on whose behalf Frederick Stewart, when Inspector of Schools, had previously proposed a floating school.[1116] Most Hong Kong boat-people have now been resettled on land. These court reports show them at a time when their life was still on the sea.

Pirates and Life at Sea: Cases.[1117]

SATURDAY 10 DECEMBER 1881[1118]
PIRACY ON THE HIGH SEAS[1119]

Wong Afuk and five others, the owner and seamen of the *Kam-ki* fishing junk, appeared on remand on a charge of piracy.

These men were originally arrested on charges of anchoring in a place not authorised by the Harbour Master, and further, with being rogues and vagabonds, and dangerous to the peace and good order of the Colony.[1120]

The first of these charges was withdrawn, and the more serious one of piracy entered against them.

Inspector Swanston said that from information he had received he now charged the six defendants with piracy on the high seas on the 28th and also on the 30th of November last. He now applied for a remand owing to two of the most important witnesses not being present.

Case remanded accordingly till the 17th instant.

SATURDAY 17 DECEMBER 1881
PIRACY ON THE HIGH SEAS[1121]

Wong Afuk and five others, the owner and seamen of the *Kam-ki* fishing junk, again appeared on remand, on a charge of piracy.

Four charges are now preferred against these men.

The first was that in which Lai Tsat Sing,[1122] a widow residing in the village of Ty Ho,[1123] is the owner of a small boat[1124] with which she plies for hire. On the 28th ultimo she, in company with two other boatwomen, took a man as a passenger from Yu Kok to Mah Wan.[1125] On the return journey, after landing this man at his destination, she was attacked by a party of men in a fishing junk, some of whom she was able to identify amongst the prisoners in the dock.

In the second case, Chan Chung Hing, cattle dealer, of Tsing-mung, in the San-on district,[1126] said – I went to buy cattle at Tsing-mung on the 28th *ultimo*; but failed to make any purchases. When near Kwo-lo-wan, a boat came suddenly alongside mine. I was in the hold at the time. Besides myself there was a crew of three on board the boat, and a man named Tun Shun Fook a cattle dealer who was with us. Five men came down into the hold with swords in their hands, who commenced to rob the ship. They searched me, and took from me my purse, twenty-five dollars in silver and four hundred cash, and my bag in which they were contained. I also saw them take a pair of shoes, a blanket, and other things. The men came on deck, and cut the ropes of the sails, so that they could not be used, and after cutting the anchor rope, took away the anchor.

His Worship: Could you identify any of the men you see before you?

Witness: No, I cannot identify any of them because I have but one eye, which is not good, and it was very dark. We then made our way to Ping Chow,[1127] and the next day we had nothing to eat, as the pirates had all our food. We got to Ping Chow on the 30th *ultimo*, and the next day we left for home. I identify the hood, bag and shoe in court as some of my property which was taken from the junk by the pirate.[1128]

The third charge was made by Leung A-i a master of a stone junk, Number 252, belonging to Toong Kong, [who] said[:] On the 28th *ultimo* my boat was anchored at Ping Chow to get in stone. We were asleep on board; I was in the cabin with my wife and daughter; and my crew of seven men were sleeping in the forehold. We went to rest at about six o'clock, and there were then no boats in sight. At midnight some men came into my cabin. I had no light, but I could see there were three men with swords. The leader searched me and took away twenty-four pieces of clothing value twenty-eight dollars, four muskets, value six dollars, and also the rice bucket, rattan pillow, rice measure, brass ladle, blue cotton bag and the rice bag in court. They also took away my anchor, value four dollars, a rope, value two dollars fifty cents, which I have seen on board the prisoner's boat used as a part of the tackle. They also damaged ropes on board the ship by cutting them[1129] to the extent of eight dollars. Besides the three men who came to my cabin, there were others on board. How many I do not know.

Four muskets were here brought into Court which the witness identified as his property, taken as he described above. He was unable to identify any of the prisoners as being the men who plundered his boat. He never saw any of them before.

His Worship: Was anyone wounded on board your boat?

Witness: My wife's wrist was cut by having a jade bangle snatched from it, value two dollars.

By the fifth defendant: – Why did not you and your men resist the thieves?

Witness: There were ten of them, and the hatches of the forehold were nailed down so that my crew could not help me.[1130]

The fourth charge was made by Puk Sing,[1131] master of the stone junk, Number 141, belonging to Hong Kong, [who] said: On the 9th moon Chinese, about the middle of November he had forgot the day but had reported it to the Police.[1132]

Inspector Swanston said the matter was reported, but he was unable to get the report as the office was closed.

The complainant continued: My boat was anchored at Ping-chow about a month ago. I went to sleep about dark, with my wife and seven children in the mainhold, my crew being asleep forward. About ten o'clock I heard a noise, and I saw four men in the forehold, two with daggers and these two men holding their weapons at my chest asked me where my money was, adding, that I had better hand the money over or they would stab me. The fourth and sixth prisoners were the two men who did this.

By his Worship: – I had no light in the cabin, but the thieves lit matches, and I am perfectly certain that the fourth and sixth defendants were in the cabin. The men took away thirty-three pieces of clothing belonging to my wife and family, value about thirty-five dollars; three quilts, worth six dollars; a silver bangle, worth three dollars; and two pairs of ear-rings, value two dollars. I identify the two pans, opium pipe, opium lamp, also several articles of old clothing and bag as property removed.

By the thieves: – A jacket belonging to myself I

found the fourth prisoner wearing in Gaol on the 16th *instant*.

The first prisoner asked witness how he made up the value of thirty-five dollars for the clothes he lost, to which the witness replied that two silk jackets were taken with two sets of silver buttons, worth one dollar fifty cents; twenty pieces of black calico, value about one dollars twenty cents.

Prisoner: Do you call an umbrella an article of clothing? No; I had forgot that. – How do you know there were ten men on board your junk? – I came up on deck as you were going away and saw about ten persons. [–] What was the size of my boat?

His Worship pointed out to the prisoner that by the way in which the last question was put he admitted his presence there, and as he was undefended he would allow him to put the question as *the* boat. The prisoner wished the question to remain as he had stated it.

The witness then replied that he was unable to give the size of the boat.

In answer to the fourth prisoner, witness said he identified the jacket he (prisoner) was wearing in Gaol by the hole in the front. There were other holes in the jacket, but he could not say how many. The prisoner became angry on hearing this and addressed the witness in loud tones, but a threat from His Worship of being placed in the stocks outside silenced him.

The sixth prisoner asked witness why he did not report the matter to the mandarin at Ping Chow to which witness answered there was no mandarin there.

His Worship remanded the case till Saturday, 24th *instant*.[1133]

WEDNESDAY 28 DECEMBER 1881
PIRACY ON THE HIGH SEAS[1134]

Wong Afuk and five others were again brought up this morning, on remand, charged with four cases of piracy. Several fresh witnesses were examined, among whom was Li Pak Shing,[1135] who gave evidence as to identifying, a week ago,[1136] the boat by which he was attacked and which belonged to the six defendants. This witness, also at this time, found some property belonging to him on board the boat. Another witness, a seaman on board a passage boat called I Li, identified a purse and anchor in court as belonging to the boat he was employed on, and which were found in the defendants' possession. The whole of the charges were again remanded till the 4th *proximo*.

WEDNESDAY 4 JANUARY 1882
PIRACY[1137]

Wong Afuk, owner of a fishing junk, and five fishermen were again placed in the dock this morning on four separate and distinct charges of piracy on the high seas in the month of November last.

The prisoners having been duly cautioned elected to reserve their defence, and were committed to take their trial at the next Criminal Sessions of the Supreme Court.[1138]

Envoi

Caught in the amber of these *China Mail* reports from Frederick Stewart's court, we see those who formerly lived in Hong Kong, or visited Hong Kong; those who have walked this earth before: most in their less socially acceptable, less happy, less successful, less admirable moments and situations. Ordinary citizens, family members, school-children and street children, unmarried workers, visitors, transients, members of travelling classes. Chinese, westerners, Macanese, Indians. Protestants, Catholics, Christians, Taoists, Moslems. The victims of theft, violence and fraud. The perpetrators of these offences: pickpockets, burglars, cheats, the violent, greedy, envious, quarrelsome, or unhappy. Those who offended against civil society itself: drunks, committers of nuisances, cutters of saplings, careless developers. People who forgot or neglected an important duty and caused incalculable inconvenience to uncountable others. Those who offended against themselves: over-passive, despairing, suicides. The unhappily married and their friends, drawn into the confused struggle to escape the bondage of incompatible proximity. Everywhere the poor, the ignorant, uneducated, lonely, weak and naïve.

Also in these reports, we can find positive human qualities and behaviour, both outside in society and within the police court itself. Responsible neighbours, friends and passers-by of any race and nationality. Sympathy, understanding and compassion.

What we see is specific of a particular time and place. But, with only a little exercise of the imagination, close parallels can be found in Hong Kong society today as well as in other societies elsewhere.

Some of those interested in the post-colonial viewpoint will doubtless find material here to support criticism of colonial Hong Kong. Equally, they might find material to give due credit (if either criticism or credit are appropriate). Certainly, we see punitive sentences handed down by a western magistrate to Chinese persons, but such were also handed down to western persons. It is more appropriate, the present writer feels, to observe how the law was used to educate all, not only to understand what was expected by the culture of the colonial administration (and this included lessons of respect and tolerance to "both" "sides"), but also as to what was needed of all in a developing multi-cultural urban society.

The law clearly also operated successfully to mediate between individuals. The law and its officers were trusted by those against whom offences were committed, or by their relatives and friends, who otherwise would not have made their complaints through the courts.

Furthermore, a very positive comment is made on a society which appoints as an officer of the law, and values the appointment of a man like Frederick Stewart, the magistrate whose cases are republished here. Usually self-effacing, his personality, qualities and behaviour are nevertheless clear. Conscientious towards the law itself and the people in his court. Alert to deficiencies in the law and responsible and effective in pointing these out for improvement. Knowledgeable as to the customs and cultures of the people he dealt with. Skilled in the Chinese and English languages. We see his kindness and patience to a child, his smoothing of ruffled feelings, his expression of appreciation for a truthful and intelligent witness.

THEN AND NOW
People and Institutions

Not surprisingly, Hong Kong's people and institutions are different today from what they were in the 1880s. For example, sailors and soldiers, so much in evidence in Hong Kong in the 1880s, are much less so today. After the return of sovereignty to the Government of Mainland China, at midnight on 30 June 1997, the ships of a later British queen and their sailors now rarely visit Hong Kong. Developments in containerization, as well as the arrival of air transport, mean that the number of merchant seamen is very much reduced, proportionate to the amount of goods traded. However, some of the facilities, put in place during the years between the 1880s and today, remain: – the Mariners' Clubs in Tsim Sha Tsui and Kwai Chung, as well as

Fenwick Pier in Wanchai, now serve the seafaring population of all nationalities.

The Queen's soldiers have also gone. Their withdrawal began early, in anticipation of the resumption of Chinese sovereignty. Today, members of the replacement garrison provided by the People's Liberation Army of the Peoples' Republic of China serve only short terms of service in Hong Kong and the soldiers are usually kept firmly in barracks.

The policemen and firemen who – fortunately, still rarely – die in the course of duty, in the present period, are still given an impressive funeral by their comrades, rich in symbolism. However, the high proportion of Chinese, compared with other members of these groups, makes it most likely that those honoured in this way will be Chinese.

As for the minimum educational requirements for joining the police force, these are now much higher. In the 1880s, some members of the Police Force could neither read nor write in their own language, let alone having competence in an additional language, as some do now. A police school was established to help them to make progress. However, as with many branches of government service, in-service training and educational opportunities are still available, including the study of English (for Chinese members) and Cantonese (for non-Chinese). The systematic and widespread corruption within the force – only hinted at in the 1880s and possibly still incipient at that time – is now a thing of the past. There is now a police public complaints bureau and an ombudsman and any complaints can be directed to these agencies rather than finding an outlet in the media, as sometimes happened in the 1880s.

As for Hong Kong teachers, these still represent a rich variety of nationalities and varying backgrounds, reflecting the schools, subjects and pupils they teach. Girls, equally with boys, are now legally required to attend school and to complete schooling up to the end of the third year of secondary education.

Cross cultural marriages between western men and Chinese women are still (perhaps increasingly) common, including what seems a significant proportion among male members of the Hong Kong Police Force. All those known to the present writer seem well-matched and happy. Nevertheless, the present writer has heard stories, similar to that of Joseph James M'Breen and Jane Francis M'Breen, of estranged wives or former live-in girlfriends making off with their man's household effects in a hired van, while he was busy at work. There is also a small – but possibly increasing – number of marriages between western women and Chinese men.

Although, for a period under British administration, concubines and their children, in Chinese families, were given certain rights under Hong Kong law (this ceased to be the case in Mainland China soon after the Communist régime won power), since 1970, this is no longer so. Nevertheless, there are still many people living in Hong Kong now who have, or have had, "two mothers". A relatively new phenomenon is the Hong Kong Chinese who has a wife, both in Hong Kong and on the Chinese Mainland. The resulting financial and emotional stress now finds an outlet in the Hong Kong courts.

Brothels are no longer licensed, although ripples in this direction from lobbying in other parts of the world sometimes reach Hong Kong. Certainly, the People's Liberation Army has not replaced the British Army as supplier of regular clients for the girls who are still at work. Lyndhurst Terrace now houses antique and home furnishing shops rather than single non-Chinese women.

When opium – the hard drug of choice among Hong Kong Chinese in the 1880s – is found smoked, as very occasionally in Hong Kong today, it is a surprising and rare anachronism, and no longer provides a popular form of suicide. Modern drugs are rife, and it is young people who are increasingly users. Gambling is still all-pervasive, newly finding expression through the internet, but still mainly contained through the outlets provided by the only legal provider of this amusement, the Hong Kong Jockey Club, which for many years has financed many charitable works from the proceeds.

Regrettably, but not surprisingly, domestic and public quarreling and violence still continue. As for burglary, a comparison of the newspaper coverage in the 1880s and today suggests (maybe wrongly) that reported offences against non-Chinese are relatively fewer proportionately than those against Chinese. Indeed, when westerners are burgled, popular prejudice believes that the culprits are "from the Mainland", since they have broken an operational rule – or a reverse prejudice – of the regular resident Hong Kong criminal world.

As for that popular Hong Kong pastime, embraced by tourists and residents alike – shopping – "Caveat Emptor" is still the rule. Buyers should still take care that the article they buy is what they suppose and that the price is right. Bargaining still applies. However, some new protections have been put in place. The Hong Kong Tourist Authority (HKTA) now exists to assist tourists and there is a Consumer Council to advise and inform consumers and provide some means of redress.

The Tung Wah Hospital, once very active in assistance for Chinese travelling through Hong Kong, to work as labourers overseas, no longer has this work, but is still active in a wide range of social services. The younger, sister society, the Po Leung Kuk, set up to mediate the abuse of kidnapping and its effects, is now also active in a similarly wide range of social services. For kidnapping is no longer a common practice, commonly feared, although the wealthy are still occasionally the objects of this crime. The children of wealthy families may have bodyguards – previously, the family servant had this job – to take them to and from school.

Pidgin English is not used – systematically or otherwise – any more; but remnants of its usage remain. Until the company ceased this aspect of their business, at the turn of the twentieth and twenty-first centuries, the phone-in order-takers at The Asia Provisions Company Limited patiently educated their western clients to ask for "ten pieces oranges" rather than "ten oranges", as they placed their orders for food, and it sometimes seems that new legal immigrants from the Chinese Mainland have studied some old textbooks on this once useful means of communication. Most Chinese who regularly need to deal with others through the medium of English can now do so adequately for the purpose. (The regularly recurring complaints, since the early 1980s, about a decline in the standard of English, are based on media-fuelled folk myth. Such complaints were first heard in the late *1870s*, when English had been taught – to a handful only – for a period of, at most, barely thirty years. These complaints naturally occur when, because of rapid economic change, the need for a high command of English, in combination with other skills, suddenly exceeds the supply of persons with that command, who are willing to give their services for the no longer acceptable previous level of pay. In time, society adjusts to the new circumstances and the complaints fade, until the next unexpected pressure on the system occurs.) In fact, there are certain local sanctions against near-perfect usage. Even among Hong Kong Chinese residents, there is still a lingering suspicion of other Chinese people, who speak fluent English; and this suspicion is particularly directed against those who have returned from privileged study overseas, speaking English with an American accent.

The mix of nationalities and cultures has changed. There are far fewer Macanese evident in Hong Kong businesses and government offices today. There are many more Australians, New Zealanders and Americans. A much smaller proportion of the population lives on boats, although an increasing (but very small) number of westerners do so. Far fewer gain their living from the sea.

Friction still exists between different groups, most obviously (because of the numbers involved) between Filipino domestic workers and their employers and also between new immigrants from China and longer term Hong Kong Chinese residents.

The social/racial divides have increasingly polarised. Different from the 1880s, apart from a few public bars (particularly during the period just prior to the return of sovereignty to China) and one or two specialist stores mainly patronised by westerners (a couple of bookshops, a military hobbyists' shop), it is unusual to find a western assistant – or even manager – at shop-floor level in Hong Kong today. Once, in the present writer's experience, when a western nanny to a Chinese family appeared in a public restaurant, carrying the baby, in company with the family she worked for, a frisson of shock went through the whole (mainly Chinese) staff and clientele.

The Street Scene

Just like the people who mill in them, the Hong Kong street scene today is both new and the same. Amongst modern businesses and premises, the old trades and professions are still quietly practised.[1139] We can easily find pawn shops, bone-setters, chinese medicine practitioners and stockists, fortune-tellers, menders of watches and knife sharpeners. Street-side shops sell freshly made traditional healthy drinks, as well as new fruit drinks. Jade or objects in stone resembling jade are still sold on the street, and joss-sticks still burned. In unbuilt areas, people still gather leaves and other herbs.

Mentally ill but apparently harmless persons still walk the streets, speaking to others or themselves, or keeping their own counsel.

New forms of transport abound: cars, taxis, double-decker buses, mini-buses, trams. Sedan-chairs have completely gone. The remaining rickshaws are used merely as photographic props, but some serviceable bicycles are still used in the urban area (as well as being recreational toys, mainly in parts of the New Territories). Cross-harbour vehicular tunnels and a subway (the Mass Transit Railway or MTR) have not succeeded in suppressing the much longer-standing cross-harbour ferry service from Central.

Fruits, flowers and vegetables are now grown mainly in the New Territories, not yet part of Hong Kong's territory in the 1880s, or flown from further afield. Fowl, cattle and pigs are no longer husbanded in the Hong Kong urban areas, but imported from the Mainland of China daily. A large proportion of Hong Kong's daily water is now, as it has been for decades, obtained from the Mainland.

Environment

The built cities that we find in Hong Kong and Kowloon in the early 2000s are a great change from the 1880s. The extent of the mass of buildings is of course the most obvious. The shore line is different as well, moved outwards by successive reclamations.

The Queen's Road seamen's bar, "The Land we Live In", and others like it are gone.[1140] And so is the ambience they created. (The nearby Lan Kwai Fong redevelopment of older premises probably aspires to a quite different tone and mood.) The Royal Naval Canteen's "Blue Buildings" in Wanchai, the Commissariat Department, and residences such as "Bellevue" are no more. The American Consulate has moved from Wanchai to the corner of Garden Road and Lower Albert Road near the Central Government Offices. The Hong Kong Cricket Club is no longer at Central but has moved to Wongneichong Gap. The Supreme Court they knew was held in a different building from the one known today as the "former Supreme Court Building", built between 1903 and 1912, which now houses the Hong Kong Legislative Council. One change has been effectively reversed however. Under the second Chinese Chief Executive, the "*former* Government House" of Tung Chi Wah, the first Chinese Chief Executive's time is now termed, "Chief Executive's Residence".

But some remains of what these people in the 1880s would have known. [1141] On Hong Kong Island, the Botanical Gardens, Flagstaff House (now the Museum of Tea Ware), St Paul's Missionary College (now Bishop's House), Wanchai Police Station (an environmental agency, appropriately, occupies it now), St John's Cathedral, the Man Mo and many other temples, the Protestant, Catholic, Moslem, Parsee and Jewish cemeteries all in Happy Valley, Bethanie and the Dairy Farm Cowsheds in Pokfulam, the former Police Station at Stanley. Government House, the former French Mission Building, the former Douglas Castle (later Nazareth House and now University Hall) also survive, but in varyingly different forms.[1142]

In spite of changes, some sites retain a similar use. There is still a school where the Government Central School (which Frederick Stewart founded) stood for twenty-seven years. There is still a Recreation Ground in Tai Ping Shan. The Hongkong Bank still has premises at No. 1 Queen's

Road Central. But at the Hollywood Road Central Police Station complex, a profound change has taken place. The Central Magistracy no longer uses the 1914 building on Arbuthnot Road, on the same site as the Old Magistracy, built in 1847, where Frederick Stewart held his court. The police station closed at the end of 2004. Victoria Prison closed in December 2005.

Although there are additions, the street names of the 1880s still remain.[1143] And so do the streets and patterns of streets. Battery Path. The curve in Queen's Road Central, near the Hong Kong Bank (although most of the beautiful buildings which graced it in the 1880s have gone).

Certain flights of steps from the period are still there: from Duddell Street to Ice House Street, Queen's Road Central to Battery Path, Queens' Road Central to Gough Street. Even the imposing Duddell Street gas lamps (now converted to electricity) may already have been there in the 1880s.

In Kowloon, some Chinese temples remain from the period. But the oldest surviving colonial buildings were all completed somewhat later. The Observatory, in late 1883,[1144] the former Marine Police Headquarters in Tsim Sha Tsui in 1884 (a third storey was added later), the former Kowloon British School and St Andrew's Church – both in Nathan Road – in 1902 and 1905, respectively, the Kowloon-Canton Railway Terminus Clock Tower in 1915.

As for the New Territories, not part of Hong Kong until 1898, several old Chinese buildings and complexes remain, including walled villages, ancestral halls, study libraries and important residences.

Crime and The Law

As for crime itself, the law, which determines what crime is, and those who deal with crime, these also have changed. Christopher Coghlan describes modern-day Hong Kong crime as more complex, more sensational and (comparing like with like), more heavily penalised. He considers the increase in criminal cases today disproportionate; very much greater than can be explained by the mass of new legislation since Stewart's day, by the acquisition of the

New Territories and Islands or by the increased population of Hong Kong; or indeed by the combination of all these factors. He comes to the sad conclusion that mankind has become both more criminal and more unpleasant.

Some offences, which exist today, were not offences in the 1880s. As commented by Garry Tallentire, the presence of vice and vice-related crimes and of bribery offences today and the relative absence of these in the 1880s both reflect changes in the law. Similarly, Tim Hamlett observes on the absence in the 1880s (when opium was legal) of any reports of crimes of theft committed to finance a drug addiction.[1145] On the other hand, some offences of the 1880s are no longer regarded as crimes: suicide, Unlawful Possession, being a Rogue and a Vagabond.[1146]

The one known piece of Hong Kong Legislation formerly applicable to one race only – the "Light and Pass" rules – has long gone.[1147] Now Anti-Discrimination Laws exist to combat at least gender and disability discrimination. But resistance to anti-racial discrimination legislation is strong in the broader Hong Kong community.

Punishments

In Hong Kong, as in the United Kingdom, punishments no longer include capital punishment, caning, flogging, or the stocks. And the sentencing today is seen even more from a rehabilitation rather than a punitive point of view.[1148] As both Christopher Coghlan and Garry Tallentire comment, there are now many more sentencing options, and imprisonment is now used much less frequently. An innovation already looked for in the 1880s, special provision is now made for juvenile offenders.

Legal Personnel

Legal personnel themselves have changed, as well as the circumstances of their work. Magistrates are now trained lawyers, and include Chinese and women. As Geoffrey Roper points out, the Police Force is now predominantly Chinese and so are the leaders of the Force.[1149] Barristers and solicitors, also, are now predominantly Chinese.

The advice and information available to magistrates is considerably superior.[1150] The problems of interpretation and translation and a greater use of Chinese in the courts have now partly been solved by the improvements that computer technology has brought.[1151]

As for defendants, their circumstances also have changed. A Duty Lawyer Scheme now exists to assist those who otherwise could not afford private representation in court.[1152] Opinions may vary as to whether this is better than an unaided appearance before a magistrate as fair-minded as Frederick Stewart, but – given the numbers today – this is the best option available.

The Government, History, the Community

Many types of culture – not just national cultures – have an impact on what the law is, as well as on how law is practised. These cultures do change, but slowly. Although the Hong Kong Government no longer derives considerable revenue from the legal dealing in opium, as it did in the 1880s, tobacco still contributes a considerable income. As for the "mui-tsai" system, although there is no evidence of new "mui-tsai" recruits, the past practice of buying and selling children into a status, which a multitude of western eyes saw as life-time "slavery", still has an impact. Hong Kong adoption law is cautious as to what modern law continues to see as the possible abuses of adoption.

Culture

As in the 1880s, court interpreters in today's courts serve a double role. Magistrates, unfamiliar with the local culture or the culture of a particular defendant, may rely on their interpreter for cultural advice.[1153] However, the need for this today, with today's more westernised and urbanised population, may be less.

Taking a broader point of view, Verner Bickley comments that the logic of Hong Kong law in the 1880s in some cases clashed with the cultural tradition of the majority population.[1154] Again, this seems less likely to be true today. The twelve decades of development since the 1880s, within Hong Kong society itself as well as internationally (this also, in turn, influencing Hong Kong), have made considerable changes.

More than one magistrate may take the admirable view, expressed by Garry Tallentire in, "The Hong Kong (Police) Magistrate in the 1880s and 1990s", above, that it would be in error, "to try to impose pure Western values on the society of Hong Kong which enjoys a multi-racial and multi-custom social order". But Hong Kong society itself is now much closer in temper to an international city anywhere, and aspires to be even more so.

Writing of the period, late 1956/7 to 1988/9, and seeking to predict future crime trends on the basis of an analysis of those shown by the available data from this period, sociologist Harold Traver concludes that, "crime is a normal feature of society". "Though we are reluctant to admit it, a great deal of crime appears to be an unintended by-product of such things as economic growth,[1155] the elimination of social barriers to achievement, and the expansion of individual liberties – in short, many of the things that we frequently hold up as important achievements of a modern, open society."[1156]

It is clear that crime in the Hong Kong of the 1880s took place in a society where conditions such as Traver describes existed, although not all the Hong Kong offences recorded in *A Magistrate's Court in Nineteenth Century Hong Kong: Court in Time* may seem a direct product of such circumstances.

Taking Traver's view as a basis, it may be suggested that the business of the Hong Kong magistrates' courts in the 1880s (as at other times) does not reflect colonial insensitivity, as some commentators argue, suggesting that defendants should never have been brought into such a formal place of trial at all, but – as in their own cultural setting of origin – dealt with in a more Confucian manner. Rather, it reflects the opportunities, newly presented by the colony's mere existence, for individuals of all backgrounds.

~~~~~

Cases brought for alleged Offences against "The Excise Ordinance (Opium) 1858-1879, Amendment Ordinance 1879": their results, the sentences given & notes on the relevant legislation[1157]

With a Table showing, for each opium case, the amount of the fine and the alternative period of imprisonment, showing whether the latter was with, or without, hard labour.

The Ordinance applicable to these 1881-1882 court cases is Ordinance No. 7 of 1879, "The Excise Ordinance (Opium) 1858-1879, Amendment Ordinance 1879".[1158]

All the offences against the Opium Ordinance in this set of reports concern possession of opium, unlicensed by the Opium Farmer.

Based on a study of these court case reports and from searching the legislation which relates to them, the following picture has emerged.

The term, "possession", was defined by Ordinance No. 1 of 1879, para. 1 as follows: "for the purposes of this Ordinance, any boiled or prepared opium, or utensils or vessels used for preparing the same shall be deemed to be in possession of any person if he knowingly have them in actual possession, custody, or control by himself or by any other person."

Broadly speaking, the position was that no-one in Hong Kong or in Hong Kong waters could have in their possession, whether for their own use or for sale, any prepared opium at all unless they had obtained it from the current Opium Farmer or from any of the licensed agents of the current Opium Farmer. Since the law was very strictly enforced, it would have been prudent for anyone, even with authorized possession of prepared opium from an authorized source, to keep available, in case he or she was ever requested to show it, the certificate, which it was the legal responsibility of the seller to provide each purchaser.[1159]

The position of Opium Farmer was obviously well-known

and "The Opium Farmer" (less often, "the Farmer") is referred to in some twenty-one of the twenty-three cases. (CCs 19, 91, 111, 124, 178, 210, 307, 324, 327, 329, 371, 375, 386, 434, 445, 492, 511, 535, 548, 569, 646.)

Almost all the cases refer to *prepared* opium, a few refer to *raw* opium (e.g. CCs 124, 178, 386, 548) and a similar number to opium *dross* (e.g. CCs 19, 124, 178, 371, 492) or opium refuse (CCs 178, 434). One only refers to *crude* opium (CC 124). In three cases, there is reference to opium *balls* (CCs 91, 386, 434). The term, "*boiled*", is used seldom and then only as a verb (CCs 327, 492). In one case Malwa Opium and Patna opium are named (CC 91) and in another case Malwa Opium only (CC 548). In one case, there are no details at all about the type of opium that was found (CC 264). In another, the opium could be described in none of these ways, as the defendant was in the process of boiling it (CC 445).

The charge in most cases was being in possession of prepared opium without a (valid) permit or a (valid) certificate from the Opium Farmer.

There was a legal reason for the overwhelming majority of references in these reports to "prepared" opium. Under the Ordinance, the finding of prepared or boiled opium, as well as utensils for preparing or boiling it, in unauthorized possession or unauthorized circumstances, was not only the primary offence but it was also a prerequisite for seizing raw opium.

> "All boiled or prepared opium offered or exposed for sale or retail by any unauthorized person and all boiled or prepared opium found in the possession or custody or control of any unauthorized person or in any unauthorized place, except as in the last section mentioned,[1160] and any utensils or vessels which have been used or which are manifestly intended to be used in boiling or preparing opium by any unauthorised person or in any unauthorized place, may be seized by a police or excise officer, and shall be forfeited and may be by a Magistrate delivered and adjudged to the holder of the

exclusive privilege for the time being, and any unauthorized person in whose possession any such boiled or prepared opium or utensils or vessels are found may be apprehended and taken before a Magistrate by any police or excise officer." (Ordinance No. 1 of 1879, para. 7.)

"Wherever boiled or prepared opium is so seized as last aforesaid and any such utensils or vessels are also seized as aforesaid [present writer's emphasis], the police or excise officer seizing the same may also seize any raw opium [present writer's emphasis] that may be found in the custody or control of such unauthorized person or in such unauthorized place and such raw opium shall be subject to the order of the Magistrate before whom the case is brought." (Ordinance No. 1 of 1879, para. 8.)

There was also provision under the Ordinance for an officer to seize raw opium under special circumstances, where no boiled or prepared opium was found in the possession of an unauthorized person or place.

"Whenever from any other cause [i.e. beyond that provided for in Ordinance No. 1 of 1879, paras 7 & 8] there is reasonable ground to believe that boiled or prepared opium is manufactured by any unauthorized person or in any unauthorized place within this Colony it shall be lawful for a police or excise officer to seize any raw opium found in the possession of such unauthorized person or in such unauthorised place." (Ordinance No. 1 of 1879, para. 9.)

This would have given authority in relation to CC 124, where the charge was, "possession of crude opium without a certificate", for the report quotes the Police Constable as stating that he found, "five empty tins in one of which there were traces of prepared opium".

Inadequate certificates

Some defendants produced documentation which was considered inadequate. In one case, the defendant produced three certificates for the purchase of opium designed for shipment, saying that the opium had been bought for coolies on board a barque, "which was going to a foreign country", but the certificates bore others' names, not the defendant's (CC 386). In one case the Defendant produced a number of certificates, but on examination by the Court Interpreter they were all were found to be obsolete and of no value (CC 535). The Defendant showed the Inspector six permits when he was asked to show a permit (CC 548). However, the Court Interpreter stated that, of the six permits, only two belonged to the defendant, and were only to the amount of ten taels. But the Defendant stated that he bought the two tins of prepared opium from the Opium Farm. This case was remanded to allow the defendant to bring forward the parties he said he bought the opium from, and bail was accepted. In a final case of this type, the Defendant, "a compradore, belonging to Canton", "produced a permit for a portion of the opium, but some of it being proved to be eight or nine years old, no permit could have been procured for it as the Opium Farmer did not have the monopoly at that time, and as he had failed to inform the Opium Farmer of having it in his possession since, an offence was proved. The case was remanded till to-day to allow the defendant to procure a permit, as he said he had forgot about its being on his premises. The Opium Farmer, however, [c?/w?]ould not grant the permit at this late date, as the rules would be infringed by doing so. The defendant should have applied for a permit when the notice was issued." (CC569). The sentence in this last case was relatively low — $10 or two days' imprisonment and confiscation of the opium — and this maybe reflects that the Magistrate was taking into consideration that the Defendant lived outside Hong Kong (in Canton), as well perhaps as indicating his view that the Opium Farmer was being rather literal in his application of the rules.

The sentences

In most of the cases, it is stated that the unauthorised opium found was to "go to", "be handed over to", "be delivered to", "be given to", or "be forfeited to" the Opium Farmer. In those cases where the opium was "to be forfeited" (CC 327, 535), it seems likely that this is shorthand for, "forfeited to the Opium Farmer". Presumably the same may be true of the two cases where the opium was to be "confiscated". (CC 569, 646) In some reports, nothing is said about what was to happen to the opium. (E.g. CCs 264, 375, 434, 445.) Possibly this was an oversight on the reporter's part or maybe the editor cut these reports.

In several cases, the sentence was a fine or a period of imprisonment, but, unlike the cases involving offences against the gambling ordinance, where most give an alternative of imprisonment with hard labour, in a few only of these opium cases (e.g. CCs 324, 434, 492, 200, 646) does the sentence mention imprisonment, "with hard labour".

The following table shows the amounts of the fine in each case, together with the alternative penalty available. It seems that there was no standard equivalence between the amount of the fine and the length of the alternative period of imprisonment. In one case the alternative to a fine of $15 was five days (CC 19), in another, the alternative to a $5 fine was seven days (CC 33). The alternative to a $25 fine was in one case one month's imprisonment (CC 91), and in another, 21 days (CC 124). In one case, the alternative to a $100 fine was six months with hard labour (CC 434); in another, the alternative to $200 fine was two months with hard labour.

It seems unlikely that the alternatives were set, based on how the Magistrate was feeling on any particular day. (This is a claim that E. J. Eitel made about cases relating to paupers.) [1161] Probably there were other considerations, practices of the court at the time, not indicated in the Ordinances, in which the alternative sentences were carefully based on the particulars of each and every individual case, including the evidence and the Magistrate's view of the witnesses in court. Some of the witnesses, the Magistrate would have known better than others — the members of the Police Force, the excise officers, possibly even the informers — and he would have built up over time an impression of their reliability as witnesses.

60. Table showing, for each opium case, the amount of the fine and the alternative period of imprisonment, showing whether the later was with or without hard labour ("hard").

CC	Amount of fine	Alternative jail period	CC	Amount of fine	Alternative jail period
19	$15	5 days	33	$5	7 days
91	$25	1 month	111	$10	14 days
124	$25	21 days	178	$20	14 days
210	$20	21 days	264	$20	14 days
307	100	2 months	324	$50	6 weeks w. hard
327	$100	6 weeks	329	$25	10 days
371	$50	2 months	375	$50	2 months
386	Remanded		434	$100	6 months w hard
445	$10	7 days	492	$25	6 months w. hard
511	$200	2 months w. hard	535	$25	6 weeks
548	Remanded		569	$10	2 days
646	1st Def-endant	Remanded	646	2nd Def-endant: $50	6 months w. hard

As for the primary sentence, did it match the apparent offence? In one case, where only a tael of opium was found (in a house in Sai Wan village), the sentence was $100 or two months' imprisonment, which seems to a lay person exceptionally severe (CC 307). Perhaps there were other circumstances, not mentioned in the report, but hinted at by the presence of a brass boiler and opium strainer at the premises.

Repeat offenders?

None of the defendants is said to have been sentenced for the offence before. It is true that this point is mentioned in a case, where the defendant, having unlawful possession of stolen goods, had gone with them to an opium divan. (CC 232.) But this is an opium-related case, not an opium case as such.

Informers, Excise Officers and Police

Some of the defendants in these cases are explicitly stated to have been informed against and subsequently arrested by a member of the Police Force, with a warrant in his possession. In one case, an Inspector of police, excise officer and informer all gave evidence (CC 91); in another, an Inspector, two excise officers and an informer had searched the premises together (CC 548); in another it was an Acting Sergeant, an informer and two Excise Officers (CC 535). In one case, an informer purchased opium from the defendant, informed the Opium Farmer and laid information (CC 124). In another case, we are told that the informer bought opium from the defendant, "laid an information" with the Opium Farmer, and the search warrant was then issued at the instance of the Opium Farmer (CC 492). In another case, the informer purchased opium from the defendant, and then, "laid an information" with the police (CC 307).

Informers

Why did the informers act as they did? — The answer seems simple. Rewards were evidently involved and presumably they did it for the money. It seems no coincidence that several of the informers were unemployed. More than one was an unemployed servant (e.g. CCs 375, 492). At least three were unemployed coolies (CCs 386, 511, 548).[1162] However, unlike in some of the cases dealing with other offences, none of these opium case reports state explicitly that any of the fine was going to an informer. Did Frederick Stewart really not award any part of any fine to informers in these cases? (He was entitled to award up to one half of the fine to an informer under Ordinance No. 7 of 1879, para. X.) Similarly, although he is reported as awarding the opium, the subject of the cases in question, to the Opium Farmer, no report states that he awarded any of the fine to, "the holder of the exclusive privilege", that is, the Opium Farmer. Again, under Ordinance No. 7 of 1879, para. X, any part of the fine not awarded to an informer was to be paid over to the Opium Farmer. Had the law changed? Or the practice of the law? Was it simply too complicated for the Court Reporter or too lengthy for the Editor to include this information in the published reports?

Excise Officers

As for the Excise Officers, they were not government officials as such but "agents or servants" of the Opium Farmer, appointed or licensed by the Governor of Hong Kong. (Ordinance No. 1 of 1879, para. 11.) Consistent with this, there is no listing of Excise Officers in the "Index to Establishments" in the Hong Kong Government Blue Books, during the relevant period; which tends to confirm that they were not remunerated by the Hong Kong Government. The names and places of residence of every excise officer "were to be posted in a conspicuous place at the Police Court." (Ordinance No. 1 of 1879, para. 12.) They were to wear a badge, "bearing such sign or mark of office as may be directed by the Governor". Before acting against any person under the provisions of the Ordinance, every excise officer was to declare his office and show his badge to the person against whom he was about to act." (Ordinance No. 1 of 1879, para. 13.) Impersonation of an Excise Officer was punishable by, "a penalty not exceeding one hundred dollars." (Ordinance No. 1 of 1879, para. 11.)

Police

Police acting in such cases were also to show evidence of their position. "Every Police officer acting under the provision of this or the said recited Ordinance [i.e. Ordinance No. 2 of 1858], if not in the uniform proper to his service[,] shall in like manner [i.e. similar to what the Excise Officers were required to do] declare his office and produce to the person against whom he is about to act such part of his public equipment as the Captain Superintendent of Police shall have directed or may direct to be carried by Police officers when employed on secret or special service." (Ordinance No. 1 of 1879, para. 13.)

Warrants

A warrant is mentioned in eight of these opium cases. (CCs 371, 375, 386, 434, 445, 492, 511, 535.)

Search warrants could be issued by a Justice of the Peace as follows:

> Seizure under search warrant. "Any Justice of the Peace may issue a search warrant under section 9 of the said recited Ordinance [i.e. Ordinance No. 2 of 1858], [1163] and such search warrant may be executed by any police or excise officer and the person executing any such search warrant may seize and hold any utensils or vessels which have been used or which are manifestly intended to be used in boiling or preparing opium and in any case where boiled or prepared opium is found under the circumstances mentioned in the said section of the said recited Ordinance [i.e. Ordinance No. 2 of 1858] or any such utensils or vessels as last aforesaid are found, may also seize any raw opium found in the possession of any person having such boiled or prepared opium, utensils, or vessels, or in any such tenement, place, or vessel as is mentioned in the said section." (Ordinance No. 1 of 1879, para. 10.)

It seems likely that, when there is no mention of a warrant

but an Informer or Excise Officer or both are mentioned (e.g. CCs 91, 124, 327), the search was in fact conducted under the authority of a warrant.

In some circumstances, action could be taken by a Police Inspector without a warrant.

> "It shall be lawful for an Inspector of Police having reasonable ground for believing that there is boiled or prepared opium in any ship within the waters of the Colony contrary to the provisions of the Opium Ordinances, (such ship not being a ship of war or vessel having the status of a ship of war) to proceed without warrant on board such ship and search for boiled or prepared opium and seize any boiled or prepared opium so found, and it shall be lawful for such Inspector to take the opium so found together with the person in whose custody possession or control it is found before a Police Magistrate, to be dealt with according to law." (Ordinance No. 7 of 1879, VIII.)

There is one case where Police Inspector Swanston was clearly acting under this authority. For, although he boarded a junk at sea and seized the opium that he found there, as well as arresting the Defendant, no mention is made of any search warrant (CC178). In fact, no direct evidence is reported in *The China Mail*, to the effect that he had "reasonable ground for believing" that there was "boiled or prepared opium" on the ship, "contrary to the provisions of the Opium Ordinances", unless the statement, "Had known defendant for two years as the master of the junk", is intended to convey this.

In this same case (CC 178), it seems that the opium equipment was seized under Ordinance No. 1 of 1879, para. 7, which reads as follows:

> "All boiled or prepared opium offered or exposed for sale or retail by any unauthorized person and all boiled or prepared opium found in the possession or custody or control of any unauthorized person or in any unauthorized place, except as in the last section mentioned,[1164] and any utensils or vessels which

have been used or which are manifestly intended to be used in boiling or preparing opium by any unauthorised person or in any unauthorized place, may be seized [present writer's emphasis] by a police or excise officer, and shall be forfeited and may be by a Magistrate delivered and adjudged to the holder of the exclusive privilege for the time being, and any unauthorized person in whose possession any such boiled or prepared opium or utensils or vessels are found may be apprehended and taken before a Magistrate by any police or excise officer." (Ordinance No. 1 of 1879, para. 7.)

In other circumstances, action could be taken by any Police or Excise Officer without a warrant.

"It shall be lawful for any Police or Excise Officer to arrest, without warrant, any person within the Colony whom he reasonably suspects [present writer's emphasis] to be conveying or to have concealed on his person boiled or prepared opium which has not paid duty to the holder of the exclusive privilege, and to convey such person to the nearest Police Station, there to be dealt with according to law." (Ordinance No. 7 of 1879, IX.)

The above would seem to be the authority under which an excise officer arrested the defendant arriving from the Canton steamer (CC 324).

The attendance of an Excise Officer at the arrival of steamers from Canton or Macau (rather like Customs Officers at some ferry piers and airports today) was clearly appropriate, given the nature of their official duties. The following wording was particularly appropriate to their doing so: "No person shall bring into this Colony, or the waters thereof, or have in his possession or custody within the same, any boiled prepared opium without having a valid certificate under section 7 of Ordinance No. 2 of 1858, as amended." (Ordinance No. 7 of 1879, para. V.)

There are several cases where there is no mention of a warrant, of an informer or an excise officer. We cannot speculate by what authority the defendant in each of these cases came to appear in court. But the evidence suggests that the Opium Ordinances were well understood and conscientiously acted upon by those enforcing the law. It seems unlikely that there was any illegality in the arrests that had been made.

Pleading guilty, co-operating with the police, being caught in a lie

Some may have improved their situation by pleading guilty. The man who pleaded that he had shown the opium he had to the Inspector immediately on his producing the warrant (CC 445) may have improved his position by doing and stating this.

However, several defendants were caught in a lie, either in court, or (according to witnesses) in what they said during the search that had been made. Most spectacular perhaps is the case of the woman who, admitting that she had no permit, claimed that the opium had been that of her husband, who had died two months previously. However, the informer stated that he had bought opium from her husband only a few days previously (CC 375). Perhaps reflecting her lie, her sentence (HK$50 or two months' imprisonment) was relatively severe. In another case, which could have been one of absent-mindedness or forgetfulness when under pressure perhaps, the defendant, when visited in his house and asked to open a safe, sent a coolie to find a key. But the coolie returned saying he could not find it. After the Police Inspector said that the safe would have to be broken open and the defendant would have to go along to the Police Station, the defendant produced the key from an inner pocket! (CC 386.)

Denials, excuses and defences

Some defendants denied they had any opium. Some defendants offered excuses. Some may include what defendants understood to be mitigating circumstances. One, admitting that he had boiled the opium, stated that it was for his own use (CC 327). Two denied selling the opium that had been found and each said that what was found was for his own use (CCs 307, 323). One said that it really had been bought from the Opium Farmer, by his son, and produced tickets showing the purchase of opium (CC 178). One said some friends had brought it from Macau and given it him (CC 210); another that some man brought the opium and boiling utensils that had been found, from on board a ship; and that he himself had nothing to do with them (CC 434). Another denied having sold any opium to the informer, admitted having opium in his possession, but explained that some of this he had purchased from the Opium Farmer and the remainder he had received from friends (CC 535). This last defendant was fined $25 or six weeks imprisonment.

A traveler from Macao said that he came from Macao and knew nothing of the laws of Hong Kong. He smoked over a tael a day and what he had was for his own use (CC 329). He was still fined $25, in default ten days' imprisonment; the opium to be forfeited to the Farmer. He seems to have been treated no differently from other defendants, despite his non-resident status and his plea of ignorance about the laws of Hong Kong.

In one of the cases where the defendant's documentation was said to be inadequate (CC 548), the Defendant nevertheless stated that he bought the two tins of prepared opium from the Opium Farm. He also said he was a dealer in Malwa Opium, and had bought the raw opium from Hadjee Ali, Yuk-ün and U-ün. He denied selling any opium to the informer. The pans in Court he used for boiling his food and the scales were used for weighing raw opium. This case was remanded to allow the defendant to bring forward the parties he said he bought the opium from, and bail in two sureties of $100 each was accepted. It seems that the Magistrate entertained the suspicion at least that the informer might have been telling a lie and was willing to believe that the man was an opium dealer and might therefore indeed have purchased opium in a legal manner.

One defendant offered what seems to have been an informed defence, stating that the material found was for medicinal use (CC 386) (which was allowable under Ordinance No. 2 of 1858, para. 5, still current at the time). Another — the master of the junk (CC 178) — said that, "the pan was only used when they were at sea"; apparently showing knowledge that it was an offence to be found in possession of unauthorized opium at sea only in Hong Kong waters and apparently hoping therefore that this statement would somehow help him to be exempt, even though it was in fact in Hong Kong waters that he had been found with unauthorized opium and equipment for preparing it.

Who were these defendants?

All the names mentioned are Chinese names and it seems that, in these cases as a whole (as in the gambling cases), no-one other than a Chinese is arrested for opium or opium-related offences. One only was a woman (CC 375), described as a, "married woman". Her fine was relatively heavy, probably influenced by the strong indication that she told a lie, stating that the opium had belonged to her husband who had died two months previously, whereas the informer said that he had bought opium from her husband some days previously.

Generally, the age of defendants is not mentioned. We do know, however, that at least some were youngish men and some fairly elderly. Of the four described as "unemployed", one was twenty-two, one was thirty-two and one was sixty-eight years old. Another (no occupation given) was seventy-four. The occupations of the men were fairly varied. One was master of a licensed fishing junk. There was a cook, a sixty-year old pig dealer, a seaman, a carpenter, an opium dross dealer, an accountant, a driver, a fishmonger, a shop-coolie, a shopkeeper and a compradore belonging to Canton.

Time of day and place where the opium was found

The time of day is mentioned in several of these cases, usually the evening, but in a couple of cases, the afternoon. This detail appears to be a means of making the witness's statement more realistic, rather than for any other reason.

The place of the offence is not detailed with the same frequency as in the gambling cases, although the following are mentioned, mainly in the central area of Hong Kong Island or less often in Wanchai: Number 9, Canton

Bazaar; Number 12, Chi Mi Lane; top floor of Number 8, Shin Hing Lane; Hing Lung Lane; Number 15, Stanley Street; Number 3, Tung-man Lane; Number 51, Wanchai Street; Number 80, Wellington Street; Number 40, Wellington Street. It is interesting, however, that one raid took place following information at Sai wan village (CC 307) and another at Stanley (CC 375). In some cases, the actual floor of a building or the room is mentioned: bedroom; top floor. From today's perspective, it is amusing to read that some opium was being kept in the servants' quarters at the back of the Hong Kong Club. In some cases, the opium was found in a dwelling: — defendant's house; defendant's bedroom; a junk. In one case, although the place searched was described as the defendant's house, there were ten or twelve men "laying about smoking opium" (CC 371).

One place is significant though. As mentioned above, it seems that the excise officer made it a practice to go to meet both the Canton steamer (CC 324) and the Macau steamer (CC 329). Sometimes however, opium was successfully brought in. In one case the defendant said that the opium that had been found had been brought from Macau by some friends and given to him (CC 210).

In another case, discussed in other contexts in this essay, including under the sub-heading, "An unusual case", immediately below, the arrest was made at sea, on board a junk in Shau-ki-wan Bay (CC 178). (As this was, "Within the waters of the Colony", this was allowed under Ordinance No. 7 of 1879, VIII.)

An unusual case

In the case where opium was found on board a junk in Shau-ki-wan Bay (CC 178), the charge was, "unlawful possession of a quantity of prepared opium without a valid certificate from the Farmer". But the Defendant said that the opium belonged to his son, who bought it from the Opium Farmer. He produced in court two tickets showing the purchase of 2 taels, 6 mace, 3 candareens on August 11, and 1 tael, 2 mace on August 26th. There was another ticket for 2 taels in June.

It is not explained whether there was a difference

between a "permit from the Opium Farmer", which the Excise Officer, Mr Santos, said that the Defendant did not have, and "tickets showing purchase", such as the Defendant produced in court.

The amount of opium was reported in different ways by the Police Inspector who made the seizure and Mr Santos, the Excise Officer. The Inspector said there were two sets of scales bearing traces of opium, two horn boxes nearly full of prepared opium, a pillow box containing three other horn boxes, nearly full of prepared opium, five earthenware jars containing more or less opium; a tin box with opium dross, and a piece of about four oz. of raw opium, several empty pots containing traces of prepared opium, a small box three parts full of prepared opium, a strainer containing opium refuse, and a large horn box containing about three taels of opium. The Excise Officer said there was about ten or twenty taels of prepared opium, and three taels of raw opium. The tickets produced by the Defendant related to a total of five taels, eight mace and three cadareens. One cadareen = ten mace and one mace = ten taels. It is clear from this that the amount of opium found was much less than the amount which the tickets showing purchase accounted for.

The ticket for the largest amount was dated 11 August, that for the next largest quantity was dated 26 August, and the ticket for the smallest amount was dated 2 June. Was the court sceptical about this evidence? Did Frederick Stewart feel that the tickets belonged to another person than the Defendant? Did he feel that the amounts were greater than could be consumed by one person (the Defendant's son, whose opium the Defendant declared it to be)?

It seems that the most damning evidence was the finding of equipment for preparing opium, particularly the strainer containing opium refuse and the brass pan, which the Defendant clearly admitted using, as his evidence was that, "the pan was only used when they were at sea".

The Defendant was fined $20 or 14 days' imprisonment; and all the opium, raw and prepared, was to go to the Opium Farmer.

Medicinal Use (CC 386)

In one case, the Defendant made the defence that the opium found was for medicinal use only. "The opium in Court was simply washings, and it was deposited in the safe to prevent his coolies from smoking it. About four years ago he bought some raw opium from a wreck. When boiled it was good for skin diseases. He denied having ever sold any opium." (CC 386.)

The accountant to the opium farm, Chan Sing Tai, was present in court, apparently as an expert witness. Having first stated that he was well acquainted with opium and its preparation, he expressed the opinion that the prepared opium in Court was made from the samples of raw opium shown, although it would be of poor quality unless mixed with some of a better kind.

This was disputed by the Defendant, who said that the raw opium in court would not produce opium at all if boiled.

Disputing this view in turn, the accountant to the opium farm declared he could boil the raw material and realise the same quality of the drug as that in Court.

The decision made by the Magistrate was a practical one, first to determine which of the statements — the accountant's or the Defendant's — was correct. He instructed that the raw opium should be boiled under the supervision of the police. To allow time for this to be done, the case was then remanded until a set date, bail being accepted "in one householder in the sum of $50".

If the evidence was that the material was for medical use (because it could not be used for smoking), then the case would perhaps be dropped, because this was allowed by Ordinance No. 2 of 1858, para. 5, which was still current.[1165]

Opium equipment

Equipment for making and using opium, as well as containers bearing evidence of having contained opium is mentioned in several cases.

Attempts to avoid discovery

There is no doubt that most of the defendants knew that possession of opium without a license from the Opium Farmer was illegal. Some took measures to avoid discovery of the opium. While an Inspector was speaking to the defendants in the servants' quarters at the Hong Kong Club, an excise officer observed the first defendant crawl under the bed, and caught him with two boxes of opium in his hands. (511) In another case, immediately the defendant became acquainted with the object of the Sergeant's visit, he put his hand behind him and upset a pot containing about four taels of opium. (CC 434) This seems to have been a common ploy. The Defendant in another case first denied having any opium, but the constable found a pot of prepared opium (produced) in a bed-room, that had been upset after witness entered the house. (CC 371) One man kept opium in an earthenware jar, similar to one in which he kept medicine (CC 492) and, although admitting that the opium found had been boiled from opium dross, and that he had done so himself, he asserted that it was only a medicine and could not be smoked. The dross had accumulated during the last twelve months." However, an informer testified that he had bought opium from the man recently.

Interestingly, none of the defendants showed the terrible fear of arrest that the gamblers in the gambling cases show.

Not surprisingly, at least some of those professionally concerned with the provision of opium could be associated with other offences and knew some pretty tough characters. A fifty-two year old licensed opium dealer, who kept an opium divan at 45, Praya at Yau-mah-ti, British Kowloon, was charged with receiving stolen goods there. (CC 170 & CC 200) The *China Mail* Editor was in no doubt what this said about him. "Thieves Friend", the caption to the report on the second hearing proclaims. A seventy-year old man, living at Number 63, Temple Street, Yau-mah-ti, a fellow clansman's house that he said he was looking after, deposed that three men came in there. One seized him by the throat, rubbed his face with pepper, tied a cravat round his throat and nearly strangled him. The other two men in the meantime ransacked the house, taking—with other goods—some of his property. After the theft, the thieves went to the Defendant's opium divan and the stolen goods were later found in his possession there. He refused to say who brought them. He also refused to give the police any information to enable them to get hold of the thieves, saying it would cause too much trouble. So firmly did he believe in the trouble that his giving information would case, that he was willing to incur a sentence of six weeks' imprisonment with hard labour to avoid it.

This was not the only case in these Reports where stolen goods were taken to an opium divan. One man was informed on for taking two bundles to an opium divan in Square Street in the middle of the night and was found on a bed there, using the stolen blanket for a pillow, with one of the bundles, containing two jackets, under the bed (CC 232). This defendant seems to have lived on the fringes of society, for he had been in gaol three times before and the arresting policeman said he often saw him prowling about the streets. On this occasion, he tried to avoid arrest by pointing out a blind boy as their owner of the goods. In spite of this, the sentence seems to have been relatively light for the time, thirty days with hard labour or a fifteen shillings fine.

The opium habit gave rise to other offences. It seems that people carried opium boxes about their person[1166] — in a purse or pocket maybe — and that others might pickpocket them to obtain these.[1167] And as we have just seen (in relation to CC 232), those in possession of stolen goods might think of an opium establishment as a good place to hide them.[1168]

Appendix

The Excise Ordinance (Opium) 1858-1879, Amendment Ordinance 1879: Selections to explain the opium and opium-related cases before Frederick Stewart, July 1881 to March 1882.

A discussion of opium is often regarded as central to a discussion of the early relations between China and the West. An early discussion appears in J. R. Eames, *The English in China* (1909). He states that, after the signing of the treaties of Nanking, "the opium traffic took a new lease of life", although the law against the importation of opium into China remained unaltered.[1169]

> At every Treaty Port a flourishing trade in opium arose, connived at by the officials and openly prosecuted by the Foreigners. The new colony of Hong-kong became the centre of illicit trade, the smugglers finding no difficulty in transporting across the frontier goods that could lawfully and openly be taken into the port. So great became the scandal, that in 1858[1170] Lord Elgin came to the conclusion that legalization was the only remedy. In this view the Chinese acquiesced, and opium was admitted subject to a duty of 30 taels per chest, on the same footing as general imports under the Treaty of Nanking. After importation it was to pass into Chinese hands and become subject to such duties as the Government should think proper. Since that date opium has been more and more grown in China, with the result that the importation from abroad is but a fraction of the whole."[1171]

Eames specifically refers to the later Chefoo Convention of 1876,[1172] which had provisions relating to opium,[1173] which were modified by a supplementary agreement made on 18 July 1885 in London,[1174] ratified 6 May 1886. But he states that soon after, 11 September 1886, "the Opium Convention was signed, by which the importation of opium into

Hong-kong was further regulated." [1175]

The cases of breaches of the Opium Ordinance, reported in *The Complete Court Cases*, took place after the legalization of the opium trade in 1858 and the much later Chefoo Convention of 1876 on the one hand and the supplementary agreement of 18 July 1885, ratified 6 May 1886 on the other hand.

There are several nineteenth-century local Hong Kong Ordinances relating to opium, including Ordinance No. 11 of 1844, No. 5 of 1845, No. 4 of 1853, No. 2 of 1858, No. 7 of 1858, No. 1 of 1879, No. 7 of 1879, No. 4 of 1883, No. 8 of 1883, No. 1 of 1884, No. 17 of 1886 and No. 22 of 1887. [1176]

The Ordinance applicable to these 1881-1882 court cases before Frederick Stewart is clearly Ordinance No. 7 of 1879, "The Excise Ordinance (Opium) 1858-1879, Amendment Ordinance 1879".

A reading of the relevant Opium Ordinances, together with the opium cases among the Court Cases of Frederick Stewart, July 1881 to March 1882, helps to illuminate each.

The purpose of the Opium Ordinances during the period in question was clearly to protect the monopoly of the Opium Farmer, [1177] and thus to protect also the revenue which the Hong Kong Government obtained by means of selling the monopoly. [1178] — In 1879, the monopoly was sold for three years for the annual sum of $205,000. [1179] In 1882, the monopoly was sold for one year for HK$210,000. [1180]

If any case, infringing the Ordinance, was proved, some recompense was to be given to the Opium Farmer. "If any charge or complaint shall be preferred under 'the Excise Ordinance (Opium) 1858-1879' or under any of the said regulations made thereunder and upon the said charge or complaint the accused shall be convicted, the pecuniary penalty imposed upon the offender shall, after the adjudication of a portion of the same not exceeding one half at the discretion of the Magistrate to the informer, be paid to the holder of the exclusive privilege, and all the boiled or prepared opium to which the same relates shall be forfeited and by the magistrate adjudged and delivered to the holder of the privilege." (Ordinance No. 7 of 1879, para. X.)

Several paragraphs in the Ordinances are aimed at protecting the interests of an incoming Opium Farmer, ruling as to what should and should not be done by the outgoing monopoly holder towards the end of the period during which he held the license. For example, he was not to produce more opium than usual at that particular time of year or to sell off stock at prices less than the current going price.

Thus, Ordinance No. 7 of 1879, paragraph 7, reads: "Neither the holder of the exclusive privilege nor his licensees shall, during the three months preceding the end of his term, manufacture more than the usual quantity of boiled or prepared opium, or during the said three months sell any boiled or prepared opium at less than the average current prices of the day, or in greater quantities than usual at the time of the year, and at the end of his term shall not sell, export, or otherwise make away with, or dispose of any of his stock of boiled or prepared opium, but shall make over to the new holder of the said exclusive privilege the full and complete stock of raw or boiled and prepared opium then in his possession at the marketable value thereof and in the event of any difference arising as to quantities of boiled and prepared opium manufactured or sold during the last three months of the term and the price of the same and of the nature and quantity of the raw or boiled or prepared opium so to be purchased or made over and the prices thereof such difference shall be determined by three arbitrators, one to be appointed by the new holder of the exclusive privilege, one by the person whose exclusive privilege has expired or is about to expire, and one by the Governor, and the award of such arbitrators or a majority of them shall be final, and the arbitration or such other settlement shall be held at such time after the end of the term of the outgoing holder of the exclusive privilege as to the Governor may seem reasonable, and any award made may be filed in Court pursuant to the provisions of 'the Hong Kong Code of Civil Procedure.'" (Ordinance No. 7 of 1879, paragraph 7.)

This concern extended to those to whom the outgoing Opium Farmer had issued a certificate and to their own stock of opium. Their certificate would cease to be valid after noon of the third day from the date of the expiration of "his privilege" (Ordinance No. 7 of 1879, section 4.)

Shortly after Frederick Stewart had heard his last case as Police Magistrate, when he was Acting Colonial Secretary, he issued a Government Notification of "Supplementary Conditions, made by the Governor in Council, to which licenses granted under the Excise Ordinances (Opium), 1858-1879, are to be subject".[1181] Clearly there was concern that the Opium Farmer was being cheated by those to whom he granted licences. From now onwards, among other regulations, licensees were to pay the Opium Farmer a monthly fee in advance and report to him daily "the quantity of Opium sold per day".[1182]

Preamble to Ordinance No. 1 of 1879

The Preamble to Ordinance No. 1 of 1879 refers to Ordinance No. 2 of 1858 which re- established an Opium monopoly.[1183] (Presumably it is no coincidence that this was the year when the opium trade was legalized.)

"Whereas by Ordinance No. 2 of 1858 it is enacted (amongst other things) that the Governor in Council may grant unto any persons for such considerations and upon such conditions and for such terms and periods and in such form as from time to time shall be by the Governor in Council regulated and determined and also previously notified to the pubic in the *Hong Kong Government Gazette* the sole privilege of boiling and preparing opium and of selling and retailing within this Colony or the waters thereof opium so boiled and prepared".

The Preamble also states that Ordinance No. 2 of 1858 enacts, "that the person, if any, actually holding any such privilege is thereby empowered to grant licenses to all proper persons authorizing them to boil and prepare opium and to sell and retail opium so boiled and prepared".

Among those provisions of **Ordinance No. 2 of 1858** which were still current up to and beyond 1881-1882,

some are particularly relevant to the "The Complete Court Cases of Magistrate Frederick Stewart as Reported in *The China Mail*, July 1881 to March 1882". For instance: —
"From henceforward, no person not holding any such privilege or licence, or save as he may be by such privilege or licence in that behalf authorized, shall, within this Colony or the waters thereof, boil or in any way prepare opium, or sell, retail, or offer or expose for sale or retail, any boiled or prepared opium; yet so that no medical practitioner, chemist, or druggist, not being a Chinaman, or (being such) not having an European or American diploma, shall be prevented from preparing or selling opium *bona fide* for medicinal purposes, the burthen of proof whereof shall be upon any person alleging the same in his defence." (Ordinance No. 2 of 1858, para. 5)

Some of the paragraphs of Ordinance No. 1 of 1879 are as follows:

Defining the terms, "Excise Officer" and "Possession": --
"The term 'Excise Officer' shall mean the person appointed by the Governor under section 11 of this Ordinance, and for the purposes of this Ordinance, any boiled or prepared opium, or utensils or vessels used for preparing the same shall be deemed to be in possession of any person if he knowingly have them in actual possession, custody, or control by himself or by any other person." (Ordinance No. 1 of 1879, para. 1.)

Prepared opium, &c., found in possession of unauthorized persons, or in unauthorized places may be seized. "All boiled or prepared opium offered or exposed for sale or retail by any unauthorized person and all boiled or prepared opium found in the possession or custody or control of any unauthorized person or in any unauthorized place, except as in the last section mentioned,[1184] and any utensils or vessels which have been used or which are manifestly intended to be used in boiling or preparing opium by any unauthorised person or in any unauthorized place, may be seized by a police or excise officer, and shall be forfeited and may be by a Magistrate delivered and adjudged to the holder of the exclusive privilege for the time being, and any unauthorized person in whose possession any such boiled or prepared opium or utensils or vessels are found may be apprehended and taken before a Magistrate by any police or excise officer." (Ordinance No. 1 of 1879, para. 7.)

<u>Raw opium found in possession of unauthorised persons or in unauthorised places may be seized</u>. "Wherever boiled or prepared opium is so seized as last aforesaid and any such utensils or vessels are also seized as aforesaid, the police or excise officer seizing the same may also seize any raw opium that may be found in the custody or control of such unauthorized person or in such unauthorized place and such raw opium shall be subject to the order of the Magistrate before whom the case is brought." (Ordinance No. 1 of 1879, para. 8.)

<u>Officer may seize raw opium under special circumstances</u>. "Whenever from any other cause there is reasonable ground to believe that boiled or prepared opium is manufactured by any unauthorized person or in any unauthorized place within this Colony it shall be lawful for a police or excise officer to seize any raw opium found in the possession of such unauthorized person or in such unauthorised place." (Ordinance No. 1 of 1879, para. 9.)

<u>Seizure under search warrant.</u> "Any Justice of the Peace may issue a search warrant under section 9 of the said recited Ordinance [i.e. Ordinance No. 2 of 1858],[1185] and such search warrant may be executed by any police or excise officer and the person executing any such search warrant may seize and hold any utensils or vessels which have been used or which are manifestly intended to be used in boiling or preparing opium and in any case where boiled or prepared opium is found under the circumstances mentioned in the said section of the said recited Ordinance [i.e. Ordinance No. 2 of 1858] or any such utensils or vessels as last aforesaid are found, may also seize any raw opium found in the possession of any person having such boiled or prepared opium, utensils, or vessels, or in any such tenement, place, or vessel as is mentioned in the said section." (Ordinance No. 1 of 1879, para. 10.)

<u>Excise officer. Warrant of appointment</u>. "The Governor may, for the purposes of this Ordinance, grant his warrant in form

of schedule (B)[1186] to such agents or servants of the holder of the exclusive privilege for the time being as may be approved of by him to act as excise officers: and no persons except those so appointed shall be competent to act as excise officers under this and the said recited Ordinance [i.e. Ordinance No. 2 of 1858]. Such warrants may at any time be withdrawn by the Governor and any person without lawful authority assuming to act as an excise officer under this Ordinance shall be liable to a penalty not exceeding one hundred dollars." (Ordinance No. 1 of 1879, para. 11.)

Excise officers' names to be posted at Police Court [*sic*]. "The names and places of residence of every excise officer so appointed as aforesaid shall be posted in a conspicuous place at the Police Court." (Ordinance No. 1 of 1879, para. 12.)

Excise officers to be supplied with badges. "Every excise officer appointed under this Ordinance shall be supplied with a badge bearing such sign or mark of office as may be directed by the Governor and before acting against any person under the provisions of this Ordinance every such excise officer shall declare his office and produce to the person against whom he is about to act his said badge.

Police officer to produce part of his public equipment when acting as excise officer. Every Police officer acting under the provision of this or the said recited Ordinance [i.e. Ordinance No. 2 of 1858], if not in the uniform proper to his service[,] shall in like manner declare his office and produce to the person against whom he is about to act such part of his public equipment as the Captain Superintendent of Police shall have directed or may direct to be carried by Police officers when employed on secret or special service. (Ordinance No. 1 of 1879, para. 13)

Penalties to be recovered summarily. "All penalties under the said recited Ordinance [i.e. Ordinance No. 2 of 1858] or under this Ordinance may be recovered in a summary way before any Magistrate. (Ordinance No. 1 of 1879, para. 14.)

Proceedings in case of prepared opium, &c., found without being apparently in possession of any one. "In case any boiled or prepared opium or utensils or vessels used for preparing the same are found without being apparently in the possession of any one, it shall be lawful for the Magistrate to cause a notice to be affixed at the place where any such article may be found calling upon the owner thereof to claim the same, and in case no person shall come forward to make a claim within one week from the date of such notice, the same together with any raw opium that may be found in the same place shall be forfeited and may be handed over by the Magistrate to the holder of the exclusive privilege for the time being." (Ordinance No. 1 of 1879, para. 15.)

Forfeiture of raw opium found where opium is unlawfully boiled or prepared. "Where any boiled or prepared opium, or utensils or vessels used for preparing the same are found in the possession of any unauthorized person, or in any unauthorized place, and it appears to a Magistrate that such boiled or prepared opium was boiled or prepared by such person, or in such place, or if any utensil or vessel used for boiling or preparing opium be found in the possession of such person or in such place, it shall be lawful for such Magistrate to declare any raw opium found in the possession of such person or in such place to be forfeited and to direct that the same shall be delivered to the person holding the exclusive privilege at the time when the same was so found as aforesaid." (Ordinance No. 1 of 1879, para. 16.)

Ordinance No. 7 of 1879

Under Ordinance No. 7 of 1879, action without a warrant was permitted as follows on certain ships:
"It shall be lawful for an Inspector of Police having reasonable ground for believing that there is boiled or prepared opium in any ship within the waters of the Colony contrary to the provisions of the Opium Ordinances, (such ship not being a ship of war or vessel having the status of a ship of war) to proceed without warrant on board such ship and search for boiled or prepared opium and seize any boiled or prepared opium so found, and it shall be lawful for such Inspector to take the opium so found together with the person in whose custody possession or control it is found before a Police Magistrate, to be dealt with according to

law." (Ordinance No. 7 of 1879, VIII.)

Under Ordinance No. 7 of 1879, action without a warrant was also permitted as follows:

"It shall be lawful for any Police or Excise Officer to arrest, without warrant, any person within the Colony whom he reasonably suspects to be conveying or to have concealed on his person boiled or prepared opium which has not paid duty to the holder of the exclusive privilege, and to convey such person to the nearest Police Station, there to be dealt with according to law." (Ordinance No. 7 of 1879, IX.)

Under Ordinance No. 7 of 1879, fines were authorized as follows:

"If any charge or complaint shall be preferred under 'the Excise Ordinance (Opium) 1858-1879' or under any of the said regulations made thereunder and upon the said charge or complaint the accused shall be convicted, the pecuniary penalty imposed upon the offender shall, after the adjudication of a portion of the same not exceeding one half at the discretion of the Magistrate to the informer, be paid to the holder of the exclusive privilege, and all the boiled or prepared opium to which the same relates shall be forfeited and by the magistrate adjudged and delivered to the holder of the privilege." (Ordinance No. 7 of 1879, para. X.)

~~~~~~~~~~~~

56. Table One: Hong Kong Police Force Strength
1880-1882[i]

	1880	1881	1882	Average 1880-1882
Europeans	107 א	109 א	108 א	108
Indians	175 ℨ	172 ℨ	172 ℨ	173
Chinese	206 ℜ	199 ⊗	199	201.33
Chinese (water police)	151	131	133 ⊗	138.33
Portuguese	1 ℘	1 ℘	1 ℘	1
Chinese Coolies	52	52	52	52
Total (excludes coolies)	640	612	613	621.66
% Europeans	16.718	17.810	17.618	17.362
% Chinese (includes water police)	55.78	53.921	54.159	54.62
% Indians	27.343	28.104	28.058	27.83
% Portuguese	0.156	0.163	0.163	0.160

א   Includes 1 clerk/accountant and 1 clerk
ℨ   Includes 1 interpreter
ℜ   Includes 1 clerk and interpreter, 1 clerk, 14 interpreters
℘   Includes 1 clerk
⊗   Includes 2 clerks and 14 interpreters

---

[i] Based on The Hong Kong Government Blue Books, 1880, 1881, 1882, Section I. (*Compiled by the present editor.*)

57. Table Two: Hong Kong Police Force Strength 1886-1889[i]

	Race	Enlistment	Deaths	Resignations	Dismissals or Desertions
1886	Europeans	19	8	12	1
	Indians	59	2	18	8
	Chinese	98	1	12	67
	Totals	17	11	28	79
1887	Europeans	17	4	6	5
	Indians	14	1	19	5
	Chinese	44	4	30	27
	Totals	93	9	55	37
1888	Europeans	26	1	26	2
	Indians	15	4	16	5
	Chinese	59	10	35	15
	Totals	100	15	69	22
1889	Europeans	29	5	13	7
	Indians	28	4	32	6
	Chinese	36	5	24	4
	Totals	93	14	69	17
Averages for 1886-1889	Europeans	25.2	4.5	14.2	3.7
	Indians	26.5	2.7	23.7	6
	Chinese	61	5	28.2	28.2
	Totals	116	12.2	62	39.2

[i] The Table, "Hong Kong Police Force Strength 1886-1889", is based upon Table E of the Annual Reports of the Captain Superintendent of Police. These are the earliest years that these figures become available in this form. The percentage for the size of the Chinese contingent is slightly over the fifty percent policy figure mentioned in "The Police Role in Magistrate Frederick Stewart's Court", but the actual working strength in 1886-1889 would have been *under* fifty percent because of the time needed to process the high level of Chinese dismissals and enlistments. The Table, "Police Force Strength, 1880-1882", based on the Hong Kong Government Blue Book Returns for those years, shows a slightly higher number of Indians and a somewhat lower number of Chinese. — *Geoffrey Roper (table compiler)*

Combined Works Cited
&
Select Bibliography

Materials used for this study include many in public and private archives, specialist libraries, and newspaper and photograph collections, some of which only are available in microform. For example, Colonial Office Records (CO/129, CO/131); *The China Mail* (Hong Kong Public Records Office, University of Hong Kong Special Collections), the [Hong Kong] *Daily Press* (University of Hong Kong, 1867 (MF 5942-5943; 1868 - June 1870, MF 5944-5948; *Hong Kong Daily Press*, Hong Kong Baptist University, 1870 - 1941 [but not always complete within individual years]); materials at the University of Hong Kong, the Hong Kong Public Records Office, the Scottish Record Office, the Public Record [*sic*] Office at Kew.

      The following is a further indication of a very small selection of the material that was useful.

Books, book chapters, CD publications, journal articles, talks and typescripts

Airlee, Shiona, *Thistle and Bamboo: The Life and Times of Sir James Stewart Lockhart*, Hong Kong, Oxford University Press, 1989.

Bayley, David H., "Modes and Mores of Policing the Community in Japan", in *Law and Society, Culture Learning Through the Law*, Honolulu, Culture Learning Institute, East-West Centre, November 1977, pp. 71-82.

Bickley, Gillian, "Arrival back in Hong Kong: 21 March 1879; Loss of the Inspectorship: effective, 25 March 1879; Award of Honorary Aberdeen LL.D.: decided, 8 March 1879; awarded April 1879", manuscript and word-processed file in preparation, Personal Archive, [LossInsp].

— compiler and editor, "Before Frederick Stewart, Esquire: The Court Cases of Frederick Stewart, Police Magistrate, Hong Kong, July 1881-March 1882 as published in *The China Mail*", unpublished typescript, 1998-1999. Planned to be made available as a CD publication in 2005 or 2006.

— "Chinese Language Study by Frederick Stewart and other British Teachers in Hong Kong Schools in the Nineteenth Century: A Response to the book review [by Professor Ruth Hayhoe] of *The Golden Needle: the Biography of Frederick Stewart (1836-1889)*, David C. Lam Institute for East-West Studies, Hong Kong Baptist University, 1997 in APJLE Vol. 1 (1)", *Asia Pacific Journal of Language in Education*, December 1998, Vol. 1 (2), pp. 151-153.

— [CourtCases:Weights], TS, Personal Archive.

— "Deceived by his own Desires", manuscript and word-processed file in preparation, Personal Archive, [Desires].

— *The Development of Education in Hong Kong, 1841-1897: as*

Revealed by the Early Education Reports of the Hong Kong Government, 1848-1896, Hong Kong, supported by the Council of the Lord Wilson Heritage Trust, distributed by the Chinese University of Hong Kong Press, 2002.

— *The Golden Needle: the Biography of Frederick Stewart (1836-1889),* Hong Kong, David C. Lam Institute for East-West Studies, Hong Kong Baptist University, 1997.

— "The Gratification of their Fancies", *TGN*, Hong Kong, David C. Lam Institute for East West Studies, 1997, pp. 129-139.

[Bickley, Gillian] Gillian Workman "The Medium of Instruction in Hong Kong: Why was it Ever English?", in Verner Bickley, Ed., *Language Use, Language Teaching and the Curriculum*, Hong Kong, Institute of Language in Education (Hong Kong Government Education Department), January 1991, pp. 6-47

Bickley, Gillian, "The New Interpretation Department: Proposal and Resistance", manuscript and word-processed file in preparation, Personal Archive, [Interp].

— "Police Magistrates 1841-1898 (alphabetical order)", Personal Archive, [Coroner:PolMagCh].

— "Police Magistrates (alphabetical order)" and "Police Magistrates Succession List, 1841 - 1898", table, word-processed document, [Coroner:PolMagCh].

— "Police Magistrates: Succession List 1841-1898", Personal Archive, [Coroner:PolMagCh].

— "Registrar General: 1883-1887", manuscript and word-processed file in preparation, Personal Archive, [RegGen].

— "The Student-interpreters' Scheme and the Chinese Teacher's Allowance: Translator Education in Nineteenth-century Hong Kong", in, *Translation in Hong Kong: Past, Present and Future*, Ed. Chan Sin-wai, Hong Kong, The Chinese University Press, 2001, pp. 8-19.

— "Trust not in princes or men's sons", manuscript and word-processed file in preparation, Personal Archive, [Losspt2].

Bickley, Verner, "The Diversified Whole: Mediation And The Language Mosaic In the Hong Kong Education System", in *Languages in Education in a Bilingual or Multi-lingual Setting*, Ed. Verner Bickley, Hong Kong, Hong Kong Government Education Department, 1989, pp. 192-209.

Blackshield, A. R., "Capital Punishment in India: The Impact of the Ediga Anamma Case", in *Law and Society: Culture Learning Through the Law*, Honolulu, Culture Learning Institute, East-West Centre, November 1977, pp. 83-98.

Biggerstaff, Knight, *The Earliest Modern Government Schools in China*, Ithaca, New York, Cornell University Press, 1961.

Blue, A. D., "Piracy on the China Coast", *JRAS(HK)*, Vol. V, pp. 69-85, p. 75.)

British Parliamentary Papers: China: Correspondence, Dispatches, Reports, Ordinances and Other Papers relating to the Affairs of Hong Kong 1846-1860, Irish University Press area studies series. Shannon, Irish University Press, 1971. 42 vols, vols. 22-26.

Carnoy, Martin, *Education as Cultural Imperialism*, New York, David McKay Company, Inc., 1974.

Chan Man Kam, "A Comparative Study on Mythology of Korea and China", MA thesis, submitted to, Shung Kyun Kwan University, Korea, 1975.

Chan, Samson, Development of the Hong Kong Penal Policy and Programme under the British Administration (1841-1945), unpublished thesis, University of Leicester, United Kingdom.

— "Differential Treatment for Chinese Offenders: A Historical Study of Early Colonial Policies in Hong Kong", TS, pp. 1-24.

Chen, Albert H. Y., in "Justice after 1997", in Ed. Traver and Vagg, *Crime and Justice in Hong Kong*, 1991, pp. 172-188.

Cheng, T. C., "Chinese Unofficial Members of the Legislative and Executive Councils in Hong Kong up to 1941", *JRAS(HK)*, 1969, Vol. 9, pp. 7-30.

Cheung, Anne, "Language Rights and the Hong Kong Courts," *Hong Kong Journal of Applied Linguistics*, Vol. 2, No. 2, December 1997, pp. 49-75.

The China Directory, 1885.

"Chinese Emigration from Hong Kong", *HKGG*, 11 February 1882, pp. 83-120.

Coates, Austin, *China Races*, Hong Kong, Oxford University Press, 1983.

— *Myself a Mandarin*, Hong Kong, Heinemann Educational Books, [1968]; republished by Oxford University Press, 1987.

Coates, P. D., *The China Consuls: British Consular Officers, 1843-1943*, Hong Kong, Oxford University Press, 1988.

Crisswell, Colin and Mike Watson, *The Royal Hong Kong Police (1841-1945)*, Hong Kong, Macmillan Hong Kong, 1982.

Crowley, David and Paul Heyer, *Communication in History*, New York, Longman, 1995.

Cross, I. Grenville and Patrick W. S. Cheung, *Sentencing in Hong Kong*, Butterworths, 1994.

Dyson, Anthony, *From Timeball to Atomic Clock*, Hong Kong, Hong Kong Government, 1983.

Eames, James Bromley, *The English in China*, London, Curzon Press, 1909, new impression, 1974.

Eitel, E. J., "Chinese Studies and Official Interpretation in the Colony of Hongkong", *China Review*, Vol. VI (July 1877-June 1878), No. 1, pp. 1-13.

— *Europe in China: the History of Hong Kong, from the beginning to the year 1882*, Hong Kong, Oxford University Press, 1983 (first published by Kelly and Walsh, Ltd., 1895).

— "Materials for a History of Education in Hong Kong", *The China Review*, Vol. XIX, March and April 1891, pp. 308-324; 335-368.

— "The Protestant Missions of Hong Kong", *Chinese Recorder*, 1891, Vol. VII, pp. 309-324; 335-368.

— Report (requested by John Pope Hennessy, 2 April 1880), "Treatment of Paupers in Hong Kong", 22 April 1880, *HKGG*, 9 June 1880, pp. 466-473.

Empson, Hal, *Mapping Hong Kong: A Historical Atlas*, Hong Kong, Government Information Services, 1992.

Endacott, George B., *A Biographical Sketch-Book of Early Hong Kong*, Singapore, D. Moore for Eastern Universities Press, 1962.

— *A History of Hong Kong*, 2nd ed. Hong Kong, Oxford University Press, 1964, first published 1958.

— *A History of Hong Kong*, Hong Kong, Oxford University Press, 1975.

England, Vaudine, *The quest of Noel Croucher: Hong Kong's quiet philanthropist*, Hong Kong, Hong Kong University Press, 1998.

Evans, Dafydd Emrys, "Chinatown in Hong Kong: the Beginnings of Taipingshan," *JRAS(HK)*, Vol. 10, 1970, pp. 69 - 78.

Fairbank, J. K., *The United States and China*, 4th ed., Cambridge, Mass, Harvard University Press, 1980.

Faure, David, James Hayes, Alan Birch, Eds, *From Village to City: Studies in the traditional roots of Hong Kong society*, Hong Kong, Centre of Asian Studies, University of Hong Kong, Occasional Papers and Monographs Number 60, 1984.

Faure, David, Ed., *Society: A Documentary History of Hong Kong*, Hong Kong, Hong Kong University Press, 1997.

Fok, K. C., *Lectures on Hong Kong History*, Hong Kong, The Commercial Press (Hong Kong) Ltd., 1990.

Forster, E. M., *A Passage to India*, New York, Harcourt, Brace & Co., 1924.

The Gospel according to Saint Matthew, chapter 18.

Grant, Ian, ["The Scottish equivalent to the Hong Kong stipendiary magistrates"], TS, 1999, Personal Archive.

Greenwood, Walter, "John Joseph Francis, Citizen of Hong Kong, A Biographical Note," *JRAS(HK)* , Vol. 26, 1986, pp. 17-45.

Ha, Louis, "The Sunday Rest Issue in 19th Hong Kong", paper presented at the International Conference on Hong Kong and Modern China, University of Hong Kong, 3-5 December 1997.

Hacker, Arthur, *Arthur Hacker's Wanchai*, Hong Kong, Odyssey Publications, 1997.

— *The Hong Kong Visitors Book: A Historical Who's Who*, Odyssey Publications, 1997.

Hamilton, Sheilah E., A History of the Medical Profession in Hong Kong's Criminal Justice System, thesis for the award of a MSocSc degree, Hong Kong, University of Hong Kong, 1994 [MSoc.Sc.94H].

— "Hong Kong's Colonial Surgeons and their civilizing influence on prison life 1843-1897", unpublished TS of a paper presented at a Centre of Asian Studies/History Department Symposium at the University of Hong Kong March 1998.

— "Private Security and Government: A Hong Kong Perspective,

1841-1941", Hong Kong, University of Hong Kong, thesis for the award of a Ph.D. degree, 1999, [Ph.D.99 H12].

Hampton, C., *Criminal Procedure*, 3rd ed., London, Sweet and Maxwell, 1982.

Harfield, Alan, *British and Indian Armies on the China Coast, 1785-1985*, Farnham, Surrey, A. and J. Partnership, 1990.

Harrison, Brian, *Waiting for China: The Anglo-Chinese College at Malacca, 1818-1843*, Hong Kong, Hong Kong University Press, 1979.

Hase, Patrick, talk given to the Royal Asiatic Society at the City Hall, Hong Kong, 1999-2000.

Hayes, James, "The Hong Kong Region", *JRAS(HK)*, Vol. 14, 1974, Hong Kong, 1974, pp.108-135

Hemyng, Bracebridge, "Prostitution in London", [1861/62], in, Henry Mayhew, *London Labour and the London Poor*, first published by Griffin, Bohn, and Company in 1861-1862, reprinted in New York, Dover Publications, Inc., 1968, 4 vols., Vol. IV, pp. 210-272.

Herskovits, Melville Jean, *Man and His Works*, New York, A. A. Knopf, 1948.

Hobson, J. A., "Imperialism in Asia", *Imperialism: A Study*, London, 1902, revised edition, 1905; 3rd ed., London, Unwin Hyam, 1988, pp. 285-327.

Hoe, Susanna, *The Private Life of Old Hong Kong: Western Women in the British Colony, 1841-1941*, Hong Kong, Oxford University Press, 1991.

Hurley, R. C., *A Handbook to the British Crown Colony of Hong Kong and Dependencies*, Hong Kong, Kelly and Walsh, 1920.

— *Picturesque Hong Kong (British Crown Colony) and its Dependencies*, Hong Kong, The Commercial Press Ltd., 1925.

Hyam, Ronald, *Empire and Sexuality*, Manchester, Manchester University Press, 1990.

Ingrams, Harold, *Hong Kong*, London, Her Majesty's Stationery Office, 1952.

[J. T.] See [Terry, J.?].

James, Lawrence, *The Rise and Fall of the British Empire*, London, Little, Brown and Co., 1994.

Jarrett, V. H. G., ["Old Colonial"], "Old Hong Kong", TS. (A series of articles on the history of Hong Kong taken from *The South China Morning Post, 17 June 1933 - 13 April 1935*, and rearranged alphabetically by subject.)

Jaschock, Maria, *Concubines and Bondservants: the Social History of a Chinese Custom*, Hong Kong, Oxford University press, 1988.

Keeton, G. W. and D. Lloyd, Eds, *The United Kingdom: The Development of its Laws and Constitutions*, London, Stevens, 1955.

King, Frank H. H., Ed. and Preston Clark, *A Research Guide to China-Coast Newspapers, 1822-1901*, Cambridge, Harvard University, 1965.

Ko Tim Keung and Jason Wordie, *Ruins of War: A Guide to Hong Kong's Battlefields and Wartime Sites*, Hong Kong, Joint Publishing Co., Ltd., 1996.

Koss, Stephen, *The Rise and Fall of the Political Press in Britain*, London, Fontana, 1990.

Kyshe, J. W. Norton, *The History of the Laws and Courts of Hong Kong*, 2 Vols, Hong Kong 1898, reprinted Hong Kong, Vetch and Lee Ltd, 1971.

Lam, Clare Branson, *Looking Back with Pride and Glory: Hong Kong Auxiliary Police History Book (1914-1997)*, [Hong Kong, Hong Kong Auxiliary Police Force?, 1997?]

Legge, James, "The Colony of Hong Kong. From a Lecture... in the City Hall, 5 November 1872," *The China Review*, 1872-1873, Vols 1 and 2, pp. 163-176. Reprinted as James Legge, "The Colony of Hong Kong", text of/based on a talk given at the City Hall, Hong Kong, 5 November 1872, *JRAS(HK)*, Vol. XI, 1971, pp. 172-193.

Lethbridge, Henry James, "Condition of the European Working Class in Nineteenth Century Hong Kong", *JRAS(HK)* , Vol. 15, 1975, pp. 88-112.

— "The District Watch Committee: 'The Chinese Executive Council of Hong Kong'", *JRAS(HK)* , Vol. XI, 1971, pp. 116-141.

— "Hong Kong Cadets, 1862-1941", *JRAS(HK)*, Vol. X, 1971, pp. 36-56, with an additional errata slip.

— *Hong Kong: Stability and Change, a collection of Essays*, Hong Kong, Oxford University Press, 1978.

[McBryde, Margaret], "Crime and Punishment: The complete text of an exhibition of documents from the national archives [of Scotland], held at General Register House [Edinburgh]", [1998].

Michie, Alexander, *The Englishman in China during the Victoria Era, as illustrated in the career of Rutherford Alcock, K.C.B., D.C.L., for many years consul and minister in China and Japan*, Edinburgh and London, William Blackwood and Sons, 1900. 2 vols. Reprint, Taipei, Ch'eng Wen Publishing Co., 1966.

Mills, Lennox A., "Hong Kong", Part II of *British Rule in Eastern Asia*, London, Oxford University Press, 1942.

Miners, Norman, *Government and Politics of Hong Kong*, 4th Edition, Hong Kong, Oxford University Press, 1986, revised 1989.

— "The Localization of the Hong Kong Police Force, 1842-1947", *The Journal Of Imperial and Commonwealth History*, Volume 18, No. 3, October 1990, Frank Cass & Co.

Miners, R. J., "State Regulation of Prostitution in Hong Kong, 1857 to 1941", *JRAS(HK)* , Vol. XXIV, 1984, pp. 143-161.

Morgan, W. P., *Triad Societies in Hong Kong*, Hong Kong, Government Press, 1960, third impression, 1989.

Morris, Jan, *Hong Kong*, Penguin, Second edition published by Penguin, 1993, reprinted with an additional chapter, 1997.

— *Hong Kong: Epilogue to an Empire*, Penguin Books, 1990, first published Viking, 1988.

Mühlhäusler, Peter, *Pidgin & Creole Linguistics*, Oxford, Basil Blackwell, 1986.

Munn, Christopher, "'An Anglo-Chino [*sic*] conspiracy in crime': the Caldwell Scandal, 1857-1861", TS, nd.

— *Chinese People and British Rule in Hong Kong, 1841-1880*,

Routledge, 2001.

— "The Criminal Trial under Early Colonial Rule", in *Hong Kong's History*, ed. Tak-Wing Ngo, London and New York, Routledge, 1999, pp. 46-73.

Nacken, J., "Chinese Street-Cries in Hong Kong", *China Review*, 1873, Vol. II, reprinted in *JRAS(HK)*, 1968, Vol. 8, pp. 128-134.

Norton-Kyshe, James William, *The History of the Laws and Courts of Hong Kong*, London, Unwin, 1898, 2 Vols.

Orwell, George, *Burmese Days*, New York, Harcourt Brace Jovanovich, 1934.

— "A Hanging", *The Collected Essays, Journalism and Letters of George Orwell*, ed. Sonia Orwell and Ian Angus, Penguin in association with Martin Secker and Warburg, 1970.

— "Shooting an Elephant", in *Shooting an Elephant and Other Essays*, London, Secker & Warburg, 1953.

Pryor, E. G., "A Historical Review of Housing Conditions in Hong Kong", *JRAS(HK)*, 1972, Vol. 12, pp. 89-116.

Rodwell, Sally, "Monuments from 19th-Century Colonial Hong Kong', in *Historic Hong Kong*, Hong Kong, Odyssey Guides, 1991, 2nd printing, 1992, pp. 68-95.

Roper, Geoffrey, "Hong Kong Police/Former Hong Kong Police, Royal Naval Dockyard, District Watchmen, Informers", unpublished table.

— "Notes for a Royal Asiatic Society (Hong Kong Branch) tour of Central District, Hong Kong", mimeograph.

Sayer, G. R., *Hong Kong, 1841-1862. Birth, Adolescence and Coming of Age*, Hong Kong University Press, 1980. Originally published by Oxford University Press in 1937 as, *Hong Kong: birth, adolescence, and coming of age*.

— *Hong Kong 1862-1919*, Hong Kong, Hong Kong University Press, 1975.

Shepherd, Bruce, *Index to the Streets, Houses and Leased Lots . . . . in the Colony of Hong Kong*, Hong Kong, Kelly and Walsh, 1894.

Sinclair, Kevin, *Asia's Finest*, Hong Kong, Unicorn, 1983.

Sinclair, Kevin and Nelson Ng Kwok-cheung, *Asia's Finest Marches On: Policing Hong Kong from 1841 into the 21st century*, Hong Kong, Kevin Sinclair Associates Limited, 1997.

Sinclair, Kevin, *Society's Guardians: a history of correctional services in Hong Kong, 1841 - 1999*, Hong Kong, Correctional Services Department, 1999.

Sinn, Elizabeth, *Index to CO/129, 1842-1926*, History Department, University of Hong Kong, CD publication, 1997.

— *Power and Charity: The Early History of the Tung Wah Hospital, Hong Kong*, Hong Kong, Oxford University Press, East Asian Historical Monographs, 1989.

Tsai Jung-fang, *Hong Kong in Chinese History: Community and Social Unrest in the British Colony, 1842-1913*, New York, Columbia University Press, 1993.

Smith, Reverend Carl T., *A Sense of History: Studies in the Social and Urban History of Hong Kong*, Hong Kong, Hong Kong Educational

Publishing Co., 1995.

— "Dr Legge's Theological School," *Chung Chi Bulletin*, 1971, No. 50, pp. 16-22.

— "The First Child Labour law in Hong Kong", *JRAS(HK)*, Vol. 28, 1988, pp. 44-69.

— *Chinese Christians: Elites, Middlemen, and the Church in Hong Kong*, Hong Kong, Oxford University Press, 1985.

— Schools and Scholars: English Language Education in the China Mission in the First Half of the Nineteenth Century and Its Results, unpublished MA Thesis, submitted to Union Theological Seminary, New York, 1962.

— "A Study of the Missionary Educational Philosophy of Samuel R. Brown", *Ching Feng: Quarterly Notes on Christianity and Chinese Religion and Culture*, Vol. X11, No. 2, 1969, pp. 2-28.

— "Ng Akew, One of Hong Kong's 'Protected Women'", *Chung Chi Bulletin*, June, Vol. 46, pp. 13-17, 27.

Smith, George, Reverend, M. A., of Magdalen Hall, Oxford, and late Missionary in China, *A Narrative of an Exploratory Visit to each of the Consular Cities of China, and to the Islands of Hong Kong and Chusan, in Behalf of the Church Missionary Society, in the years 1844, 1845, 1846*, Seeley, Burnside, and Seeley, London, 1847.

Spierenburg, P., *The Spectacle of Suffering*, London, Cambridge University Press, 1984.

The *Sunday Morning Post*, "HK catches Euro 2000 betting fever", 18 June 2000, p. 1.

[Terry, J.?] [J. T.], *Dates and Events Connected with the History of Education in Hong Kong*, Hong Kong, December 1877.

Traver, Harold and Jon Vagg, eds, *Crime and Justice in Hong Kong*, Hong Kong, Oxford University Press, 1991.

Traver, Harold, "Crime Trends," in Traver, Harold and Jon Vagg, eds, *Crime and Justice in Hong Kong*, Hong Kong, Oxford University Press, 1991, pp. 10-24.

Ward, Iaian, *Sui Geng: The Hong Kong Marine Police, 1841-1950*, Hong Kong Hong Kong University Press, 1991.

Wang Jen-Huong, "Some Cultural Factors Affecting Chinese in Treaty Negotiation", in *Cultural Factors in International Relations*, Ed. R. P. Anand, New Delhi, Abhinav Publications, 1981, pp. 97-112.

Wesley-Smith, Peter, "Cultural Problems in Negotiation of the Convention of Peking, 1898", in *Cultural Factors in International Relations*, *op. cit.*, pp. 113-128.

Welsh, Frank, *A History of Hong Kong*, London, Harper Collins, 1993.

Workman, Gillian. See Bickley, Gillian.

Wright, Arnold, Ed., *Twentieth Century Impressions of Hong Kong, Shanghai, and other Treaty Ports of China: Their History, People, Commerce, Industries, and Resources*, London, 1908.

Yee, Albert H., *A People Misruled: Hong Kong and The Chinese Stepping Stone Syndrome*, Hong Kong, UEA Press Ltd., 1989.

Yu, Patrick Shuk-siu, *A Seventh Child and the Law*, Hong Kong, Hong Kong University Press, 1998.

Government Archives, Documents and Publications
Great Britain, Colonial Office Records

Series CO/129, Governor's Despatches and Replies from the Secretary of State for the Colonies, 1841-1926. (For most individual documents and minutes, see notes to individual chapters.)

Series CO/131, Executive Council Minutes. (For specific meetings, see notes to chapters.)

Series CO/882, Confidential Prints, Eastern, 1860-1913. CO/882/4 (i) Eastern No. 33.

Brothel Slavery, 1882 (CO/129/202/658r. - 668r.)

Eitel, E. J., Report [on Slavery], dated Hong Kong, 25 October 1879 (CO/129/194/27r.-30r.).[1187]

Eitel, E. J., Report on Domestic Servitude, 25 October 1879, *British Parliamentary Papers: China 26*, pp. 218-219.

Eitel, E. J., Translation of Fung Ming-shan (Member of the Tung Wa Hospital Committee), document, dated Hong Kong, 25 October 1879 (CO/129/194/24r.-30r.).

Her Majesty's Stationery Office (HMSO), *Correspondence respecting the Alleged Existence of Chinese Slavery in Hong Kong, presented to Parliament, March 1882*, London, HMSO, 1882 [C.-3185], in, *British Parliamentary Papers: China*, Vol. 26, pp. 161-288.

Her Majesty's Stationery Office (HMSO), *Papers respecting the flogging of prisoners in Hong Kong 1878-79* [C. 2438], in *British Parliamentary Papers: China*, Vol. 25, pp. 457-505.

Her Majesty's Stationery Office (HMSO), *Correspondence relating to the working of the Contagious Diseases Ordinances of the Colony of Hong Kong*, presented to both Houses of Parliament by command of Her Majesty, August, 1881, [C. - 3,093], London, HMSO, 1881, in *British Parliamentary Papers: China*, Vol. 25, pp. 573-639.

Her Majesty's Stationery Office (HMSO), *Report of the Commission to inquire into the working of the Contagious Diseases Ordinance*, 1867, printed for the House of Commons, 11 March 1880, in, *British Parliamentary Papers: China*, Vol. 25, pp. 507-572.

Her Majesty's Stationery Office (HMSO), *Correspondence regarding the Measures to be Adopted for Checking the Spread of Venereal Disease, Presented to Parliament September 1899*, [C. 9523], London, HMSO, 1899, in *British Parliamentary Papers: China*, Vol. 26, pp. 487-.

Chadwick, Osbert, *Reports on the Sanitary Conditions of Hong Kong*, dated 18 July 1882, London, Her Majesty's Stationery Office, 1882, in, *British Parliamentary Papers: China*, Vol. 26, pp. 93-160.

Hong Kong Government

"Authorities", Hong Kong Records Series (HKRS) 275, Hong Kong Public Records Office.

Captain Superintendent of Police, "Annual Report and Returns" for 1881, *HKGG*, 1882.

Captain Superintendent of Police, "Annual Report" for 1886, *HKGG*, 1887.

Colonial Surgeon, Report for 1862, dated 6 February 1863, *HKGG*, 7 March 1863, pp. 73-78.

Colonial Surgeon, Report for 1865, dated 3 March 1866, *HKGG*, 17 March 1866, pp. 122-125.

"Criminal Calendar – December Sessions, 1880", *HKGG*, 8 January 1881.

"Criminal Calendar – February Sessions, 1881", *HKGG*, 26 March 1881.

"Criminal Calendar – April Sessions, 1881", *HKGG*, 30 April 1881.

"Criminal Calendar – August Sessions, 1881", *HKGG*, 3 September 1881.

"Criminal Calendar – December Sessions, 1881", *HKGG*, 31 December 1881.

Hong Kong Government Blue Books (HKGBB)

The Hong Kong Government Gazette (HKGG)

"Index to Establishments", HKGBB, 1882, Appendix I, p. I2.

"List of Officers", HKGBB, 1882, Appendix I, pp. I3 - I13.

Pennefather-Evans, J. P., Commissioner of Police, "Report" (CR/31 1536/1946, HKPRO).

"Police Force," HKGBB, 1880, Appendix I, pp. I44 - I50.

"Police Force," HKGBB, 1881, Appendix I, pp. I48 - I53.

"Police Force," HKGBB, 1882, Appendix I, pp. I48 - I53.

"Police Magistrates' Office," HKGBB, 1881, Appendix I, pp. I46 - I47.

Registrar General, Annual Report for March 1883 - March 1884.

Wright, George Bateson, Headmaster of Queen's College, Annual Report for 1895, dated 28 January 1896, *HKGG*, 15 February 1896, pp. 117-118.

Newspapers

(For most individual articles and columns, see notes to individual chapters.)

The China Mail

"Sir John Smale on the Evils of Hong Kong", *CM*, 26 January 1882, p. 3, cc. 6-7, c. 6. (Report of a speech given to members of the National Association for the Promotion of Social Science on 21 November 1881.)

The [*Hong Kong*] *Daily Press*

Sunday Morning Post, 2000.

Websites

"History of Gambling in the United States", <http://www.library.ca.gov/CRB/97/03/Chapt2.html>.

"Marine Terms Dictionary", <http://www.marineterms.com>.

General Reference Books

Encyclopedia Americana – International Edition, Grolier Incorporated, 1993.

The Oxford Encyclopedic English Dictionary, Oxford, Oxford University Press, 1991.

The Oxford English Dictionary, 2nd edition, Oxford, Clarendon Press, 1989, 20 Vols.

Other useful sources

Hong Kong Museum of History.

Museum of Teaware, Hong Kong (formerly Flagstaff House).

The Police Museum, Combe Road, Hong Kong.

The Museum, Macau (in the old fort).

Act of South Australia

An Act to regulate and restrict Chinese Immigration, assented to 18 November 1881, *HKGG*, 25 February 1882, pp. 212-213.

Ordinances of Hong Kong
(See also endnotes for individual Ordinances)

Chronological Table of Ordinances. Laws of Hong Kong. Index. [HKU Law Library. PR KT 4353.1 H7 F90.]

The Ordinances of Hong Kong for the years 1844-1846. [HKU Law Library. KT 4351 H7 S1]

The Ordinances of Hong Kong for the years 1847-1859. [HKU Law Library. KT 4351 H7 S1]

The Ordinances of Hong Kong, 1888, printed by Noronha and Co., Government Printers, Hong Kong, 1889. [HKU Law Library. KT 4351 H7 S1]

The Ordinances of Hong Kong, 1889, printed by Noronha and Co., Government Printers, Hong Kong, 1890. [HKU Law Library. KT 4351 H7 S1]

The Ordinances of Hong Kong, 1897, printed by Noronha and Co., Government Printers, Hong Kong, 1898. [HKU Law Library. KT 4351 H7 S1]

The Ordinances of Hong Kong, 1930, printed by Noronha and Co., Government Printers, Hong Kong. [HKU Law Library. KT 4351 H7 S1]

The Ordinances of Hong Kong, Hong Kong, 1937, University of Hong Kong Library Special Collections, [HK.348.5125 H7]

Editor's Note (2009)

All contributors took as their starting point, "Before Frederick Stewart, Esq. The Court Cases of Frederick Stewart, Police Magistrate, Hong Kong", being the present editor's unpublished typescript of an edited and annotated database of over 700 cases reported in *The China Mail*, which came before the Hong Kong Police Magistrate, Frederick Stewart, during the period 26 July 1881 to 29 March 1882. This database, improved and with additional material, is now incorporated into *The Complete Court Cases of Magistrate Frederick Stewart as Reported in The China Mail, July 1881 to March 1882,* published in CD format in December 2008 and supported by the Council of the Lord Wilson Heritage Trust.

In one way or another, all the contributors, as well as the editor, learnt from and in turn enhanced the work of all other members of the group.

Nevertheless, the opinions and points of view of each contributor are his or her own. Although of course responsible for her own contributions, the editor does not necessarily agree with or endorse those of other contributors. Nor does any other contributor necessarily agree with or endorse the opinions and points of view, either of fellow contributors, or of the editor herself. Similarly, the editor and contributors, as a group, do not necessarily share the attitudes of the anonymous *China Mail* court reporter or reporters of the 1880s, nor of the magistrate, nor of any of the many individuals that the following pages present.

~~~~~

Notes on the Contributors

EDITOR AND CONTRIBUTOR

GILLIAN BICKLEY, PhD (Leeds), MLitt, BA (Hons), CertEd (Brist), FRSA, is the author of *The Golden Needle: The Biography of Frederick Stewart (1836-1889)* (David C. Lam Institute for East-West Studies, Hong Kong Baptist University, 1997); and *The Stewarts of Bourtreebush* (Centre for Scottish Studies, University of Aberdeen, 2003); and compiler, editor and author of *The Development of Education in Hong Kong, 1841-1897: as Revealed by the Early Education Reports of the Hong Kong Government 1848-1896* (distributed by the Chinese University of Hong Kong Press, 2002). She contributed a new entry on Frederick Stewart in the *Oxford Dictionary of National Biography* (2004). She has taught at the University of Hong Kong, the University of Lagos (Nigeria), and the University of Auckland (New Zealand); and recently retired as Associate Professor in the Department of English Language and Literature, Hong Kong Baptist University, where she taught for twenty-two years. Now an Honorary Research Fellow at the Centre of Asian Studies, University of Hong Kong, she is also Managing Editor of Proverse Hong Kong.

CONTRIBUTORS

VERNER BICKLEY, MBE, PhD (London), MA, BA (Hons), DipEd, FIL, FRSA, has led culture and language learning projects in seven countries. He first experienced other national cultures in India and Sri Lanka as a Sub-Lieutenant in the Royal Naval Volunteer Reserve (Special Branch). After demobilisation, he added to this experience as an Education Officer with the Singapore Government, as a British Council Officer in Burma, Indonesia and Japan (where he was also First Secretary in the British Embassy Cultural Department, Tokyo), as Head of Language Training for Saudi Arabian Airlines, as Full Professor of English at the University of Hawaii and as Director of the Culture Learning Institute of the East-West Centre in Honolulu. In Hong Kong, he was Assistant Director of Education and Director of the Government's

Institute of Language in Education. His *Searching for Frederick and Adventures Along the Way* (2001) describes his and his wife, Gillian Bickley's research into the life and work of Frederick Stewart, the Magistrate whose cases are reported and discussed in *Court in Time*. Now an Honorary Research Fellow at the Centre of Asian Studies, University of Hong Kong and Chairman of the Executive Committee of The English Speaking Union (Hong Kong), he is also Managing Director of Proverse Hong Kong.

CHRISTOPHER COGHLAN, BCL, was born in Karachi, then in India, on 12 October 1943. After public school at Ampleforth in Yorkshire and university in Dublin, he started his working life as an articled clerk to a firm of accountants in London. After two years he entered the Inner Temple and was called to the Bar in 1972. He practised on the South Eastern Circuit, latterly specialising in crime. Christopher arrived in Hong Kong in January 1986 as a Crown Counsel in the Attorney General's Chambers. His work as a Crown Counsel was solely criminal, specialising in appellate work. He left the Legal Department in 1994 and returned to England to practise. Within eighteen months he was back in Hong Kong, again as a barrister but this time at the private Bar, in which he continues.

TIM HAMLETT, BA (Hons), DipEd (Oxford); MA (London), worked on provincial newspapers in England before moving to Hong Kong in 1980. He held senior editorial positions on several Hong Kong publications, including leading an award-winning investigative team for the *Hong Kong Standard*, before joining Hong Kong Baptist University as a Lecturer in Journalism in 1988. When an Associate Professor at this University, he continued (as he still does) to write extensively for both the print and broadcast media and was a presenter of the Radio Television Hong Kong (RTHK) Mediawatch programme. His column, 'Tim Hamlett's Hong Kong' appears regularly in the *South China Morning Post*.

GEOFFREY ROPER, QPM, CPM, BA (Hons). Born in Peterborough, England in 1937, a Year of the Rat, Geoffrey had an urge to roam, fuelled largely by tales of overseas Christian missionaries at his local Anglo-Catholic church. After education at King's School, Peterborough, and two years of National Service spent applying unsuccessfully for overseas postings, Geoffrey finally reached the East when he flew into Hong Kong on a Bristol Britannia on 22 November 1958, to become Probationary Sub-Inspector of Police. After retirement from the Police in 1993, in the rank of Assistant Commissioner, he has furthered his education by travelling widely, mostly in China, and obtaining an Honours Degree in Arts and Humanities at the Open University of Hong Kong.

GARRY TALLENTIRE was born in North East England and educated at Teesdale Grammar School, Barnard Castle. He achieved a BA (Hons) (Law) at Nottingham University with subsidiary subjects Politics and Economic and Social History. His first post was as a Court Clerk at Nottingham City Magistrates' Court where he was articled to the Clerk to the Justices. In 1975, he was admitted as a Solicitor of the Supreme Court of England and Wales. In 1977, he was appointed Deputy Clerk to the Justices of Worksop and East Retford Nottinghamshire. From 1980 to 1988, he was Clerk to the Justices at three courts – Barrow-in-Furness, Lonsdale North of the Sands and Millom, Cumbria – working from two offices, the main one being at Barrow. In 1988, he left an idyllic Lakeland Village of four hundred people to come to Hong Kong as a Magistrate! In 1997, he was appointed a Principal Magistrate (there is one at each of the Hong Kong Magistracies), the post held at the time of writing his contribution to *Court in Time*. From time to time he has acted as a District Court Judge.

THE HON. SIR TI LIANG YANG, GBM, JP was knighted in 1988; and has received the following honours and honorary degrees: the Order of Chivalry, First Class, SPMB of Negara Brunei Darussalam, 1990; the Grand Bauhinia Medal, 1999; Hon. LLD Chinese Unversity of Hong Kong, 1984; Hon. DLitt Hong Kong University, 1991; Hon. LLD, Hong Kong Polytechnic, 1992. He was a member of the Executive Council, Hong Kong SAR, 1997-2002; Chief Justice of Hong Kong, 1988-1996; Lord President of The Court of Appeal of Negara Brunei Darussalam 1988-92; Justice of Appeal, Hong Kong, 1980; Judge of the High Court, Hong Kong, 1975; District Judge, District Court, 1968; Rockefeller Fellow, London University 1963-64; Senior Magistrate, 1963; Magistrate, Hong Kong, 1956; Chairman, Kowloon Disturbances Claims Assessment Board, 1966; Compensation Board, 1967; Commission of Inquiry into the Rainstorm Disasters, 1972; Commission of Inquiry into the Leung Wing-sang Case, 1976; Commission of Inquiry into the MacLennan Case, 1980. He was a Member of The Law Reform Commisison, 1980 (Chairman, Sub-Committee on Law Relating to Homosexuality, 1980); a Member of The Chinese Language Committee (Chairman, Legal Sub-Committee), 1970. In 1996, he campaigned for the post of Chief Executive, Hong Kong Special Administrative Region. He was Chairman, University and Polytechnic Grants Committee, 1981-1984; Chairman, Hong Kong University Council, 1985-2001; Pro-Chancellor, Hong Kong University, 1994-2001; President of the Bentham Club, University College London, 1988. He is adviser of The Society for the Rehabilitation of Offenders, Hong Kong. His publications include translations of three Chinese novels, *General Yue Fei*, *The Peach Blossom Fan* and *Officialdom Unmasked*.

Glossary

After hatch: after hatchway: "the hatchway nearest the stern" (<*http://www.marineterms.com*>)

Covid: "a lineal measure formerly used in India: its length varied, at different times, from 36 to 14 inches" (*OED*)

Forecastle: a short raised deck at the fore end of a vessel. In early vessels, raised like a castle to command the enemy's decks (*OED*)

'Tween decks = "between decks": "the space between any two decks of a ship" OR "the name of the deck or decks between the ceiling and main deck." (<*http://www.marineterms.com*>)

Lan: guild, guild's premises, warehouse

Lukong/lukwong: green jackets = during the period of these reports, this term refers to Chinese police constables. However, the word came into use in the 1840s when the European police force wore green coats and this is the meaning of the nickname.[1188]

Purlin: a horizontal beam along the length of a roof, resting on principals and supporting the common rafters or boards (*Oxford Encyclopedic English Dictionary*, 1991)

Samshu: "the generic name for Chinese spirits distilled from rice or sorghum" (*OED*); OR, "a diabolical mixture of alcohol, tobacco juice, sugar and arsenic" (Arthur Hacker)

Shroff: cashier, money-changer, banker (cf. Hindi, śarāf; Urdu sharāf; Arbic sarrāf).

Spelling Conventions

The romanisation of Chinese personal and geographical names in the Court Case transcriptions remains as it appears in the original newspaper reports. Elsewhere in the text, the Wade-Giles system of romanization is normally followed.

Referencing Conventions

The method of referencing used is based on the MLA (Modern Language Association of America) Style Sheet.

Key to Abbreviations
used in editorial comment & notes in this book

aka: also known as
CM: *The China Mail*
DevEd: Gillian Bickley, compiler and editor, *The Development of Education in Hong Kong, 1841-1897: as Revealed by the Early Education Reports of the Hong Kong Government 1848-1896*, 2002
HK: Hong Kong
HKGG: *The Hong Kong Government Gazette*
HKPRO: Hong Kong Public Records Office
HKGBB: Hong Kong Government Blue Book(s)
HKRS: Hong Kong Records Series, HKPRO
HMS: Her Majesty's Ship
HRH: His Royal Highness
JRAS (HK): *Journal of the Royal Asiatic Society (Hong Kong Branch)*
MS: Manuscript
No.: Number
OED: *Oxford English Dictionary*
Personal Archive: Gillian and Verner Bickley personal archive
Revd: Reverend
Rt Revd: Right Reverend
TGN: Gillian Bickley, *The Golden Needle: The Biography of Frederick Stewart (1836-1889)* 1997
TS: Typescript

Notes with Contributors' Acknowledgements

1. The main source for all commentary on Frederick Stewart's Court Cases in *A Nineteenth Century Magistrate's Court: Court in Time*, for references to cases and newspaper reports on cases, and for quotations from the reports in *The China Mail* is as follows: Gillian Bickley, compiler and editor, "Before Frederick Stewart, Esq: The Court Cases of Frederick Stewart, Police Magistrate, Hong Kong, July 1881-March 1882, as published in *The China Mail*", unpublished typescript, created 1998-1999 (referred to below as "Court Cases 1881-1882"). In this unpublished typescript, the cases transcribed are numbered in chronological sequence of reporting, each report being given a number. Hence "Court Case 1" is the first in the sequence; "Court Case 50" the fiftieth. – It is planned that this typescript will be made available as a CD publication in 2005 or 2006. – When "new number" appears, this indicates an addition to this typescript, at a time after it had already been made available to others to read and use.

2. Christopher Munn, "The Criminal Trial under Early Colonial Rule", in Ed. Tak-Wing Ngo, *Hong Kong's History*, London and New York, Routledge, 1999, pp. 46-73, p. 47.

3. In addition to Frederick Stewart, Nineteenth Century Police Magistrates and acting Police Magistrates included the following: Captain Bruce, William Caine, C. V. Creagh, Tudor W. (or H. T.) Davies, John Joseph Francis, E. W. Goodlake, Captain Haly, C. B. Hillier, W. C. H. Hastings, William Holdforth, Charles May, William Henry Mitchell, Norman Gilbert Mitchell-Innes, Ng Choy, C. B. Plunkett, J. C. Power, James Russell, C. C. Smith, H. G. Thomsett, M. S. Tonnochy, John Charles Whyte, A. G. Wise, H. E. Wodehouse. (Sources: Gillian Bickley, "Police Magistrates 1841-1898 (alphabetical order)", [Coroner:PolMagCh]; "Police Magistrates: Succession List 1841-1898" [Coroner:PolMagCh]).

4. Case heard on 10 August 1881 (Court Case 58).

5. E. J. Eitel, *Europe in China: the History of Hong Kong, from the beginning to the year 1882*, Hong Kong, Oxford University Press, 1983 (first published by Kelly and Walsh, Ltd., 1895), pp. 540-546.

6. See *HKGG*, 19 November 1881, p. 1007.

7. H. J. Lethbridge, "Condition of the European Working Class in Nineteenth Century Hong Kong", *JRAS (HK)*, Vol. 15, 1975, pp. 88-112, p. 89.

8. Tsai Jung-Fang, "Introduction", in Tsai Jung-Fang, *Hong Kong in Chinese History: Community and Social Unrest in the British Colony, 1842-1913*, 1993.

9. Tsai Jung-Fang, *Hong Kong in Chinese History*, op. cit., p. 103.

10. Fewer than ten in "Coolies in the British Colony", the chapter which comments on the rarity of scholarly publications on the working people in Hong Kong from 1842-191. Apparently none at all in the chapter,

"Coolie Unrest and Elitist Nationalism, 1887-1900".

11. Christopher Munn, "The Criminal Trial", *op. cit.*, p. 50.

12. *Ibid.*, p. 47.

13. Tsai Jung-Fang, *Hong Kong in Chinese History*, *op. cit.*, p. 115.

14. *Ibid.*, p. 115.

15. *Ibid.*, p. 116.

16. *Ibid.*, p. 115.

17. See *TGN* (pp. 233-234, 234-235) for extracts from these.

18. Editorial practices are explained in the Editor's Note. Their objective has been to produce an accurate text and to supply simple and basic explanations of terms, events, personalities and background, when it seemed absolutely necessary. No material has been cut or otherwise modified.

19. See also Gillian Bickley, "Police Magistrate" in *TGN*, pp. 218-222.

20 . "R. M.", Colonial Office, Minute, dated 13 May 1881. (CO/129/193/57r.-57v.; 57v.)

21. From shortly after 30 March 1883, when the new Governor, Sir George Bowen, arrived (*CM*, 30 March 1883), Stewart was evidently acting as Registrar General, the post to which he was later confirmed, at which time his appointment was backdated.

22. [Government Notification no. 262], 3 May 1880, Authorities, 1880, HKRS 275, HKPRO.

23. *CM*, 28 March 1882, p. 3, c. 1.

24. *CM*, 28 March 1882, p. 2, cc. 6-7.

25. *CM*, 28 March 1882, p. 2, c. 7.

26. *CM*, 30 March 1883.

27. Gillian Bickley, unpublished table, "Police Magistrates (alphabetical order)" and "Police Magistrates Succession List, 1841-1898", word-processed document, [Coroner: PolMagCh].

28. Ordinance No. 16 of 1875.

29. See *HKGG*, 19 November 1881, p. 1007. See also this chapter, below.

30. Governor John Pope Hennessy, Despatch, dated 28 April 1879, reports death of "Mr C. May, Senior Police Magistrate". (CO/129/184/179r.-181r.) (For a comment on the designation, "Senior", see elsewhere in this chapter.)

31. Colonial Office official, Minute to Sir M. Hicks Beach, dated 1 July 1879. (CO/129/184/266r.-266v.)

32. See Frederick Stewart, Acting Colonial Secretary, Letter No. 193 to Governor Sir John Pope Hennessy, dated 2 February 1881. (CO/129/192/265r.-265v.)

See also John Bramston, Colonial Office official, Minute dated 9 June 1879: "Mr Stewart, writing on the 29th, gives me the news of Mr May's death, which reached the Colony on the day previous, the date of this dispatch [28 April 1879]: and he informs [sic] me that he intended [sic] to apply for the post." (Colonial Office Minute Sheet,

CO/129/184/177r.-178r., attached to, Governor John Pope Hennessy, Despatch, dated 28 April 1879, CO/ 129/ 184/ 179r.-181r.)

It is not clear when Stewart actually put in his application through Governor Pope Hennessy. Given the speed at which he wrote to John Bramston (the day after news of the death of May reached Hong Kong), it would be strange if he delayed doing so until 2 May, the date when the Governor forwarded his application to London.

And why did Stewart take the unusual step of writing privately to his former Hong Kong colleague in London, John Bramston? (All we know of him suggests that this was not the sort of thing that he would do. He did write to Bramston twice, on other occasions, both to beg him to intervene so that first, Governor Sir George Bowen's plan and then, his renewed intention to recommend Stewart for the award of the CMG, might not be acted on in London.)

It may not be surprising that the Governor wrote the very same day that news of the death of May reached Hong Kong, suggesting two other names for the position – Charles V. Creagh and Ng Choy.

However, it seems at least possible that the following took place. That Stewart did in fact put in his application, whether verbally or in writing, to the Governor on 28 April, and that two things followed. Firstly, the Governor, not wanting Stewart to receive the position, speedily wrote to put forward two other names, not mentioning Stewart's interest. Secondly, Stewart, perceiving the Governor's opposition to his application, decided that he should write directly to London to express his interest.

It is hoped that Frederick Stewart's letter, applying for the post, as well as his letter to John Bramston, will be found, since both may be extremely interesting.

33. Stewart's second letter of application refers to his earlier application. (Frederick Stewart, Acting Colonial Secretary, Letter No. 193 to Governor Sir John Pope Hennessy, dated 2 February 1881. (CO/129/192/265r.-265v.))

However, no copy of this earlier application has been found with the Governor's covering despatch and the related Colonial Office Minute Sheets. (CO/129/192/265r.-273r.)

34. Governor Hennessy, Confidential Despatch, dated 2 May 1879, to Sir Michael Hicks Beach. (CO/129/184/272r.-272v.) The present writer has been unable to find Stewart's letter of application.

35. Presumably this reference must be to the period during which Stewart acted for James Russell as Acting Police Magistrate and Coroner (22 July 1876 to 4 January 1877).

36. Pope Hennessy gives no reason to explain why the "present moment" would be a particularly unfortunate one for Stewart to be transferred from the Central School.

37. "R. M." [i.e. Mr Meade], Minute to Mr Bramston, dated 17 June 1879. (CO/129/184/265r.)

38. Sir Michael Hicks Beach, Minute [no addressee], dated 20 June 1879.

(CO/129/184/265v.)

39. Colonial Office official, Minute to Sir M. Hicks Beach, dated 1 July 1879. (CO/129/184/266r.-266v.)

40. Mr R. W. G. Herbert, Minute to Sir M. Hicks Beach, dated 23 July 1879. (CO/129/184/267r.-267v., 267r.)

41. Frederick Stewart, Acting Colonial Secretary, Letter No. 193 to Governor Sir John Pope Hennessy, dated 2 February 1881. (CO/129/192/265r.-265v.)

42. Governor John Pope Hennessy, Despatch No. 9, dated Hong Kong, 5 February 1881, CO/129/192/264r.-264v.

43. C. P. Lucas, Colonial Office, Minute to Mr Meade, dated 15 March 1881. (CO/129/192/263r.)

44. See the following manuscripts and word-processed files by Gillian Bickley in preparation, in Personal Archive: "The new Interpretation Department: Proposal and Resistance", [Interp]; "Arrival back in Hong Kong: 21 March 1879; Loss of the Inspectorship: effective, 25 March 1879; Award of Honorary Aberdeen LL.D.: decided, 8 March 1879; awarded April 1879", [LossInsp]; "Trust not in princes or men's sons", [Losspt2]; Registrar General: 1883-1887, [RegGen]; "Deceived by his own Desires", [Desires].

45. The same.

46. Frederick Stewart took his place today at the Police Magistrate's Bench. (*CM*, 26 July 1881, p. 2, c. 6.)

47. See Verner Bickley, "Beware: You are in a Court of Justice", below.

48. *CM*, 24 January 1882.

49. See "Police", below, Court Case 293.

50. "Creating a Disturbance", "Police Intelligence," *CM*, Tuesday, 15 November 1881, p. 3, cc. 4-5; "Court Cases 1881-1882", Number 383.

51. *CM*, 15 November 1881, p. 3, c. 7-p. 4, c. 1.

52. Tsai Jung-fang, *Hong Kong in Chinese History*, *op. cit.*, p. 105.

53. Court Case 206.

54. *CM*, 27 September 1881, p. 3, cc. 5-6.

55. *CM*, 3 October 1881, p. 2, c. 7-p. 3, c. 1, reads as follows: "Ordinance No. 22 of 1844, entitled, "An Ordinance for establishing standard weights and measures and for preventing the use of such as are false and dishonest," with a translation of the same into Chinese, is published in the "Gazette" by command of H. E. the Administrator. We noted the other day, in our Police Intelligence columns, in reporting eighteen cases in which Chinese shopkeepers were fined 50 cents for each false measure in their shops, a remark made by the presiding Magistrate, Dr Frederick Stewart, to the effect that he 'inflicted this nominal penalty, as the Trade had been representing to the Government a "custom" not recognised by Ordinance adding that he did not know that the "custom" would ever be recognised by the Legislature, but he hoped the Ordinance would be translated and circulated so as to remove all doubt as to what the Law on the subject really was.' It is satisfactory to see the ordinance in [question?] was promptly published in the form [required?]."

A Chinese translation of the "Ordinance for Establishing Standard Weights and Measures, and for preventing the Use of such as are false and deficient", No. 22 of 1844, dated 30 December 1844, appeared under Government Notification No. 349 in *HKGG*, 8 October 1881, pp. 915-919.

When Frederick Stewart was Registrar General, he continued to be concerned with these differences between English and Chinese measures. The Executive Council Minutes of a meeting held on 22 April 1885 (which refer to the Weights and Measures Ordinance of 1885) refer to Stewart's petition for permission to use Chinese, not English, measures of length. (CO/131/14/288-)

The Executive Council Minutes of a meeting held on 1 May 1885 refer to a report by the Registrar General (Frederick Stewart) and the Colonial Treasurer on the use of the Chinese foot measure. It has been decided not to alter the law. (CO/131/14/295-)

56. *CM*, 3 October 1881, p. 2, c. 7-p. 3, c. 1.

57. *HKGG*, 8 October 1881, p. 915.

58. Magistrate Garry Tallentire explains (personal communication) that, today, changes in Law come about by a constant process of representation to the Department of Justice (formerly the Attorney-General's Department) often via the Judiciary or interested bodies, and the Government is then consulted.

59. See "Children and Students", below.

60. Court Case 483.

61. There is a reference, dated 26 February 1880, to Ordinance No. 2 of 1875, which gave a person, charged with an offence, the option of being tried by a jury. (CO/129/241/190)

62. Personal communication.

63. The newspaper makes no comment about the fact that the two men had identical surnames. Were they perhaps brothers?

64. "Police Intelligence", *CM*, Wednesday, 1 March 1882, p. 3, cc. 2-3. [Court Case 660]

65. A Special Session [*sic*] was held on 10 March 1882. See "Criminal Calendar" – March Special Session 1882", *HKGG*, 18 March 1882, p. 296. John Bryant was unanimously found not guilty of shooting with intent to murder and not guilty of shooting with intent to do some grievous bodily harm but he was found guilty of common assault. The sentence, also given on 10 March 1882, was three months' imprisonment with hard labour.

66. See "Soldiers", below.

67. *CM*, 3 October 1881, p. 2, c. 7 - p. 3, c. 1.

68. Alan Harfield, *British and Indian Armies on the China Coast, 1785-1985*, Farnham, Surrey, A. and J. Partnership, 1990, p. 161.

69. "Local and General", *CM*, 10 December 1881, p. 2, c. 7.

70. *Ibid.*, A few undecipherable words are guessed at in this transcription.

71. "Local and General", *CM*, 10 December 1881, p. 2, c. 7.

72. Court Case 79.

73. Court Case 472. "Police Intelligence", *CM*, Tuesday, 13 December 1881, p. 3, cc. 5-6.

74. *Sic.*

75. Court Case 533.

76. Court Case 531.

77. See "Public Obstruction", reported on 16 November 1881, when Mr Francis acted for the defendant and Stewart supported the Police.

78. Presumably he is the "A. Spencer", No. 268 on the school roll, nationality English, who appears in a list of pupils, dated 5 March 1878, aged 13, then having attended the school for 5 months.

79. Court Case 721.

80. The title, "Police Magistrate", is not given after Stewart's name, as it is in the case of Wodehouse.

81. See above.

82. See also Ordinance No. 8 of 1889, which, "provides for the exercise by one Police Magistrate of jurisdiction which, under Ordinance No. 2 of 1875 and 16 of 1875, was vested in two magistrates sitting together, but with a limit to the power of punishment to one year instead of two, and it provides also for the forfeiture of articles illegally hawked." (CO/129/241/192r.-192v.)

83. *CM* seems to believe – erroneously – that Frederick Stewart was a cadet, one of the élite group appointed after examination in the United Kingdom, later succeeded by "Administrative Officers" of any background.

84. *CM*, 25 February 1876, p. 2, c. 6-p. 3, c. 1.

85. *CM*, 28 February 1876, p. 3.

86. *CM*, 16 May 1881, p. 2, c. 7.

87. *Ibid.*

88. *Ibid.*

89. *CM*, 23 May 1881, p. 2, c. 5.

90. *CM*, 16 May 1881, p. 2, c. 7.

91. *CM*, 2 June 1881, p. 2, c. 6. See also above, this essay.

92. "Local and General", *CM*, 15 November 1881, p. 2. c. 7-p. 3, c. 1.

93. See "Urban Life", below.

94. *CM*, Editorial.

95. See also "Prostitutes, their Clients and Associates", below.

96. See Garry Tallentire, "The Hong Kong (Police) Magistrate in the 1880s and 1990s", below.

97. See note in "Urban Life", below.

98. "Counterfeit Coin", 6 January 1882.

99. "The Senior Police Magistrate, though not a Chinese scholar himself, has through his long residence in Hong Kong (since 1844) acquired a good practical acquaintance with Chinese modes of thought...". (E. J. Eitel, "Chinese Studies and Official Interpretation in the Colony of Hong Kong", *The China Review*, Vol. VI, 1877, pp. 1-13, p. 9, c. 2-p. 10, c. 1.)

100. Eitel's essay, published in 1877, argues for a better system of interpretation in the Supreme Court at Hong Kong. By stating that the

situation in the Police Courts was better than in the Supreme Court, Eitel confirms that satisfactory interpretation was important here also. Writing of James Russell, Eitel says: "There is ... one Police Magistrate, who also acts as Coroner, who has gone through a course of thorough Chinese study as one of the ... Student-Interpreters, and he is perfectly able to check the interpretation going on in his Court...". (E. J. Eitel, "Chinese Studies and Official Interpretation in the Colony of Hong Kong", *op. cit.*)

101. See Gillian Bickley, "Chinese Language Study by Frederick Stewart and other British Teachers in Hong Kong Schools in the Nineteenth Century: A Response to the book review of *The Golden Needle: the Biography of Frederick Stewart (1836-1889)*, David C. Lam Institute for East-West Studies, Hong Kong Baptist University, 1997 in APJLE Vol. 1 (1)", *Asia Pacific Journal of Language in Education*, December 1998, Vol. 1 (2), pp. 151-153 and Gillian Bickley, "The Student-interpreters' Scheme and the Chinese Teacher's Allowance: Translator Education in Nineteenth-century Hong Kong", in, *Translation in Hong Kong: Past, Present and Future*, Ed. Chan Sin-wai, Hong Kong, The Chinese University Press, 2001, pp. 8-19.

102. See Garry Tallentire, "The Hong Kong (Police) Magistrate in the 1880s and 1990s", below.

103. Tim Hamlett, "Reporting the Cases of Frederick Stewart", below.

104. E. J. Eitel, *Europe in China*, *op. cit.*, p. 170.

105. For the relationship between Hong Kong and British law, see also Christopher Coghlan, "Thoughts about the Practice of Law in Hong Kong," below.

106. In some commentary or references to flogging, during this period, it is not clear whether the term refers to the cat or whip only, or whether it is also used to refer to the use of the cane or rattan.

107. E. J. Eitel, *Europe in China*, *op. cit.*, p. 171.

108. *Ibid.*, p. 171.

109. Albert H. Y. Chen, in "Justice after 1997" (pp. 172-188, pp. 176-177), in Eds Traver and Vagg, *Crime and Justice in Hong Kong*, 1991, gives a useful brief historical comment on comparisons between Chinese and British systems:

"If contemporary Western systems seem to approximate the ideals of justice and protection of human rights to a greater extent than the Chinese system, there did exist many points in history where the prevailing institutions and practices would be considered uncivilized, underdeveloped, or irrational by present-day standards. For example, as a leading scholar on the English law of criminal procedure points out, until recent times the treatment of the accused under the English legal system can only be described as barbarous (Hampton 1982:1). Similarly, two other authors observed:

"'Until the nineteenth century the criminal law [in England] was barbarous in operation and antiquated in structure. The death penalty could be inflicted for over 200 offences, sometimes with gruesome incidents. Executions were in public, transportation [to overseas colonies for convict labour] was in full vigour, a person accused of felony was subject to heavy disadvantages in presenting his case, and the law of criminal evidence was unsystematic and uncertain (Keeton and Lloyd 1955: 101).'"

Chen continues, "It is interesting to note in this regard the comment by an expert in Chinese history on changing Western images of Chinese justice: 'Early European observers had been well impressed with Chinese justice. It was only after the eighteenth and nineteenth century reforms of law and punishments in the modern West that China was left behind' (Fairbank 1980: 117-118)."

The references are to:

Fairbank, J. K., *The United States and China*, 4th ed., Cambridge, Mass, Harvard University Press, 1980.

Hampton, C., *Criminal Procedure*, 3rd ed., London, Sweet and Maxwell, 1982.

Keeton, G. W. and D. Lloyd, eds, *The United Kingdom: The Development of its Laws and Constitutions*, London, Stevens, 1955.

110. *The Daily Press*, 29 September 1897, p. 3.

111. James Legge, "The Colony of Hong Kong", text of/based on a talk given at the City Hall, Hong Kong, 5 November 1872, reprinted in *JRAS (HK)*, Vol. XI, 1971, pp. 172-193, p. 181.

112 . Lethbridge, "The District Watch Committee: 'The Chinese Executive Council of Hong Kong'", pp. 116-117.

113. *Ibid.*, p. 117.

114. *Ibid.*, p. 117.

115. E. J. Eitel (doubtless to please the governor) reported that these measures were becoming effective. (CO/129/194/24v., paragraph 2.)

116. Christopher Munn, "'An Anglo-Chino [*sic*] conspiracy in crime': the Caldwell Scandal, 1857-1861", TS, p. 16. Munn is speaking of the 1860s, but this comment was true throughout the nineteenth century at least.

117. Lethbridge, "The District Watch Committee", *op. cit.*, p. 117.

118. See also "Police", below.

119. See "Pirates and Life at Sea", below.

120. Patrick Hase, talk given to the Royal Asiatic Society at the City Hall, Hong Kong, 1999-2000. See also "Pirates", below.

121. Acting Superintendent of Police, Annual Report for 1877, *HKGG*, 6 April 1878, pp. 125-126, paragraph 4.

122. Samson Chan, "Differential Treatment for Chinese Offenders: A Historical Study of Early Colonial Policies in Hong Kong", TS, p. 5.

123. Frank Welsh has an interesting account of this incident. (Frank Welsh, *A History of Hong Kong*, London, Harper Collins, 1993, pp. 214-215.)

124. Frederick Stewart, Inspector of Schools Report for 1868, dated 15 February 1869 (referring back to 1862), paragraph 39. See *DevEd*, p. 125.

125. Minutes of an Executive Council Meeting, held on 16 August 1889, CO/131/17/169.

126. *HKGG*, 30 September 1882, p. 783. The Ordinance in question was Ordinance No. 14 of 1879, Section 18.

127. *Sic*. Quoted in Frank Welsh, *A History of Hong Kong*, *op. cit.*, p. 244.

128. E. J. Eitel, *Europe in China*, *op. cit.*, pp. 238-239.

129. *Ibid*.

130. Ordinance No. 12 of 1865 and Ordinance No. 3 of 1868.

131. Ordinance No. 7 of 1870.

132. "Public Flogging", *The Daily Press*, 7 September 1870, p. 3 (?), c. 2.

133. Mr F. Douglas was "Superintendent of Victoria Gaol". See "List of Officers", HKGBB for 1870, p. 53.

134. E. J. Eitel, *Europe in China*, *op. cit.*, pp. 227-228.

135. See also Tim Hamlett, "Reporting the Cases of Frederick Stewart", below.

136. *Sic*. E. J. Eitel, *Europe in China*, *op. cit.*, pp. 449-450. Samson Chan, however, states that it ended in April, 1870. ("Differential Treatment for Chinese Offenders", *op. cit.*, p. 8.)

137. Samson Chan, "Differential Treatment for Chinese Offenders", *op. cit.*, p. 8.

138. E. J. Eitel, *Europe in China*, *op. cit.*, pp. 488-489, 541-542.

139. 16 April 1872 to 1 March 1877.

140. E. J. Eitel, *Europe in China*, *op. cit.*, p. 489.

141. Governor Hennessy, despatch to the Earl of Carnarvon, 6 July 1877, in CO/882/4 (i) Eastern No. 33, pp. 5-7, p. 5, paragraph 5.

142. Governor Hennessy to the Earl of Carnarvon, 13 June 1877, in, CO/882/4 (i) Eastern No. 33, pp. 1-2, p. 2, paragraph 19.

143. Governor John Pope Hennessy to Earl of Carnarvon, Despatch dated 6 July 1877: "As far as I am aware there is no code of laws in any part of her Majesty's Empire in which the power of flogging is so extensively given to Magistrates and Judges as in Hong Kong." (In, CO/882/4 (i) Eastern No. 33, p. 5, paragraph 1.)

144. E. J. Eitel, *Europe in China*, *op. cit.*, p. 541.

145. *HKGG*, 19 November 1881, p. 1006.

146. *CM*, 3 March 1882, p. 3, c. 3.

147. Colonial Office Minute, dated 20 November 1880. (CO/129/189/324r.)

148. E. J. Eitel, *Europe in China*, *op. cit.*, p. 545.

149. Samson Chan, "Differential Treatment for Chinese Offenders ", *op. cit.*, p. 13.

150. E. J. Eitel, *Europe in China*, *op. cit.*, p. 450.

151. *Ibid.*, pp. 541-545.

152. See two reports of earring snatching ("Court Cases 1881-1882", Court Case 6, reported on 26 July 1881 and Court Case 605, reported on 7 February 1882) and also "Theft of a Hair Pin", Court Case 225, reported on 30 September 1881. See also below, this essay.

153. *CM*, 20 September 1881, p. 2, c. 6.

154. "Sir Edmund Hornby [Late Her Majesty's Chief Judge for China and

Japan] on the Residents in Hong Kong", *CM*, 31 December 1877, p. 3, cc. 2 -3 (reprinted from the "Spectator", where it appeared as a letter to the Editor).

155. "Police Intelligence," *CM*, Tuesday, 13 December 1881, p. 3, cc. 5-6. See also "Court Cases 1881-1882", Court Case 467.

156. See "Inquests", *CM*, 24 January 1882, p. 2, c. 6.

157. E. J. Eitel, *Europe in China, op. cit.*, p. 545.

158. Minutes of an Executive Council Meeting, held on 23 April 1884, CO/131/14/57.

159. Samson Chan, "Differential Treatment for Chinese Offenders", *op. cit.*, p. 16. Chan supports his point by reference to, *Report of the Commission Appointed to Consider the Question of Insufficient Accommodation in Victoria Gaol*, 1 June 1886.

160. Samson Chan, "Differential Treatment for Chinese Offenders", *op. cit.*, p. 17.

161. P. Spierenburg, *The Spectacle of Suffering*, London, Cambridge University Press, 1984, p. 78.

162. Samson Chan, "Differential Treatment for Chinese Offenders", *op. cit.*, p. 20.

163. Case heard on 19 August 1876, reported in the *Daily Press*, 21 August 1876, p. 2, c. 3.

164. CO/882/4 (i) Eastern No. 33, p. 14, p. 15.

165. Samson Chan, "Differential Treatment for Chinese Offenders", *op. cit.*, p. 15.

166. See Garry Tallentire, "The Hong Kong (Police) Magistrate in the 1880s and 1990s", below.

167. Court Case 342 refers to a second sentence in a single year (1876), for larceny from a dwelling house, which included two applications of the rod, as well as a term in prison and time in the stocks.

168. See also below, this essay.

169. See "Urban Life", below, note 16.

170. Frederick Stewart, Inspector of Schools, Annual Report for 1870, paragraph 34. (See *DevEd*, pp. 144-145.)

171. [Margaret McBryde], "Crime and Punishment: The complete text of an exhibition of documents from the national archives [of Scotland], held at General Register House [Edinburgh]", [1998], p. 8.

172. *Ibid.*, p. 11.

173. *Ibid.*, p. 11.

174 . *Encyclopedia Americana – International Edition*, Grolier Incorporated, 1993, p. 732.

175. *CM*, 3 August 1881, p. 3, c. 1.

176. See also above, this essay.

177. Some of these alleged offences seem rather minor to have been remitted to the Supreme Court and one is tempted to find an explanation in a new rule, described above. However, the Table, "Sentences to the Stocks in Frederick Stewart's Court", below, shows five defendants with twenty-four prior sentences between them, none of whom were remitted

to the Supreme Court and all of whom were sentenced by Stewart in his Magistrate's Court.

178. Court Case 131.
179. Court Case 156.
180. Court Case 162.
181. Court Case 163.
182. Court Case 164.
183. Court Case 220.
184. Court Case 221.
185. Court Cases 255, 292, 293. The sentence in this case was later given by Magistrate Stewart, since a technicality prevented the case being treated as one of embezzlement.
186. Court Case 342.
187. Court Case 343.
188. Court Case 356.
189. Court Case 388.
190. Court Case 420.
191. Court Case 455.
192. Court Case 491.
193. Court Case 520.
194. Court Case 522.
195. Court Case 529.
196. Court Cases 558, 567, 634, 665.
197. Court Case 604.
198. Court Case 619.
199. Court Case 633.
200. Court Case 687.
201. Court Case 694.
202. Court Case 721.
203. See note above, this essay.

NOTES TO, "DIFFERING PERCEPTIONS OF SOCIAL REALITY IN DR STEWART'S COURT" — *VERNER BICKLEY*

204. For example, Melville Jean Herskovits, *Man and His Works*, New York, A. A. Knopf, 1948.
205. Court Case 112. Court Case numbers refer to, "Court Cases 1881-1882". Over one hundred of these are included in Section Two, below.
208. Jen-Huong Wang, "Some Cultural Factors Affecting Chinese in Treaty Negotiation", in *Cultural Factors in International Relations*, Ed. R. P. Anand, New Delhi, Abhinav Publications, 1981, pp. 97-112, p. 100.
207. Peter Wesley-Smith, "Cultural Problems in Negotiation of the Convention of Peking, 1898", in *Cultural Factors in International Relations, op. cit.*, pp. 113-128, p. 120.
208. Court Case 4, heard on 26 July 1881.
209. Court Case 686, heard on 15 March 1882.
210. Court Case 180, heard on 20 September 1881.

211. Present writer's italics.

212. More often than not, the Chinese calendar begins later than January (the first month — and the first moon — of the western calendar).

213. Court Case 51, heard on 9 August 1881.

214. Court Case 53, heard on 10 August 1881.

215. By Ordinance No. 10 of 1872, "to prevent certain nuisances", the lighting of crackers or fireworks without previous permission was illegal. (*HKGG*, 1872, p. 388.)

216. Court Case 259, heard on 8 October 1881. It is the eighth moon of the *Chinese* calendar, which is referred to. See note above.

217. Court Case 620, heard on Monday, 13 February 1882.

220. The permission was given under Ordinance 10 of 1872. In districts West of the Cross Roads and of Shing Wong Street, permission was from 4pm on 17 February to 4pm on 19 February. For Districts East of the Cross Roads and of Shing Wong Street, the permitted period was a little shorter, from 4pm on 17 February to 9pm on 18 February. ("Government Notification No. 32", *HKGG*, 28 January 1882, p. 48.)

221. David H. Bayley, "Modes and Mores of Policing the Community in Japan", in *Law and Society, Culture Learning Through the Law*, Honolulu, Culture Learning Institute, East-West Centre, November 1977, pp. 71-82.

220. A. R. Blackshield, "Capital Punishment in India: The Impact of the Ediga Anamma Case", in *Law and Society: Culture Learning Through the Law*, Honolulu, Culture Learning Institute, East-West Centre, November 1977, pp. 83-98, p. 97.

221. "Theft of a Watch", Court Case 112, heard on 2 September 1881. See "Police", below.

222. Punctuation *sic*.

223. Court Case 360, heard on 9 November 1881.

226. "A Dangerous Lunatic", Court Case 372, heard on 12 November 1881.

225. Elizabeth Sinn, *Power and Charity: The Early History of the Tung Wah Hospital, Hong Kong*, Hong Kong, Oxford University Press, East Asian Historical Monographs, 1989, p. 97.

226. "An Ordinance for the better protection of Chinese Women and Female children and for the repression of certain abuses in relation to Chinese Emigration", *HKGG*, 1875, pp. 76-77, 105-106, 259.

227. Court Case 343, heard on 4 November 1881. See, "Kidnappers and Traffickers in Human Beings", below.

228. "Kidnapping". First heard as Court Case 575, heard on 27 January 1882; and then as Court Cases 587, 600, 619 ("Alleged Kidnapping"), heard on 31 January, 4 and 12 February 1882. See "Kidnappers and Traffickers in Human Beings", below.

229. *Sic*.

230. Contents of square brackets are supplied by the present writer.

231. See Gillian Bickley, "Chinese Language Study by Frederick Stewart and other British Teachers in Hong Kong Schools in the Nineteenth

Century: A Response to the book review of *The Golden Needle*, *op. cit.*
See also *TGN*, e.g. pp. 80-81, 268, 280.

232. Verner Bickley, "The Diversified Whole: Mediation And The Language Mosaic In the Hong Kong Education System", in *Languages in Education in a Bilingual or Multi-lingual Setting*, Ed. Verner Bickley, Hong Kong, Hong Kong Government Education Department, 1989, pp. 192-209, p. 202.

233. See Peter Mühlhäusler, *Pidgin & Creole Linguistics*, Oxford, Basil Blackwell, 1986, p. 5.

234. Court Case 51, heard on 9 August 1881. See also above, this essay.

235. "Alleged Assault", Court Case 83, heard on 15 March 1882. See also "Prostitutes, their Clients and Associates", below.

236. Court Case 86, heard on 17 August 1881 and again (Court Case 87) on 18 August 1881 and (Court Case 94) on 20 August 1881. See also "Wives and Husbands" etc., below.

237. "Silly Billy", 2 September 1881, Court Case 113.

NOTES TO, "THOUGHTS ABOUT THE PRACTICE OF LAW IN HONG KONG" — *CHRISTOPHER COGHLAN*

238. "A Goose Plucked", 20 September 1881, Court Case 180; "A Needy Customer Provided For", 28 September 1881, Court Case 213.

239. Writing to Frederick Stewart, Acting Colonial Secretary, on 2 September 1880, J. J. Francis, who had recently been acting as Police Magistrate, expresses the view that the bulk of the cases currently brought before the Magistrates' Courts, "are petty larcenies, most of them the result of poverty and destitution in the accused." (CO/129/189/327r.-329v., 327v.-328r.) In his view, the solution for this lay in finding a way, "to deal with the increasing mass of poverty in the Colony". (CO/129/189/327r.-329v., 329r.-329v.)

240. "Theft from the Person", 6 September 1881, Court Case 127.

241. "Pocket Picking", 8 September 1881, Court Case 139.

242. "Theft from the Person", 15 September 1881, Court Case 158.

243. "Mendicancy", 6 September 1881, Court Case 122.

244. In 1995, the number of criminal cases heard in the Magistrates' Courts in Hong Kong was 609,000, whereas 1,322 were heard in the District Courts and 1,652 in the High Court. The percentage heard in the Magistrates' Courts was therefore ninety-nine point five percent.

245. Strictly speaking, the Court of Appeal and the Court of Final Appeal do not try appeals, they hear them.

246. "Committal", 12 October 1881, Court Case 280.

247. In England, this was the clerk's duty. In Hong Kong, magistrates may have had to make their own notes.

248. See for example, "Committed for Trial", 4 November 1881, Court Case 342.

249. *CM*, 15 December 1881, p. 2, c. 7 (defective original), commented on the contemporary method of prosecution as follows: "The growls which we have heard [from] more than one source, as to the . . . expense

to which a resident may be put in prosecuting a dishonest servant, appeared to be almost unprecedentedly well-founded until we stumbled over . . . [another] expression of the same grievance [outside Hong Kong]. As a matter of fact, however, we have always looked upon the Head of the Police, and his Inspectors, as Public Prosecutors, and generally found them to be ever ready to undertake such a duty."

A further clarification is offered in James Russell, Acting Attorney General, letter to W. H. Marsh, Colonial Secretary, dated, Hong Kong, 14 October 1890, where he writes: "The Attorney General here is not a public prosecutor in the sense in which the Chief Justice puts it. He has nothing to do with the prosecution of offences as a rule until the cases are committed for trial, when he is then called upon to perform the functions of a grand jury and either files an information or not. If he files an information he takes the responsibility of Prosecutor. Up to that time the Police generally and the Crown Solicitor in special cases under directions of the Government conduct public prosecutions. Besides by Ordinance 2 of 1869 Sec: 9 – The Attorney General may send back cases to the Magistrate to be reopened for further evidence, or for summary disposal."(CO/129/187/111r.-116r., 113v.-114r.)

250. This essay was written in 1999.

251. Jan Morris, *Hong Kong*, Penguin, Second edition published by Penguin, 1993, reprinted with an additional chapter, 1997, pp. 222-223.

252. Frank Welsh, *A History of Hong Kong*, *op. cit.*, Chapter Sixteen, p. 488.

255. This story is referred to again in, *Foreign Devils: Expatriates in Hong Kong* by May Holdsworth with additional text by Caroline Courtauld, OUP, 2002.

254. "Leaving His Employer Without Notice," 5 October 1881, Court Case 249.

255. *"The Bolton Abbey* – False Report", 4 October 1881, Court Case 242.

256. "All is not Gold which Glitters", 6 September 1881, Court Case 131. See "Urban Life", below.

257. James William Norton-Kyshe, *The History of the Laws and Courts of Hong Kong*, London, Unwin, 1898, 2 vols, Vol. II, p. 416.

258. See E. J. Eitel, *Europe in China*, *op. cit.*, p. 488.

NOTES TO, "THE HONG KONG "LIGHT AND PASS" RULES" – *GILLIAN BICKLEY*

259. See "An Old Offender", 20 October 1881.

260. Colin Crisswell and Mike Watson, *The Royal Hong Kong Police (1841-1945)*, Hong Kong, Macmillan Hong Kong, 1982, p. 14.

261. In an editorial, which appeared on 29 March 1882 *CM* (p. 2, c. 1) states that flogging for being out without a light or pass had never come into force or had, "practically become inoperative".

262. *Sic.*

266. George Smith, Letter to Earl Grey, dated, Church Missionary House, 16 January 1847, Stamped, "Received Colonial Office, 18 January 1847", CO/129/22/269r.-272v. ["77 Hong Kong"] Stamped, "Printed for Parliament May 1852". A marginal note reads, "Extract to War Office, 18 March 1847; Copy to Governor, No. 77-19; Answered 19 March 47".

    See also CO/129/135/64 LH -, where this text is given again, but in printed form.

    The printed version has differences in capitalisation and punctuation from those in George Smith's original manuscript: but otherwise it seems to be an accurate word for word transcription. The following is "corrected" by reference to the printed version.

264. Revd George Smith, M. A., of Magdalen Hall, Oxford, and late Missionary in China, *A Narrative of an Exploratory Visit to each of the Consular Cities of China, and to the Islands of Hong Kong and Chusan, in Behalf of the Church Missionary Society, in the years 1844, 1845, 1846*, Seeley, Burnside, and Seeley, London, 1847, p. 53.

265. *Ibid.*, p. 180.

266. CO/129/22/276r.-277r.

267. Draft of Earl Grey, Despatch to Sir J. Davis, later dated 19 March 1847. (CO/129/29/288r.-289r.)

268. According to Lethbridge, although unsuccessful, there was a proposal to reintroduce "the night pass system" in 1903. (Lethbridge, "The District Watch Committee", p. 137, n. 25.)

269. See the amended Ordinance for the better Securing the Peace of the Colony (No. 9 of 1857), dated 15 July 1857, *HKGG*, 18 July 1857, p. 2.

270. See Ordinance No. 14 of 1870, paragraphs XXIII-XXIV, *HKGG*, 10 September 1870, p. 455.

271. See below.

272. Frank Welsh, *A History of Hong Kong*, *op. cit.*, pp. 214-215, p. 215, gives a reference to, *HKGG*, 25 June 1857 and *HKGG*, 14 February 1857. The text of the amended Ordinance for the better Securing the Peace of the Colony, dated 15 July 1857, was published in *HKGG*, 18 July 1857, p. 2.

273. *HKGG*, 18 July 1857, p. 2 (only).

274. Ordinance No. 9 of 1857, Section V, *HKGG*, 18 July 1857, p. 2.

275. Ordinance No. 9 of 1857, Section II.

276. *Ibid.*

277. Executive Council Minutes of meeting, 17 March 1858, CO/131/4/456v.

278. Government Notification No. 52, dated 29 March 1865, *HKGG*, 1 April 1865, p. 173.

279. *HKGG*, 13 September 1870, p. 453.

280. Present writer's emphasis.

281. Letter dated 6 August [*sic*] 1870, *Daily Press*, 7 September 1870, p. 3, c. 2.

282. *Daily Press*, 7 September 1870, p. 3?, c. 2.

283. *Sic*.

284. Letter dated 6 September 1870, *Daily Press*, 7 September 1870, p. 3?, cc. 2-3.

285 . Executive Council Minutes of meeting, 5 January 1871, CO/131/7/3473.

286. *CM*, 29 January 1876, p. 2.

287. Hennessy arrived in Hong Kong in April 1877. (G. B. Endacott, *A History of Hong Kong*, 2nd ed. Hong Kong, Oxford University Press, 1964, first published 1958.)

288. *CM*, 20 December 1877, p. 2, cc. 5-6.

289. It seems that the report is slightly in error, and that the regulation was that *either* a pass *or* a lantern should be carried, not both. See above.

290. *CM*, 27 September 1878, p. 3, c. 3.

291. *HKGG*, 23 July 1879, p. 444.

292. Court Case 207.

293. *CM*, 20 January 1882, p. 2, c. 7.

294. *CM*, speaks of *three* nights of illuminations. (*CM*, 27 December 1881, p. 3, cc. 1-4.)

295. The modern word for this might be "wow".

296. *CM*, 20 January 1882, p. 2, c. 7.

297. "The Illuminations", *CM*, 27 December 1881, p. 3, cc. 1-4, c. 3.

298. Court Cases 498, 502, 504 and 506. See also Geoffrey Roper, below.

299. Court Case 502.

303. Ordinance No. 13 of 1888, paragraph 30, *The Ordinances of Hong Kong for 1888*, Noronha, 1889.

301. Ordinance No. 13 of 1888, paragraph 31, *The Ordinances of Hong Kong for 1888*, Noronha, 1889.

302. Ordinance No. 6 of 1897, *The Ordinances of Hong Kong for 1897*, Noronha, 1898.

303. Chronological Table of Ordinances: Laws of Hong Kong: Index. [HKU Law Library. PR KT 4353.1 H7 F90]

304. Court Case 47.

305. Court Case 155.

306. Court Case 165.

307. Court Case 179.

308. Court Case 184.

309. Court Case 267.

310. Court Case 275.

311. Court Case 301.

312. Court Case 339.

313. Court Case 368.

314. Court Case 393.

315. By Ordinance No. 9 of 1857, paragraph XI, "If any Chinaman, not being the holder of a Night Pass, shall cary abroad with him, whether by night or day, any deadly weapon whatsoever, he shall be guilty of a misdemeanour." By Ordinance No. 14 of 1870, paragraph XVIII, "Every

Chinese not being the lawful holder of a Pass who shall, without reasonable excuse, the proof of which shall lie upon him, carry any deadly weapon whatever about him, whether by night or day, shall be liable on summary conviction thereof, to a fine not exceeding one hundred dollars, or to imprisonment with hard labour for any period not exceeding six nonths, and such weapon to be forfeited to the Crown."

316. Court Case 446.

317. Court Case 517.

318. Court Case 599.

319. Court Case 630.

320. On the basis of these reports only, it is unclear whether it was an offence only if you had neither a lamp nor a pass, or if it was also an offence if you had one but not the other. Some reports mention the absence of both lamp and pass throughout. Some mention the absence of both in one part of the report and the absence of one only in another part. Three cases mention the absence of a pass only, but, given the variability described, this could be an aspect of the reporting of the cases, rather than a reflection of the law or its application at this time. On the other hand, it could be that the *time* of the offence was the significant factor; that you had to have a lantern earlier in the evening than you had to have a pass. (See above.) In the three cases where the absence of a pass only is mentioned, the specific time of the offence is not stated. However, no time is given for two other cases, where the absence of both light and pass are mentioned. As stated in a note above, however, the rule was that, if you had no pass, you had to have a lantern.

321. Court Case 184. The rate of exchange was about four dollars eighty cents to one pound sterling.

In May 1889, an Editorial appeared in the Hong Kong newspaper, *CM* (9 May 1889, p. 2, c.7), containing a comparison of the purchasing power of money in Hong Kong as between 1876 and 1889 in regard to general commodities. It says: "A very good test of this is obtained from the Market Prices which have been published every week for nearly a score of years." Comparing the figures for 27 April 1876 and 27 April 1889, and giving the prices in "Cash" (which in 1876 stood at 1090 to HK$1), it shows that, on 27 April 1876, English bacon cost 400 to 300; corned beef, 160 to 140; roast beef, 180 to 160; soup beef, 100 to 80; steak beef, 180 to 160; American hams, 350; Chinese Hams, 200 to 160; English Hams, 400 to 360; mutton chop, 90 to 180; mutton leg, 200 to 180; mutton shoulder, 160 to 140; a catty of veal, 180 to 160; a catty of capons, 200 to 180; a catty of ducks, 110 to 100; a turkey cock, 500 to 400; a turkey hen, 400 to 350; Macao potatoes, 30 to 20; Japan Potatoes 25 to 20.

Fares for Jinrickshas with one coolie ranged from 5 cents for fifteen minutes or less to fifty cents for one day (considered as twelve hours). (*HKGG*, 16 September 1882, p. 760, Government Notification No. 367.)

322. Court Case 393.

323. Court Case 368.
324. Court Case 267.
325. Court Case 275.
326. Court Case 339.
327. Court Case 517.
328. See also Geoffrey Roper, "The Police Role in Magistrate Frederick Stewart's Court", below.
329. Court Case 179.
330. Court Case 630. Solitary confinement seems to have been regarded as a privilege, rather than an additional punishment.
331. Court Case 47.
332. Court Case 155.
333. Court Case 301.
334. Court Case 179.
335. See "Sailors", below.
336. "I have known men to be let out from gaol in the morning and passed the same evening in that place and why? Chiefly because they had no home, and often to my knowledge some of the men have boldly asked the Magistrate to commit them to jail and on refusal would go down to the town and commit a nuisance with the object of obtaining food and shelter." ("Junius", "Destitutes", Correspondence, *CM*, 2 December 1881, p. 3, c. 4.)
337. See above comments on the different means taken by homeless westerners and homeless Chinese to obtain shelter in a prison for some days.
338. There are fifteen reports and fourteen cases, one being before the court twice.

NOTES TO, "THE POLICE ROLE IN MAGISTRATE FREDERICK STEWART'S COURT" – *GEOFFREY ROPER*

343. Acknowledgements:
I thank Dr Gillian Bickley and Dr Verner Bickley, MBE, for the invitation to write this essay and their continuing patience and support. My thanks go also to Mr N. K. Wong, the Curator of the Hong Kong Police Museum, for his assistance. Dr Norman Miners' article, "The Localization of the Hong Kong Police Force, 1842-1947", has been a major source of influence on my thinking on localization. Like all writers on the history of the Hong Kong Police, I salute Mike Waters as the *doyen* of the corps.
340. "A Batch of Rogues", 16 January 1882, Court Case 545.
341. "A Novel Use of a Queue", 23 January 1882, Court Case 561.
342. See Court Cases: 58, 124, 146, 307, 331, 375, 399, 405, 434, 438, 475, 485, 492, 493.
343. See Court Cases: 575, 587, 600, 627.
344. Colonial Surgeon's Report, 1879, courtesy Public Records Office of Hong Kong (Hong Kong Public Records Office).

345. "An Unhappy Inmate of a Brothel", 15 February 1882, Court Case 631.

346. See Court Cases: 48, 153, 189, 276, 278, 364, 494.

347. See "Assault", 16 September 1881, Court Case 160.

348. See "Assault", 16 September 1881, Court Case 160.

349. See Court Cases 103, 557.

350. "Public Gambling", 10 August 1881, Court Case 58.

351. See also, "Prostitutes, Associates and Clients", below.

352. See also, "Prostitutes, Associates and Clients", below.

353. See Court Case 364.

354. Court Case 561.

355. Geoffrey Roper, Notes, Royal Asiatic Society (Hong Kong Branch) tour of Central District, Hong Kong, mimeograph.

356. See Court Cases: 80, 132, 258, 359, 397.

357. Captain Superintendent of Police, "Annual Report and Returns" for 1881, *HKGG*, 1882, p. 102, courtesy Hong Kong Public Records Office.

358. Figures based on Geoffrey Roper's table, "Hong Kong Police Force Strength 1886-1889", based on Table E of the Annual Reports of the Captain Superintendent of Police, 1886, 1887, 1888, 1889 and the present editor's table, "Hong Kong Police Force Strength 1880-1882", based on Section I, HKGBBs, 1880, 1881, 1882. The drop in numbers of the Chinese members, and the increase in numbers of the Indian members of the force, seen in a comparison between the two periods, 1880-1882 and 1886-1889, seem to be a result of a major corruption case brought against Chinese members of the force in 1886.

359. See cases 446, 522.

360. Many of the European members of the force had inadequate literacy. See "Police", below.

361. See Court Cases 423, 436.

362. See, for example, "A Rogue and Vagabond", 20 October 1881, Court Case 308, where he secured a conviction, leading to three months' imprisonment with hard labour. Pang Alui also appears in these reports as "Pang Lui" and "Pang Aloi", and before appearing as Police *Sergeant* 199, seems to appear earlier in the reports as Police *Constable*.

363. Wong Tsan also appears in these court reports as "Wong Tsau".

364. See cases: (for Pang Alui) 117, 236, 240, 308, 496, and (for Wong Tsan) 61, 232, 418.

365. "Rogue and Vagabond", 20 October 1881, Court Case 304.

366. "The Tables Turned", 1 February 1882, Court Case 596.

367. "Editorial", *CM*, 9 March 1882.

368. See Court Cases: 58, 331, 375, 399, 405, 475, 492, 493, 499, 511, 525, 548.

369. *CM*, 15 December 1881, p. 2, c. 7 speaks of, "Secret Service and Detection monies". – *Editor*.

370. See Court Cases 439, 484, 485.

371. J. P. Pennefather-Evans, Commissioner of Police, "Report" (CR/31 1536/1946, Hong Kong Public Records Office).

372. For example, Court Case 295.

373. See Court Cases 47, 107, 396, 437, 441, 495.

374. "Rogue and Vagabond", 12 October 1881, Court Case 277.

375. See Court Cases 422, 444, 473, 482, etc. See also, "Urban Life", below.

376. "Highway Robbery", 16 September 1881, Court Case 162.

377. "A bean-curd makers' row", 24 September 1881, Court Case 193.

378. See "Wilful Damage", 24 October 1881, Court Case 317.

379. See "Fighting in the Streets", 30 July 1881, Court Case 21.

380. See "Creating a Disturbance", 7 December 1881, Court Case 446.

381. "Assault with a Lethal Weapon", 29 October 1881, Court Cases 335, 339.

382. "Editorial", *CM*, 9 March 1882. See also, "Prostitutes, their Associates and Clients", below.

383. W. P. Morgan, *Triad Societies in Hong Kong*, Hong Kong Government Press, 1960, p. 63.

384. There are at least a few instances in our corpus where bribery was offered to a policeman. See Garry Tallentire, "A Flavour of the Times", below, note four. Crisswell and Watson
(*The Royal Hong Kong Police, op. cit.*, p. 49) state that, in 1867, a constable was acquitted of taking a bribe on the grounds that there was no ordinance under which he could be charged. — *Editor.*

385. Captain Superintendent of Police, "Annual Report" for 1886, *HKGG*, 1887, p. 32, courtesy Hong Kong Public Records Office.

386. See "Country Life", below, Court Cases 422, 444, 473, 482, 491.

387. See "Mariners Bold", Court Case 74.

388. See Court Cases 498, 504, 506.

389. Court Case 461.

390. Forty-five Scots were recruited in about 1872 and another twenty in 1876 (Crisswell and Watson, *The Royal Hong Kong Police, op. cit.*, p. 57, p. 59).

NOTES TO, "REPORTING THE CASES OF FREDERICK STEWART"
– *TIM HAMLETT*

391. Even in English-speaking countries this did not become an important outlet until the great increase in circulations in the decade around 1890. See Michael Schudson, "The New Journalism", in Crowley and Heyer (eds.) *Communication in History,* pp. 159-166. For the United Kingdom, see the discussion of the birth of the *Daily Mail* in Stephen Koss, *The Rise and Fall of the Political Press in Britain,* pp. 369-370.

392. This does not mean by five in the evening. Each edition of *CM* has a line saying when "publication commenced". This is usually about 7.50pm, though when the Legislative Council was sitting it might be as late as 9.25pm. Some readers probably had the paper delivered at home; many no doubt read it at the Club. [Subscription orders are mentioned in *CM*, 19 October 1881, p. 4, c. 1, and "subscribers" are mentioned in *CM*, 1 October 1881, p. 3, c. 1. – *Editor.*]

393. "Theft of sweet potatoe [*sic*] sprouts", *CM*, 12 September 1881, Court Case 152.

394. "Theft", *CM*, 5 August 1881, Court Case 45.

395. "Gambling", 14 February 1882, Court Case 628.

396. "No light or pass", *CM*, 17 November 1881, Court Case 393.

397. "A needy customer provided for", *CM*, 28 September 1881, Court Case 213.

398. 26 July 1881, Court Case 4.

399. "A Medicine Man", 26 July 1881, Court Case 5.

400 . "[Fighting, petty assaults, hawking against the regulations, obstruction]", *CM*, 26 September 1881, Court Case 204.

401. "Public gambling", *CM*, 5 December 1881, Court Case 442.

402. "Public gambling", *CM*, 15 December 1881, Court Case 475.

403. "Street Gambling", 30 September 1881, Court Case 222.

404 . See for example "Breach of the Market Ordinance", *CM*, 30 September 1881, Court Case 226.

405. For a splendid exception see Tsai Jung-Fang, *Hong Kong in Chinese History*, *op. cit.*, Chapter Four.

406. Tsai Jung-Fang, *Hong Kong in Chinese History*, *op. cit.*, p. 118, and Gillian Bickley, *TGN*, pp. 208-222. See also "Magistrate Frederick Stewart", above.

407. See also "Magistrate Frederick Stewart", above.

408. "The 'rickshaw question", *CM*, 8 October 1881, Court Case 258.

409. See "Sailors", below.

410. The fate of "poor whites" in Hong Kong was a recurring topic of concern in *CM*. For one family's life at the bottom of white society see Vaudine England, *The Quest of Noel Croucher: Hong Kong's quiet philanthropist,* Chapter Two.

411. An ancient and historic regiment, the Fusiliers were first raised in 1689 as Wetham's foot, and in the days when British regiments were numbered in order of seniority they were the 27th. This seniority spared them the first phase of post-imperial amalgamations but in the 1960s they were merged with two other regiments to form the Royal Irish Rangers, in turn amalgamated with the Ulster Defence Regiment in 1992 to form the Royal Irish Regiment, which still serves.

412. See also "The 'Light and Pass' Rules", above.

413. 13 (*sic*) for 14 September 1881, Court Case 155.

414. See also "The 'Light and Pass' Rules", above.

415. See Crisswell and Watson, *The Royal Hong Kong Police*, *op. cit.*, p. 89.

416. *Ibid.*, p. 18.

417. "Dispatch of a steamer without woman", *CM*, 4 October 1881, Court Case 248.

418. "Fokien": *sic.*

419. "An offence under the Post Office regulations", *CM*, 24 January 1882, Court Case 563.

420. The *OED* states that "samshu" is the generic name for chinese spirits distilled from rice or sorghum.

NOTES TO, "THE HONG KONG (POLICE) MAGISTRATE IN THE 1880S AND 1990S" – *GARRY TALLENTIRE*

421. This essay was written in 1999.

422. "On fiat": a barrister in private practice who is instructed by the Department of Justice and paid a fee by the prosecution (the Government) to prosecute the case.

423. See also Christopher Coghlan's essay, "White Gloves and Patience," above.

424 . See "Prostitutes, their Associates and Clients", below, and "Kidnappers and Traffickers in Human Beings", also below. Registration of Brothels ceased in 1897. (Crisswell and Watson, *The Royal Hong Kong Police*, *op. cit.*, p. 78.)

425. See "Prostitutes, their Associates and Clients", below.

426 . It also made possible action against "brothel slavery". (See "Kidnappers and Traffickers in Human Beings", below.)

427. Relating to Frederick Stewart's earlier period as *Acting* Police Magistrate, in 1876 to 1877, the report of one case before him has been found where the charge was "committing an unnatural act". – *Editor*.

428. In fact, Frederick Stewart had heard such a case on 29 December 1876. (*The Daily Press*, 30 December 1876, p. 2, cc. 3-4.) "Mak Alok, a marine hawker, was charged with exposing on a stall in Taipingshan eight indecent photographs". – *Editor*.

429. This is the technical wording of the charge.

430. There are at least a few instances in our corpus where bribery was offered to a policeman. In two cases, it formed part of the charge; in another, it was mentioned as an additional incriminating factor; and in a third case, the bribe – which the accused had succeeded in slipping to the policeman – was confiscated. (See the following cases: "Without a Licence", 26 July 1881 (Court Case 1); "Bribing a Constable", 11 November (Court Case 368); "A Rogue and Vagabond", 23 November 1881 (Court Case 410); "Gamblers' Watchman", 29 March 1882 (Court Case 722).) Another such case is 20 October 1881, Court Case 304.

431. E. J. Endacott, *A History of Hong Kong*, *op. cit.*, p. 150.

432. Crisswell and Watson, *The Royal Hong Kong Police*, *op. cit.*, p. 91.

433 . See Verner Bickley's description of a trial at a Hong Kong Magistrate's Court in 1989 in, "Differing Perceptions of Social Reality in Dr Stewart's Court", below. – *Editor*.

434. This does not mean that the magistrate did not know, or was not learning, Cantonese. See Gillian Bickley, "The Student-interpreters' Scheme and the Chinese Teacher's Allowance", *op. cit.* This essay shows the efforts made by the Hong Kong Government to secure western government officials (including magistrates) who were knowledgeable in the local language – Cantonese – as well as in written Chinese.

435. See Gillian Workman (Gillian Bickley), "The Medium of Instruction

in Hong Kong: Why was it Ever English?", in Verner Bickley, Ed., *Language Use, Language Teaching and the Curriculum*, Hong Kong, Institute of Language in Education (Hong Kong Government Education Department), January 1991, pp. 6-47, p. 6, p. 41-42, n. 27.

436. See also, "Magistrate Frederick Stewart", above.

437. See also *Ibid.*

438. See Tim Hamlett's essay, "Reporting the Cases of Frederick Stewart", above, when he attributes the relatively mild sentencing to the effect of Governor John Pope Hennessy's intervention in the law and its application. – *Editor.*

439. See "Court Cases 1881-1882", Court Cases 215, 612 and 676. In Court Case 215, "Love Me, Love My Cat", one man was charged with threatening another with intent to provoke a breach of the peace. Found guilty, he was, "Bound over in $20 to keep the peace towards complainant for two months." ("Police Intelligence," *CM*, Wednesday, September 28, p. 3, cc. 5-6.)

In Court Case 612, "Drunk and Disorderly", an unemployed watchman, who admitted the charge and also nine previous convictions, was ordered to be bound over with two sureties in one recognizance of L10 [*sic* for "$10"], with condition to be of good behaviour, in default to be committed for six weeks." ("Police Intelligence", *CM*, Saturday, 11 February 1882, p. 3, cc. 3-4.)

In Court Case 676, "Chinese Female Rowdies", one woman, "was fined 50 cents with the alternative of two days' imprisonment." She and another woman had had a fight. Both "were bound over in personal security of $2, to keep the peace towards each other for two months." ("Police Intelligence", *CM*, Saturday, 11 March 1882, p. 3, c. 7.) – *Editor.*

440. The power derives from the Justices of the Peace Act of 1361.

441. See Tim Hamlett, "Reporting the Cases of Frederick Stewart", above. Stewart's term on the bench in the early 1880s coincided with a period of greater lenience of punishment in Hong Kong. – *Editor.*

442. See above.

443. Justice of the Peace Act, 1361.

444. See "Children and Students", below, for comments on the West Point Reformatory.

445. Maybe they did not even have this. Comment was made at some point during the Nineteenth Century that a printed standard updated version of the laws was lacking. Each magistrate and judge had his own hand-annotated copy. In August 1882, Frederick Stewart was included on a commission to produce a revised edition of the Ordinances. (*CM*, 12 August 1882, p. 2, c. 6) – *Editor.*

446. This was introduced piecemeal, but all courts since about 1996 have had this facility.

447. Reference to the giving of statements is mentioned in our corpus. See "Court Cases 1881-1882" Court Cases 449 and 507.

The report of Court Case 449, "Obtaining Goods under False Pretences", it states that, "Defendant this morning made a long statement in his defence". ("Police Intelligence," *CM*, Wednesday, 7 December 1881, p. 3, c. 2.)

The report of Court Case 507, "Assault", reports the defendant's statement and Stewart's comments when giving sentence: "His Worship, in sentencing prisoner to fourteen days' imprisonment with hard labour, remarked that on the evidence adduced he could hardly have committed him to prison, but after his own statement he had no doubt that prisoner had used the bar to strike the complainant, and the use of those bars must be put down, they being almost as dangerous as knives were." ("Police Intelligence," *CM*, Wednesday, 28 December 1881, p. 3, cc. 3-4.) – *Editor.*

[448]. GN No. 367, 16 September 1882, *HKGG*, 16 September 1882, p. 760.
449 . Attachment (CO/129/202/444r.-444v.) to J. Russell, Acting Registrar General, Letter No. 34 to Frederick Stewart, Acting Colonial Secretary, dated 17 June 1882. (CO/129/202/440r.-443v.) Enclosure No. 2 in Administrator Marsh, Despatch No. 98, dated Hong Kong, 19 June 1882, to Lord Kimberley, Secretary of State for the Colonies. (CO/129/202/435r.-436v.) See also cutting from the *Daily Press* of 29 September 1882. (CO/129/202/666r.)
450. Attachment to J. Russell, Acting Registrar General, Letter No. 34 to Frederick Stewart, Acting Colonial Secretary, dated 17 June 1882. For full reference, see note above.
[451]. *HKGG*, 8 October 1881, pp. 918-919.
[452]. *HKGG*, 10 September 1870, p. 456.

453. *HKGG*, 10 December 1881, p. 1076.
454. *HKGG*, 28 January 1882, p. 48.
455. *The China Directory*, 1885.

NOTES TO SECTION TWO
456. *CM*, 1 October 1881, p. 3, c. 1.
457. Frank H. H. King (editor) and Prescott Clarke, *A Research Guide to China-coast Newspapers, 1822-1911*, East Asian Research Centre, Harvard University, 1965.
458. Christopher Munn names Thomas Dick, "an employee of *CM* who read Chinese", May 1856, probably much too early to be a candidate for our court reporter. (Christopher Munn, "'An Anglo-Chino conspiracy in crime': the Caldwell Scandal, 1857-1861", TS, p. 24, note 131.)
459. *CM*, 7 February 1882, p. 3, c. 5.
460. *Ibid.*
461. "Drunk and Disorderly", *CM*, 21 November 1881, p. 3, c. 4, Court Case 400.
462. See "Mr Driscoll's Amah Again", in "Wives and Husbands, Amahs and Cooks, Widows and Protected Women, Sons and Adopted Daughters. Burglars. The Domestic Scene", below.

463. Wednesday, 13 September 1881, erroneously given for 14 September 1881. (See "Larceny of Jewelry", Court Case 153.)

464. "Court Cases 1881-1882", Court Case 131.

465. "The Tai Tam Attack", *CM*, 14 December 1881. See "Country Life", below.

466. See "Soldiers", below, "Assault with Intent", *CM*, 10 December 1881, Court Case 454.

467. "A Raid on Gamblers", *CM*, 22 October 1881, Court Case 311. See "Urban Life", below.

468. "Public Obstruction", *CM*, 16 November 1881, Court Case 387. See "Urban Life", below.

469. For editing conventions, please see, "The Original Writer and the Present Text".

470. The one ship stated to be Canadian, however, is elsewhere stated to be British.

471. *CM*, 21 September 1881, p. 2, cc. 6-7.

472. *CM*, 31 December 1877, p. 3, c. 1.

473. Leading article, *CM*, 3 January 1882, p. 2, c. 7. - p. 3, c. 1.

474. See, e.g., "Charge of Cutting and Wounding When at Sea", case brought before Frederick Stewart on 24 October 1876. (*Daily Press*, 25 October 1876.)

475. The complete set of reports in connection with this case in "Court Cases 1881-1882" is: Court Cases 233, 237.

476. In the reports of this case, this name is given as both "Naylor" and "Taylor".

477. "50 England yards". The original has not been corrected.

478. "By Mr Wotton:" This formula is used throughout these reports. It seems to mean (in this case), "in answer to Mr Wotton".

479. It is not clear what the "Shanghai dodge" was. Was it the same as "Shanghai-ing", that is "kidnapping"?

480. The complete set of reports in connection with this case in "Court Cases 1881-1882" is: Court Cases 224, 242, 250.

The Captain and nineteen men of the "Bolton Abbey" arrived in Hong Kong on 11 October and a detailed account of their experiences based on the Captain's Reports appeared in *CM* the same day. Not only had they been dismasted during a severe typhoon, but after continuing on their way in very trying circumstances had subsequently run onto a reef, the Pratas Shoal. Five men were later drowned in attempts to reach the shore. A Marine Court of Enquiry was held in Hong Kong, the Harbour Master, Captain Thomsett, presiding. The findings included a recommendation that the Pratas Shoal should be provided with lights.

At the time the men were falsely reported to have arrived in Hong Kong, they still had several days of dangerous ordeal ahead.

481. In the reports of this case, this name is given as "Cameron", "Cannron" and "Cannon".

482. Since Cameron, Cannron or Cannon's ship *Twilight* did not arrive in Hong Kong until (probably) 27th September (see *CM*, 27 September

1881, p. 3, c. 2 and 4 October 1881 report, quoted above), "20th" must be a misprint for "28th" (Wednesday) or "30th" September (Friday).

483. Gilman and Co. were Lloyd's agents. (See *CM*, 5 October 1881, p. 3, c. 1.)

484. Captain Thomsett was the Harbour Master at Hong Kong.

485. Cannron, Cameron or Cannon's ship was in fact the *Twilight*. (See 30 September 1881 report above.) For the purposes of his story, however, he pretended he was from the *Bolton Abbey*. (See 4 October 1881 report above.)

486. The complete set of reports in connection with this case in "Court Cases 1881-1882", is: Court Cases 291, 296, 300, 388.

487. In the reports of this case, this name is given as both "H. Sewart" and "Herbert Servant".

In "Court Cases 1881-1882", we find "Herbert Servant", "H. Sewart" and "H. Stewart". Quite possibly these are one and the same. However, as the number is given only with "Herbert Servant, P. C. No. 4", it is not possible to say this for certain.

488. Deposition taken by F. Stewart at the Civil Hospital. Court Case 296 (new number). "The Stabbing Case", *CM*, Monday, 17 October 1881, p. 3, cc. 1-2.

489. In the reports of this case, this name is given as both "Finlay" and "Findlay".

490. This is the age given in the "Certified Copy of an Entry in a Register of Deaths kept in Terms of the Births and Deaths Registration Ordinance", dated 16 April 1999. However, other details in this document are incorrect, probably due either to the physical condition of the original and/or difficulty in reading the handwriting of the original. Hence, the name of the District Registrar is given as "John Gerrad" for "John Gerrard". The name of the Coroner is given as "Tradehouse" for "Wodehouse". The cause of death is given as "Effects of a Normal respired in the chest"!

491. The British ["Canadian" as stated in the court report] barque, 693, *Helen Marion* (Captain Robert J. Robinson) is reported as arriving in Hong Kong on 27 September 1881, having left Cardiff on 23 May with a cargo of coal. (*CM*, Tuesday 27 September 1881, p. 2, c. 3.)

492. The original is difficult to decipher and deficiencies have been silently supplied as well as possible.

493. In the reports of this case, this name is given as both "Powers" and "Power".

494. In the reports of this case, this name is given as both "Parry" and "Perry".

495. Probably short for "Edward".

496. Resumed Investigation at the Magistracy "before Dr Stewart". Court Case 300 (new number). "The Stabbing Case", *CM*, Tuesday, 18 October 1881, p. 3, cc. 1-2.

497. This reads abruptly; but the report really does end here.

498. Court Case 388 (new number). "Stabbing Case on Board *The Helen*

Marion", [Police Magistrate's Court,] *CM*, Wednesday, 16 November 1881, p. 3, c. 1.

499. The Superintendent of the Civil Hospital, Mr Wharry, was on leave.

500. At the Criminal Sessions held on Monday, 19 December 1881, Mr Francis, representing Parry, stated the prisoner's intention to plead guilty to a charge of manslaughter, agreed by both the Attorney General and the presiding Judge, the Hon. F. Snowden, Acting Chief Justice. Permission was asked and given for an affidavit to be prepared in mitigation of Parry's crime. Sentence was given on Friday, 23 December. Snowden said that he had read the affidavit very carefully and had come to the conclusion that Parry had not improved his position by making his statement. The prisoner might be thankful that he had not been tried for murder, as the evidence given at the Police Court proved that the stabbing was not the result of an accident. The sentence was ten years' imprisonment.

501. Court Case 354.

502. Court Case 358

503. Court Case 421.

504. Court Case 448.

505. This case does not appear among the *CM* reports of Frederick Stewart's court cases on 9 December 1881.

506. Court Case 490.

507. Court Case 523.

508. Original has, "No. 10 Room".

509. Court Case 526. *CM*, Saturday, 7 January 1882, p. 3, c. 6.

510. Court Case 611.

511. Court Case 618.

512. The British steamer, *Anjer Head* (Captain Alfred Roper) had been in Hong Kong recently, arriving on 7 October 1881 from Singapore and Saigon, with 340 Chinese passengers. Douglas Lapraik and Co. are listed as the agents. (*CM*, 7 October 1881, p. 2, cc. 4, 5.)

513. During this period, the Harbour Master had his own Magistrate's Court.

514. "Local and General", *CM*, Friday, 17 February 1882, p. 3, cc. 2-3. Court Case 635.

515. Court Case 655. The complete set of reports in connection with this case in "Court Cases 1881-1882", is: Court Cases 655, 660.

516. The original omits the words, "was charged".

517. Court Case 660.

518. A Special Session [*sic*] was held on 10 March 1882. See "Criminal Calendar" – March Special Session 1882", *HKGG*, 18 March 1882, p. 296. John Bryant was unanimously found not guilty of shooting with intent to murder and not guilty of shooting with intent to do some grievous bodily harm but he was found guilty of common assault. The sentence, also given on 10 March 1882, was three months' imprisonment with hard labour.

519. Court Case 695.

520. For details about individual soldiers, barracks, etc., for a slightly later period in general (1890s), see Gillian Bickley, *Hong Kong Invaded! A '97 Nightmare*, Hong Kong, Hong Kong University Press, 2001 (particularly the notes and Appendices).

521. Major General China, Hong Kong and Straits Settlements, 1878-1882 was Lieutenant General E. W. Donovan and from 1882-1885, Major General J. N. Sargent CB. (Alan Harfield, *British and Indian Armies on the China Coast, op. cit.*, p. 483.)

522. *CM*, 31 December 1881, p. 3, c. 3.

523. Recent printed programmes for Hong Kong Players' productions state in their brief historical note that the Hong Kong Players are a product of a merging in 1991 of the Garrison Players and the Hong Kong Stage Club. They trace the origins of the two former groups only to the end of the Pacific War, however.

524. *CM*, 18 October 1877, p. 2, c. 6.

525. See *CM*, 27 December 1881, p. 3, cc. 4-5.

526. *CM*, 12 September 1881, p. 3, c. 2.

527. *CM*, 2 December 1881, p. 3, c. 3.

528. *CM*, 15 December 1881, p. 3, c. 2.

529. See, for example, *CM*, 31 December 1881, p. 3, c. 1.

530. Harfield lists the Regiments stationed at Hong Kong and China 1841-1900. (Alan Harfield, *British and Indian Armies on the China Coast, op. cit.*, pp. 485-489.) Retitled the First Battalion, Royal Inniskilling Fusiliers with effect from 1 July 1881 (p. 161), this unit replaced the 74th Foot (who embarked on 10 March 1879).

531. "Christmas in Garrison", *CM*, 27 December 1881, p. 3, cc. 4-5.

532. "Mutiny."

533. *CM*, 4 October 1881, p. 3, c. 2.

534. See *CM*, 11 March 1882, p. 3, c. 1. "The troopship *Tyne*, under Commander J. E. Stokes, R. N., arrived from Singapore with the head-quarters of the second battalion of the 3rd Buffs, East Kent Regiment, numbering 12 officers, 318 non-commissioned officers and men, 14 women and 14 children."
See also Alan Harfield, *British and Indian Armies on the China Coast, op. cit.*, p. 161. The Inniskillings embarked on 25 March 1882.
      In its description of the open house at the Garrison, kept at Christmas 1881, *CM* mentions the Royal Artillery and the Royal Engineers, as well as the Inniskillings.

535. *CM*, 25 March 1882, p. 3, c. 2.

536. *CM*, 23 March 1882, p. 3, c. 1.

537. Some British soldiers were demobilised in Hong Kong. When removed from the sheltered cocoon of army peace-time life, they may have been more subject to appear in Court. One appeared before Stewart, charged with Embezzlement. See the Section, "Police", below.

538. *CM*, 9 December 1881, p. 3, cc. 1-2.

539. Alan Harfield, *British and Indian Armies on the China Coast, op.*

cit., p. 161.

540. "Local and General", *CM*, 10 December 1881, p. 2, c. 7.

541. "Local and General", *CM*, 10 December 1881, p. 2, c. 7. A few undecipherable words are guessed at in this transcription.

542. "Local and General", *CM*, 10 December 1881, p. 2, c. 7.

543. Court Case 454. The complete set of reports in connection with this case in "Court Cases 1881-1882" is: Court Cases 454, 456.

544. The original reads "intend" [*sic* for "intent"].

545. On 20 December 1881, Lieutenant Davidson had played a part in the visit of the two Princes. "A guard of honour, consisting of fifty rank and file, the Band and Regimental Colours of the Royal Inniskilling Fusiliers, under the command of Lieutenant Davidson, was drawn up at the landing place, and the Royal Artillery fired a salute as the Admiral landed." (*CM*, 20 December 1881, p. 3, c. 2.)

546. Court Case 456.

547. This road, which in some places runs more or less parallel with Queensway, at a higher level, is now the location of Zetland Hall (the Masonic building), St Joseph's College and many high-rise residential buildings. Bowen Road, further up the hill, is now the favourite place for nearby residents to take a leisurely walk or to jog.

548. The Jurors List for 1897 lists "Hormusjee Meherwanjee Mehta as a Special Juror. (*HKGG*, 27 February 1897, pp. 119-131, p. 119.)

549. Mr Byramjee, Mr Mehta and Mr Billia are identified as Parsees in a later article on this case, in *CM*, 10 December 1881, p. 2, c. 7.

550. The building previously known as "Head-Quarter House" was renamed "Flagstaff House" in 1932/33 and now houses the Hong Kong Tea Museum. Built in 1846, it was the residence of the Commanding General in Hong Kong until the closure of Victoria Barracks and the construction of the new Headquarter House on the Peak in the late 1970s. (Ko Tim Keung and Jason Wordie, *Ruins of War: A Guide to Hong Kong's Battlefields and Wartime Sites*, Hong Kong, Joint Publishing Co., Ltd., 1996, p. 171.)

551. At the time of writing, Kennedy Road still runs above the former Victoria Barracks area. The "Plan of the City of Victoria Hong Kong, 1889", reproduced in Hal Empson, *Mapping Hong Kong: A Historical Atlas*, Hong Kong, Government Information Services, 1992, pp. 162-163, p. 163 clearly shows the magazine in question.

552. There is an image of Victoria Barracks stated to date from this time in Arthur Hacker. (*The Hong Kong Visitors Book: A Historical Who's Who*, Odyssey Publications, 1997, p. 62.) It shows one large building and several other buildings, set in an otherwise empty space, linked by paths which traverse a slightly grassy landscape and lead up into treeless hills containing no buildings whatsoever. Today, much of the land previously used for Victoria Barracks is now the Hong Kong Park in Central District. One of the buildings shown in the image described above is recognisable as the former Flagstaff House. It and Hong Kong Park as a whole can

conveniently be reached by escalator from Queensway, near Admiralty Mass Transit Railway Station.

553 . Mr Horspool is identified below as the Acting Deputy Superintendent of Police.

554. Mr Aarons is identified as a German in another article on this case, in *CM*, 10 December 1881, p. 2, c. 7.

555. The original has "Co.'s".

556. The original says, "He heard a cried [*sic* for cry] of 'Police'".

557 . The "Magazine above Victoria Barracks" has already been mentioned above.

558 . Mr Horspool has already stated that he shouted, "Stop that blackguard". Unless the witness could not see the faces of the running men clearly, it seems surprising that the witness, Mr H. MacCallum, Apothecary and Analyst at the Government Hospital, did not know the Acting Deputy Superintendent of Police by sight.

559. Lieutenant Davidson is stated earlier to be watching the case "on behalf of the Military Authorities".

560 . *CM*, 27 December 1881, p. 3, c. 4, names the Iniskillings' Sergeant-Major as "Mr Williams".

561. "made down his bed": *sic*.

562. "in the verandah": *sic*.

563. "when he was woke up": *sic* for, probably, "when he woke up".

564. For commentary on their work, from a police perspective, see Geoffrey Roper's essay, "The Police Role in Magistrate Frederick Stewart's Court", above.

565. See, e.g., "Wives and Husbands", below.

566. See "Country Life", below.

567. *CM*, 21 February 1882, p. 3, c. 2. Neither Easur Singh nor Police Constable Robert Anderson are listed in the "Roll of Honour: the Supreme Sacrifice", presented in Kevin Sinclair's, *Asia's Finest Marches On*. (Kevin Sinclair Associates Ltd., 1997, p. 144.) Sinclair admits that the names are not known of all those law enforcement officers who have died in the course of duty, since the first were sworn in 1841. Taking Sinclair's list as a reference, however, Easur Singh should be listed second, the second policeman and the second Indian policeman, to die in this way, while Robert Anderson is the first European and the third policeman to die in Hong Kong in the execution of his duty.

568. *CM*, 28 November 1881, p. 3, cc. 2-3. See below. See also note above.

569. *CM*, 21 February 1882, p. 3, c. 2.

570. *CM*, 10 December 1881, p. 3, c. 1.

571. *CM*, 19 June 1886, p. c, c. 4.

572. *CM*, 7 January 1882, p. 3, cc. 2-3.

573. *The Daily Press*, 17 October 1870, p. 3, c. 1

574. *CM*, 21 September 1881, p. 2, cc. 6-7.

575. *CM*, 28 January 1876, p. 2, c. 6.

576. *CM*, 4 October 1878, p. 2, c. 6.

577. *CM*, 7 June 1886, p. 3, c. 4.
578. The Mong-kok Tsui Burglary is reported today "Before H.E. Wodehouse".
579. *CM*, 1 February 1882, p. 3, c. 1.
580. Frederick Stewart, Coroner, No. 9, to J. Gardiner Austin, Colonial Secretary, dated 27 August 1869, HKRS 275, 1869.
581. *CM*, 24 February 1882, p. 3, c. 2.
582. *CM*, 20 March 1882, p. 3, c. 1.
583. Newspaper report of Finance Committee meeting held on 27 October 1888. CO/129/239/262r.-269r.; f. 265.
584. *CM*, 21 September 1881, p. 2, cc. 5-6.
585. *CM*, 6 April 1881, p. 2, c. 6.
586. Newspaper report of Finance Committee meeting held on 27 October 1888. CO/129/239/262r.-269r.; f. 265.
587. *CM*, 17 October 1881, p. 2, c. 6.
588. *CM*, 21 October 1881, p. 2, c. 7.
589. *Sic.*
590. "Yesterday's Storm", *CM*, 15 October 1881, p. 2, c. 7-p. 3, cc. 1-2; p. 3, c. 1.
591. e.g. *CM*, 11 March 1882, p. 3, c. 1.
592. *CM*, 11 March 1882, p. 2, c. 7.
593. *CM*, 15 November 1881, p. 3, c. 1.
594. *CM*, 28 July 1881, p. 2.
595. *CM*, 12 September 1881, p. 3, c. 1.
596. Also "Li Fan". He appears in our corpus as "P. C. 280, Li Fan". See "Court Cases 1881-1882", Court Cases 390, 410 (17 and 23 November 1881).
597. *CM*, 16 July 1886, p. 2, c. 7.
598. *CM*, 19 July 1886, p. 3, c. 1.
599. *CM*, 17 August 1886, p. 2, cc. 6-7.
600. See also "Gamblers", below.
601. Crisswell and Watson, *The Royal Hong Kong Police*, *op. cit.*, p. 89.
602. *Ibid.*, pp. 91-92.
603. See also "Magistrate Frederick Stewart", above.
604. *The Daily Press*, 17 November 1870, p. 3, c. 1.
605. Court Case 144.
606. Court Case 361.
607. Court Case 516.
608. Court Case 244.
609. Court Case 112. "Police Intelligence," *CM*, Friday, 2 September 1881, p. 3, c. 5.
610. *Sic.*
611. "Police Intelligence," *CM*, Friday, 7 October 1881, p. 3, c. 4.
612. Court Case 255. The complete set of reports in connection with this case in "Court Cases 1881-1882" is: Court Cases 255, 292, 293.
613. Court Case 292. "Police Intelligence," *CM*, Friday, 14 October 1881, p. 3, c. 6.

614. *Sic.*
615. "Stopped": "stayed" or "lived", an English colloquialism still used today.
616. Connor.
617. "Gone on": "gone on duty".
618. The head of the British Navy, based in Hong Kong. See "Sailors", above.
619. Court Case 293, "Police Intelligence," *CM*, Saturday, 15 October 1881, p. 3, c. 5.
620. Court Case 294, "Police Intelligence," *CM*, Saturday, 15 October 1881, p. 3, c. 5.
621. There was a severe typhoon on the night of 14 October 1881.
622. There is only very brief reporting from the Magistrates' Courts on 17 October 1881 (due to typhoon stories). There is nothing about this case in *CM* of this date (nor of the 18 October).
623. Court Case 287.
624. Court Case 305.
625. The original has "Percy" for "Piercy".
626. Court Case 374.
627. This gives the impression that Sergeant Campbell had a permanent "interpreter". There was, however, a policy of encouraging non-Chinese policemen to learn Chinese. Today, non-Chinese policemen in Hong Kong are among the few non-Chinese in Hong Kong who are fluent in Cantonese.
628. Chinese were frequently referred to as "celestials" at this time, alluding to their own terminology and self-concept.
629. Court Case 472.
630. There are three images of the Basel Missionary station at Sai Ying Pun, Hong Kong Island, in Revd Carl T. Smith, *Chinese Christians: Elites, Middlemen, and the Church in Hong Kong*, Hong Kong, Oxford University Press, 1985, which are dated pre 1870, post 1870, and undated, respectively. Only the earliest of these suggests that the surrounding space was at all open and even that hardly appears verdant. No wonder that the cows sought pastures new.
631. Court Case 498. "Police Intelligence," *CM*, Saturday, 24 December 1881, p. 3, c. 5.
632. See "The Chinese Illuminations, *CM*, 23 December 1881, p. 3, c. 5.
    "Last night was certainly not favourable for illuminations, being so drizzly and wet, that the roads were greasy and slippery in the last degree. The fireworks in the Parade Ground began about seven o'clock and were of various descriptions, the designs being mostly of a rather ludicrous and amusing design.
    "The procession was the feature of the night's proceedings, and was certainly rather elaborate; – fishes were supplied, as we mentioned, by the fish lans; the porkers, &c., by the butchers; and various other designs were carried by coolies, – all the devices being illuminated by

candles. A dragon, of monstrous length, wound up the whole affair. This in the crowding of the street was occasionally apt to get shortened and crammed up considerably, but its sinuous length of tinsel was a great attraction.

"Along Queen's Road decorations were, at intervals, suspended in front of various places of business. The Man On Insurance Office was tastefully illuminated, and otherwise by having plants placed all round the entrances; but the great point of the illumination was Bonham Strand, which was covered in from the one end to the other, and at intervals of about six yards were suspended historic figures sketches, which were done up in a very pretty and artistic style. Between the different sketches were 81 lamps which showed the figures to perfection, and certainly made the street brilliant in the extreme."

These events were part of the celebrations of the visit of the two young sons of Queen Victoria, as junior officers on board the *Bacchante*.

633. Court Case 533.

634. Court Case 552.

635. See Geoffrey Roper, "The Police Role in Magistrate Frederick Stewart's Court", above, on the changed policy of appointing expatriates to the rank of "Inspector" only.

636. The Gun Lascars allegedly taking English-language tuition were Indian artillerymen.

Alan Harfield lists the Artillery units in the China and Hong Kong Command, 1881 to 1900, divided into "British" and "Colonial" Units. He shows one company of Gun Lascars during the years 1881 to 1883 inclusive, and two companies from 1884 to 1889 inclusive. He states that during this period from 1881 to 1889, the command was shown as China, Hong Kong and Straits Settlements, without showing the breakdown between Hong Kong and Singapore. During 1889, the command structure was changed and units serving in China and Hong Kong were listed separately from those stationed in the Singapore Garrison. From 1889 to 1892, four companies of Gun Lascars were stationed in China and Hong Kong. (Alan Harfield, *British and Indian Armies on the China Coast*, *op. cit.*, p. 489.)

In 1882, *CM* commented that, "the Gun Lascar Company is never up to its full complement, is recruited with difficulty, and compelled to accept those rejected by the other services." ("Editorial Notes," *CM*, 24 February 1882, p. 3, c. 2.) The men, it observed, preferred serving in the Hong Kong Police.

637. Court Case 694.

638. "Leang" *is* the correct spelling of the name as given in the *Mail*.

639. The following information appears in the Criminal Calendar for the April Sessions, 1882, *HKGG*, 6 May 1882, p. 461, where this case is No. 6.

Chu A-ying [*sic*], Wong A-wing [*sic*] and Chiu A-po [*sic*] were tried on 19 April 1882 on five counts: 1) Larceny, 2) Larceny, 3)

Receiving stolen goods, 4) Previous conviction (summary) and 5) Previous conviction (summary).

Chu A-ying was found not guilty on all counts and discharged.

Wong A-wing pleaded guilty to 1) Larceny and 2) Larceny, and was found guilty on 3) Receiving stolen goods and was sentenced on 24 April 1882 to nine months' imprisonment with hard labour.

Chiu A-po was found guilty of 3) Receiving stolen goods, and pleaded guilty to 4) Previous conviction (summary) and 5) Previous conviction (summary) and was sentenced on 24 April 1882 to three years' penal servitude.

640. Court Case 708.

641. See also Verner Bickley, "Differing Perceptions of Social Reality in Dr Stewart's Court", above, which comments on this case.

642. The building's name, "Bellevue", evidently refers to its good view.

643. See *TGN*, pp. 226-227.

644. See *CM*, 29 March 1882, p. 3, c. 5.

645. See also Geoffrey Roper, "The Police Role in Magistrate Frederick Stewart's Court", above.

646. Executive Council Minutes of meeting, 4 April 1871, CO/131/8/67.

647. See also "Magistrate Frederick Stewart", above.

648.   Ordinance No. 7 of 1866 provides for "the better Registration of Householders and Chinese Servants in the Colony of Hong Kong", *HKGG*, 25 August 1866, pp. 336-340, p. 336. Chinese Servants were to be given "a numbered certificate of registration" (paragraph XXIV).

649. Revd Carl Smith uses the term, "protected woman", usually for the Chinese mistress of a western man and Susanna Hoe has an interesting discussion of such situations, in her monograph, *The Private Life of Old Hong Kong: Western Women in the British Colony, 1841-1941*, Hong Kong, Oxford University Press, 1991, pp. 69-71.

650. Court Case 86. The complete set of reports in connection with this case in "Court Cases 1881-1882", is: Court Cases 86, 87, 94.

651. Court Case 87.

652. This is further identified below as "the Commissariat Department" and then as "the Ordnance Store". M'Breen was subject to the Commissary General's regulations. Presumably this was a department for military supply.

653. Sergeant Blake was concerned about this statement. As we see later, he was at pains to state that M'Breen had not stayed with him; and others in court then reassured him that this was not what people had understood.

654. According to Arthur Hacker, the Royal Naval Canteen in Wanchai was known as "the Blue Buildings" and was the forerunner of the China Fleet Club. (*Arthur Hacker's Wanchai*, 1997, pp. 71, 78.) There is a postcard of it on p. 78 of Hacker's book. It shows a long collonaded building with three main stories, fronting the Harbour. Each outside room has a covered terrace or balcony with railings. A few have washing hung out to dry and flags are flying.

655. This is identified below as No. 208, Queen's Road Central. From

what Mrs M'Breen says about wanting her husband "to manage the tavern", when they first married, it seems that No. 208, Queen's Road Central may have been a bar.

656. Chief Clerk of the Magistracy.

657. Judging from her use of pigeon English, Mrs M'Breen seems to be Chinese or Eurasian. She seems to have children from a previous husband, now buried in Happy Valley.

658. Perhaps Mr Mossop had been confused into thinking that James M'Breen had lived with Sergeant Blake by the ambiguity of the possessive pronoun, thinking that it referred to a singular, not a plural subject. See also note above.

659. Mrs M'Breen uses the Chinese calendar.

660. "costs": for "cost".

661. Internal evidence suggests that the "rooms next door to the American Consulate" were the rooms in the "Blue Buildings".

662. She shouted out in Cantonese, "Save Life!"

663. That is, 208, Queen's Road, where his wife lived.

664. Court Case 94. The available copy of *CM* is difficult to read. The present editor has supplied apparently missing words as best possible.

665. This statement seems to be based on the legal situation at this time, that a husband owned his wife's property.

666. In the reports of this case, this name is given as both "Siemund" and "Seimund" in the originals.

667. She was screaming, "Police!"

668. That is, he let go of his wife.

669. See notes above.

670. The original says, "he was sure that Mr Mossop would do nothing which was not proper." It is clear from the context that this is a mistake for "Mr Blake".

671. "infer": for "imply".

672. See notes above.

673. See notes above.

674. George Blake.

675. This is exactly what Mr Seimund is earlier reported to have said.

676. Court Case 169. The complete set of reports in connection with this case in "Court Cases 1881-1882", is: Court Cases 169, 205.

677. "I want go home". Does the little girl mean, "I *won't* go home", meaning her present home? Or does she mean, I *want* to go home, meaning her paternal home?

678. That is, the woman is part of a polygamous family.

679. Court Case 205.

680. Court Case 191. The complete set of reports in connection with this case in "Court Cases 1881-1882", is: Court Cases 191, 236.

681. The finding of the watch had been noticed separately in the newspaper. See *CM*, 15 September 1881, p. 3, c. 3. "Some praise is due to the vigilance of the police that the lady's gold watch stolen from the villa "Bellevue" about two months ago has now been recovered. Facts

such as this show that although cases may drop from the notice of the public, they remain green in the memory of the ubiquitous policeman. The watch was found in a pawnshop, the number having been carefully erased."

682. Court Case 236.

683. This surely irregular prompting of a witness did not seem to strike the reporter.

684. The original has "L10", which it is assumed is a mistake for "$10".

685. Court Case 363.

686. See note above.

687. "Sterling" is mistakenly used for "dollar" on a few occasions in these reports. The pound sign is also mistakenly used for the "dollar" sign on occasion.

688. Court Case 510.

689. Court Case 661.

690. Court Case 715.

691. Crisswell and Watson, *The Royal Hong Kong Police, op. cit.*, p. 18, refer to the "Omnibus" Ordinance of 1845 which made it an offence – among other things – to expose one's sores in order to obtain alms [I, 17], to be abroad at night without a satisfactory reason [III, 6; XVI] and *to leave one's employer before he had time to engage a successor* [III, 3] [present writer's emphasis and references to the text of the Ordinance (No. 14 of 1845)].

692. "Mr Driscoll's Amah Again", *CM*, 29 March 1882, p. 3, c. 5.

693. This is the only case quoted in this way in the present book, which was not heard before Frederick Stewart.

694. This situation existed by the time of Stewart's court. Carl Smith refers to a list of brothels licensed for foreigners only, dated 1877. See Reverend Carl T. Smith, *A Sense of History: Studies in the Social and Urban History of Hong Kong*, Hong Kong, Hong Kong Educational Publishing Co., 1995, p. 150.

695. Ronald Hyam, *Empire and Sexuality*, Manchester, Manchester University Press, 1990, p. 142.

696. Editorial, *CM*, 5 August 1880, p. 2, cc. 6-7.

697. Crisswell and Watson, *The Royal Hong Kong Police, op. cit.*, p. 17.

698. Crisswell and Watson, *The Royal Hong Kong Police, op. cit.*, p. 73.

699. See R. J. Miners, "State Regulation of Prostitution in Hong Kong, 1857 to 1941", *JRAS (HK)*, Vol. XXIV, 1984, pp. 143-161, pp. 143-144.

700. *Ibid.*, p. 144.

701. Executive Council Minutes, 2 July 1884, CO/131/14/98-.

702. Executive Council Minutes, 5 June 1884, CO/131/14/81-.

703. "There was a time when these women could not make their appearance in Wellington Street, but then came a recommendation from the Registrar General that they should be allowed to come nearer this end of the town, to accommodate the gentlemen residing there, and so the sound and sanitary rules were broken through." (Report of the Legislative

Council Meeting held on 19 November 1877, *CM*, 19 November 1877, p. 3, cc. 1-5, c. 4.)

704. George Bateson Wright, Headmaster of Queen's College, Annual Report for 1895, dated 28 January 1896, *HKGG*, 15 February 1896, pp. 117-118, paragraph 8.

705. Report of the Legislative Council Meeting held on 19 November 1877, *CM*, 19 November 1877, p. 3, cc. 1-5, cc. 3-5. See also the *Daily Press*, 17 November 1877, p. 2, c. 5.

706. *CM*, 20 November 1877, p. 3, c. 3.

707. See Gillian Bickley, "The Gratification of their Fancies", in *TGN*, pp. 129-139 and "Prostitutes and their Associates", below.

708. Susanna Hoe refers to the effects of the Tai Ping Rebellion, saying that this brought large numbers of families to Hong Kong, fleeing to safety. (Susanna Hoe, *The Private Life of Old Hong Kong, op. cit.*, p. 79.)

709. *CM*, 11 March 1882, p. 2, cc. 6-7.

710. One case was before the court twice, making twenty hearings (as counted in this book).

711. The two Caucasian women lived in Gage Street, the defendant at number fifteen and her friend at number twenty-two. (One at least was a prostitute, and probably both of them were.)

712. "Assault", 16 September 1881.

713. In the section that follows this, "Kidnappers and Traffickers in Human Beings", another brothel in Taipingshan – 32, West Street – is named.

714. R. J. Miners says, "Regulations made by the Governor segregated the licensed brothels catering for Europeans at the east end of the city and those for Chinese to the west end." (R. J. Miners, "State Regulation of Prostitution in Hong Kong", *op. cit.*, p. 144.)

Hoe refers to "Chinese prostitutes for soldiers and sailors and such permanent European residents as policemen, all of the women being confined to Wanchai towards the east". (Susanna Hoe, *The Private Life of Old Hong Kong, op. cit.*, p. 144.)

715. The two names given are Chinese. The assumption is made that all these others are Chinese because the other names in the case are Chinese, because it is assumed that Caucasians would be named, because of the street or area (where named) and because of the terminology "brothel" and "inmate of a brothel". See above.

716. For comments about the Square Street Brothel, and this particular evidence, see also Geoffrey Roper, "The Police Role in Magistrate Frederick Stewart's Court: A Personal Commentary", above.

717. David Faure, Ed., *Society: A Documentary History of Hong Kong*, Hong Kong, Hong Kong University Press, 1997, pp. 65-66.

718. The names of two prostitutes only are given, Lai Su Lin and Lo Chun. One brothel mistress is named, but initially, the court did not know that this was her occupation, and this seems to be why her name appears, in this case.

719. *Sic.*

720. Editorial, *CM* , 5 August 1880, p. 2, cc. 6-7.

721. See CO/129/189/323r/-325r., particularly 324r.

722. *CM*, 11 March 1882, p. 2, cc. 6-7.

723. *Ibid.*

724. Editorial, *CM*, 11 March 1882, p.2, cc. 6-7.

725. Crisswell and Watson, *The Royal Hong Kong Police*, *op. cit.*, p. 123.

726. "Sir John Smale on the Evils of Hong Kong", *CM*, 26 January 1882, p. 3, cc. 6-7. See a discussion of the number of "female slaves and prostitutes" on Hong Kong Island from time to time, in Christopher Munn, "'An Anglo-Chino [*sic*] Conspiracy in Crime': the Caldwell Scandal, 1857-1861'", TS, nd, note 138.

Bracebridge Hemyng, in his essay, "Prostitution in London", states that there were probably eighty thousand prostitutes in London then [1861/62], out of a population of more than two million. (See Henry Mayhew, *London Labour and the London Poor*, first published by Griffin, Bohn, and Company in 1861-1862, reprinted in New York, Dover Publications, Inc., 1968, 4 vols, Vol. IV, pp. 210-272, p. 213, c. 2, p. 211, c. 1.)

As in Hong Kong, so in London, girls were brought up to become prostitutes later. (p. 213. c. 1.)

727. Government Notification No. 387, *HKGG*, 30 September 1882, p. 788.

728. *Ibid.*

729. Court Case 48.

730. Court Case 97.

731. "Police Intelligence," *CM*, Wednesday, 14 September 1881, p. 3, c. 3, Report relating to "Wednesday 13" [*sic* for "Wednesday 14"] September 1881.

732. Court Case 153.

733. Court Case 160.

734. The original does not provide inverted commas.

735. Court Case 166.

736. Court Case 189.

737. Court Case 276.

738. Court Case 278.

739. Court Case 297.

740. Court Case 310.

741. "Police Intelligence," *CM*, Friday [*sic*], 29 October 1881, p. 3, cc. 4-5.

742. Court Case 335. The complete set of reports in connection with this case in "Court Cases 1881-1882" is: Court Cases 335, 339.

743. Court Case 339. The complete set of reports in connection with this case in "Court Cases 1881-1882" is: Court Cases 335, 339.

744. "Court Cases 1881-1882", does not have any earlier report on this case.

745. Court Case 364.

746. See an Editorial, *CM*, 9 March 1882, quoted below.

747. Court Case 460.

748. Court Case 494.

749. The original does not use inverted commas.

750. Court Case 557. The complete set of reports in connection with this case in "Court Cases 1881-1882", is: Court Cases 557, 593.

751. In the reports of this case, the first name is given as both "Cheong Yak Fong" and "Cheong Tak-fong"; and the second name as both "Tsung Yang Kiu" and "Tsung Yang-kin".

752. There is nothing for 9 or 10 January 1882 in "Court Cases 1881-1882".

753. There is nothing on this case in "Police Intelligence", *CM*, 17 January 1882.

754. It is impossible to read clearly up to the margin of the copy supplied to the present Editor. It seems possible that a first digit is missing.

755. There is nothing on this case in "Police Intelligence", *CM*, 23 January 1882.

756. Court Case 593.

757. Court Case 594.

758. *Sic*.

759. Court Case 631.

760. The consumption of opium was a common method of suicide among the Chinese.

761. "Local and General", *CM*, Thursday, 9 March 1882, p. 3, c. 2. No number is assigned to this, as it does not describe a case as such. Nevertheless, it is included here since it does give some of the content of the case.

The Square Street Brothel is referred to above also. See "Disorderly Conduct", *CM*, 10 November 1881, p. 3, c. 2. See also "Court Cases 1881-1882", Number 364.

762. Court Case 683.

763. *Sic*.

764. *Sic*.

765. "persisted on having" *sic*.

766. As stated by R. J. Miners, the former purpose was of particular concern to the naval and army authorities; and the second purpose was accepted by the Secretary of State in London. (See R. J. Miners, "State Regulation of Prostitution in Hong Kong", *op. cit.*, p. 158.) Miners argues, that in practice the first aim always had priority and was largely achieved; although he also states that control over Chinese prostitutes catering for Chinese clients was less comprehensive and less strictly enforced. In Miners's view, licensed prostitution probably failed in the ostensible purpose of preventing brothel slavery. The period Miners discusses is the whole period, 1857 to 1889, and it would not be surprising if his comments do not seem perfectly accurate for a small number of years within these dates. Certainly, the cases quoted below show no slackness in the protection of women and children from offences and crimes

associated with their enslavement.

767. "Slavery", *The Times*, cutting attached to Colonial Office Minute Sheets, dated April 1882. (CO/129/204/309r.-310v., 310r., c. 2.)

768. For some comment on and references to further discussion of the changing roles of the Po Leung Kuk and the Registrar General's Department at this time, see note below to Court Case 37.

769. Men also were being exploited at this time, shipped overseas as indentured labourers. In the case, "Larceny of Clothing", reported on 17 November 1881, and quoted in "Urban Life", in the present book, the defendant claims he had been brought to Hong Kong by a man who intended to sell him and send him off to Singapore, but he had refused to go.

770. See also Verner Bickley, "Differing Perceptions of Social Reality in Dr Stewart's Court", above.

771. See J. Stewart Lockhart, Acting Registrar General, 9 August 1884, Enclosure (CO/129/217/174r.-177r.; f. 174r.) in Governor Sir George Bowen, Despatch No. 282 to the Earl of Derby, dated 11 August 1884. (CO/129/217/172r.-173r.)

772. See J. Stewart Lockhart, *Ibid.*, ff. 174r.-176r.

773. See J. Stewart Lockhart, *Ibid.*, f. 176r.

774. See Elizabeth Sinn, *Power and Charity, op. cit.*, pp. 113-114.

775. See David Faure, Ed., *Society: A Documentary History of Hong Kong*, Hong Kong, Hong Kong University Press, 1997,
p. 62, foonote **, which confirms that this was the regular arrangement. This note also presents a view of the relationship between these two organisations during this early period.

776. John Smale, Chief Justice, letter dated Hong Kong, 20 October 1879, printed, CO/129/194/21v.-22r. See also Frederick Stewart, Inspector of Schools, annual report for 1865, paragraph 44, in *DevEd*, p. 98.

777. E. J. Eitel, Inspector of Schools, annual report for 1882, 20 February 1883, paragraph 19. See *DevEd*, p. 248.

778. Vivien Cui, "Missing inaction", *South China Morning Post*, 9 June 2004.

779. No. 2, "Criminal Calendar – December Sessions, 1880", *HKGG*, 8 January 1881, p. 20.

780. No. 4, "Criminal Calendar – April Sessions, 1881", *HKGG*, 30 April 1881, p. 303.

781. "Kidnapping", Court Case 37.

782. "Wholesale [Decoying] of Boys and Girls", Court Case 235.

783. No. 7, "Criminal Calendar – August Sessions, 1881", *HKGG*, 3 September 1881, p. 817.

784. No. 1, "Criminal Calendar – December Sessions, 1881", *HKGG*, 31 December 1881, p. 1106.

785. No. 3, "Criminal Calendar – December Sessions, 1880", *HKGG*, 8 January 1881, p. 20.

786. "Criminal Calendar – February Sessions, 1881", *HKGG*, 26 March 1881, p. 212.

787. At the first hearing on 15 July, the case was remanded or adjourned, and again on 22 and 29 July, and 5, 12, 19 and 26 August. The case was further remanded on 3, 10, 17, and 24 September. On 1 October, it was remanded again until 8 October.

All the relevant newspaper reports found have been included below.

788. "A woman" in the house had said that one of the children had been in the house for two months, and this would seem, therefore, to be Chan Hing.

789. There is a printer's error, and the report published on 1 October does not state whether or not the uncle had reappeared by then.

790. This is the court's reckoning. Using Chinese reckoning, the boys himself says he is twelve.

791. E. J. Eitel, Inspector of Schools, Annual Report for the year 1881, dated 8 May 1882, paragraph 5. See *DevEd*, pp. 225-226.

792. Chan Man Kam, "A Comparative Study on Mythology of Korea and China", MA thesis, submitted to, Shung Kyun Kwan University, Korea, 1975.

793. Frank Welsh, *A History of Hong Kong*, *op. cit.*, p. 394.

794. See also Verner Bickley, "Differing Perceptions of Social Reality in Dr Stewart's Court", above.

795. R. J. Miners, "State Regulation of Prostitution in Hong Kong", *op. cit.*, p.144.

796. Susanna Hoe states that the lists were on display *outside* the brothel. (Susanna Hoe, *The Private Life of Old Hong Kong*, *op. cit.*, p. 145.)

797. R. J. Miners, "State Regulation of Prostitution in Hong Kong", *op. cit.*, p. 144.

798. It could be that the practice at this particular short period of time was different to other times and that Governor John Pope Hennessy's attempt to reallocate among other officers the previous duties of the Registrar General's department had had a knock-on effect in this area also. After Pope Hennessy had left, comment is made by Administrator Marsh that the return to the previous practice had been very successful in improving the control of brothels. "I think your Lordship will agree with me that the successful proceedings in the three cases [two, where a person was convicted for bringing females to Hong Kong for the purpose of prostitution, and one, where a person was convicted for having a female in her brothel who had not been registered] . . . demonstrate the advantage of having restored to the Registrar General the duties which formerly attached to that office." (Administrator Marsh, Despatch No. 98, to the Secretary of State for the Colonies, dated Hong Kong 19 June 1882. (CO/129/202/435r.-436v., 436r.-436v.)

799. See "Urban Life", below.

800. See J. Russell, Acting Registrar General, Letter No. 34 to Frederick Stewart, Acting Colonial Secretary, dated 17 June 1882. (CO/129/202/440r.-443v.) Enclosure in Administrator Marsh, Despatch No. 98, dated Hong Kong, 19 June 1882, to Lord Kimberley, Secretary of State for the Colonies. (CO/129/202/435r.-436v.)

801. See the text displayed on p. 288.

802. See the text displayed on p. 288.

803. Enclosure in the Registrar General's letter, dated 19 September 1882, to the Acting Colonial Secretary, who forwarded it to Administrator Marsh, who enclosed it and the Registrar General's letter in his despatch No. 209 to the Secretary of State for the Colonies, dated 27 September 1882. (CO/129/202/659r.-666r., f. 664r.)

804. *Ibid.*

805. See *TGN*, p. 223.

806. See *TGN*, p. 224.

807. Frederick Stewart, Registrar General, Sub-enclosure dated 26 March 1884 (CO/129/217/178r.) in J. Stewart Lockhart, Acting Registrar General, 9 August 1884, Enclosure (CO/129/217/174r.-177r.) in Governor Sir George Bowen, Despatch No. 282 to the Earl of Derby, dated 11 August 1884. (CO/129/217/172r.-173r.)

808. E. J. Eitel refers to, "purchased children whose parents are in most cases not living in Hong Kong". (Inspector of Schools Report for the year 1881, paragraph 5. See *DevEd*, pp. 225-226.)

809. E. J. Eitel, Inspector of Schools Report for the year 1881, *op. cit.*, paragraph 5.

810. The reporting in the four cases given in this section is very detailed. Probably, as is still done today, and as the present writer witnessed on Wednesday, 7 June 2000, in His Honour Justice Wilson's court, District Courts, Wanchai, Gloucester Road, Hong Kong, interpretation was given in open court.

811. Court Case 20. The complete set of reports in connection with this case in "Court Cases 1881-1882" is: Court Cases 20, 93, 235, 238.

      The caption to this report, "Detaining a Boy" is an example of the misleading captions that Tim Hamlett writes of in, "Reporting the Cases of Frederick Stewart", above.

812. In the reports of this case, this name is given as both "Tong" and "Fong".

813. In the reports of this case, this name is given as both "Wong Ang" and "Wong a Ng".

814. This is consistent with the evidence of "a woman", given on 14 July, that all but one of the children had been in the house for "about ten days".

815. The case is not reported among Tonnochy's cases in *CM* on either 15 or 22 July 1881.

816. Later, this gentleman is identified as a detective of the Po Leung Kuk.

817. In the reports of various cases, the name of this informer/Po Leung Kuk detective is given as "Wong Way Fu", "Wong Man Yu" and "Wang Mun Yu". In the reports of this particular case, there is also "Wong Man In". This name is sufficiently similar to the other variations to suggest that "Wong Man In" is the same person, particularly since another Po Leung Kok detective uses this name to refer to his absent colleague.

818. There is nothing on this case in "Police Intelligence," *CM*, 5 August

1881.
819. Court Case 93.
820. Previously named as, "Police Sergeant".
821. A very big case was reported on 26 and 27 August 1881, and page three carries coverage of the Police Courts only on 27 August 1881. This case is not mentioned.
822. Court Case 235.
823. This statement is misleading. The complete set of reports in connection with this case in "Court Cases 1881-1882", is: Court Cases 20, 93, 235, 238. Some of these were published earlier than this report. Perhaps the reporter meant that the case had not been written about *at length* before.
824. In fact, as shown below, the case continued before the court until at least 8 October 1881. It has not been possible, however, to trace it any further.
825. It was evidently expected that the case would go before the Supreme Court.
826. This is consistent with "a woman" in the house saying, on 14 July, that four of the children had been in the house for about ten days.
827. See note above. This gentleman is later identified as a detective of the Po Leung Kuk.
828. *Sic*, perhaps for "in".
829. "were" is in italics in the original. It seems more likely that "five" should have been in italics, since this is a correction of the Detective Sergeant Fisher's expectation of six children.
830. *Sic*.
831. In the original, there is a comma following "when", which occurs one third of the way into a line and then the rest of the line is blank. As the present writer interprets the sense, a whole line of content is missing, or perhaps more.
832. Earlier, this gentleman is – apparently inaccurately – referred to as an "informer". Elizabeth Sinn refers to the use the Po Leung Kuk made of "Detectives and informers" (*Power and Charity, op. cit.*, pp. 115-116; p. 248, n. 176.)
833. Wong Man Yu, himself.
834. In the reports of this case, this name is given as "Fung Kwok Tai" and "Kwong Kwok Tai".
835. Fung Kwok Tai.
836. The name "Amui" is given to both this boy and a girl in the report, possibly a mistake.
837. Wong Man Yu.

838. Kwong Kwok Tai would have been a practitioner of Chinese medicine.
839.   Is this perhaps the same as "Tan Afau", mentioned previously?
840. Kwan Atsu.
841. The informer/detective, Wong Man Yu.

842. The doctor, Kwong Kwok Tai.

843. See above. The second defendant asks both the informer/ detective, Wong Man Yu, and the doctor, Kwong Kwok Tai, about a person called Afau.

844. Chinese Police Constable 192.

845. His occupation is given above as "marine hawker".

846. *Sic* for "others"?

847. *Sic*.

848. Court Case 238.

849. In the original, the rest of the line following "when" is left blank. There is certainly a missing word or two and maybe also one or more missing lines at this point.

850. *Sic* for "Kuk".

851. There is no report of this case in *CM* on this day.

852. The names of the defendants have been checked in the Criminal Calendar for the following Sessions – October, November and December 1881, January, February and April 1882. (The March 1882 Criminal Calendar seems not to have been included in the *HKGG*.) In none, have they been found.

853. Court Case 37.

854. See previous case, in which Wang Mun Yu is also involved.

855. Earlier, January 1878, Lai Shik Kai (apparently employed within the Registrar General's Department) is named as "the kidnapping detective". (*CM*, 16 January 1878, p. 2, c. 5.) If only judging from a comparison of this reference with this court report, it would seem that the Po Leung Kuk has taken over some functions of the Registrar General's Department.

Frank Welsh also reports this situation, as well as the later return to the previous arrangements. He quotes Hong Kong public opinion (undated), that the *Tung Wah* (the senior and closely associated society) had "taken over the responsibilities that the Registrar-General was meant to fulfil", and reports that, "When Hennessy left William Marsh . . . succeeded in reinstating the office of Registrar-General, and appointing a cadet officer with good Cantonese to the post [of Registrar-General]". (Frank Welsh, *A History of Hong Kong, op. cit.*, pp. 303-304.)

For other discussions of the temporary changes in the role of the Registrar General's Department, see *TGN*, pp. 223-224 and Gillian Bickley, "Registrar General: 1883-1887", manuscript and word-processed file in preparation, Personal Archive, [RegGen].

856. This was a clever thing to do. On the one hand, it gave credence to the detective's professed interest in buying the child. On the other hand, effecting a bill of sale would be proof that the boy was being offered for sale.

857. This is by "Chinese reckoning". The official account is that he was only eleven.

858. Pun Yu is a district of Canton.

859. Wang Man Yu, the detective. It appears that it was at this point that

the detective "blew his cover".

860. Here, a report of direct speech is embedded in reported speech with no use of quotation marks.

861. This is the boy's direct speech.

862. This is the boy's reported speech, given in note form. It seems that, in cases like these, the alleged victim or victims were lodged at the Tung Wah Hospital, whose important social role is carefully described by Elizabeth Sinn in her monograph, *Power and Charity, op. cit.*, throughout.

863. This report gives a rather full description of the police procedures of the time, including, in this instance, the cautioning of people likely to be accused of an offence.

864. This case was not heard at the August Criminal Sessions, which took place on 19 and 20 August, the first possible occasion when it could have been heard. The report of the Criminal Sessions held on 19 August states, that the Attorney General had said that two cases only would be brought before the Court on the following day, which seems to imply that other cases would be outstanding.

The following Criminal Calendars also have been checked: September, October, November and December 1881, January, February and April 1882. It does not appear in any of these. (The March 1882 Criminal Calendar seems not to have been published in *HKGG*.)

It also does not feature in *CM*'s December Criminal Session reports.

865. Court Case 343.

866. This is the only report of this case in "Court Cases 1881-1882". But see the report itself below, which refers to "the first enquiry". This was not the first time the case had come to court.

867. The reporter is being ironic. Revd Carl Smith gives quite a few details about Ship Street. See *A Sense of History, op. cit.,* pp. 115, 124, 128-130, 143. Smith also states that, "In an 1877 list of brothels licensed for foreigners only, there were six on Ship Street." (*Ibid.*, p. 150)

868. The case was not heard at the November Criminal Sessions, but at the December Criminal Sessions, before the Hon. F. Snowden, Acting Chief Justice, on Monday, 19 December 1881.

The case was reported in *CM*, Monday, 19 December 1881, p. 3, c. 2, as follows.

"Unlawful Detention

"The first case was one of unlawful detention, in which Ng Sam Mui, Li Akwai, Wong Awa, Kam Asam, and Lau Asam, were charged with detaining, for the purpose of selling her, one Pang Afuk. The prisoners pleaded not guilty, and the following gentlemen were sworn as jurors: – Messrs A. de Costa, T. Hashi, J. F. Broadbent, J. M. de J. P. Collaço, H. A. Ritchie, A. Soares, and C. F. Grossman.

"The Attorney General (the Hon. E. L. O'Malley) prosecuting, said the prisoners were indicted for taking part in the detention of a woman, unlawfully and by force, for the purpose of selling her. The complainant was a married woman whose husband had been in Singapore for three years, and with whom she corresponds. In the month of September last, she received money from him to pay her passage to Singapore. She made arrangements to leave her native place, and on the way had been detained by the prisoners who had promised to procure her passage, receiving in payment thereof $50 sent by her husband.

"The evidence led was substantially the same as that given in the Police Court.

"After evidence was heard, the Attorney General acknowledged that there had been very little evidence to sustain the charge of unlawful detention, and that there appeared to have been persuasion used rather than force. His Lordship agreed with the Attorney General that there was very little convicting evidence – insufficient to justify him in laying the case before the jury. The jury found the prisoners not guilty. His Lordship then dismissed the prisoners advising them to inform all their friends that no person was allowed to sell another in this Colony."

The Criminal Calendar for the December Sessions gives the names of the defendants as Ng Sam Mui, Li A-kwei, Wong A-wa, Kam A-sam and Lau A-sam, and the name of the complainant as Pun A-fung. The crime is described as, "Unlawfully and by force detaining within this Colony a woman named Pun A-fung, for the purpose of selling her."

The verdict was "not guilty", and the following remarks are given: "In this case there was no evidence whatever that the woman was detained by force or fraud. The evidence shewed [sic] that the prisoners wanted to obtain a sum of money by negociating [sic] to marry her to a man who was called as a witness. F. S. [Francis Snowden, (Acting Chief Justice)]"

869. See also the *Daily Press*, 28 January 1882.

870. Court Case 575. The complete set of reports in connection with this case in "Court Cases 1881-1882", is: Court Cases 575, 587, 600, 619.

871. In the reports of this case, this name is given as "Pang Asun", "Pang Asum". See also the *Daily Press*, where this name is given as "Tang Asun" (28 January 1882), but "Pang Asun" (4 February 1882).

872. See the *Daily Press*, 28 January and 4 February 1882, where this name is given as "Chun Acheung".

873. In the reports of this case, this place name is given as "Lo-kong" and "Lukong". See also the *Daily Press*, where this place name is given as "Lo Kong" (28 January 1882) and "Lo Keng" (Monday, 6 February 1882).

874. In the reports of this case, this name is given as "Kiu-lan" and "Mui Lan".

875. The address of this is given below, as No. Thirty-two, West Street.

876. Original defective. Date supplied by reference to later account of this same case. See below.

877. The "List of Officers" in the HKGBB for 1882 lists J[ohn] Lee as Assistant Inspector of [Registered] Brothels, Lock Hospital. He seems to have been a European, since he was *accompanied* by an interpreter on his

visit to the brothel, described below.

878. Court Case 587.

879. The Assistant Inspector of Brothels. (See above.)

880. Chan Nui had earlier given "Chung Tai Fuk" as her husband's name on 27 January 1882.

881. The "List of Officers" in the HKGBB for 1882 lists James Russell as Registrar General.

882. It is the defendant, not the alleged victim, who ran towards Inspector Lee, falling on her knees.

883. Inspector Lee.

884. The appearance of a barrister-at-law for the defence suggests that the defendants had decided that they were now in need of assistance. Mr Holmes is reported in the next two reports as continuing to appear for the defence. Not until the report of the hearing on 11 February 1882, however, does a barrister-at-law appear for the Crown, to prosecute.

885. See discussion of this in the introductory essay to this section.

886. This is also reported in the *Daily Press*, 6 February 1882.

887. Court Case 600.

888. The *Daily Press* names the interpreter as "Alam".

889. If this interpreter was, "Tso lam", it may be that this is one of the examples of his work, which led to him soon leaving this work. J. Russell, Registrar General, wrote to Frederick Stewart, Acting Colonial Secretary, on 1 June 1882, stating that Tso Lam wished to resign his provisional appointment as Interpreter to the Inspector of Brothels. "The Man is utterly unfit for the post, and he cannot be said to speak English at all – he tells me he was a boy of Dr. Eitel, who had him appointed." (J. Russell, Registrar General, to Frederick Stewart, Acting Colonial Secretary, 1 June 1882, C.S.O. No. 1843, HKRS 275, 1882, Vol. II.)

890. Court Case 619.

891. Original has "Arrived at" for "on arrival at", as given here.

892. This case does not appear in the Criminal Calendar for the February or April Sessions. (It seems that the March 1882 Session is not reported in the *HKGG*.) It is not reported in the 27 February 1882 *China Mail* account of the Criminal Sessions.

893. GN No. 344, *HKGG*, 26 August 1882, p. 712. A Chinese translation was published alongside this in the original.

894. See also two cases quoted in, "Urban Life", below. In "Theft of a Hair Pin", a twelve year old boy gives evidence about the snatching of his mother's silver hair pin.

An editorial note to the second of these, "Cutting Earth without a License", suggests that the complainant, H. Gustave, who states he is a pupil at St Joseph's College, might be a mature pupil. He might equally, however, be a young pupil, appearing as complainant in this case because his parents had inadequate language skills.

895. See also, T. C. Cheng, "Chinese Unofficial Members of the Legislative and Executive Councils in Hong Kong up to 1941", *JRAS (HK)*, 1969, Vol. 9, pp. 7-30.

896. E. J. Eitel, Annual Report on Education for 1881, 8 May 1882, paras 2-4. See *DevEd*, pp. 224-225.

897. Frederick Stewart, Annual Report on Education for 1867, 15 February 1868, paragraph 10. See *DevEd*, p. 111.

898. Frederick Stewart, Annual Report on Education for 1871, paragraph 36. See *DevEd*, p. 154.

899. This topic is also mentioned in "Kidnappers and Traffickers", in the present book.

900. The Gospel according to Saint Matthew, the Christian Bible, chapter 18, verse 6.

901. Another case, involving a young person, was heard by Stewart on Friday, 30 September 1881. (See "Urban Life", below.) Committed for trial at the Criminal Sessions, the defendant was found guilty and sentenced to three years' penal servitude.

902. *CM*, 29 March 1882, p. 3, c. 4.

903. *Ibid.*

904. *Ibid.*

905. *Ibid.*

906. The following discussion is based on Gillian Bickley, mimeograph, "The Grant-in-aid Scheme" [1873Prt1].

907. [J. T.], *Dates and Events Connected with the History of Education in Hong Kong*, Hong Kong, December 1877, p. 11.

908. Frederick Stewart, Annual Report on Education for 1865, 12 February 1866, last paragraph. See *DevEd*, p. 103.

909. Editorial, *CM*, 29 March 1882, p. 2, c. 1.

910. There had been some discussion of this at a meeting of the Hong Kong Executive Council held in December 1886. (Minutes of Meeting held on 10 December 1886, CO/131/15/237.)

911. *CM*, 31 August 1886, p. 2, cc. 4-5.

912. E. J. Eitel, Annual Report on Education for 1893, *HKGG*, 5 May 1894, paragraph 19. See *DevEd*, p. 402.

913. Court Case 142.

914. Court Case 171.

915. This is commented on above, in "Children and Returned Students as Defendants, Victims, Accomplices and Witnesses".

916. Court Case 232.

917. *Sic.*

918. Court Case 251 (additional number). "Local and General", *CM*, Thursday, 6 October 1881, p. 3, c. 1.

919. The original has several words that are difficult to decipher. They have been supplied as best possible.

920. This communication between the British consul at Nagasaki, in Japan, and the Hong Kong police, on a criminal charge, is most interesting.

921. Here, and twice further in the reports of this case, quoted below, it is implied that the magistrate needed advice from the Central Hong Kong Government on the extent of his jurisdiction, and on the proper procedure

in such a case.

922. *CM*, Friday, 7 October 1881, p. 2, c. 7.

923. Court Case 365.

924. Nothing is published about this case in *CM*, 9 November 1881.

925. The "List of Officers" in the HKGBB for 1881 lists Leong A-tsau as Chinese Clerk and <u>Shroff</u>, Magistracy, stating that he was appointed on 15 October 1881.

A similar list in the Blue Book for 1880 lists as Chinese Clerk and Shroff, Sung Cheung Kam, whose appointment is given as dating from 1 April 1878.

No-one of the name, "Leon" is listed in either. Possibly, therefore, "Leon" is a mistake for "Leong".

Although a "shroff" is not a "sheriff", a "sheriff's officer" might have the functions of clerk and shroff.

926. According to Crisswell and Watson, No. Seven Police Station was located at the junction of Queen's Road and Pokfulam Road. (Crisswell and Watson, *The Royal Hong Kong Police*, *op. cit.*, "Appendix 1".)

927. The original has "were" (*sic* for "where").

928. The machine meant is the defendant's rickshaw.

929. Court Case 468.

930. Presumably, the child was considered too young to swear an oath, of whatever kind.

931. Court Case 570.

932. Kelly & Walsh had a bookshop in Central Hong Kong (Ice House Street, off Queen's Road) up to at least the 1980s. At the time of writing, it has an outlet in Pacific Place, Admiralty, Hong Kong. Similary-named stores existed elsewhere in Asia, e.g. Singapore, Yokahama and Shanghai.

933. Court Case 616.

934. Court Case 638.

935. Court Case 640.

936. Court Case 643.

937. Court Case 691.

938 . See "History of Gambling in the United States", <http://www.library.ca.gov/CRB/97/03/Chap2.html>.
It is assumed that these rules in the USA derive from the parent country, England.

939. Frank Welsh, *A History of Hong Kong*, *op. cit.*, pp. 236-237.

940. *CM*, 6 April 1867, p. 3, cc. 2-3, c. 2.

941. Additional perspective can be derived from considering the history of gambling in the USA, in which Chinese gambling deserves separate mention. In the mid 1800s to the early 1900s, the desire for respectability and a recognition of the social ills tied to gaming led to limits on gambling. The Legislature made most types of gambling illegal. Scandals and the rise of Victorian morality led to the end of legal gambling. By 1910, virtually all forms of gambling were prohibited in the USA. The only legal betting that occurred was in three states which allowed horse

racing. (See, "History of Gambling in the United States", <http://www.library.ca.gov/CRB/97/03/Chapt2.html>.)

942. Crisswell and Watson, *The Royal Hong Kong Police, op. cit.*, p. 7.

943. E. J. Eitel, *Europe in China, op. cit.*, pp. 207, 283. The first race meeting at Happy Valley was on 17-18 December 1846 (Austin Coates, *China Races*, Hong Kong, Oxford University Press, 1983, p. 67.) Before that, the first race meeting took place in Pokfulam in 1845. (Austin Coates, *Ibid.*, p. 67.)

944. Austin Coates does not tell us in so many words when the number of race-meetings increased. We can deduce from his book, however, that the meeting was still an annual event as late as the 1920s (*China Races*, Hong Kong, Oxford University Press, 1983, pp. 245-247), but that racing had taken place once a week from at least 1966. (*Ibid.*, p. 291.)

944. Austin Coates indicates that facilities for betting existed as of 1890, when Hong Kong Governor Sir William Robinson (1891-1898) decreed that all such facilities should be removed. (Austin Coates, *China Races, op. cit.*, p. 142.) Betting resumed in 1892. (*Ibid.*, p. 143.)

946. "Hong Kong catches Euro 2000 betting fever", *The Sunday Morning Post*, 18 June 2000, p. 1. This article was brought to the present writer's attention by Dr Verner Bickley.

947. *CM*, 6 April 1867, p. 3, cc. 2-3, c. 2.

948. See Frank Welsh, *A History of Hong Kong, op. cit.*, especially pp. 236-241; E. J. Eitel, *Europe in China, op. cit.*, pp. 428-440.

949. E. J. Eitel, *Europe in China, op. cit.*, p. 440.

950. *Daily Press*, 10 August 1876.

951. See "Reporting the Cases of Frederick Stewart", above.

952. *CM*, 6 April 1867, p. 3, cc. 2-3, c. 2.

953. Geoffrey Roper, "The Police Role in Magistrate Stewart's Court", above.

954. *CM*, 6 December 1881, p. 2, cc. 6-7.

955. *CM*, 14 August 1886, p. 3, cc. 3-4.

956. *CM*, 6 April 1867, p. 3, cc. 2-3, c. 2.

957. Court Case 146.

958. *Sic.*

959 . Examples of these gambling instruments and the weapons mentioned can be seen at the Hong Kong Police Museum.

960. The reporter omitted to expand his notes when writing his report.

961. There seems to be no further mention of the eighth prisoner in "Court Cases 1881-1882".

962. Court Case 484. "Police Intelligence," *CM*, Monday, 19 December 1881, p. 3, cc. 3-4.

963. Court Case 485. The case is a larceny case, but the caption writer has chosen to focus on the profession of the defendants.

964. This is an instance where two similar names in the report(s) of one case are not variations on the same name. "Lau Aluk" is a different person from "Lum Afuk".

965. This implies that Lau Aluk was charged with permitting illegal

gambling on his premises.

966. Supplied for the sake of clarity.

967. Queen Victoria's two young sons, junior officers on the ship, *Bacchante*, were on a world cruise, during which they visited Hong Kong.

968. Probably the first defendant, rather than the complainant in this case, the occupant of the premises, who was evidently the defendant in the previous case, in relation to gambling, and must therefore also have been arrested.

969. This is a mistake. Sergeant Rae must have been part of the police party. The "He" here must refer to another of the informers.

970. The informers.

971. The sequence of arrival at the premises was evidently: the four informers, the party of police, including Inspectors Lindsay, Perry and Thomson, Sergeant Rae and others.

972. The first witness was Lau Aluk, the owner of the alleged gambling establishment. The first defendant (an informer) seems to be accusing this gentleman of trying to frame him and Inspector Thomson of collusion.

973. The employment referred to is that of gambling informers.

974. The Police.

975. Urinated.

976. "Commital of Nuisance", 28 January 1882. However, sometimes this was a deliberate act, intended to secure arrest, and hence food and shelter for an indigent. See "The Light and Pass Rules", above.

977. In the Museum at Macau, located in the former fort, one section shows such tradesmen. Pushing a button produces the sound of their cries.

978. Court Case 131.

979. Original has "offence" for "defence"!

980. The case is reported as No. Five in the Criminal Calendar – September Sessions, 1881. "Chan A-sai" was tried by Francis Snowden, Acting Chief Justice, on 20 September 1881, for "Obtaining money by false pretences", and found "Not guilty". ("Criminal Calendar – September Sessions, 1881", *HKGG*, 1 October 1881, p. 875.)

The hearing is reported in *CM* (20 September 1881, p. 3, cc. 1-2).

"Obtaining Money by False Pretences

"Chan Asai was charged with falsely obtaining from Chan Afook a certain sum of money and some jewellery by selling to her certain pieces of metal which he led her to believe were gold.

"Prisoner pled [*sic*] not guilty.

"The following Jury was impanelled:–

"D. H. Billia, H. C. Maclean, R. dos Remedios, Erich Georg, Charles L. Gorham, E. Herbst, and Harry Wicking.

"The Attorney General went over the circumstances of the case as already detailed and said that he believed the defence was mistaken identity. [The original has "identify".]

"Evidence was heard for the prosecution, in which it came out that on the prisoner being searched two $10 notes, two $5 notes, and a $1 note–the exact values of the notes given by the woman to prisoner–were found.

"Mr Hayllar who, instructed by Messrs Brereton and Wotton, appeared for the prisoner, said his case would be one of mistaken identity. The evidence against the prisoner depended entirely upon the woman. He held that the similarity of the notes was merely a coincidence. It was obvious that the woman had been trying to cheat too. He would call witnesses (opium dealers) to prove that prisoner during the whole of the period during which the offence was said to have been committed was in their shop.

"Lam Afat salesman [– the original has "salesmen" –] in an opium shop in Wing-lok Street, gave evidence as to the prisoner being there, and as to his having large transactions with him. The master of the shop gave similar evidence.

"Mr Hayllar addressed the Jury and the Attorney General replied. His Lordship having gone over the evidence, the jury returned a verdict of not guilty.

"Prisoner discharged."
981. Court Case 220.
982. The case was heard at the Supreme Court Criminal Sessions before the Acting Puisne Judge, the Hon. J. Russell, on Tuesday, 18 October 1881. Mr Francis, under instructions from the Attorney General, prosecuted. The jurors were Messrs J. W. Crocker, R. Steil [?], A. S. Garfit, A. F. Gonsalves, F. H. G. Lorberg, E. Vogel, and S. V. dos Remedios.

"Theft of an Umbrella
"Chan Ayau was charged with stealing an umbrella on the 17th Sept. It will be recollected that complainant had set his umbrella down at the side of a stall near the Harbour-master's office while drinking some sugared water. Defendant took it up and ran, but was stopped by a Police Constable. Prisoner was also charged with a previous conviction.

"The Jury found him guilty.

"His Lordship said he was a bad boy. Although only seventeen years of age he had been convicted a great many times. It was only a waste of time to go on giving him short punishments. The sentence would be three years' penal servitude."
(CM, Tuesday, 18 October 1881, p. 3, c. 4.)
983. Court Case 221.
984. No. Seven Police Station was at the junction of Queen's Road and Pokfulam Road.
985. Usually spelt, "a-missing". An old-fashioned construction.
986. Lum Amui appeared before the Acting Puisne Judge, the Hon. J. Russell, at the Criminal Sessions held on Tuesday, 18 October 1881. The report which appeared in CM reads as follows:

"Lum Amui was charged with the theft of twenty-two articles

of clothing and two red handkerchiefs on the 6th inst. The circumstances of the case were that the owner (a hawker) had gone to Station Street to sell his wares. He had a boy to carry them. While engaged in completing a bargain the bundles were set on the ground, and one of them was lifted by prisoner, who was seen doing so by the boy. The goods had been pawned at Kowloon by the prisoner. The pawn tickets were found on him.

"His Lordship, in sentencing prisoner to five years' penal servitude, remarked that it would be cheaper for the rate-payers to keep him in gaol than to have him prowling about in the Colony."

987. Court Case 225.

988. One would expect that a government employee would be likely to assist the authorities in promoting law and order.

989. This is variably called the "Harbour Office" and the "Harbour Department" in this report.

990. Court Case 281.

991. It was common at this time for adults to attend school. Many at the Government Central School were married, and some had children at school at the same time as they themselves attended it.

992. For purposes of land sale, ownership and rating valuation, etc., Hong Kong was divided into Inland and Marine Lots at the beginning of British occupation.

993. Crisswell and Watson, *The Royal Hong Kong Police*, *op. cit.*, p. 45) speak of two types of stocks, one portable. Apparently, both types bore details of the crime committed and the portable type was used in connection with flogging, which would be administered to the prisoner after he had been paraded around town in this manner. None of the reported cases heard before Frederick Stewart in the 1880s, however, include both flogging and the stocks (or cangue).

994. Court Case 285. "Police Intelligence," *CM*, Thursday, 13 October 1881, p. 3, cc. 3-4.

995. See Court Case 206, heard on September 1881, "Court Cases 1881-1882". Frederick Stewart's comments as magistrate led to the order being translated. See Gillian Bickley, [CourtCases3:Weights], for a documented transcript of relevant material from *CM*.

996. The same system was used to reward informers.

997. Court Case 286.

998. *Sic* for "an unemployed cook".

999. This colloquialism or regionalism for "staying at" is a broad clue as to the origins at least of our court reporter.

1000. Similar turnings of tables are recorded in cases involving prostitutes or brothel managers. (See "Prostitutes, their Associates and Clients", above, p. 270.)

1001. Court Case 301.

1002. See "Unenlightened law? The 'Light and Pass' Rules", above.

1003. Court Case 311.

1004. The name appears as "Chan Cheung" and "Chan Acheung" in this report.

1005. Chan Cheung.

1006. The second witness, Chan Cheung.

1007. Li Asing.

1008. Tse Akum.

1009. This bond was now forfeited. See below, this report.

1010. Chan Cheung.

1011. Tsang Ayui.

1012. That is, he had to find two householders to agree to put up ten dollars each, as a guarantee that the defendant would do what was required. If he did not, the sum would be forfeited, as had already happened as a result of the appearance in this case of the third defendant.

1013. Chu Aping.

1014. The first defendant.

1015. Tse Akum.

1016. For the first reference to this bond, see above, this report.

1017. These brackets are in the original.

1018. Li Asing.

1019. These brackets are in the original.

1020. Court Case 368.

1021. See "Unenlightened law? The 'Light and Pass' Rules", above.

1022. Christopher Coghlan comments on the use of the Poor Box in Stewart's Court, in his essay, "Thoughts about the Practice of Law in Hong Kong, arising from the Court Cases of Frederick Stewart, Esq.", above.

1023. Court Case 387.

1024. Ordinance No. 14 of 1845 reads:

"II. And be it further enacted and ordained, That every person shall be liable to a penalty not exceeding Five Pounds, who, within the Colony of Hong Kong, shall, in any thoroughfare or public place, or adjacent thereto, commit any of the following offences: that is to say: – . . .

"11. Every person who, upon any public footway, shall roll or carry any barrel, cask, butt, or other thing calculated to annoy or incommode the passengers thereon, except for the purpose of housing them or of loading any cart or carriage on the other side of the footway."

1025. A sedan chair. Unlike 'rickshaws, sedan chairs were also used in urban environments in England.

1026. This last statement seems to be in response to a question asked.

1027. Lo Ayau.

1028. The defendant's men.

1029. Court Case 389.

1030. See "Kidnappers and Traffickers in Human Beings", above, which discusses and quotes cases where people attempted to sell girls, boys and women for prostitution or domestic slavery.

During an earlier period, Hong Kong had been a centre for what was called the "coolie trade", involving the immigration from China of workers for lengthy terms of service in other countries, including the

USA. Following legislation in Hong Kong, this activity seems to have ceased. However, a similar trade through Macau – mainly (because of the common language, Portuguese) to Peru, Cuba and Chile – continued, until the pressure of international opinion brought it to an end in about 1875. (Reverend Carl Smith is thanked for his comments, in personal communication, about the Macau "coolie" trade.)

In the 1880s, several items, relating to the Immigration of Chinese, particularly directed towards ascertaining the free decision of immigrants to immigrate and the protection and good treatment of the immigrants while on board ship, or after arrival, were published in *HKGG*.

For example, *HKGG* of 11 February 1882 (p. 83) contains a Government Notification (No. 48), that an "Act of the Imperial Parliament for the Regulation of Chinese Passenger Ships, together with the Ordinances now in force, Proclamations and Regulations under it, with copies or extracts of correspondence or documents bearing on the subject of Contract Emigration, have been laid before the Legislative Council." This is followed by the documents in question (pp. 83-120).

Other items include:

Correspondence and Minutes, relating to the collecting of evidence (by Frederick Stewart, Acting Colonial Secretary, John Gerrard, Acting Registrar General, E. J. Eitel, Acting Chinese Secretary) from proposed emigrants to enable the questioners, "to determine whether they are really free emigrants and under no contract of service whatever." (*HKGG*, 23 July 1881, pp. 621-633.)

Despatches relating to Chinese Immigration to Australia, *HKGG*, 4 March 1882, pp. 242-243.

A Notice, signed by the Emigration Officer, "to Charterers and Masters of Ships carrying Chinese Emigrants under the Chinese Passengers Act 1855 and Local Ordinances, that the undersigned will not give the Certificate provided for in Section A to the above-mentioned Act, unless the Lime-juice supplied for the said Emigrants is fully approved of, as an anti-scorbutic, by the Colonial Surgeon and the Health Officer". (*HKGG*, 25 March 1882, p. 294.)

From New Zealand, "An Act to regulate the Immigration of Chinese", *HKGG*, 1 July 1882, pp. 594-595.

26 August 1882, Frederick Stewart, as Acting Colonial Secretary, authorised the publication of the following notice, signed by H. G. Thomsett, R.N., Emigration Officer, and dated 21 August 1882:

"The Emigration Officer gives notice that for the better protection of Emigrants, it is hereby notified that on and after the 1st proximo women and children who are taken before him for the purpose of emigrating should be provided with one photograph each.

"If the woman or child is passed [for emigration], one photograph will be stamped and given back to the Emigrant. The Emigrant will show this photograph to the proper Officer on board the vessel before departure, and again to the Protector of Chinese or proper

Officer on the Emigrant's arrival at Port of destination". (CO/129202/663r.)

Two months later, following a suggestion for improvement, made by the Po Leung Kok (see CO/129/202/662r.), the number of photographs required was increased to two.

On 21 October 1882, Frederick Stewart, as Acting Colonial Secretary, authorised the publication of the following notice, signed by H. G. Thomsett, R.N., Emigration Officer and dated 21 October 1882:

"The Emigration Officer gives notice that for the better protection of Emigrants, it is hereby notified that on and after the 1st proximo women and children who are taken before him for the purpose of emigrating should be provided with two photographs of each.

"If the woman or child is passed [for emigration], one photograph will be stamped and given back to the Emigrant. The Emigrant will show this photograph to the proper Officer on board the vessels before departure, and again to the Protector of Chinese or proper Officer on the Emigrant's arrival at Port of destination". (*HKGG*, 21 October 1882, p. 831.)

Other items on the topic were sent for the information of the Governor. For example, an article from the San Francisco *Weekly Chronicle* respecting "Emigrant Slavery in Hawaii" was sent to Governor Pope Hennessy in a letter dated 6 September 1881. (CO/129/195/93r.-96v.)

1031. The present writer has seen a comment by Frederick Stewart, in another capacity, in which he comments on the extreme simplicity of some of those who entered as labourers into the system for supplying Chinese workers overseas. This would be an example that would have gone to inform this point of view.

1032. Court Case 418

1033. Court Case 478.

1034. Spelling of "Yau-ma Ti", *sic*. For a comment on ferries, see a quotation in Arthur Hacker, *Arthur Hacker's Wanchai*, pp. 100-101. Iain Ward states that a ferry service run by the "Yow-Ma-Tee Ferry Company" had been running from Pedder's Wharf in Central to Yau Ma Tei since 1873. (Iain Ward, *Sui Geng: the Hong Kong Marine Police 1841-1950*, Hong Kong, Hong Kong University Press, 1991, p. 34, n. 8.) The first "proper ferry service" to Tsim Sha Tsui was started by Mr Dorabjee Nowrojee, and the Star Ferry Company was incorporated in 1898, when it took over Mr Nowrojee's assets. (Iain Ward, *Sui Geng, op. cit.*, p. 34, n. 9.)

1035. In the paragraph below, this man is named as "Leung Anam".

1036. Presumably, a paper wrapper around a bundle of a certain number of notes.

1037. *CM*, Friday, 6 January 1882, p. 3, c. 4.

1038. Court Case 525. The complete set of reports in connection with this case in "Court Cases 1881-1882", is: Court Cases 525, 529.

1039. A false bottom can obviously be presented as a suspicious matter, indicating that one wants to hide something from the authorities. Equally, it can indicate that one wants to hide valuables from potential thieves.

1040. Leung A-tsau was appointed Chinese Clerk and Shroff on 15 October 1881 (HKGBB, 1881).

1041. Bedell Lee Yung (listed as "Bedell Ayune" in the Blue Book for 1862) was first appointed to the Hong Kong Government on 1 November 1861. (See the HKGBB for 1869, pp. 105-106 [208-209].) From 1862 at least, his entire subsequent career in the Hong Kong Government was spent in the Police Magistrates' Court, although additional responsibilities were added. In 1862, he was Assistant Chinese Interpreter; from at least 1867 he was second Chinese Interpreter; and he was promoted to First Chinese Interpreter on 1 March 1876, continuing in this position up to 1886 or early 1887 when he is no longer listed on the Government's establishment.

From 1 October 1868 (see Blue Book for 1872) up to 1878 or early 1879, he was also Interpreter of the Fire Brigade.

From 1876 up to 1886 or early 1887, he was also Clerk and Chinese Interpreter to the Coroner.

1042. Presumably, a permanent notice or advertisement usually hung outside the defendant's premises, such as those that can be seen today in English, "Old books wanted", "We buy used clothes. Best prices paid".

1043. Court Case 529. *CM*, Monday, 9 January 1882, p. 3, c. 6.

1044. The following information appears in the Criminal Calendar for the January Sessions, 1882, *HKGG*, 4 February 1882, p. 61, where this case is No. Eight.

Kan A-kut was tried on 18 January on two counts, 1) Selling counterfeit coin and 2) Being in possession of counterfeit coin.

He was found not guilty of 1) Selling counterfeit coin and not guilty of 2) Being in possession of counterfeit coin. The jurors voted six to one on the second count.

Kan A-kut was discharged.

The *CM* report of the Supreme Court Criminal Sessions shows that the case was tried, "Before His Honour the Acting Puisne Judge, J. Russell, Esq.", with the following jury: Messrs A. W. Mactavish, E. A. Jorge, A. H. M. da Silva, J. M. do Rozario, G. A. Wieler, J. B. Gomes, and E. Holst. Mr Mackean prosecuted on behalf of the Attorney General. The report reads as follows:

"Counterfeit Coin Case

"Kow Akut [*sic*] was charged with selling two counterfeit dollars to one Ng Ahoi, at less value than they purported to bear, on the 3rd of January; and on a second count, with having in his possession a number of counterfeit coins.

"Evidence was given by an informer to the effect that the prisoner had sold him two counterfeit dollars, and Inspector Perry proved finding the coins in his possession.

"The defendant said he went about teaching the occupation of shroffing, and two witnesses attested to this statement.

"His Lordship pointed out to the jury that there was not much reliance to be placed on the statement of the informer, as it was unsupported.

"The jury after some deliberation found the prisoner not guilty unanimously on the first count; and not guilty by six to one on the second." (*China Mail*, Wednesday, 18 January 1882.)

1045. *CM*, Saturday, 28 January 1882, p. 3, c. 2.

1046. Court Case 577.

1047. According to Crisswell and Watson, No. One Police Station was located in Percival Street, Happy Valley. (Crisswell and Watson, *The Royal Hong Kong Police*, *op. cit.*, Appendix One.)

1048. CC new Number 695. "Local and General," *CM*, 17 March 1882, p. 3, c. 2.

1049. *Sic* for "Poor".

1050. *CM*, Monday, 23 January 1882, p. 3.

1051. See Geoffrey Roper, "The Police Role in Magistrate Frederick Stewart's Court", above.

1052. *CM*, 19 January 1882, p. 3.

1053. The Blue Book for 1881 lists Chan A-fook, appointed Acting Second Clerk at the Magistracy on 10 September 1881, stating that he was first appointed to the Hong Kong Government on 1 January 1867. In the Blue Book for 1867, "Chun A Fuk" is listed as Chinese Registration Clerk, Registrar General's Office. Immediately previous to this, the Blue Book for 1880 lists him as Third Clerk, Surveyor General's Department. Some years later, in the Blue Book for 1888, he is listed as Second Clerk, Public Works Department.

The two men in this account are distinguishable by the fact that one has a "k" at the end of his name, whereas the other does not.

1054. *CM*, 28 November 1881, p. 3, cc. 2-3.

1055. *Sic.*

1056. *CM*, Monday, 23 January 1882, p. 3, cc. 3-4, c. 3.

1057. *Ibid.*

1058. Court Case 347. The complete set of reports in connection with this case in "Court Cases 1881-1882", is: Court Cases 347, 356.

1059. In the reports of this case, this name is given as both "Blockhead" and "Blackhead".

1060. The original says variably, "pig" and "pigs".

1061. Original does have "of Mr Smith's"; an error in syntax.

1062. Court Case 356.

1063. It was unusual for a case to be reported the day *after* it was heard. Usually, cases are reported the same day or not at all.

1064. "Hung Ham": *sic* for "Hung Hom".

1065. The "Criminal Calendar – November Sessions, 1881", published in *HKGG*, 26 November 1881, p. 1043, lists this case as No. Five. Chan A-po was charged with "unlawfully and maliciously destroying and damaging certain Saplings and Shrubs, the property of John Henry Smith". The day of trial was 18 November 1881. The verdict or plea was "guilty". Chan A-po was sentenced on 24 November 1881 to six calendar months' imprisonment with hard labour.

The *CM* report of the Criminal Sessions of the Supreme Court, before the Acting Chief Justice, the Hon. Francis Snowden, on Friday, 18 November 1881, names the jury as consisting of Messrs J. R. White, F. D. Bush, C. Danenberg, J. Gourlay, J. d'Almeida [*sic*], L. D. Collaço and J. Edgar, and reports that,

"Chan Apo, a gardener, was charged with destroying flowers and vegetables belonging to Mr J. H. Smith, of the firm of Blackhead & Co. He pleaded not guilty. This case was fully reported when it was before the Police Court, and the evidence given today was to the same effect. The Jury returned a unanimous verdict of guilty, and sentence was deferred."

In its report of the Criminal Sessions of Thursday, 24 November 1881, *CM* states that, "Chan Apo, convicted of wilful and malicious damage to the garden of his employer, received six months' imprisonment with hard labour."

1066. Court Case 422. The complete set of reports in connection with this case in "Court Cases 1881-1882", is: Court Cases 422, 444, 473, 482, 491.

1067. The house is identified elsewhere in *CM* as that of "Mr Chan Afuk, second clerk in the Magistracy". His brother was the person at home at the time of the armed robbery and the person, therefore, who appears as a witness.

1068. The following variations of this name occur in the reports of this case: "Easur Singh" and "Eassur Singh".

1069. "Pokfulum": *sic*.

1070. *CM*, 28 November 1881, p. 3, cc. 2-3.

1071. "Purlin": a horizontal beam along the length of a roof, resting on principals and supporting the common rafters or boards. (*Oxford Encyclopedic English Dictionary*, 1991.)

1072. "Pok-fu Lam": *sic*.

1073. In the reports of this case, this name is given as both "Easur" and "Eassur".

1074. Court Case 444.

1075. Court Case 473.

1076. The original mistakenly uses the word, "deceased's", twice, once in mistake for "witness's". From elsewhere in *CM*, it seems that the witness's beat was Number One, and hence, the deceased's beat was Number Two.

1077. This translation is provided in *CM* report.

1078. In the reports of this case, this name is given as both "Chang Au Fuk" and "Chan Afoo". This is the gentleman who was in the house when it was attacked. As we know from elsewhere in *CM*, he was the master of an opium shop in Stanley and the brother of the house-owner.

1079. Court Case 482.

1080. That is, the man whose house was attacked. See above.

1081. Original has "P. C. Duncan, 21". It was not usual to give the ages of the policemen, although the ages of defendants were frequently given. Perhaps what was meant was "Duncan, P. C. 21", but perhaps his initials were not known and this led to confusion?

1082. Court Case 491.

1083. *CM* report of the Criminal Sessions (19 January 1882, p. 3, c. 4 and 23 January 1882, p. 3, cc. 3-4) names three of these men as Lai Aloi, Ng Akow, and Chun Atak.

This enables us to identify the listing in the "Criminal Calendar – January Sessions, 1882", *HKGG*, 4 February 1882, p. 61, as No. Eleven.

This states that Li A-loi, 'Ng [*sic*] A-kau and Chung A-tak were charged on five counts, the first of burglary, the second, third and fourth of larceny and the fifth of receiving stolen goods. The day of the trial was 19 January 1882 and all the prisoners were found guilty on the first count, and not guilty on the second, third, fourth and fifth counts. Sentence was given on 23 January 1882, and each was sentenced to twelve years' penal servitude.

1084. A. D. Blue, "Piracy on the China Coast", *JRAS (HK)*, Vol. V, pp. 69-85, p. 75.)

1085. James Hayes, "The Hong Kong Region", *JRAS (HK)*, Vol. 14, 1974, Hong Kong, 1974, pp.108-135, p. 121.

1086. James Hayes, "The Hong Kong Region", *op. cit.*, p. 123.

1087. Christopher Munn, "The Criminal Trial", *op. cit.*, pp. 57-58.

1088. *Ibid.*, pp. 57-58.

1089. E. J. Eitel, *Europe in China, op. cit.*, p. 409.

1090. *Ibid.*, p. 451.

1091. James Hayes, "The Hong Kong Region", *op. cit.*, p. 123.

1092. Iaian Ward, *Sui Geng, op. cit.*, p. 21.

1093. Patrick Hase, talk given to the Royal Asiatic Society at the City Hall, Hong Kong, 1999-2000.

1094. Ordinance "For the Rendition in Certain Cases of Chinese subjects charged with Piracy", No. 13 of 1865. See *HKGG*, 8 July 1865, p. 410 (only).

1095. Iaian Ward, *Sui Geng, op. cit.*, p. 22.

1096. Christopher Munn, "The Criminal Trial", *op. cit.*, p. 62.

1097. *The Daily Press*, 5 January 1882.

1098. James Legge, "The Colony of Hong Kong", *op. cit.*, pp. 179-180.

1099. E. J. Eitel, *Europe in China, op. cit.*, p. 452.

1100. James Hayes, "The Hong Kong Region", *op. cit.*, p. 123.

1101. Iaian Ward, *Sui Geng, op. cit.*, p. 32.

1102. *Ibid.*, p. 34.

1103. *Ibid.*, p. 58.

1104. *Ibid.*, p. 58.

1105. *Ibid.*, p. 58.

1106. *Ibid.*, p. 7.

1107. Since the four cases included acts of piracy committed on each of

28 and 30 November, and since, also, the first three are specifically stated to have occurred on 28 November 1881, the fourth must have occurred on 30 November 1881.

1108. The Supreme Court hearing names it as a junk.

1109. This familiarity may not necessarily have been from events prior to the present case. For, as reported, they ask no questions of the complainant in the first and second cases, one only in the third, and several in the fourth. This may not, as suggested in the present writer's essay, reflect the level of concern they felt about the evidence of the different witnesses, but the learning curve they experienced during the present sequence of cases. A further possible interpretation is that it reflects either the interest of the reporter or his (partly mistaken) understanding of the significance of the four cases,

1110. To a person unfamiliar with police procedure, this is a little puzzling, since this would put the date at 21 December 1881, whereas the boat was searched by Inspector Swanston several days previously, 2 December 1881.

1111. *CM*, Wednesday, 18 January 1882, p. 3, cc. 2-3, c. 2.

1112. It is not made quite clear that this was done in court, rather then at the same time as identifying the boat at Shaukiwan. Perhaps it was done on both occasions.

1113. *CM*, Monday, 23 January 1882, p. 3, cc. 3-4.

1114. *Ibid.*

1115. There is a strong similarity with the family scene on a boat, formerly shown in the Hong Kong Museum of History, when in Kowloon Park.

1116. TGN, p. 193.

1117. Missing question-marks are silently supplied to the original reports. The convention, "By . . ." means, "in response to a question by . . .".

1118. "Police Intelligence," *CM*, Saturday, 10 December 1881, p. 3, cc. 4-5.

1119. Court Case 452. The complete set of reports in connection with this case in "Court Cases 1881-1882", is: Court Cases 452, 483, 508, 520. None of these relates to the earlier arrest of the men on two charges, anchoring in a place not authorised by the Harbour Master, and with being rogues and vagabonds and dangerous to the peace and good order of the Colony.

1120. At the later Supreme Court hearing, Inspector Swanston gives evidence of having searched the defendants' boat on 2 December, when at Shaukiwan.

1121. Court Case 483. "Police Intelligence," *CM*, Saturday, 17 December 1881, p. 3, cc. 2-3.

1122. In the report of the Supreme Court hearing, the boatwoman's name is given as, "Toat Shing" throughout.

1123. *Sic* for "Tai O", the spelling given in the report of the hearing at the Supreme Court. For variations, "Tyhoo" and "Tyho", see James Hayes, "The Hong Kong Region", *op. cit.*, p. 124, n. 2. In the Supreme Court hearings, Tai O is described as, "near Iu Kok, the S. W. point of Lantow [*sic* for "Lantau"] Island".

1124. The Supreme Court hearings identify this as a junk.

1125. *Sic* for "Ma Wan"?

1126. Sun On is the district of China, within Canton Province, to which Hong Kong belongs. (Hal Empson, *Mapping Hong Kong*, *op. cit.*, p. 12, c. 2.)

1127. Peng Chau, off southeast Lantau, seems to have been familiar with pirates. An inscribed tablet, dated 1834, outside the Tin Hau Temple there, records a petition from fishermen against the local officials' practise of using their craft as decoys to catch pirates. (See James Hayes, "The Hong Kong Region", *op. cit.*, p. 123.)

1128. *Sic*: "pirate" not "pirates".

1129. Corrected from the original, which has "than".

1130. The report of the Supreme Court hearing describes this more clearly: – "His crew had been previously nailed down by the pirates, and therefore he had no assistance from then."

1131. The following variations occur in the newspaper reports of this case: Puk Sing, Li Pak Shing. We know that both these refer to the same gentleman, because both Court Case 508 and the report of the Supreme Court hearing use the version, Li Pak Shing, and because the two latter reports and Court Case 483 (this present report), together, establish that Puk Sing and Li Pak Shing are the same person.

1132. The later Supreme Court hearing gives the date as 13 November.

1133. There is no report of this hearing published on either Saturday 24 or Monday 27 December 1881.

1134. Court Case 508. "Police Intelligence," *CM*, Wednesday, 28 December 1881, p. 3, cc. 3-4.

1135. The following variations occur in the newspaper reports of this case: Puk Sing, Li Pak Shing. See also note above.

1136. *Sic*.

1137. Court Case 520. *CM*, Wednesday, 4 January 1882, p. 3, cc. 4-5.

1138. The following information appears in the Criminal Calendar for the January Sessions, 1882, *HKGG*, 4 February 1882, p. 61, where this case, tried on 18 January 1882, appears as Nos. 9 and 10.

As Case No. 9, 1) Wong A-fuk [*sic*], 2) Lung A-fong, 3) Wong A-yiu, 4) Wong Mun Tong, 5) Wong A-hoi and 6) Ching A-u were tried on the two following counts of 1) Piracy and Assault and 2) Receiving goods piratically stolen.

1) Wong A-fuk [*sic*], 2) Lung A-fong, 3) Wong A-yiu and 5) Wong A-hoi were found guilty of receiving goods piratically stolen and not guilty of piracy and assault. 4) Wong Mun Tong and 6) Ching A-u were found guilty on both counts.

Sentence was given on 23 January 1882.

4) Wong Mun Tong and 6) Ching A-u were sentenced to six years' penal servitude each on the first count, and four years' penal servitude each on

the second count to be concurrent with sentence on first count. This sentence to take effect after expiration of the sentences past [*sic*] on the same prisoners in case No. 10.

1) Wong A-fuk [*sic*], 2) Lung A-fong, 3) Wong A-yiu and 5) Wong A-hoi were sentenced to four years' penal servitude each to take effect after expiration of the sentence passed on the same prisoners, in case No. 10.

<u>As Case No. 10</u>, 1) Wong A-fuk [*sic*], 2) Lung A-fong, 3) Wong A-yiu, 4) Wong Mun Tong, 5) Wong A-hoi and 6) Ching A-u were tried on the two counts of 1) Piracy and Assault and 2) Receiving goods piratically stolen.

1) Wong A-fuk [*sic*], 3) Wong A-yiu, 4) Wong Mun Tong and 5) Wong A-hoi were found guilty of 2) Receiving goods piratically stolen and not guilty of 1) Piracy and assault.

2) Lung A-fong and 6) Ching A-u were found guilty of both 1) Piracy and Assault and 2) Receiving goods piratically stolen.

2) Lung A-fong and 6) Ching A-u were sentenced to six years' penal servitude for 1) Piracy and Assault and four years' penal servitude for 2) Receiving goods piratically stolen to be concurrent with their sentence for 1) Piracy and Assault.

1) Wong A-fuk [*sic*], 3) Wong A-yiu, 4) Wong Mun Tong and 5) Wong A-hoi were sentenced to four years' penal servitude each.

1139. See also "Urban Life", above.

1140. See "Wives and Husbands, Amahs and Cooks, Widows and Protected Women, Sons and Adopted Daughters. Burglars. The Domestic Scene," above, for a reference to the bar at 208 Queen's Road managed by Mr and Mrs M'Breen.

1141. See also "Urban Life", above.

1142. Sally Rodwell, "Monuments from 19th-Century Colonial Hong Kong", in *Historic Hong Kong*, Hong Kong, Odyssey Guides, 1991, 2nd printing, 1992, pp. 68-95.

1143. See also "Urban Life", above.

1144. Anthony Dyson, *From Timeball to Atomic Clock*, Hong Kong, Hong Kong Government, 1983, p. 23.

1145. See Tim Hamlett, "Reporting the Cases of Frederick Stewart", above.

1146. See Geoffrey Roper, "The Police Role in Magistrate Frederick Stewart's Court", above.

1147. See *Ibid*.

1148. See Garry Tallentire, "The Hong Kong (Police) Magistrate in the 1880s and 1990s", above and Christoper Coghlan, "Thoughts about the Practice of Law in Hong Kong", above.

1149. Geoffrey Roper, "The Police Role in Magistrate Frederick Stewart's Court", above.

1150. See Garry Tallentire, "The Hong Kong (Police) Magistrate in the 1880s and 1990s", above.

1151. See Christopher Coghlan, "Thoughts about the Practice of Law in Hong Kong", above.

1152. Garry Tallentire, "The Hong Kong (Police) Magistrate in the 1880s and 1990s", above.

1153. *Ibid.*

1154. See Verner Bickley, "Differing Perceptions of Social Reality in Dr Stewart's Court", above.

1155. Unintended by society, that is.

1156. Harold Traver, "Crime Trends," *Crime and Justice in Hong Kong*, 1991, pp. 10-24, p. 23.

[1157] See also the Appendix, "The Excise Ordinance (Opium) 1858-1879, Amendment Ordinance 1879: Selections to explain the opium and opium-related cases before Frederick Stewart, July 1881 to March 1882". Referred to after this as, "The Excise Ordinance (Opium) 1858-1879".

[1158] See also the Appendix, "The Excise Ordinance (Opium) 1858-1879".

[1159] The amendments to section 7 of Ordinance No. 2 of 1858, effected by Ordinance No. 7 of 1879, had resulted in the following wording: "It shall be the duty of every person selling or retailing prepared opium under this Ordinance [i.e. Ordinance No. 2 of 1858], to deliver therewith a sealed certificate, specifying the amount so sold; which certificate shall be evidence of the facts therein stated, and shall not be transferable and shall contain a notice printed in English and Chinese, in the following form: —

'Notice is hereby given that the monopoly of the Hong Kong opium farm, at present held by the undersigned, expires on the ...., and that the boiled or prepared opium now purchased and sold cannot be legally used or retained in your possession after noon of the 3rd day from the above date, without the consent of the new holder of the monopoly or of the Governor. [There follow three blank lines for signatures.]'"

[1160] This relates to Paragraph 6, which was repealed by Ordinance No. 7 of 1879 and so does not apply to these 1881-1882 cases.

[1161] "Treatment of Paupers in Hong Kong", 22 April 1880, in HKGG, 9 June 1880, pp. 466-473.

[1162] "If any charge or complaint shall be preferred under 'the Excise Ordinance (Opium) 1858-1879' or under any of the said regulations made thereunder and upon the said charge or compliant the accused shall be convicted, the pecuniary penalty imposed upon the offender shall, after the adjudication of a portion of the same not exceeding one half at the discretion of the Magistrate to the informer, be paid to the holder of the exclusive privilege, and all the boiled or prepared opium to which the same relates shall be forfeited and by the magistrate adjudged and delivered to the holder of the privilege." (Ordinance No. 7 of 1879, para. X.)

[1163] Section 9 of Ordinance No. 2 of 1858 reads as follows:

"Power to issue search warrants upon lawful evidence of facts." "Upon lawful evidence being first given to the reasonable satisfaction of a Stipendiary Magistrate or the Superintendent of Police (duly constituted under Ordinance No. 12 of 1844), that any person within this Colony or the waters thereof hath in his possession or custody any opium contrary to section 8, or any opium prepared, sold, or retailed, contrary to this Ordinance, it shall be lawful for the said Magistrate or Superintendent to issue a search warrant in that behalf, and under such warrant any member of the Police Force may enter any tenement, place, or vessel, within this Colony or the waters thereof, and search for, and (if found) seize and hold, subject to the order of the Court hereinafter mentioned, any prepared opium within such tenement, place, or vessel, and whereof no satisfactory explanation shall have been given by the person aforesaid." (Section 9 of Ordinance No. 2 of 1858.)

NB Section 8 of Ordinance No. 2 of 1858 was partly repealed by and partly amended by Ordinance No. 7 of 1879. Section 8 of Ordinance No. 2 of 1858, among other points, refers to Section 7 of Ordinance No. 2, which was itself amended by Ordinance No. 7 of 1879.

The amendments resulted in the following wording: "No person shall bring into this Colony, or the waters thereof, or (except in cases to which section 7 applies) have in his possession or custody within the same, any boiled prepared opium without having a valid certificate under section 7 of Ordinance No. 2 of 1858, as amended."

And the amendments to section 7 of Ordinance No. 2 of 1858, effected by Ordinance No. 7 of 1879, resulted in the following wording: "It shall be the duty of every person selling or retailing prepared opium under this Ordinance [i.e. Ordinance No. 2 of 1858], to deliver therewith a sealed certificate, specifying the amount so sold; which certificate shall be evidence of the facts therein stated, and shall not be transferable and shall contain a notice printed in English and Chinese, in the following form: —
'Notice is hereby given that the monopoly of the Hong Kong opium farm, at present held by the undersigned, expires on the ...., and that the boiled or prepared opium now purchased and sold cannot be legally used or retained in your possession after noon of the 3rd day form the above date, without the consent of the new holder of the monopoly or of the Governor. [There follow three blank lines for signatures.]'"

[1164] This relates to Paragraph 6, which was repealed by Ordinance No. 7 of 1879 and so does not apply to these 1880-1881 cases.

[1165] "From henceforward, no person not holding any such privilege or licence, or save as he may be by such privilege or licence in that behalf authorized, shall, within this Colony or the waters thereof, boil or in any way prepare opium, or sell, retail, or offer or expose for sale or retail, any boiled or prepared opium; yet so that no medical practitioner, chemist, or druggist, not being a Chinaman, or (being such) not having an European or American diploma, shall be prevented from preparing or selling opium *bona fide* for medicinal purposes, the burthen of proof whereof shall be upon any person alleging the same in his defence." (Ordinance No. 2 of 1858, para. 5.)

[1166] See CC 127.

[1167] See again CC 127.

[1168] E.g. CC 232.

[1169] J. R. Eames, *The English in China*, London, Curzon Press, 1909, new impression, 1974, p. 564. Referred to after this as, "J. R. Eames, *The English in China*".

[1170] Eitel — inaccurately, it seems — gives 185<u>3</u> as the date when the "present state of legitimate commerce" began, attributing it as arising "through the decision of the Chinese Government to legalise the importation of opium." (*Europe in China*, p. 274.) But this may quite possibly be a typographical error. A later historian, G. B. Endacott implies that legalization occurred during the Governorship of Sir Hercules Robinson (for which he gives the dates, September 1859 to March 1865) (G. B. Endacott, *A History of Hong Kong*, Oxford University Press, 1964, p. 327). The Index to Geoffrey Robley Sayer, *Hong Kong 1841-1862: Birth, Adolescence and Coming of Age*, Hong Kong University Press, 1980, reprint of the original 1937 edition, published by Oxford University Press under the title *Hong Kong: Birth, Adolescence and Coming of Age*, lists, "Opium: legalized by tariff convention of 1858" (p. 229). The text referred to reads as follows: "In 1858, consequent, one presumes, on the legalization of the import of opium into China, an opium monopoly was reintroduced in Hong Kong for the first time since its abandonment in 1848." (G. R. Sayer, p. 185.)

[1171] J. R. Eames, *The English in China*, 1909, pp. 564-566.

[1172] J. R. Eames, *The English in China*, 1909, p. 542.

[1173] J. R. Eames, *The English in China*, 1909, p. 543.

[1174] J. R. Eames, *The English in China*, 1909, p. 543.

[1175] J. R. Eames, *The English in China*, 1909, p. 543.

[1176] Of Ordinance No. 22 of 1887, Traver and Gaylord write that it was passed in response to treaty requirements and they take the view that its role was entirely symbolic. Its net effect was, they write, "an incease in the flow of opium to China and a rise in the value of the opium monopoly." In their view, the next major piece of legislation on this topic was the Ordinance passed in 1909. (Traver, Harold H. "Colonial Relations and Opium Control Policy in Hong Kong, 1841-1945", in Traver, Harold H and Mark S. Gaylord, *Drugs, Law and the State*, University of Washington Press, 1991, pp. 135-148, p. 142.)

[1177] See Ordinance No. 1 of 1879, paras 2, 3, 4, 5, 6; and Ordinance No. 7 of 1879, sections III, IV, V, VI, VII.

[1178] E. J. Eitel has useful information about the sums gained by the Hong Kong Government through the sale of the opium monopoly and he also refers to a Commission appointed by Governor Sir Arthur Kennedy on 8 June 1872, "to enquire into the working of the opium monopoly, because there was very good reason to suppose that the amount received from this farm was far short of what it ought to have realized." (*Europe in China*, p. 485.) Eitel states that from 1858 until 1878, the monopoly had been "held by a Chinese syndicate in Hongkong at an unfairly low rate". (*Europe in China*, p. 536.)

[1179] See HKGN No. 12, dated 21 January 1879, HKGG, 22 January 1879, p. 28. With effect from 28 February 1879, The Opium Farm was leased for 3 years to Mr Banhap by his Attorney, Mr Tan-King-Sing, for the sum of $205,000 p.a. (Presumably this means that Mr Tan-King-Sing acted for Mr Banhap in this transaction.) E. J. Eitel describes Mr Tan-King-Sing as "a partner of the Singapore Syndicate" and states that the public was not satisfied with the manner in which the monopoly was sold. (*Europe in China*, p. 536.)

[1180] HKGN No. 55, "Sale of the Opium Farm", HKGG, 11 February 1882, p. 126.

[1181] HKGN No. 221, HKGG, 13 May 1882, p. 475.

[1182] "Supplementary Conditions, made by the Governor in Council, to which licenses granted under the Excise Ordinances (Opium), 1858-1879, are to be subject", HKGG, 13 May 1882, pp. 475-476.

[1183] E. J. Eitel describes the establishment in 1844 of a short-lived earlier Opium Monopoly, replaced in 1845 by a system of opium retail licences (*Europe in China*, pp. 235-236, 265) and refers to the re-establishment of the opium monopoly by Governor Sir John Bowring on 1 April 1858 (*Europe in China*, p. 336).

The first holders of the renewed monopoly seem to be those named in HKGN No. 26, 23 March 1858, *Gazette Extraordinary*, 23 March 1858, pp. 1-5, p. 5, where we read: "Privilege for Sale of Prepared Opium" granted to Chun-Tai-Kwong of the Man-Cheong shop for Twelve Months from 1 April 1858.

[1184] This relates to Paragraph 6, which was repealed by Ordinance No. 7 of 1879 and so does not apply to these 1881-1882 cases.

[1185] Section 9 of Ordinance No. 2 of 1858 reads as follows: "Power to issue search warrants upon lawful evidence of facts." "Upon lawful evidence being first given to the reasonable satisfaction of a Stipendiary Magistrate or the Superintendent of Police (duly constituted under Ordinance No. 12 of 1844), that any person within this Colony or the waters thereof hath in his possession or custody any opium contrary to section 8, or any opium prepared, sold, or retailed, contrary to this Ordinance, it shall be lawful for the said Magistrate or Superintendent to issue a search warrant in that behalf, and under such warrant any member of the Police Force may enter any tenement, place, or vessel, within this Colony or the waters thereof, and search for, and (if found) seize and hold, subject to the order of the Court hereinafter mentioned, any prepared opium within such tenement, place, or vessel, and whereof no satisfactory explanation shall have been given by the person aforesaid."

NB Section 8 of Ordinance No. 2 of 1858 was partly repealed by and partly amended by Ordinance No. 7 of 1879. Section 8 of Ordinance No. 2 of 1858, among other points, refers to Section 7 of Ordinance No. 2, which was itself amended by Ordinance No. 7 of 1879. The amendments resulted in the following wording: "No person shall bring into this Colony, or the waters thereof, or (except in cases to which section 7 applies) have in his possession or custody within the same, any boiled prepared opium without having a valid certificate under section 7 of Ordinance No. 2 of 1858, as amended."

And the amendments to section 7 of Ordinance No. 2 of 1858, effected by Ordinance No. 7 of 1879, resulted in the following wording: "It shall be the duty of every person selling or retailing prepared opium under this Ordinance [i.e. Ordinance No. 2 of 1858], to deliver therewith a sealed certificate, specifying the amount so sold; which certificate shall be evidence of the facts therein stated, and shall not be transferable and shall contain a notice printed in English and Chinese, in the following form: --

'Notice is hereby given that the monopoly of the Hong Kong opium farm, at present held by the undersigned, expires on the ...., and that the boiled or prepared opium now purchased and sold cannot be legally used or retained in your possession after noon of the 3rd day from the above date, without the consent of the new holder of the monopoly or of the Governor. [There follow three blank lines for signatures.]'"

[1186] A template for appointing such an excise officer is given in Schedule B.

1187. This seems to be the discussion of slavery in Hong Kong, written by E. J. Eitel, which Sir John Smale states was written on behalf of the Chinese community, and referred to in "Sir John Smale on the Evils of Hong Kong", *CM*, 26 January 1882, p. 3, cc. 6-7, c. 7. (Report of a speech given to members of the National Association for the Promotion of Social Science on 21 November 1881.)

Mentioned by John Bramston (July 1880) as subsequently having appeared in *The China Review*. (CO/129/187/107v.)

1188. Crisswell and Watson, *The Royal Hong Kong Police*, *op. cit.*, p. 14.

~~~~

Captions for page 6, back & front cover

Page 6. Top left: Botanical Gardens (previously known as Public Gardens). Young Chinese men, gardeners and amah with western toddler. Top right: Chinese shroffs testing for counterfeit silver coins; The shroffs took up two coins at a time, poised on the tips of their fingers, then struck and sounded them to detect the tone of base metal. – Although Hong Kong's British royal coinage was introduced as early as 1863, foreign coins, especially Mexican silver dollars, continued to circulate alongside them until the early 20th century. Bottom left: Ng Choy (1842-1922), c. 1880. Also known as Wu Ting Fang. The first Chinese Barrister and Member of the Legislative Council in Hong Kong. Bottom right: Chinese merchant in the foreground, western woman with young girls (one Chinese, two western) in Wellington Street, crowded with pedestrians. The bilingual signboards advertise millinery, drapery, cigars, cigarettes, sedan chairs and bamboo.

Cover. Front: The Supreme Court Hong Kong (second building) in recent times (now housing the Hong Kong Legislative Council). Back: Coloured German woodblock engraving of the Pedder Street clocktower (erected in 1863 but now removed), at its intersection with Queen's Road Central. Background: The Supreme Court Hong Kong (second building) shortly after completion. The photograph also shows the Hong Kong Club and Queen Victoria's statue (now relocated to Victoria Park, Causeway Bay, Hong Kong).

Index

(main text)

Booth, Revd C. Gilbert (Military Chaplain), 205, 206

Bolton Abbey (ship), 184, 185

Bonham, Sir George, 54

Bonham Strand, 472

Böning, G.D., 60

Botanical Gardens, 44, 232, 384

Bowen, Sir George, 32

Bowring, Dr, 54

Bramston, John, 35, 441, 442, 509

branding, 25, 34, 55, 56, 57, 60, 61, 62, 65, 124

Bremer, Commodore, 51

Brereton and Wotton, 202, 492

Breslin, Philip (Able Seaman), 188

British Empire, 7, 205, 263

Brothel, Mui Lan, 305, 307

Brothels, Registered, Inspector of, 130, 245, 246, 284, 294, 295, 309

Brothel bouncer(s) / bully(ies), 97, 100, 105, 109, 111, 112, 269, 278

Brothels closed, 274

Brothel keeper(s) / manager(s) / mistress(es), 14, 167, 269, 270, 271, 294, 295

Brothels, licensed / registered, 106, 135, 273, 276

Brothels, licensing ceased, 463

Brothels, locations of, 270, 272, 280, 283, 284

Brothels, unlicensed / illegal, 14, 265, 270, 273, 275

Brown, Christini, 271, 283

Bryant, John (boatswain), 41, 201, 202

Bryant, Samuel (ship's fireman), 41, 201, 202

Bryce, Mr W. (3rd engineer), 192

Buffs (Army Regiment), 207

Bury, Captain, 207

Butlin, John (Police Sergeant), 103, 195, 236

Butterfield & Swire, 198

Byramjee, Mr D., 210-215

C

Caine Road, 253, 266, 277, 281, 333, 341

Caine, James (seaman), 194

Caine, William (Captain of the 29th Cameronian Regiment, Police Magistrate HK), 32, 51, 87

Caldwell, Richard, 324

Cameron, Inspector, 355

Campbell, Sergeant, 104, 232

Cannron (aka Cannon, Cameron), George (seaman), 184

Canberra (ship), 365

Canton, 51, 52, 53, 73, 74, 92, 94, 190, 221, 224, 232, 233, 234, 242, 264, 268, 280, 282, 289, 291, 294, 304, 305, 307, 324, 346, 379, 385, 394, 401, 404, 405

Canton Authorities, the, 242

Canton Bazaar, 405

Canton Medal (1857), 221

Canton steamer, 280, 401, 405

Canton Register, The, 324

Canton Wharf, 190

Cantonese (language), 22, 49, 73, 74, 106, 134, 379

Cape Collinson, 184
Cape D'Aguilar, 184
Capitulino Priamo Marçal, 173
Carnarvon, Earl of, 56
Carysfort, HMS., 195
Cassumbhoy, Mr, 252
Catholic Register, The, 265
Catholic Truth Society, The, 106
Centre Street, 111, 260, 329
Central Market, 334, 337
Central Magistracy, 107, 385
Central Police Station, 22, 103, 106, 114, 149, 150, 181, 289, 302, 334, 352, 359
*Central School: does it justify its raison d'être?,*45
Central Station, 194, 247, 249, 252, 300, 302, 357, 359
Centre Street, 111, 260, 329
Chan Acheung, 72, 73, 304, 343
Chan Afoo, 353, 361, 362
Chan Afuk, 353, 358, 359, 499
Chan Ahoi, 343
Chan Akan, 317
Chan Akok (District Watchman), 226
Chan Alam, 275
Chan Ang, 301
Chan Asai, 337, 492
Chan Asan, 249
Chan Ayan, 281
Chan Cheung, 342
Chan Chung Hing, 372
Chan Hing, 289, 300
Chan Man Kam, 290
Chan Mui, 339
Chan Nui, 72, 73, 291, 292, 293, 294, 304, 305
Chan, Samson, 61

Chan Sing (District Watchman), 226
Chan Yau Mui, 288
Chang Au Fuk, 357
Chang Apo, 355, 356
Cheung On Lane, 299, 300
Cheong Alam, 242
Cheong Tak-fong (aka Cheong Yak Fong), 281
Cheung, Akwai, 338
Cheung Chau, 140, 141, 366
Cheung Kong Centre, 205
Cheung On Lane (Sai-Ying-Pun), 299, 300
China Mail, 19, 20, 22, 29, 31, 32, 39, 40, 46, 47, 48, 57, 58, 60, 62, 64, 69, 75, 77, 92, 93, 95, 98, 103, 108, 117, 118, 119, 121, 123, 124, 127, 128, 129, 131, 134, 173, 175, 176, 180, 181, 205, 207, 208, 220, 221, 222, 223, 265, 266, 269, 272, 286, 289, 314, 315, 323, 327, 328, 352, 377, 400, 409, 415
China Review, The, 64
Chinese Festivals, 291, 304
Chinese Manchu Empire, 223
Chinese police constables (*lukwongs*), 327, 328
Ching Agan, 254
Chiu Apo, 236
Chiu Ayau, 338
Chiu Ayuk, 341
Cho Aluk, 327
Chow Young Chan, 279, 281
Chu Apin, 261
Chu Aping, 259, 342
Chü Tak Mong (Revd), 232, 236, 237
Chu Atam, 259
Chu Azing, 236

G

Gage Street, 266, 283
Garrison Theatre, 205, 206
Geddes, Lieutenant Colonel Andrew David (Royal Inniskillings), 42, 209
George, HRH Prince (son of Queen Victoria), 206
Gibb, the Hon. H.G., 92
Gilman & Company, 184
Glaholm, John, 196
Glenelg (ship), 204
Gleniffer (ship), 200
Golden Needle: the Biography of Frederick Stewart (1836-1889) (by Gillian Bickley), 18
Gomes, E.J., 345
Government Civil Hospital, 186, 190, 282, 334, 349
Graham Street, 334, 346
Grant, C. (Manager, Kelly & Walsh, HK), 320
Grant, J.C. (Police Sergeant), 357
Grastin, Henry, 203
Great Britain, 7, 22, 54, 66
Greenberg, Joseph, 274
Greenstang, Nocheum, 104, 274
Grey, Earl (British statesman), 88, 89
Grey, Inspector, 360
Gustave, H., 65, 340

H

Ha Wan Market, 334, 341
Hacker, Arthur, 272,
Haines, William (seaman), 195
Hamlett, Timothy, 3, 4, 5
Hansen, George (ship's fireman), 194
Harmsworth, St. John, 80
Haines, William (seaman), 197

Hansen, George, 192
Happy Valley, 76, 208, 239, 252, 324, 334, 360, 384
Haye, Colvin, 18
Hayhoe, Dr Ruth, 18
Heerman, C. O., 369
Helen Marion (ship), 185, 186, 187, 188, 189, 190
Hennessy, Sir John Pope (HK Governor), 31, 35, 124
Herbert, Mr, 36, 190, 198
Hewart, Lord, 79
High Street, 233
Hill, Police Constable, 360
Hillier, C.B., 37
Hilton Hotel, 205
History of Hong Kong (by G. B. Endacott), 134
History of the Laws and Courts of Hong Kong (by Norton Kysshe), 17
Ho Achi, 281
Ho Amang, 347
Ho Apak, 234
Ho Apui, 233
Ho Asing, 183
Ho Ayau, 275
Hollywood Road, 36,59, 105, 106, 158, 195, 226, 280, 334, 343, 385
Holmes (Messrs Stephen and Holmes) / Holmes, Mr, 73, 104, 306, 307, 361, 362, 363
Hong Kong Arts Development Council, 19
Hong Kong Club, 207, 405, 408
Hong Kong Cricket Club, 207, 224, 384
Hong Kong Government Central School for Boys, 231
Hong Kong Daily Press, 19, 173

Liu Luk, 260
Lloyd's agent, 83
Lo Ai (coolie), 196
Lo Aping, 339
Lo Asam, 331
Lo Awai, 345
Lo Ayau, 344
Lo Chun, 282
Lo Fan (San Shui District), 289, 300
Lockhart, J. Stewart (Registrar General), 105, 285
Lo-Kong Village, 304
London and China Express, 92
Lord Wilson Heritage Trust, 19
Louis, Thomas, 61
Lucas, C.P., 36, 37
Lui Ahoi, 322
Luk Achü, 283
Luk Akun, 321
Lukong (village), 307
Lukong(s) (green jackets) i.e. Chinese policemen, 65, 108, 230
Lul Singh, 340
Lum Afuk, 330
Lum Amui, 339
Ly Aying, 320
Lyndhurst Terrace, 380
Lynsaght, William (Inspector of Naval Police, HM Dockyards, HK), 228

M
MacCallum, Mr H., 215
MacDonnell, Sir Richard, 54, 56, 57, 325, 366
Mackanery, P. (Private), 128
Mackie, Inspector, 104, 190
Macmillan, Pioneer-Sergeant, 205
Maconnachie, Mr., 211

Mah Wan [*sic*], 367, 372
Mahomedan Cemetery, 71
Malacca, 71
Malacca Straits, 365
Malacca-man (person from Malacca), 221, 227
Man Kwong Village, 301
Man Mo Temple, 105
Mandarin Hotel, 291
Marçal, Capitulino Priamo, 173
Mardtfieldt, J.F., 60
Marks and Spencer, 137
Marques, Dr (Civil Hospital), 259, 282
Marr, Thomas, 173, 174
Marsh, W.H. (Administrator of Hong Kong), 31, 32, 294
Mason, Richard, 272
Mathieson, Inspector, 104, 302, 360
May, Charles (HK Magistrate), 20, 34, 35, 49
May, F.H (Captain Superintendent of Police, later Sir F.H. May (HK Governor), 225
Mayne, Lieutenant, J.G., 206
M'Breen, James, 43, 239, 245, 249, 380
M'Breen, Jane, 43, 239, 245
McCallum, Mr (public analyst), 277, 349
McCormick, W.J., 217
McDonald, Donald (Police Constable), 235
Meade, Mr, 35
Mehta, Mr, 210, 211, 212, 213
Milton, Mr (boatswain), 205
Mok Aping, 194
Mok Awa, 339
Mok Awang, 339

ABOUT PROVERSE HONG KONG

Proverse Hong Kong is based in Hong Kong with long-term and expanding regional and international connections.

Proverse has published novels, novellas, fictionalized autobiography, non-fiction (including autobiography, biography, history, memoirs, sport, travel narratives), single-author poetry collections, children's, teens / young adult and academic books. Other interests include diaries, and academic works in the humanities, social sciences, cultural studies, linguistics and education. Some Proverse books have accompanying audio texts. Some are translated into Chinese.

Proverse welcomes authors who have a story to tell, wisdom, perceptions or information to convey, a person they want to memorialize, a neglect they want to remedy, a record they want to correct, a strong interest that they want to share, skills they want to teach, and who consciously seek to make a contribution to society in an informative, interesting and well-written way. Proverse works with texts by non-native-speaker writers of English as well as by native English-speaking writers.

The name, "Proverse", combines the words "prose" and "verse" and is pronounced accordingly.

THE PROVERSE PRIZE

The Proverse Prize, an annual international competition for an unpublished book-length work of fiction, non-fiction, or poetry, was established in January 2008. It is open to all who are at least eighteen on the date they sign the entry form. Unusually for a competition of this nature, there is no restriction based on nationality, residence or citizenship.

The objectives of the Proverse Prize are: to encourage excellence and / or excellence and usefulness in publishable written work in the English Language, which can, in varying degrees, "delight and instruct". Entries are invited from anywhere in the world. Semi-finalists to date include writers born or resident in Andorra, Australia, Canada, Germany, Hong Kong, New Zealand, Nigeria, Singapore, South Africa,

Taiwan, The Bahamas, the Peoples' Republic of China, the United Arab Emirates, the United Kingdom, the USA.

FOUNDERS: Verner Bickley and Gillian Bickley. To celebrate their lifelong love of words in all their forms as readers, writers, editors, academics, performers, and publishers.
HONORARY LEGAL ADVISOR: Mr Raymond T. L. Tse.
HONORARY ACCOUNTANT: Mr Neville Chow.
HONORARY JUDGES: Anonymous.
HONORARY ADVISORS: Bahamian poet Marion Bethel; UK translator, Margaret Clarke; UK linguist & lexicographer David Crystal; Canadian poet and academic, Jonathan Hart; Swedish linguist Björn Jernudd; Hong Kong University Librarian, Peter Sidorko; Singapore poet Edwin Thumboo; Czech novelist & poet Olga Walló.
HONORARY UK AGENT AND DISTRIBUTOR: Christine Penney
HONORARY ADMINISTRATORS: Proverse Hong Kong.

PROVERSE PRIZE WINNERS WHOSE BOOKS HAVE ALREADY BEEN PUBLISHED BY PROVERSE HONG KONG

Laura Solomon, Rebecca Jane Tomasis, Gillian Jones, David Diskin, Peter Gregoire, Sophronia Liu, Birgit Linder, James McCarthy, Celia Claase, Philip Chatting.

Summary Terms and Conditions
(for indication only & subject to revision)

The information below is for guidance only. Please refer to the year-specific Proverse Prize Entry Form & Terms & Conditions, which are uploaded in April each year onto the Proverse Hong Kong website:
<www.proversepublishing.com>.

The free Proverse E-Newsletter includes ongoing information about the Proverse Prize. To be put on the E-Newsletter mailing-list, email: info@proversepublishing.com with your request.

The Prize
1) Publication by Proverse Hong Kong, with
2) Cash prize of HKD10,000 (HKD7.80 = approx. US$1.00)

Supplementary publication grants may be made to selected other entrants for publication by Proverse Hong Kong.

Depending on the quality of the work in any year, the prize may be shared by at most two entrants or withheld, as recommended by the judges.

In 2015, the entry fee was: HKD220.00 OR GBP32.00.

Writers are eligible, who are at least eighteen on the date they sign The Proverse Prize entry documents. There is no nationality or residence restriction.

Each submitted work must be an unpublished publishable single-author work of non-fiction, fiction or poetry, the original work of the entrant, and submitted in the English language. School textbooks and plays are ineligible.

Translated work: If the work entered is a translation from a language other than English, both the original work and the translation should be previously unpublished. The submitted work will not be judged as a translation but as an original work.

Extent of the Manuscript: within the range of what is usual for the genre of the work submitted. However, it is advisable that novellas be in the range 30,000 to 50,000 words); other fiction (e.g. novels, short-story collections) and non-fiction (e.g. autobiographies, biographies, diaries, letters, memoirs, essay collections, etc.) should be in the range, 75,000 to 100,000 words. Poetry collections should be in the range, 5,000 to 25,000 words. Other word-counts and mixed-genre submissions are not ruled out.

Writers may choose, if they wish, to obtain the services of an Editor in presenting their work, and should acknowledge this help and the nature and extent of this help in the Entry Form.

KEY DATES FOR THE PROVERSE PRIZE IN ANY YEAR
(subject to confirmation and/or change)

Receipt of Entry Fees / Entry Documents	14 April to 31 May of the year of entry
Receipt of entered manuscripts	1 May to 30 June of the year of entry
Announcement of semi-finalists	July-September of the year of entry
Announcement of finalists	October-December of the year of entry
Announcement of winner/ max two winners (sharing the cash prize)	December of the year of entry to April of the year that follows the year of entry
Cash Award made	At the same time as publication of the work(s) adjudged the winner / joint-winners of the Proverse Prize
Publication of winning work(s)	In or after November of the year that follows the year of entry

NON-FICTION (INCLUDING BIOGRAPHY)
Published by Proverse Hong Kong

The Chinese of Macau a decade after the handover, by Jean Berlie. HK & UK, November 2012. Pbk. c.248pp. with 8pp. colour illustrations. ISBN-13: 978-988-8167-37-1.

The complete court cases of Magistrate Frederick Stewart as reported in The China Mail, July 1881 to March 1882. Edited with commentary and chapters by Gillian Bickley. Essay by Dr Ian Grant. HK & UK, 2008. Preface by The Hon. Mr Justice Bokhary PJ, Court of Final Appeal. CD. 761pp. inc. notes. Supported by the Council of the Lord Wilson Heritage Trust. ISBN-13: 978-988-17724-1-1

The development of education in Hong Kong, 1841-1897: as revealed by the early Education Reports of the Hong Kong Government, 1848-1896. Ed. Gillian Bickley. HK & UK, 2002. Hbk. 633pp., inc. bibliography. Supported by the Council of the Lord Wilson Heritage Trust.
ISBN-10: 962-85570-1-7; ISBN-13: 978-962-85570-1-1.

The diplomat of Kashgar: A Very Special Agent. The Life of Sir George Macartney, 18 January 1867 to 19 May 1945, by James McCarthy. HK & UK, 2014.
ISBN 13: 978-988-8227-62-4.

Forward to Beijing! a guide to the Summer Olympics, by Verner Bickley. HK & UK, 2008. Message by Timothy Fok. Preface by The Hon. Dr Arnaldo de Oliveira Sales. With an essay, "A big idea" by Chris Wardlaw. Pbk. 260pp. with 16 b/w photographs. ISBN-13: 978-988-99668-3-6.

The Golden Needle: the biography of Frederick Stewart (1836-1889), by Gillian Bickley. David C. Lam Institute for East-West Studies, Hong Kong Baptist University. HK & UK, 1997. Foreword by Lady Saltoun. Introduction by Sir David Wilson (now Lord Wilson). Pbk. 308pp., inc. bibliography, archival photographs.
ISBN-1: 962-8027-08-5; ISBN-13 978-962-8027-08-8.

The Golden Needle: the biography of Frederick Stewart (1836-1889). Full audio version on 14 CDs. Read by Verner Bickley.
ISBN: CD-962-8027-08-5;ISRC: HK-D94-00-00001-40.

Also, Teachers' and students' guide to the book and audio book, 'The Golden Needle: the biography of Frederick Stewart (1836-1889)'. Proverse Hong Kong Study Guides. E-book.
ISBN-10: 962-85570-9-2; ISBN-13: 978-962-85570-9-7.
24Reader e-book edition (2010),
ISBN-13: 978-988-19320-5-1.

A magistrate's court in nineteenth century Hong Kong: Court in Time. Contributing Editor, Gillian Bickley. Contributors: Garry Tallentire, Geoffrey Roper, Timothy Hamlett, Christopher Coghlan, Verner Bickley. Preface by Sir T. L. Yang. 1st edn. HK & UK, 2005. Pbk. 531pp. inc. bibliography, notes, archival illustrations.
ISBN-10: 962-85570-4-1; ISBN-13: 978-962-85570-4-2.

A magistrate's court in nineteenth century Hong Kong, with additional discussion of "The Opium Ordinance": Court in Time. 2nd edn. HK & UK, 2009. Pbk. 536pp. inc. bibliography, notes, archival illustrations.
ISBN-13: 978-988-17724-5-9.

Searching for Frederick and adventures along the way, by Verner Bickley. Hong Kong, 2001. Pbk. 420pp. Supported by the Hong Kong Arts Development Council. ISBN-10: 962-8783-20-3; ISBN-13: 978-962-8783-20-5.

The Stewarts of Bourtreebush, by Gillian Bickley. Aberdeen, UK, Centre for Scottish Studies, University of Aberdeen, 2003. Pbk. 153pp. Extensive documentation of the Scottish family of Frederick Stewart, founder of Hong Kong Government Education.
ISBN-10: 0-906265-34-7; ISBN-13: 978-0-906265-34-5.

AUTOBIOGRAPHY, MEMOIRS, LETTERS, DIARIES, TRAVEL
Published by Proverse Hong Kong

Chocolate's brown study in the bag by Rupert Kwan Yun Chan. HK & UK, March 2011. Pbk. 112pp. + 16 colour pp. illustrations. Proverse Prize Finalist (2009). ISBN: 978-988-19932-1-2.

Footfalls echo in the memory: a life with the colonial education service and the British Council in Asia, by Verner Bickley. London and New York, 2010. Forewords by Rt Hon the Lord Hunt of Wirral, MBE and Valerie Mitchell, OBE, Director-General, the English-Speaking Union of the Commonwealth. Signed Copies. Hbk. xviii+314pp. inc. 20 b/w photographs. Supported by the Hong Kong Arts Development Council. ISBN: 978-1-84885-085-9.

Gin's tonic: ocean voyage, inner journey, by Virginia MacRobert. HK & UK, 2010. Preface by Ed Vaughan. Pbk. 600pp., inc. index, illustrations: colour photographs, author portrait. Supported by Hong Kong Arts Development Council. ISBN-13: 978-988-17724-3-5.

In time of war, by Richard Collingwood-Selby. HK & UK, 2013. ISBN-13: 978-988-8167-36-4. Supported by Lord Wilson Heritage Trust.

A personal journey through sketching: the sketcher's art, by Errol Patrick Hugh. HK & UK, 2009. Introduction by Li Shiqiao. Hbk. 96pp. inc. 100+ original sketches and photographs by the author & author's portrait. 300mm x 215mm x 14mm. w. CD-ROM. ISBN-13: 978-988-18479-1-1.

Semper fi! The story of a vietnam era marine, by Orville Leverne Clubb. HK & UK, 2012. Pbk. 216pp. + 6pp photographs, sketch-map, inc. glossary. ISBN-13: 978-988-19933-4-2.

Wannabe backpackers: the Latin American & Kenyan journey of five spoiled teenagers by Gerald Yeung. HK & UK, 2009. Pbk. 164pp. inc. several b/w pix.
ISBN 978-988-17724-2-8.

NON-FICTION – CHINESE LANGUAGE

The Golden Needle: the biography of Frederick Stewart (1836-1889):
Selections《香港開埠時的雙語教育——史劍域和母語教學》by Gillian Bickley. Translated by Hong-Lok Kwok. 2010. E-book. ISBN-13: 978-988-18905-4-2.

GENRES

Proverse publishes novels, novellas, short story collections and poetry collections; non-fiction including autobiography, biography, children's illustrated books, educational books, Hong Kong educational and legal history, memoirs, teenage / young adult books, and travel. Other genres may be added.

FIND OUT MORE ABOUT OUR AUTHORS AND BOOKS

Visit our website
http://www.proversepublishing.com

Visit our distributor's website
<www.chineseupress.com>

Follow us on Twitter
Follow news and conversation: <twitter.com/Proversebooks>
OR
Copy and paste the following to your browser window and follow the instructions: https://twitter.com/#!/ProverseBooks

Request our E-Newsletter
Send your request to info@proversepublishing.com.

Availability
Most titles are available in Hong Kong and world-wide from our Hong Kong based Distributor, The Chinese University Press of Hong Kong, The Chinese University of Hong Kong, Shatin, NT, Hong Kong SAR, China. Web: chineseupress.com

All titles are available from Proverse Hong Kong and the Proverse Hong Kong UK-based Distributor.

We have stock-holding retailers in Hong Kong, Singapore (Select Books), Canada (Elizabeth Campbell Books), Principality of Andorra (Llibreria La Puça, La Llibreria).

Orders can be made from bookshops in the UK and elsewhere.

Ebooks
Most of our titles are available also as Ebooks.

www.ingramcontent.com/pod-product-compliance
Lightning Source LLC
Chambersburg PA
CBHW061229220326
41599CB00028B/5379